How the Brain Learns
Fifth Edition

David A. Sousa

FOR INFORMATION:

Corwin
A SAGE Company
2455 Teller Road
Thousand Oaks, California 91320
(800) 233-9936
www.corwin.com

SAGE Publications Ltd.
1 Oliver's Yard
55 City Road
London EC1Y 1SP
United Kingdom

SAGE Publications India Pvt. Ltd.
B 1/I 1 Mohan Cooperative Industrial Area
Mathura Road, New Delhi 110 044
India

SAGE Publications Asia-Pacific Pte. Ltd.
3 Church Street
#10-04 Samsung Hub
Singapore 049483

Program Director: Jessica Allan
Senior Associate Editor: Kimberly Greenberg
Editorial Assistant: Katie Crilley
Production Editor: Amy Schroller
Copy Editor: Diana Breti
Typesetter: C&M Digitals (P) Ltd.
Proofreader: Dennis W. Webb
Indexer: Sheila Bodell
Cover Designer: Gail Buschman
Marketing Manager: Jill Margulies

Copyright © 2017 by David A. Sousa

Printed in the United States of America

ISBN 978-1-5063-4630-4

This book is printed on acid-free paper.

SUSTAINABLE
FORESTRY
INITIATIVE

Certified Chain of Custody
Promoting Sustainable Forestry
www.sfiprogram.org
SFI-01268

16 17 18 19 20 10 9 8

Contents

List of Practitioner's Corners   x

Preface to the Fifth Edition   xii

Publisher's Acknowledgments   xiv

About the Author   xv

Introduction   1

Looking Inside the Brain   1
    Types of Brain Imaging   2
Implications for Teaching   4
    Some Important Findings   5
Why This Book Can Help Improve Teaching and Learning   6
    Chapter Contents   7
    Who Should Use This Book?   8
    Try It Yourself—Do Action Research   9
What's Coming Up?   11

Chapter 1: Basic Brain Facts   15

Some Exterior Parts of the Brain   16
    Lobes of the Brain   16
    Motor Cortex and Somatosensory Cortex   18
Some Interior Parts of the Brain   18
    Brain Stem   18
    The Limbic System   18
    Cerebrum   20
    Cerebellum   21
    Brain Cells   21
    Brain Fuel   25
Neuron Development in Children   25
    Windows of Opportunity   26
The Brain as a Novelty Seeker   30
    Environmental Factors That Enhance Novelty   31
What's Coming Up?   36

Chapter 2: How the Brain Processes Information   43

    The Information Processing Model   44
       Origins of the Model   44
       Usefulness of the Model   44
       Limitations of the Model   45
       Inadequacy of the Computer Model   46
       The Senses   47
       Sensory Register   47
       Short-Term Memory   48
       Long-Term Storage   57
       The Cognitive Belief System   58
       Self-Concept   59
       Variations in Processing With Age   61
       Learning Profiles (Styles)   62
       What's Coming Up?   64

Chapter 3: Memory, Retention, and Learning   86

    How Memory Forms   87
       The Temporary Stimulus   87
       Forming the Memory   88
    Stages and Types of Memory   90
       Stages of Memory   90
       Types of Memory   90
       Emotional Memory   93
    Learning and Retention   96
    Factors Affecting Retention of Learning   97
       Rehearsal   97
       Retention During a Learning Episode   99
       Implications for Teaching   101
    Learning Motor Skills   108
       Brain Activity During Motor Skill Acquisition   108
       Does Practice Make Perfect?   110
    Daily Biological Rhythms Affect Teaching and Learning   115
       Circadian Rhythms   115
       The Importance of Sleep in Learning and Memory   116
    Intelligence and Retrieval   119
       Intelligence   119
       Retrieval   122
       Chunking   126
       Forgetting   129
       A Word About Brain-Training Programs   133
    What's Coming Up?   134

Chapter 4: The Power of Transfer   153

    What Is Transfer?   154
       Transfer During Learning   154

Types of Transfer 155

Transfer of Learning 156

Teaching for Transfer 157

Factors Affecting Transfer 159

Teaching Methods 165

Transfer and Constructivism 167

English Language Learners (ELLs) and Transfer 167

Technology and Transfer 168

Additional Thoughts About Transfer 169

What's Coming Up? 170

Chapter 5: Brain Organization and Learning 187

Brain Lateralization 188

Left and Right Hemisphere Processing (Laterality) 189

What Causes Specialization? 191

Specialization Does Not Mean Exclusivity 191

The Gender Connection 193

Schools and Brain Organization 198

Spoken Language Specialization 199

Learning Spoken Language 201

Learning a Second Language 204

Learning to Read 205

Is Reading a Natural Ability? 205

Neural Systems Involved in Reading 206

Skills Involved in Reading 207

Phases of Learning to Read 209

Problems in Learning to Read 209

Implications for Teaching Reading 214

Learning Mathematics 215

Number Sense 215

Teaching Brain-Friendly Mathematics 218

Difficulties in Learning Mathematics 223

Environmental Factors 223

Neurological Factors 226

Mathematics for English Language Learners 227

What's Coming Up? 228

Chapter 6: The Brain and the Arts 243

The Arts Are Basic to the Human Experience 244

Why Teach the Arts? 245

The Arts and the Young Brain 245

The Arts Develop Cognitive Growth 246

The Arts and Creativity 248

The Sciences Need the Arts 250

Impact of the Arts on Student Learning and Behavior 251

Arts Education and Arts Integration 251

Other Areas of Impact 253

Music   255
   Is Music Inborn?   255
   Effects of Listening to Music
      Versus Creating Instrumental Music   256
   How the Brain Listens to Music   257
   The Benefits of Listening to Music   258
   Creating Music   260
   Benefits of Creating Music   260
   Creating Music Benefits Memory   261
   Does Creating Music Affect Ability in Other Subjects?   262
   Student Attitudes Toward Music in the Schools   265
The Visual Arts   266
   Imagery   266
   Research on Visual Arts and Learning   267
Movement   269
   Movement and the Brain   269
   Implications for Schools   270
What's Coming Up?   272

Chapter 7: Thinking Skills and Learning   **282**

Characteristics of Human Thinking   282
   Types of Thinking   283
   Thinking as a Representational System   284
   Thinking and Emotion   284
   Technology May Be Affecting How Students Think   285
The Dimensions of Human Thinking   285
   Designing Models   285
   Are We Teaching Thinking Skills?   286
   Modeling Thinking Skills in the Classroom   287
Revisiting Bloom's Taxonomy of the Cognitive Domain   288
   Why Start With This Model?   288
   The Model's Structure and Revision   289
   Important Characteristics of the Revised Model   293
   Cognitive and Emotional Thinking   293
   Testing Your Understanding of the Taxonomy   294
   The Taxonomy and the Dimensions of Thinking   295
   The Critical Difference Between Complexity and Difficulty   295
   Curriculum Changes to Accommodate the Taxonomy   298
Other Thinking Skills Programs   299
What's Coming Up?   300

Chapter 8: Putting It All Together   **312**

Students Should Know How Their Brains Learn   312
What About the Flipped Classroom?   313
Daily Planning   314
   General Guidelines   314
   Daily Lesson Design   314

Twenty-Two Questions to Ask During Lesson Planning 319
Unit Planning 321
    Teacher's Work Sample 321
Maintaining Skills for the Future 322
    The Building Principal's Role 322
    Types of Support Systems 322
Conclusion 324

Resources 327

Glossary 332

References 338

Index 366

List of Practitioner's Corners

Introduction   1

    What Do You Already Know?   12
    How Brain-Compatible Is My Teaching/School/District?   13
    Using Action Research   14

Chapter 1: Basic Brain Facts   15

    Fist for a Brain   37
    Arm for a Neuron   38
    Review of Brain Area Functions   39
    Using Novelty in Lessons   40
    Preparing the Brain for Taking a Test   41

Chapter 2: How the Brain Processes Information   43

    Walking Through the Brain   65
    Redesigning the Information Processing Model   66
    Developing Students' Growth Mindset   67
    Determining Your Sensory Preferences   68
    Developing a Classroom Climate Conducive to Learning   71
    Using Humor to Enhance Climate and Promote Retention   73
    Increasing Processing Time Through Motivation   75
    Creating Meaning in New Learning   78
    Using Closure to Enhance Sense and Meaning   79
    Testing Whether Information Is in Long-Term Storage   80
    Using Synergy to Enhance Learning   82
    NeuroBingo   84

Chapter 3: Memory, Retention, and Learning   86

    Guidelines for Teaching the Emotional Brain   135
    Avoid Teaching Two Very Similar Motor Skills   136
    Using Rehearsal to Enhance Retention   137
    Using the Primacy-Recency Effect in the Classroom   139
    Strategies for Block Scheduling   141

Using Practice Effectively 143
Relearning Through Recall 144
Impact of Circadian Rhythms on Schools and Classrooms 145
Using Wait Time to Increase Student Participation 147
Using Chunking to Enhance Retention 148
Using Mnemonics to Help Retention 150

Chapter 4: The Power of Transfer **153**

General Guidelines on Teaching for Transfer 171
Strategies for Connecting to Past Learnings 172
Avoid Teaching Concepts That Are Very Similar 173
Identifying Critical Attributes for Accurate Transfer 175
Teaching for Transfer: Bridging 179
Teaching for Transfer: Hugging 181
Using Metaphors to Enhance Transfer 183
Using Journal Writing to Promote Transfer and Retention 185

Chapter 5: Brain Organization and Learning **187**

Teaching to the Whole Brain—General Guidelines 229
Strategies for Teaching to the Whole Brain 231
Concept Mapping—General Guidelines 233
Acquiring Another Language 236
Considerations for Teaching Reading 238
Reading Guidelines for All Teachers 240
Instructional Considerations for
    Teaching PreK–12 Mathematics 241

Chapter 6: The Brain and the Arts **243**

Including the Arts in All Lessons 273
Using Music in the Classroom 274
Using Imagery 276
Visualized Note Taking 277
Strategies for Using Movement 279

Chapter 7: Thinking Skills and Learning **282**

Understanding Bloom's Revised Taxonomy 301
Take a Concept/Situation Up the Taxonomy! 302
Tips on Using Bloom's Revised Taxonomy 304
Bloom's Taxonomy: Increasing Complexity 305
Understanding the Difference
    Between Complexity and Difficulty 306
Questions to Stimulate Higher-Order Thinking 309
Activities to Stimulate Higher-Order Thinking 310

Chapter 8: Putting It All Together **312**

Reflections on Lesson Design 325

Preface to the Fifth Edition

Publishing a fifth edition of this book is an encouraging sign that more educators are recognizing that research in cognitive neuroscience is providing exciting new insights into how the brain develops and learns. Because teachers are essentially "brain changers," they realize that the more they know about how the brain learns, the more likely they are to be successful at helping their students succeed.

One major development since the fourth edition of this text is that the academic discipline called *educational neuroscience* or *mind, brain, and education science* is now firmly established. This field of inquiry explores how research findings from neuroscience, education, and psychology can inform our understandings about teaching and learning and whether they have implications for educational practice. This interdisciplinary approach ensures that recommendations for teaching practices have a foundation in solid scientific research.

For this fifth edition, I have made numerous changes that reflect new advances in our understanding of the learning process. Specifically, I have

- expanded the explanations of brain facts;
- added a section on the importance of mindset;
- added an explanation of how brain processing varies with the student's age;
- updated the section on memory systems, especially on emotional memory;
- added the Gradual Release of Responsibility (GRR) model;
- added a section on brain-training programs;
- updated new research findings on how the explosion of technology may be affecting the brain;
- significantly expanded the section on learning to read;
- added a section on learning mathematics;
- added a section on integrating the arts into STEM to produce STEAM;
- added a new section on how technology is affecting students' thinking;
- added short descriptions of other thinking skills models;
- added a section on the importance of telling students how their brains learn;
- added a section on the flipped classroom model;

- added several new Practitioner's Corners;
- updated the Resources section to include more Internet sites selected for their reliable information on the brain; and
- added or updated more than 300 references, most of which are primary sources for those who wish to explore the actual research studies.

This continues to be an exciting time to be in education. Granted, never has society asked so much of its schools. At the same time, however, never have we known so much about how students learn and what we can do to make that happen successfully. This book opens the door to educational neuroscience in the hopes that educators will experience the joy of seeing more students reach their full potential.

—*David A. Sousa*

Publisher's Acknowledgments

Corwin gratefully acknowledges the contributions of the following reviewers:

Carlton Fitzgerald, EdD
Visiting Associate Professor of Education
New England College
Henniker, NH

Judith Josephs, JD, EdD
Visiting Professor
Salem State University
Salem, Massachusetts

Kathleen Kremer, PhD
Assistant Professor
University of Wisconsin
Mequon, WI

Stephanie L. Standerfer, PhD
Associate Professor of Music Education
Shenandoah University
Winchester, VA

About the Author

David A. Sousa, EdD, an international consultant in educational neuroscience, has written 16 books for educators and parents on ways to use brain research to improve teaching and learning. He has conducted workshops for more than 200,000 educators in hundreds of school districts on brain research and science education at the pre-K to Grade 12 and university levels. He has presented at national conventions of educational organizations and to regional and local school districts across the United States, Canada, Europe, Australia, New Zealand, and Asia.

Dr. Sousa has a bachelor of science degree in chemistry from Bridgewater (Massachusetts) State University, a master of arts degree in teaching science from Harvard University, and a doctorate from Rutgers University. His teaching experience covers all levels. He has taught high school science and has served as a K–12 director of science, a supervisor of instruction, and a district superintendent in New Jersey schools. He has been an adjunct professor of education at Seton Hall University and at Rutgers University. A past president of the National Staff Development Council (now called Learning Forward), Dr. Sousa has edited science books and published numerous articles in leading educational journals on staff development, science education, and brain research. He has received awards from professional associations, school districts, and Bridgewater State University (Distinguished Alumni Award), and several honorary doctorates for his commitment and contributions to research, staff development, and science education. He has been interviewed on the NBC *Today* show and on National Public Radio about his work with schools using brain research. He makes his home in south Florida.

Introduction

You start out as a single cell derived from the coupling of a sperm and egg; this divides into two, then four, then eight, and so on, and at a certain stage there emerges a single cell which will have as all its progeny the human brain. The mere existence of that cell should be one of the great astonishments of the earth.

—Lewis Thomas,
The Medusa and the Snail

The human brain is an amazing structure—a universe of infinite possibilities and mystery. It constantly shapes and reshapes itself as a result of experience, yet it can take off on its own without input from the outside world. How does it form a human mind, capture experience, or stop time in memory? Although it does not generate enough energy to light a simple bulb, its capabilities make it the most powerful force on Earth.

For thousands of years, humans have been delving into this mysterious universe and trying to determine how it accomplishes its amazing feats. How fast does it grow? What impact does the environment have on its growth? How does it learn language? How does it learn to read? What is intelligence?

Just how the brain learns has been of particular interest to teachers for centuries. Now, in the 21st century, there is new hope that our understanding of this remarkable process called teaching and learning will improve dramatically. A major source of that understanding is coming from the sophisticated medical instruments that allow scientists to peer inside the living—and learning—brain.

LOOKING INSIDE THE BRAIN

New technologies for looking inside and seeing the workings of the living brain have advanced faster than scientists predicted just a few years ago. The more we learn about the brain, the more remarkable it seems. Hardly a week goes by when some major news story about the brain appears in the press or on television. Consequently, most of us have heard about the imaging technologies, and some readers may have even experienced a brain scan. Because we will be mentioning brain scans throughout this book, here is a brief review of the more common scanning instruments that have contributed to our understanding of brain structure and function.

Types of Brain Imaging

The imaging technologies fall into two major categories: those that look at brain *structure* and those that look at brain *function*. When aimed at the brain, computerized axial tomography (CAT, or simply CT) and magnetic resonance imaging (MRI) are very useful diagnostic tools that produce computer images of the brain's internal structure. For example, they can detect tumors, malformations, and the damage caused by cerebral hemorrhages.

Different technologies, however, are required to look at how the brain works. An alphabet soup describes the five most common procedures that can be used to isolate and identify the areas of the brain where distinct levels of activity are occurring. The scanning technologies for looking at brain function are the following:

- Electroencephalography (EEG)
- Magnetoencephalography (MEG)
- Positron-Emission Tomography (PET)
- Functional Magnetic Resonance Imaging (fMRI)
- Functional Magnetic Resonance Spectroscopy (fMRS)

Here is a brief explanation of how each one works. A summary chart follows.

• **Electroencephalography (EEG) and Magnetoencephalography (MEG).** These two techniques are helpful in determining how quickly something occurs in the brain. To do that, they measure electrical and magnetic activity occurring in the brain during mental processing. In an EEG, anywhere from 19 to 128 electrodes are attached to various positions on the scalp with a conductive gel so electrical signals can be recorded in a computer. In a MEG, about 100 magnetic detectors are placed around the head to record magnetic activity. EEGs and MEGs can record changes in brain activity that occur as rapidly as one millisecond (one thousandth of a second), a typical time when the brain is processing language. When a group of neurons responds to a specific event (like a word), they activate, and their electrical and magnetic activity can be detected above the noise of the nonactivated neurons. This response is called an *event-related potential,* or ERP. ERP evidence has provided information about the time needed for the brain to do mathematical calculations or process reading. EEGs and MEGs do not expose the subject to radiation and are not considered hazardous.

• **Positron-Emission Tomography (PET).** The first technology to observe brain functions, PET involves injecting the subject with a radioactive solution that circulates to the brain. Brain regions of higher activity accumulate more of the radiation, which is picked up by a ring of detectors around the subject's head. A computer displays the concentration of radiation as a picture of blood flow in a cross-sectional slice of the brain regions that are aligned with the detectors. The picture is in color, with the more active areas in reds and yellows, and the quieter areas in blues and greens. Two major drawbacks to PET scans are the invasive nature of the injection and the use of radioactive materials. Consequently, this technique is not used with healthy children because the radioactive risk is too high.

- **Functional Magnetic Resonance Imaging (fMRI).** This technology is rapidly replacing PET scans because it is painless, is noninvasive, and does not use radiation. The technology helps to pinpoint the brain areas of greater and lesser activity. Its operation is based on the fact that when any part of the brain becomes more active, the need for oxygen and nutrients increases. Oxygen is carried to the brain cells by hemoglobin. Hemoglobin contains iron, which is magnetic. The fMRI uses a large magnet to compare the amount of oxygenated hemoglobin entering brain cells with the amount of deoxygenated hemoglobin leaving the cells. The computer colors in the brain regions receiving more oxygenated blood and can locate the activated brain region to within one centimeter (less than a half-inch).

- **Functional Magnetic Resonance Spectroscopy (fMRS).** This technology involves the same equipment as fMRI but uses different computer software to record levels of various chemicals in the brain while the subject is thinking. Like the fMRI, fMRS can precisely pinpoint the area of activity, but it can also identify whether certain key chemicals are present at the activation site. fMRS has been used to study language function in the brain by mapping the change in specific chemicals, such as lactate, that respond to brain activation during tasks involving language.

Researchers are also learning much more about several dozen brain chemicals called *neurotransmitters*. These substances bathe the brain cells and either permit signals to pass between them or inhibit them. Wide fluctuations in the concentration of neurotransmitters in certain brain areas can change our mood, affect our movement, diminish or enhance our alertness, and interfere with our ability to learn.

To determine which parts of the brain control various functions, neurosurgeons use tiny electrodes to stimulate individual nerve cells and record their reactions. Besides the information collected by these techniques, the growing body of case studies of individuals recovering from various types of brain damage is giving us new evidence about and insights into how the brain develops, changes, learns, remembers, and recovers from injury.

Techniques for Mapping Brain Functions		
Technique	**What It Measures**	**How It Works**
Electroencephalography (EEG) Magnetoencephalography (MEG)	The electrical and magnetic activity occurring in the brain during mental processing. The spikes of activity are called event-related potential (ERP).	In EEG, multiple electrodes are attached to the scalp to record electrical signals in a computer. In MEG, magnetic detectors are placed around the head to record magnetic activity. EEGs and MEGs record changes in brain activity that occur as rapidly as one millisecond. When a group of neurons responds to a specific event, they activate, and their electrical and magnetic activity can be detected. This response is called an event-related potential, or ERP.

(Continued)

(Continued)

Technique	What It Measures	How It Works
Positron-Emission Tomography (PET)	Amount of radiation present in brain regions.	The subject is injected with a radioactive solution that circulates to the brain. Brain regions of higher activity accumulate more radiation, which is picked up by a ring of detectors. A computer displays the concentration of radiation in a cross-sectional slice of the brain regions aligned with the detectors. The picture shows the more active areas in reds and yellows and the quieter areas in blues and greens.
Functional Magnetic Resonance Imaging (fMRI)	Levels of deoxygenated hemoglobin in brain cells.	Any part of the brain that is thinking requires more oxygen, which is carried to the brain cells by hemoglobin. The fMRI uses a large magnet to compare the amount of oxygenated hemoglobin entering brain cells with the amount of deoxygenated hemoglobin leaving the cells. The computer colors in the brain regions receiving more oxygenated blood and locates the activated brain region to within one centimeter (half-inch).
Functional Magnetic Resonance Spectroscopy (fMRS)	Levels of specific chemicals present during brain activity.	This technology involves the same equipment as fMRI but uses different computer software to record levels of various chemicals in the brain while the subject is thinking. fMRS can not only precisely pinpoint the area of activity, but it can also identify whether certain key chemicals are present at the activation site.

IMPLICATIONS FOR TEACHING

As we examine the clues that this research is yielding about learning, we recognize its importance to the teaching profession. Every day teachers enter their classrooms with lesson plans, experience, and the hope that what they are about to present will be understood, remembered, and useful to their students. The extent that this hope is realized depends largely on the knowledge base that these teachers use in designing those plans and, perhaps more important, on the instructional techniques they select during the lessons. Teachers try to change the human brain every day. The more they know about how it learns, the more successful they can be.

Educators in recent years have become much more aware that neuroscience is finding out a lot about how the brain works, and that some of the discoveries have implications for what happens in schools and classrooms. There is a growing interest among educators in the biology of learning and how much an individual's environment can affect the growth and development of the brain. More teacher training institutions are incorporating brain research into their courses. Professional development programs are also devoting more time to this area, more books about the brain are available, brain-compatible teaching units are sprouting up, and the journals of most major educational organizations have devoted special issues to the topic. These are all good signs. I believe this focus on recent brain research can improve the quality of our profession's performance and its success in helping others learn.

> *Teachers try to change the human brain every day. The more they know about how it learns, the more successful they can be.*

Some Important Findings

As research continues to provide a deeper understanding of the workings of the human brain, educators need to be cautious about how they apply these findings to practice. There are critics who believe that brain research should not be used at this time in schools and classrooms. Some critics say it will be years before this has any application to educational practice. Others fear that unsubstantiated claims are being made, usually referred to as "neuromyths," and that educators are not sufficiently trained to tell scientific fact from hype. The concerns are understandable but should not prevent educators from learning what they need to know to decide whether research findings have application to their practice. For those who wonder how recent discoveries about the brain can affect teaching and learning, we can tell them that this research has done the following:

- Reaffirmed that the human brain continually reorganizes itself on the basis of input. This process, called *neuroplasticity*, continues throughout our life but is exceptionally rapid in the early years. Thus, the experiences the young brain has in the home and at school help shape the neural circuits that will determine how and what that brain learns in school and later.
- Startled the scientific world with evidence that neurons in the brain do slowly regenerate, thereby enhancing learning and memory.
- Challenged the notion that the brain can multitask.
- Revealed more about how the brain acquires spoken language.
- Developed scientifically based computer programs that dramatically help young children with reading problems.
- Shown how emotions affect learning, memory, and recall.
- Suggested that movement and exercise improve mood, increase brain mass, and enhance cognitive processing.
- Tracked the growth and development of the teenage brain to better understand the unpredictability of adolescent behavior.
- Developed a deeper understanding of circadian cycles to explain why teaching and learning can be more difficult at certain times of day.
- Studied the effects of sleep deprivation and stress on learning and memory.
- Recognized that intelligence and creativity are separate abilities, and that both can be modified by the environment and schooling.
- Highlighted the degree to which a school's social and cultural climates affect teaching and learning.

- Updated our understandings about working memory.
- Added to our knowledge of how the arts develop the brain.
- Recognized that omnipresent technology is rewiring toddlers' and students' brains.

Other researchers strongly disagree with the critics and support the increased attention that educators are giving to neuroscience. Several universities here and abroad have established dedicated research centers to examine how discoveries in neuroscience can affect educational practice. As a result, educational theory and practice will become much more research based, similar to the medical model. In fact, the body of knowledge that represents this application of brain research to classroom practice has grown so much in the past two decades that it is now recognized as a separate area of study. Known as *mind, brain, and education* or *educational neuroscience*, this field of inquiry looks at how what we are learning about the human brain can affect the curricular, instructional, and assessment decisions that teachers make every day. These implications do not represent an "in-the-box program" or the "strategy du jour" that teachers sometimes view with a wary or cynical eye. Rather, the goal of educational neuroscience is to reflect on this research and decide whether it should have an impact on educational practices.

There is, of course, no panacea that will make teaching and learning a perfect process—and that includes brain research. It is a long leap from making a research finding in a laboratory to the changing of schools and practice because of that finding. These are exciting times for educators, but we must ensure that we don't let the excitement cloud our common sense.

WHY THIS BOOK CAN HELP IMPROVE TEACHING AND LEARNING

What I have tried to do here is report on research (from neuroscience as well as the behavioral and cognitive sciences) that is sufficiently reliable that it can inform educational practice. This is hardly a novel idea. Madeline Hunter in the late 1960s introduced the notion of teachers using what science was learning about learning and modifying traditional classroom procedures and instructional techniques accordingly. Her program at the UCLA School of Education came to be called "Instructional Theory Into Practice," or ITIP. Readers familiar with that model will recognize some of Dr. Hunter's work here, especially in the areas of transfer and practice. I had the privilege of working periodically with her for nine years, and I firmly believe that she was the major force that awakened educators to the importance of continually updating their knowledge base and focusing on research-based strategies and the developing science of learning.

This book will help answer questions such as these:

- When do students remember best in a learning episode?
- To what extent is technology changing the brain?

- How can I help students understand and remember more of what I teach?
- Why is focus so important, and why is it so difficult to get?
- How can I teach motor skills effectively?
- How can humor and music help the teaching-learning process?
- How can I get students to find meaning in what they are learning?
- Why is transfer such a powerful principle of learning, and how can it destroy a lesson without my realizing it?
- What classroom strategies are more likely to appeal to the brain of today's student?
- What important questions should I be asking myself as I plan daily and unit lessons?

Chapter Contents

Chapter 1. Basic Brain Facts. Because we are going to talk a lot about the brain, we should be familiar with some of its anatomy. This chapter discusses some of the major structures of the human brain and their functions. It explores how the young brain grows and develops, focusing on those important windows of opportunity for learning in the early years. There is an explanation of how students' brains today are very different from those of just a few years ago, especially in what they expect from their school experiences.

Chapter 2. How the Brain Processes Information. Trying to develop a simple model to describe the complex process of learning is not easy. The model at the heart of this chapter outlines what cognitive researchers believe are the critical steps involved in the brain's acquisition and processing of information. The components of the model are discussed in detail and updated from previous editions. Also included is an instrument to help you determine your modality preferences.

Chapter 3. Memory, Retention, and Learning. Teachers want their students to remember forever what they are taught, but that does not happen too often. The third chapter focuses on the different types of memory systems and how they work. Those factors that affect retention of learning are discussed here along with ideas of how to plan lessons that result in greater remembering. Also included are some cautions about commercial brain-training programs.

Chapter 4. The Power of Transfer. Transfer is one of the most powerful and least understood principles of learning. Yet a major goal of education is to enable students to transfer what they learn in school to solve future problems. The nature and power of transfer are examined in this chapter, including how to use past knowledge to enhance present and future learning.

Chapter 5. Brain Organization and Learning. This chapter explores how areas of the brain are specialized to perform certain tasks. It examines the latest research on how we learn to speak and read, and learn mathematics, along with the implications of this research for classroom instruction and for the curriculum and structure of schools.

Chapter 6. The Brain and the Arts. Despite strong evidence that the arts enhance cognitive development, they run the risk of being abandoned so more time can be devoted to preparing for mandated high-stakes testing. Public support for keeping the arts is growing. This chapter presents the latest evidence of how the arts in themselves contribute to the growth of neural networks as well as enhance the skills needed for mastering other academic subjects, including in the STEM areas.

Chapter 7. Thinking Skills and Learning. Are we challenging our students enough to do higher-level thinking? This chapter discusses some of the characteristics and dimensions of human thinking. It focuses on the recent revision of Bloom's taxonomy, notes its continuing compatibility with current research on higher-order thinking, and explains the taxonomy's critically important relationship to difficulty, complexity, and intelligence.

Chapter 8. Putting It All Together. So how do we use these important findings in daily practice? This chapter emphasizes how to use the research presented in this book to plan lessons. It discusses different types of teaching methods, including the flipped classroom, and suggests guidelines and a format for lesson design. Because neuroscience continues to reveal new information about learning, the chapter describes support systems to help educators maintain expertise in brain-compatible techniques and move toward continuous professional growth.

At the end of each chapter are the Practitioner's Corners. Some include activities that check for understanding of the major concepts and research presented in the chapter. Others offer my interpretation of how this research might translate into effective classroom strategies that improve the teaching-learning process. Readers are invited to critically review my suggestions and rationale to determine if they have value for their work.

Main thoughts are highlighted in boxes throughout the book. At the very end of each chapter, you will find a page called Key Points to Ponder, an organizing tool to help you remember important ideas, strategies, and resources you may wish to consider later.

Where appropriate, I have explained some of the chemical and biological processes occurring within the brain. However, I have intentionally omitted complex chemical formulas and reactions and have avoided side issues that would distract from the main purpose of this book. My intent is to present just enough science to help the average reader understand the research and the rationale for any suggestions I offer.

Who Should Use This Book?

This book will be useful to classroom teachers because it presents a research-based rationale for why and when certain instructional strategies should be considered. It focuses on the brain as the organ of thinking and learning, and takes the approach that the more teachers know about how the brain learns, the greater the number of instructional options that become available. Increasing the options that teachers have during the dynamic process of instruction also increases the likelihood that successful learning will occur.

The book should also help professional developers who continually need to update their own knowledge base and include research and research-based strategies and support systems as part of their repertoire. Chapter 8 offers some suggestions to help professional developers implement and maintain the knowledge and strategies suggested here.

Principals and head teachers should find here a substantial source of topics for discussion at faculty meetings, which should include, after all, instructional as well as informational items. In doing so, they support the attitude that professional growth is an ongoing school responsibility and not an occasional event. More important, being familiar with these topics enhances the principal's credibility as the school's instructional leader and promotes the notion that the school is a learning organization for *all* its occupants.

College and university instructors should also find merit in the research and applications presented here, as both suggestions to improve their own teaching and information to be passed on to prospective teachers.

Some of the information in this book will be useful to parents, who are, after all, the child's first teachers.

Indeed, the ideas in this book provide the research support for a variety of initiatives, such as cooperative learning groups, differentiated instruction, integrated thematic units, and the interdisciplinary approach to curriculum. Those who are familiar with constructivism will recognize many similarities in the ideas presented here. The research is yielding more evidence that knowledge is not only transmitted from the teacher to the learners but is also transformed in the learner's mind as a result of cultural and social mediation. Much of this occurs through elaborative rehearsal and transfer and is discussed in several chapters.

> *This book can help teachers, professional developers, principals, college instructors, and parents.*

Try It Yourself—Do Action Research

Benefits of Action Research

One of the best ways to assess the value of the strategies suggested in this book is to try them out in your own classroom or in any other location where you are teaching. Conducting this action research allows you to gather data to determine the effectiveness of new strategies and affirm those you already use, to acclaim and enhance the use of research in our profession, and to further your own professional development.

Other benefits of action research are that it provides teachers with consistent feedback for self-evaluation, it introduces alternative forms of student assessment, and its results may lead to important changes in curriculum. Action research can be the work of just one teacher, but its value grows immensely when it is the consistent effort of a teacher team, a department, a school staff, or even an entire district. Incorporating action research as a regular part of the K–12 academic scene not only provides useful data but also enhances the integrity of the profession and gains much-needed respect from the broad community that schools serve.

Teachers are often hesitant to engage in action research, concerned that it may take too much time or that it represents another accountability measure in an already test-saturated environment. Yet, with all the programs and strategies emerging today in the name of reform, we need data to help determine their validity. The valuable results of cognitive neuroscience will continue to be ignored in schools unless there is reliable evidence to support their use. Action research is a cost-effective means of assessing the effectiveness of brain-compatible strategies that are likely to result in greater student learning. Several studies in PreK-12 schools have shown that action research has a positive effect on teacher confidence and practice (e.g., Brown & Weber, 2016; Calvert & Sheen, 2015).

> *Using action research provides valuable data, affirms best practices, and enhances the integrity of the profession.*

The Outcomes of Action Research

The classroom is a laboratory in which the teaching and learning processes meet and interact. Action research can provide continual feedback on the success of that interaction. Using a solution-oriented approach, action research includes identifying the problem, systematically collecting data, analyzing the data, taking action based on the data, evaluating and reflecting on the results of those actions, and, if needed, redefining the problem (see Figure I.1). The teacher is always in control of the type of data collected, the pace of assessment, and the analysis of the results. This process encourages teachers to reflect on their practices, to refine their skills as practitioners, and to direct their own professional development. This is a new view of the profession, with the teacher as the main agent of change.

Building administrators have a special obligation to encourage action research among their teachers. With so much responsibility and accountability being placed on schools and teachers, action research can quickly assess the effectiveness of instructional strategies. By supporting such a program, principals demonstrate by action that they are truly instructional leaders and not just building managers. See the Practitioner's Corner: Using Action Research at the end of this chapter for specific suggestions on using action research in the classroom.

Finally, this fifth edition of the book reflects what more I have gathered about the brain and learning at the time of publication. Because this is now an area of intense research and scrutiny, educators need to constantly read about new discoveries and adjust their understandings accordingly. As we discover more about how the brain learns, we can devise strategies that can make the teaching-learning process more efficient, effective, and enjoyable.

Figure I.1 The diagram illustrates the six steps in the action research cycle.

WHAT'S COMING UP?

As neuroscience advances, educators are realizing that some basic information about the brain must now become part of their knowledge base. Educators are not neuroscientists, but they are members of the *only* profession in which their job is to change the human brain every day. Therefore, the more they know about how it works, the more likely they are to be successful at changing it. To that end, Chapter 1 will take the reader through a painless and easy-to-read explanation of some major brain structures and their functions as well as a peek at the brain of today's students.

> *Educators are in the only profession in which their job is to change the human brain every day.*

PRACTITIONER'S CORNER

What Do You Already Know?

The value of this book can be measured in part by how it enhances your understanding of the brain and the way it learns. Take the following true-false test to assess your current knowledge of the brain. Decide whether the statements are generally true or false and circle T or F. Explanations for the answers are identified throughout the book in special boxes.

1. T F The structures responsible for deciding what gets stored in long-term memory are located in the brain's rational system.

2. T F Learners who can perform a new learning task well are likely to retain it.

3. T F Reviewing material just before a test is a good practice to determine how much has been retained.

4. T F Increased time on task increases retention of new learning.

5. T F Two very similar concepts or motor skills should be taught at the same time.

6. T F The rate at which a learner retrieves information from memory is closely related to intelligence.

7. T F The amount of information a learner can deal with at one time is genetically linked.

8. T F It is usually not possible to increase the amount of information that the working (temporary) memory can deal with at one time.

9. T F Most of the time, the transfer of information from long-term storage is under the conscious control of the learner.

10. T F Bloom's taxonomy has not changed over the years.

PRACTITIONER'S CORNER

How Brain-Compatible Is My Teaching/School/District?

Directions: On a scale of 1 (lowest) to 5 (highest), circle the number that indicates the degree to which your teaching/school/district does the following. Connect the circles to see a profile.

1. I/We adapt the curriculum to recognize the windows of opportunity students have during their cognitive growth.   1—2—3—4—5

2. I/We are trained to provoke strong, positive emotions in students during the learning process.   1—2—3—4—5

3. I/We are trained to help students adjust their self-concept to be more successful in different learning situations.   1—2—3—4—5

4. I/We provide an enriched and varied learning environment.   1—2—3—4—5

5. I/We search constantly for opportunities to integrate curriculum concepts between and among subject areas.   1—2—3—4—5

6. Students have frequent opportunities during class to talk about what they are learning, while they are learning.   1—2—3—4—5

7. I/We do not use lecture as the main mode of instruction.   1—2—3—4—5

8. One of the main criteria I/we use to decide on classroom activities and curriculum is relevancy to students.   1—2—3—4—5

9. I/We understand the power of chunking and use it in the design of curriculum and in daily instruction.   1—2—3—4—5

10. I/We understand the primacy-recency effect and use it regularly in the classroom to enhance retention of learning.   1—2—3—4—5

PRACTITIONER'S CORNER

Using Action Research

Basic Guidelines

Action research helps teachers assess systematically the effectiveness of their own educational practices using the techniques of research. Because data collection is essential to this process, teachers need to identify the elements of the research question that can be measured.

- **Select the Research Question.** Because you need to collect data, choose a research question that involves elements that can be easily measured quantitatively or qualitatively. For example,

  1. How does the chunking of material affect the learner's retention? This can be measured by a short oral or written quiz.

  2. How does teaching material at the beginning or middle of a lesson affect learner retention? This can be measured by quizzes.

  3. How does changing the length of wait time affect student participation? This can be measured by comparing the length of the wait time to the number of subsequent student responses.

  4. Does using humor or music increase student focus? Can either be measured by the number of students who are on/off task with or without humor or music?

  5. Does teaching two very similar concepts at different times improve student understanding and retention of them? This can be measured by oral questioning or quizzes after teaching each concept.

- **Collect the Data.** Remember that you need baseline data before you try the research strategy to provide a comparison. Plan carefully the methods you will use to measure and collect the data. Try not to use paper-and-pencil tests exclusively. You will collect pretrial and posttrial data.

  Pretrial. Select a control group, which is usually the same group of students that will be used with the research strategy. Collect test data without using the research strategy.

  Posttrial. Use the strategy (e.g., chunking, prime-time-1, wait time, humor) and then collect the appropriate data.

- **Analyze the Data.** Use simple analytical techniques, such as comparing the average group test scores before and after using the research strategy. What changes did you notice in the two sets of data? Did the research strategy produce the desired result? If not, why not? Was there an unexpected consequence (positive or negative) of using the strategy?

- **Share the Data.** Sharing the data with colleagues is an important component of the action research process. Too often, teachers work in isolation, with few or no opportunities to interact continuously with colleagues to design and discuss their lessons.

- **Implement the Change.** If the research strategy produced the desired results, decide how you will make it part of your teaching repertoire. If you did not get the desired results, decide whether you need to change some aspect of the strategy or perhaps use a different measure.

- **Try New Practices.** Repeat the above steps with other strategies so that action research becomes part of your ongoing professional development.

1

Basic Brain Facts

With our new knowledge of the brain, we are just dimly beginning to realize that we can now understand humans, including ourselves, as never before, and that this is the greatest advance of the century, and quite possibly the most significant in all human history.

—Leslie A. Hart
Human Brain and Human Learning

Chapter Highlights

This chapter introduces some of the basic structures of the human brain and their functions. It explores the growth of the young brain and some of the environmental factors that influence its development into adolescence. Whether the brain of today's student is compatible with today's schools and the impact of technology are also discussed.

The adult human brain is a wet, fragile mass that weighs a little more than three pounds. It is about the size of a small grapefruit, is shaped like a walnut, and can fit in the palm of your hand. Cradled in the skull and surrounded by protective membranes, it is poised at the top of the spinal column. The brain works ceaselessly, even when we are asleep. Although it represents only about 2 percent of our body weight, it consumes nearly 20 percent of our calories! The more we think, the more calories we burn. Perhaps this can be a new diet fad, and we could modify Descartes' famous quotation from "I think, therefore I am" to "I think, therefore I'm thin"!

Through the centuries, surveyors of the brain have examined every cerebral feature, sprinkling the landscape with Latin and Greek names to describe what they saw. They analyzed structures and functions and sought concepts to explain their observations. These observations were often of individuals who had damage to certain areas of the brain. If the damage resulted in a specific functional deficit, then the researchers surmised that the affected area was most likely responsible for that function. For example, physicians noted that damage to the part of the brain behind the left temple often resulted in temporary loss of speech (called *aphasia*). Therefore, they inferred that this area must be related to spoken language, and indeed it is.

One early concept of brain structure divided the brain by location—forebrain, midbrain, and hindbrain. Another, proposed by Paul MacLean (1990) in the 1960s, described the triune brain according to three stages of evolution: reptilian (brain stem), paleo-mammalian (limbic area), and mammalian (frontal lobes).

For our purposes, we will take a look at major parts of the outside of the brain (see Figure 1.1). We will then look at the inside of the brain and divide it into three parts on the basis of their general functions: the brain stem, limbic system, and cerebrum (see Figure 1.2). We will also examine the structure of the brain's nerve cells, called *neurons*.

Figure 1.1 The Major Exterior Regions of the Brain

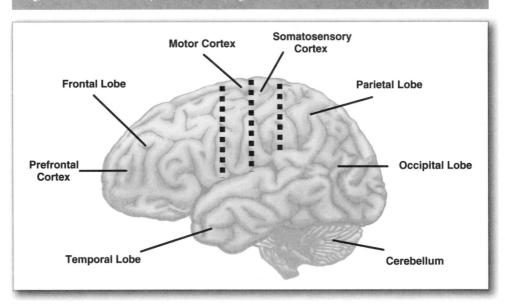

Video: For more information on structures of the brain, see

http://www.nimh.nih.gov/brainbasics/index.html

SOME EXTERIOR PARTS OF THE BRAIN

Lobes of the Brain

Although the minor wrinkles are unique in each brain, several major wrinkles and folds are common to all brains. These folds form a set of four lobes in each hemisphere. Each lobe tends to specialize for certain functions.

Frontal Lobes. At the front of the brain are the *frontal lobes*, and the part lying just behind the forehead is called the *prefrontal cortex.* Often called the executive control center, these lobes deal with planning and thinking. They comprise the rational and executive control center of the brain, monitoring higher-order thinking, directing problem solving, and regulating the excesses of the emotional system. The frontal lobe also contains our self-will area—what some might call our personality. Trauma to the frontal lobe can cause dramatic—and sometimes permanent—behavior and personality changes, including loss of speech and difficulties with memory. Because most of the working memory is located here, it is the area where focus occurs (Geday & Gjedde, 2009; Nee & Jonides, 2014). The frontal lobe matures slowly. MRI studies of postadolescents reveal that the frontal lobe continues to mature into early adulthood. Thus, the capability of the frontal lobe to control the excesses of the emotional system is not fully operational during adolescence (Dosenbach et al., 2010; Satterthwaite et al., 2013). This is one important reason why adolescents are more likely than adults to submit to their emotions and resort to high-risk behavior.

Temporal Lobes. Above the ears rest the *temporal lobes*, which deal with sound, music, face and object recognition, and some parts of long-term memory. They also house the speech centers, although this is usually on the left side only. Damage to the temporal lobes may affect hearing, the recognition of a familiar person's face, and the processing of sensory information.

Occipital Lobes. At the back are the paired *occipital lobes*, which are used almost exclusively for visual processing, including perceiving shapes and colors. Damage to these lobes can cause distorted vision.

Figure 1.2 A Cross Section of the Human Brain

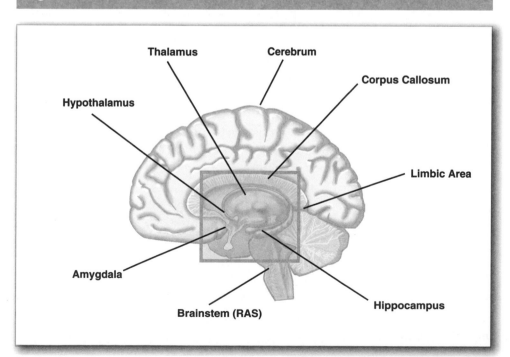

Parietal Lobes. Near the top are the *parietal lobes*, which integrate sensory information from various parts of the body (e.g., hot, cold, touch, and pain) and help with spatial orientation. Damage in this area may affect the ability to recognize and locate part of your body.

Motor Cortex and Somatosensory Cortex

Between the parietal and frontal lobes are two bands across the top of the brain from ear to ear. The band closer to the front is the *motor cortex*. This strip controls body movement and, as we will learn later, works with the cerebellum to coordinate the learning of motor skills. Just behind the motor cortex, at the beginning of the parietal lobe, is the *somatosensory cortex*, which processes touch signals received from various parts of the body.

SOME INTERIOR PARTS OF THE BRAIN

Brain Stem

The **brain stem** is the oldest and deepest area of the brain. It is often referred to as the reptilian brain because it resembles the entire brain of a reptile. Of the 12 body nerves that go to the brain, 11 end in the brain stem (the olfactory nerve—for smell—goes directly to the limbic system, an evolutionary artifact). Here is where vital body functions, such as heartbeat, respiration, body temperature, and digestion, are monitored and controlled. The brain stem also houses the **reticular activating system** (RAS), responsible for the brain's alertness and about which more will be explained in the next chapter.

The Limbic System

Nestled above the brain stem and below the cerebrum lies a collection of structures commonly referred to as the *limbic system* and sometimes called the *old mammalian brain*. Many researchers now caution that viewing the limbic system as a separate functional entity is outdated because all of its components interact with many other areas of the brain.

Most of the structures in the limbic system are duplicated in each hemisphere of the brain. These structures carry out a number of different functions, including generating emotions and processing emotional memories. Its placement between the cerebrum and the brain stem permits the interplay of emotion and reason.

Four parts of the limbic system are important to learning and memory:

The Thalamus. All incoming sensory information (except smell) goes first to the **thalamus** (Greek for "inner chamber"). From here it is directed to other parts of the brain for additional processing. The cerebrum and the cerebellum also send signals to the thalamus, thus involving it in many cognitive activities, including memory.

The Hypothalamus. Nestled just below the thalamus is the **hypothalamus**. While the thalamus monitors information coming in from the outside, the hypothalamus monitors the internal systems to maintain the normal state of the body (called *homeostasis*). By controlling the release of a variety of hormones, it moderates numerous body functions, including sleep, body temperature, food intake, and liquid intake. If body systems slip out of balance, it is difficult for the individual to concentrate on cognitive processing of curriculum material.

The Hippocampus. Located near the base of the limbic area is the **hippocampus** (the Greek word for "sea horse" because of its shape). It plays a major role in consolidating learning and in converting information from working memory via electrical signals to the **long-term storage** regions, a process that may take days to months. It constantly checks information relayed to working memory and compares it to stored experiences. This process is essential for the creation of meaning.

Its role was first revealed by patients whose hippocampus was damaged or removed because of disease. These patients could remember everything that happened before the operation, but not what happened afterward. If they were introduced to you today, you would be a stranger to them tomorrow. Because they can remember information for only a few minutes, they can read the same article repeatedly and believe on each occasion that it is the first time they have read it. Brain scans and case studies continue to confirm the role of the hippocampus in permanent memory storage (e.g., Huijgen & Samson, 2015; Postle, 2016). Alzheimer's disease progressively destroys neurons in the hippocampus, resulting in memory loss.

Studies of brain-damaged patients have revealed that the hippocampus plays an important role in the recall of facts, objects, and places. One surprising revelation in recent years is that the hippocampus has the capability to produce new neurons—a process called *neurogenesis*—into adulthood (Balu & Lucki, 2009). Furthermore, there is research evidence that this form of neurogenesis has a significant impact on learning and memory (Deng, Aimone, & Gage, 2010; Neves, Cooke, & Bliss, 2008). Studies also reveal that neurogenesis can be strengthened by diet (Hornsby et al., 2016; Kitamura, Mishina, & Sugiyama, 2006) and exercise (Kent, Oomen, Bekinschtein, Bussey, & Saksida, 2015; Pereira et al., 2007) and weakened by prolonged sleep loss (Kreutzmann, Havekes, Abel, & Meerlo, 2015) and excessive alcohol consumption (Geil et al., 2014).

The Amygdala. Attached to the end of the hippocampus is the **amygdala** (Greek for "almond" because of its shape and size). This structure plays an important role in emotions, especially fear. It regulates the individual's interactions with the environment that can affect survival, such as whether to attack, escape, mate, or eat.

Because of its proximity to the hippocampus and its activity on PET scans, researchers believe that the amygdala encodes an emotional message, if one is present, whenever a memory is tagged for long-term storage. It is uncertain whether the emotional memories themselves are actually stored in the amygdala. Research evidence is leaning toward the possibility that the emotional component of a memory is stored in the amygdala while other cognitive components (names, dates, etc.) are stored elsewhere (Hermans et al., 2014). The emotional component is recalled whenever the memory is recalled. This explains why people recalling a strong emotional memory will often experience those emotions again. Interactions between the amygdala and the hippocampus ensure that we remember for a long time those events that are important and emotional.

Neurogenesis—the growth of new neurons—can be strengthened by diet and exercise and weakened by prolonged sleep loss.

Teachers, of course, hope that their students will permanently remember what was taught. Therefore, it is intriguing to realize that the two structures in the brain mainly responsible for long-term remembering are located in the *emotional* area of the brain. Understanding the significant connection between emotions and cognitive learning and memory will be discussed in later chapters.

Test Question No. 1: The structures responsible for deciding what gets stored in long-term memory are located in the brain's rational system. True or false?

Answer: False. These structures are located in the emotional (limbic) system.

Cerebrum

A soft, jellylike mass, the cerebrum is the largest area, representing nearly 80 percent of the brain by weight. Its surface is pale gray, wrinkled, and marked by deep furrows called *fissures* and shallow ones called *sulci* (singular: sulcus). Raised folds are called *gyri* (singular: gyrus). One large sulcus runs from front to back and divides the cerebrum into two halves, called the *cerebral hemispheres*. For some still-unexplained reason, the nerves from the left side of the body cross over to the right hemisphere, and those from the right side of the body cross to the left hemisphere. The two hemispheres are connected by a thick cable of more than 200 million nerve fibers called the *corpus callosum* (Latin for "large body"). The hemispheres use this bridge to communicate with each other and coordinate activities.

The hemispheres are covered by a thin but tough laminated cortex (meaning "tree bark"), rich in cells, that is about one tenth of an inch thick and, because of its folds, has a surface area of about two square feet. That is about the size of a large dinner napkin. The cortex is composed of six layers of cells meshed in about 10,000 miles of connecting fibers per cubic inch! Here is where most of the action takes place. Thinking, memory, speech, and muscular movement are controlled by areas in the cerebrum. The cortex is often referred to as the brain's gray matter.

These cells were first discovered in the late 1800s by Santiago Ramón y Cajal (1989), a Spanish pathologist and neuroscientist. Figure 1.3 is a drawing from his notebook showing the neurons in the thin cortex forming columns whose branches extend through six cortical layers into a dense web below known as the white matter. Here, neurons connect with each other to form vast arrays of neural networks that carry out specific functions. The drawing is surprisingly accurate.

Cerebellum

The **cerebellum** (Latin for "little brain") is a two-hemisphere structure located just below the rear part of the cerebrum, right behind the brain stem. Representing about 11 percent of the brain's weight, it is a deeply folded and highly organized structure containing more neurons than all of the rest of the brain put together. The surface area of the entire cerebellum is about the same as that of one of the cerebral hemispheres.

This area coordinates movement. Because the cerebellum monitors impulses from nerve endings in the muscles, it is important in the performance and timing of complex motor tasks. It modifies and coordinates commands to swing a golf club, smooth a dancer's footsteps, and allow a hand to bring a cup to the lips without spilling its contents. The cerebellum may also store the memory of automated movements, such as touch-typing and tying a shoelace. Through such automation, performance can be improved as the sequences of movements can be made with greater speed, greater accuracy, and less neural effort. The cerebellum also is known to be involved in the mental rehearsal of motor tasks, which also can improve performance and make it more skilled. A person whose cerebellum is damaged slows down and simplifies movement and would have difficulty with finely tuned motion, such as catching a ball or completing a handshake.

The role of the cerebellum has often been underestimated. Research studies suggest that it also acts as a support structure in cognitive processing by coordinating and fine-tuning our thoughts, emotions, senses (especially touch), and memories (e.g., Hertrich, Mathiak, & Ackermann, 2016; Marvel & Desmond, 2016). Because the cerebellum is connected also to regions of the brain that perform mental and sensory tasks, it can perform these skills automatically, without conscious attention to detail. This allows the conscious part of the brain the freedom to attend to other mental activities, thus enlarging its cognitive scope. Such enlargement of human capabilities is attributable in no small part to the cerebellum and its contribution to the automation of numerous mental activities.

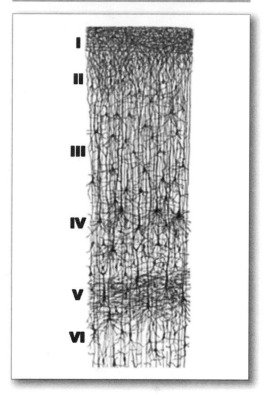

Figure 1.3 This drawing shows a cross section of the human cerebral cortex with the six layers labeled I through VI. Below layer VI is the white matter.

Brain Cells

The brain is composed of about a trillion cells of at least two known types, nerve cells and **glial cells**. The nerve cells are called *neurons* and represent about a tenth of the total—roughly 100 billion. Most of the cells are *glial* (Greek for "glue") cells that hold the neurons together and act as filters to keep harmful substances out of the neurons. Star-shaped glial cells, called **astrocytes**, have a role in regulating the rate of neuron signaling. By attaching themselves to blood vessels, astrocytes also serve to form the blood-brain barrier, which plays an important role in protecting brain cells from blood-borne substances that could disrupt cellular activity.

The neurons are the functioning core for the brain and the entire nervous system. Neurons come in different sizes, but the body of each brain neuron is about one hundredth of the size of the period at the end of this sentence. Unlike other cells, the neuron (see Figure 1.4) has tens of thousands of branches emerging from its core, called *dendrites* (from the Greek word for "tree"). The dendrites receive electrical impulses from other neurons and transmit them along a long fiber, called the *axon* (Greek for "axis"). There is normally only one axon per neuron. A layer called the *myelin sheath* surrounds each axon. The sheath insulates the axon from the other cells, prevents the electric charge from leaking into the environment, and thereby increases the speed of impulse transmission. This impulse travels along the neurons through an electrochemical process and can move through the entire length of a six-foot (183 centimeters) adult in two tenths of a second. A neuron can transmit between 250 and 2,500 impulses per second.

Neurons have no direct contact with each other. Between each dendrite and axon is a small gap of about a millionth of an inch (25 millionths of a millimeter) called a *synapse* (from the Greek, meaning "to join together"). A typical neuron collects signals from its neighbors through the dendrites, which are covered at the synapse with thousands of tiny bumps called *spines*. The neuron sends out spikes of electrical activity (impulses) through the axon to its end (called the *presynaptic terminal*) at the synapse. This activity releases chemicals stored in sacs (called *synaptic vesicles*) at the end of the axon (see Figure 1.5). These chemicals (called *neurotransmitters*) move across the synaptic gap and either excite or inhibit the end (*postsynaptic terminal*) of the neighboring neuron. The impulse then moves along this neuron's axon to other neurons, and so on. Learning occurs by changing the synapses so that the influence of one neuron on another also changes.

Video: To see an animation of neurotransmitters crossing the synaptic gap, go to

https://www.youtube.com/watch?v=mltV4rC57kM

About 100 different neurotransmitters have been discovered so far, but only about 10 of them do most of the work. The following are some of the common neurotransmitters:

acetylcholine (affects learning, movement, memory, and REM sleep)

epinephrine (affects metabolism of glucose, release of energy during exercise)

serotonin (affects sleep, impulsivity, mood, appetite, and aggression)

glutamate (most predominate one that affects learning and emotion)

endorphins (relief from pain, feelings of well-being and pleasure) and

dopamine (affects movement, attention, learning, pleasure, and reinforcement) Essentially, messages move *along* the neuron electrically but *between* neurons chemically.

A direct connection seems to exist between the physical world of the brain and the work of the brain's owner. Studies of neurons in people of different occupations (e.g., professional musicians) show that the more complex the skills demanded of the occupation, the greater the number of dendrites on the neurons. This increase in dendrites allows for more connections between neurons, resulting in more sites in which to store learnings.

We already mentioned that there are about 100 billion neurons in the adult human brain—about 14 times as many neurons as people on this planet and roughly the number of stars in the Milky Way. Each neuron can have up to 10,000 dendrite branches. This means that it is possible to have up to one quadrillion (that's a 1 followed by 15 zeros) synaptic connections in one brain. This inconceivably large number allows the brain to process the data coming continuously from the senses; to store decades of memories, faces, and places; to learn languages; and to combine information in a way that no other individual on this planet has ever thought of before. This is a remarkable achievement for just three pounds of soft tissue!

Conventional wisdom has held that neurons are the only body cells that never regenerate. However, we noted earlier that researchers have discovered that the adult human brain does generate neurons in at least one site—the hippocampus. This discovery raises the question of whether neurons regenerate in other parts of the brain

> *Believe it or not, the number of potential synaptic connections in just one human brain is about 1,000,000,000,000,000.*

and, if so, whether it is possible to stimulate them to repair and heal damaged brains, especially for the growing number of people with Alzheimer's disease. Research into Alzheimer's disease is exploring ways to stop the deadly mechanisms that trigger the destruction of neurons.

Figure 1.4 Neurons transmit signals along an axon and across the synapse (in dashed circle) to the dendrites of a neighboring cell. The myelin sheath protects the axon and increases the speed of transmission.

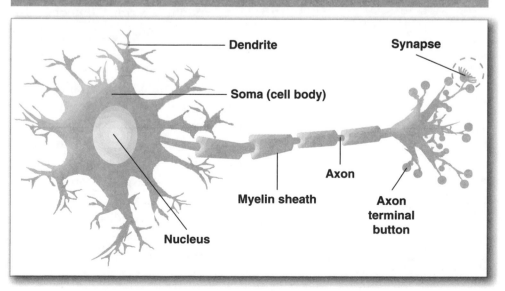

Mirror Neurons

Several decades ago, Italian scientist Giacomo Rizzolatti was doing research on motor movements in monkeys using fMRI technology (Rizzolatti, Fadiga, Gallese, & Fogassi, 1996). He discovered a set of neurons that fired both when the monkey performed an action and when it observed a similar action performed by another monkey or the experimenter. These specific neurons were named *mirror neurons* and were later discovered in humans. As with the monkeys, scientists using fMRI technology found clusters of neurons in the premotor cortex (the area in front of the motor cortex that plans movements) firing just before a person carried out a planned movement. Curiously, these neurons also fired when a person saw someone else perform the same movement. For example, the firing pattern of these neurons that preceded the subject grasping a cup of coffee was identical to the pattern when the subject saw someone else do that. Thus, similar brain areas process both the production and the perception of movement.

Neuroscientists believe these mirror neurons may help an individual to decode the intentions and predict the behavior of others (Catmur, 2015; Iacoboni, 2015). They allow us to recreate the experience of others within ourselves and to understand others' emotions and empathize. Seeing the look of disgust or joy on other people's faces causes mirror neurons to trigger similar emotions in us. We start to feel their actions and sensations as though we were doing them.

Mirror neurons probably explain the mimicry we see in young children when they imitate our smile and many of our other movements. We have all experienced this phenomenon when we attempted to stifle a yawn after seeing someone else yawning. Neuroscientists have wondered whether mirror neurons may explain a lot about mental behaviors that have remained a mystery. For instance, could children with autism spectrum disorders have a deficit in their mirror-neuron system? Wouldn't that explain why they have difficulty inferring the intentions and mental state of others? As coherent as that explanation may be, there is no solid research evidence to date linking autism spectrum disorders to deficits in the mirror neuron system (Cusack, Williams, & Neri, 2015).

Figure 1.5 The neural impulse is carried across the synapse by chemicals called neurotransmitters that lie within the synaptic vesicles.

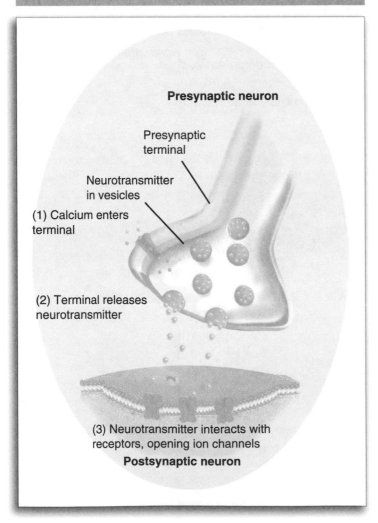

Presynaptic neuron

Presynaptic terminal

Neurotransmitter in vesicles

(1) Calcium enters terminal

(2) Terminal releases neurotransmitter

(3) Neurotransmitter interacts with receptors, opening ion channels

Postsynaptic neuron

Brain Fuel

Brain cells consume oxygen and glucose (a form of sugar) for fuel. The more challenging the brain's task, the more fuel it consumes. Therefore, it is important to have adequate amounts of these substances in the brain for optimum functioning. Low amounts of oxygen and glucose in the blood can produce lethargy and sleepiness. Eating a moderate portion of food containing glucose (fruits are an excellent source) can boost the performance and accuracy of working memory, attention, and motor function (Kumar, Wheaton, Snow, & Millard-Stafford, 2016; Scholey et al., 2013; Valentin & Mihaela, 2015) as well as improve long-term recognition memory (Sünram-Lea, Dewhurst, & Foster, 2008).

Water, also essential for healthy brain activity, is required to move neuron signals through the brain. Low concentrations of water diminish the rate and efficiency of these signals. Moreover, water keeps the lungs sufficiently moist to allow for the efficient transfer of oxygen into the bloodstream.

Many students (and their teachers, too) do not eat a breakfast that contains sufficient glucose, nor do they drink enough water during the day to maintain healthy brain function. Schools should have breakfast programs and educate students on the need to have sufficient blood levels of glucose during the day. Schools should also provide frequent opportunities for students and staff to drink plenty of water. The current recommended amount is an eight-ounce glass of water a day for every 25 pounds of body weight. Thus, a person weighing around 150 pounds should drink six eight-ounce glasses of water a day.

> *Many students (and their teachers) do not eat a breakfast with sufficient glucose or drink enough water during the day for healthy brain function.*

NEURON DEVELOPMENT IN CHILDREN

Neuron development starts in the embryo about four weeks after conception and proceeds at an astonishing rate. In the first four months of gestation, around 200 billion neurons are formed, but about half will die off during the fifth month because they fail to connect with any areas of the growing embryo. This purposeful destruction of neurons (called *apoptosis* or *synaptic pruning*) is genetically programmed to ensure that only those neurons that have made connections are preserved and to prevent the brain from being overcrowded with unconnected cells. The characteristic folds in the cerebrum begin to develop around the sixth month of gestation, creating the sulci and gyri that give the brain its wrinkled look. Any drugs or alcohol that the mother takes during this time can interfere with the growing brain cells, increasing the risk of fetal addiction and mental defects.

The neurons of a newborn are immature; many of their axons lack the protective **myelin** layer, and there are few connections between them. Thus, most regions of the cerebral cortex are quiet. Understandably, the most active areas are the brain stem (body functions) and the cerebellum (movement).

Surprisingly, neurons in a child's brain make many more connections than those in adults. A newborn's brain makes connections at an incredible pace as the child absorbs stimuli from its environment. Information is entering the brain through "windows" that emerge and taper off at various times. The richer the environment, the greater the number of interconnections that are made. Consequently, learning can take place faster and with greater meaning.

As the child approaches puberty, the pace slackens, and two other processes begin: Connections the brain finds useful become permanent; those not useful are eliminated (apoptosis) as the brain selectively strengthens and prunes connections based on experience. This process continues throughout our lives, but it appears to be most intense between the ages of 3 and 12 years. Thus, at an early age, experiences are already shaping the brain and designing the unique neural architecture that will influence how it handles future experiences in school, work, and other places.

Windows of Opportunity

Windows of opportunity represent important periods in which the young brain is highly susceptible to certain types of input from its environment in order to create or consolidate neural networks. Some windows relating to physical development are critical and are called *critical periods* by pediatric researchers. For example, if even a perfect brain doesn't receive visual stimuli by the age of 2, the child will be forever blind, and if a child doesn't hear words by the age of 12, the person will most likely never learn a language. When these critical windows taper off, the brain cells assigned to those tasks may be pruned or recruited for other tasks.

> *The brain's plasticity and resilience allow it to learn almost anything at any time, as long as the associated neural networks are developing or in place.*

The windows relating to cognitive and skill development are far more plastic but still significant. It is important to remember that learning can occur in each of the areas for the rest of our lives, even after a window tapers off. However, the skill level probably will not be as high. This ability of the brain to continually change during our lifetime in subtle ways as a result of experience is referred to as *plasticity* (also called *neuroplasticity*).

An intriguing question is why the windows taper off so early in life, especially since the average life span is now more than 75 years. One possible explanation is that these developmental spurts are genetically determined and were set in place many thousands of years ago when our life span was closer to 20 years. Figure 1.6 shows just a few of the windows that we will examine to understand their importance.

Several words of caution are necessary here. First, the notion of windows of opportunity should not cause parents to worry that they may have missed providing critical experiences to their children in their early years. Rather, parents and educators should remember that the brain's plasticity and resilience allow it to learn almost anything at any time, as long as the associated neural networks are developing or in place. In general, learning earlier is better, but learning later is certainly not a catastrophe.

Second, the initiatives and pressures to increase teacher and school accountability in recent years are changing what is happening in the primary grades. Early childhood researchers are noting that studies of instruction and content in kindergartens in the past decade show that these classrooms are becoming more like first grade (Bassok, Latham, & Rorem, 2016). Basically, kindergarten teachers are now spending time on more challenging literacy and mathematics content. However, the studies also found that this shift results in a decrease in time spent on music, art, science, and child-selected activities. Furthermore, there is much more frequent use of standardized testing. The question for further research is to examine what impact this development has on the kindergartners' cognitive and social development. It bears repeating that learning earlier is better, but learning *too* early may be counterproductive.

Motor Development

This window opens during fetal development. Those who have borne children remember all too well the movement of the fetus during the third trimester as motor connections and systems are consolidating. The child's ability to learn motor skills appears to be most pronounced in the first eight years. Such seemingly simple tasks as crawling and walking require complicated associations of neural networks, including integrating information from the balance sensors

Figure 1.6 The chart shows some of the sensitive periods for learning during childhood, according to current research. Future studies may modify the ranges shown in the chart. It is important to remember that learning occurs throughout our entire life.

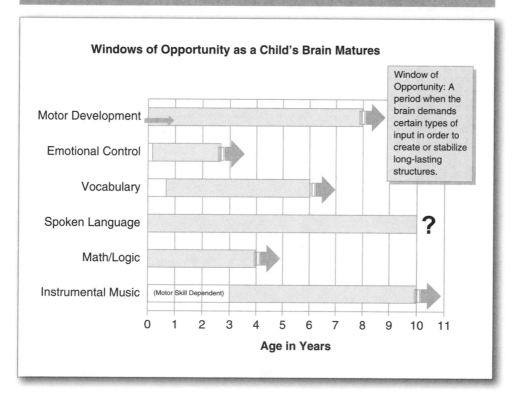

in the inner ear and output signals to the leg and arm muscles. Of course, a person can learn motor skills after the window tapers off. However, what is learned and practiced while it is open can be learned masterfully. Most concert virtuosos (e.g., cellist Yo Yo Ma), Olympic medalists (e.g., swimmer Michael Phelps), and professional players of individual sports such as tennis (e.g., Serena and Venus Williams) and golf, (e.g., Tiger Woods), began practicing their skills by the age of 8.

> *What is learned and practiced while a window of opportunity is open can be learned masterfully.*

Emotional Control

The window for developing emotional control seems to be from 2 to 30 months. During that time, the limbic (emotional) system and the frontal lobe's rational system are evaluating each other's ability to get their owner what he or she wants. It is hardly a fair match. Studies of human brain growth suggest that the emotional (and older) system develops faster than the frontal lobes (see Figure 1.7; Leventon, Stevens, & Bauer, 2014; Wessing et al., 2015). Consequently, the emotional system is more likely to win the tug-of-war for control. If tantrums almost always get the child satisfaction when the window is open, then that is the method the child will likely use when the window tapers off. This constant emotional-rational battle is one of the major contributors to the "terrible twos." Certainly, one can learn to control emotions after that age. But what the child learned during that open-window period will be difficult to change, and it will strongly influence what else is learned after the window tapers off.

Figure 1.7 Based on research studies, this chart suggests the possible degree of development of the brain's limbic area and frontal lobes. The 10- to 12-year lag in the full development of the frontal lobes (the brain's rational system) explains why so many adolescents and young adults get involved in risky situations.

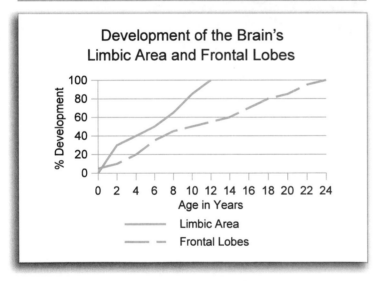

In an astonishing example of how nurturing can influence nature, there is considerable evidence confirming that how parents respond to their children emotionally during this time frame can encourage or stifle genetic tendencies. Biology is not destiny, so gene expression is not necessarily inevitable. To produce their effects, genes must be turned on. The cells on the tip of your nose contain the same genetic code as those in your stomach lining. But the gene that codes for producing stomach acid is activated in your stomach, yet idled on your nose. For example, shyness is a trait that seems to be partially hereditary. If parents are overprotective of their bashful young daughter, the toddler is likely to remain shy. On the other hand, if they encourage her to interact with other toddlers, she may overcome it. Thus, genetic tendencies toward intelligence, sociability, or

> *The struggle between the emotional and rational systems is a major contributor to the "terrible twos."*

schizophrenia and aggression can be ignited, moderated, or stifled by parental response and other environmental influences (McNamara & Isles, 2014; Zheng & Cleveland, 2015).

Vocabulary

Because the human brain is genetically predisposed for language, babies start uttering sounds and babble nonsense phrases as early as the age of 2 months. By the age of 8 months, infants begin to try out simple words like *mama* and *dada*. The language areas of the brain become really active at 18 to 20 months. A toddler can learn 10 or more words per day, yielding a vocabulary of about 900 words at age 3 years, increasing to 2,500 to 3,000 words by the age of 5.

Here's testimony to the power of talk: Researchers have shown that babies whose parents, especially fathers, talked to them more had significantly larger vocabularies (Henderson, Weighhall, & Gaskell, 2013; Pancsofar & Vernon-Feagans, 2006). Knowing a word is not the same as understanding its meaning. So it is crucial for parents to encourage their children to use new words in a context that demonstrates they know what the words mean. Children who know the meaning of most of the words in their large vocabulary will start school with a greater likelihood that learning to read will be easy and quick. These positive findings hold even for children from low-income families (Malin, Cabrera, & Rowe, 2014).

Language Acquisition

The newborn's brain is not the *tabula rasa* (blank slate) we once thought. Certain areas are specialized for specific stimuli, including spoken language. The window for acquiring spoken language opens soon after birth and tapers off first around the age of 5 years and again around the age of 10 to 12 years. Beyond that age, learning any language becomes more difficult. The genetic impulse to learn language is so strong that children found in feral environments often make up their own language. There is also evidence that the human ability to acquire grammar may have a specific window of opportunity in the early years (Pulvermüller, 2010). Knowing this, it seems illogical that many schools still wait to *start* new language instruction in middle school or high school rather than in the primary grades. Chapter 5 deals in greater detail with how the brain acquires spoken language.

Mathematics and Logic

How and when the young brain understands numbers is uncertain, but there is substantial evidence that infants have a rudimentary number sense that is wired into certain brain sites at birth (Ceulemans et al., 2015; Dehaene, 2010). The purpose of these sites is to categorize the world in terms of the "number of things" in a collection; that is, they can tell the difference between two of something and three of something. We drive along a road and see horses in a field. While we are noticing that they are brown and black, we cannot help but realize that there are four of them, even though we did not count them individually. Researchers have also found that toddlers as young as 2 years recognize the relationships between numbers as large as 4 and 5, even though they are not able to verbally label them. This research shows that fully functioning language ability is not needed to support fundamental number sense, but it is necessary to do numerical calculations (Dehaene, 2010; Lachmair, Dudschig, de la Vega, & Kaup, 2014).

Instrumental Music

All cultures create music, so we can assume that it is an important part of being human. Babies respond to music as early as 2 to 3 months of age. A window for creating music may be open at birth, but obviously neither the baby's vocal chords nor motor skills are adequate to sing or to play an instrument. Around the age of 3 years, most toddlers have sufficient manual dexterity to play a piano. (Mozart was playing the harpsichord and composing at age 4.) Several studies have shown that children aged 3 to 4 years who received piano lessons scored significantly higher in spatial-temporal tasks than a group who did not get the instrumental music training. Further, the increase was long term (Vargas, 2015). Brain imaging reveals that creating instrumental music excites the same regions of the left frontal lobe responsible for mathematics, logic, and other cognitive processes (Van de Cavey & Hartsuiker, 2016). See Chapter 6 for more on the effects of music on the brain and learning.

Research on how the young brain develops suggests that an enriched home and preschool environment during the early years can help children build neural connections and make full use of their mental abilities. Because of the importance of early years, I believe school districts should communicate with the parents of newborns and offer their services and resources to help parents succeed as the first teachers of their children. Such programs, called "parents as teachers" initiatives, are already in place on a statewide basis in Michigan, Missouri, and Kentucky, and similar programs sponsored by local school districts are springing up elsewhere. The recently passed Every Student Succeeds Act that replaced the No Child Left Behind law places greater emphasis on the importance of early childhood education. But we need to work faster toward achieving this important goal.

> *School districts should communicate with the parents of newborns and offer their services and resources to help parents succeed as the first teachers of their children.*

THE BRAIN AS A NOVELTY SEEKER

Part of our survival and success as a species can be attributed to the brain's persistent interest in novelty, that is, changes occurring in the environment. The brain is constantly scanning its environment for stimuli to determine whether they pose a potential threat. When an unexpected stimulus arises—such as a loud noise from an empty room—a rush of adrenaline closes down all unnecessary activity and focuses the brain's attention so it can assess the stimulus and be ready to spring into action. Conversely, an environment that contains mainly predictable or repeated stimuli (like some classrooms?) lowers the brain's interest in the outside world and tempts it to turn within for novel sensations.

Environmental Factors That Enhance Novelty

Craig is a good friend of mine and a high school mathematics teacher with more than 25 years' experience. He often remarks about how different today's students are from those of just a few years ago. They arrive with all their electronic gadgets and their attention darting among many tasks—usually not involving mathematics. As a conscientious teacher, Craig has incorporated more technology in his lessons, mainly because that holds his students' attention. In the past, Craig smiled skeptically whenever I talked to him about the rapidly increasing research findings about the brain and their possible applications to teaching and learning. Not anymore! He now realizes that because the brain of today's student is developing in a rapidly changing environment, he must adjust his teaching.

We often hear teachers remark that students are more different today in the way they learn than ever before. They seem to have shorter attention spans and bore easily. Why is that? Is there something happening in the environment of learners that alters the way they approach the learning process? In a word, yes!

The Environment of the Past

The home environment for many children several decades ago was quite different from that of today. For example,

- The home was quieter— less noise from gadgetry.
- Parents and children did a lot of talking and reading.
- The family unit was more stable, family members ate together, and the dinner hour was an opportunity for parents to discuss their children's activities as well as reaffirm their love and support.
- Television was in a common area and controlled by adults. What children watched could be carefully monitored.
- School was an interesting place because it had television, films, field trips, a few simple computers, and guest speakers. Because there were few other distractions, school was an important influence in a child's life and the primary source of information.
- The neighborhood was also an important part of growing up. Children played together, developing their motor skills as well as learning the social skills needed to develop relationships and interact successfully with other children in the neighborhood.

The Environment of Today

In recent years, children have been growing up in a very different environment.

- Family units are not what they once were. According to a Pew Research Survey, about 46 percent of U.S. children younger than 18 years of age are living in what was once termed the "traditional" family, that is, in a home with two married heterosexual parents in their first marriage (Livingston, 2014). Thirty-four percent are living with an unmarried parent, and 5 percent have no parent at home. Their dietary habits are changing as home cooking is becoming a lost art. As a result, children have fewer opportunities to have that important dinnertime talk with the adults who care for them.

- Many 10- to 18-year-olds can now watch television and play with other technology in their own bedrooms, leading to serious sleep deprivation. Furthermore, with no adult present, what kind of moral compass is evolving in the impressionable preadolescent mind as a result of watching programs containing violence and sex on television and the Internet?

- They get information from many different sources beside school, some of it inaccurate or false.

- They spend much more time indoors with their technology, thereby missing outdoor opportunities to develop gross motor skills and social-ization skills necessary to communicate and act directly and civilly with others. Sometimes their social media sites are places for hurtful antiso-cial expression. One unintended consequence of spending so much time indoors is the rapid rise in the number of overweight children and adolescents, now more than 17 percent of 6- to 19-year-olds. That rep-resents 12.7 million children (Ogden, Carroll, Kit, & Flegal, 2014).

- Young brains have responded to technology by changing their func-tioning and organization to accommodate the large amount of stimu-lation occurring in the environment (Sousa, 2016). By acclimating themselves to these changes, brains respond more than ever to the unique and different—what we called novelty. There is a dark side to this increased novelty-seeking behavior. Some adolescents who per-ceive little novelty in their environment may turn to alcohol or mind-altering drugs, such as ecstasy and amphetamines, for stimulation. This drug dependence can further enhance the brain's demand for nov-elty to the point where it becomes unbalanced and resorts to extremely risky behavior.

- Children's diet contains increasing amounts of substances that can affect brain and body functions. Caffeine is a strong brain stimulant, considered safe for most adults in small quantities. But caffeine is found in many of the foods and drinks that teens consume daily. Too much caffeine causes insomnia, anxiety, and nausea. Some teens can also develop allergies to aspartame (an artificial sugar found in children's vitamins and many "lite" foods) and other food additives. Possible symptoms of these allergic reactions include hyperactivity, difficulty concentrating, and headaches (Sharma, Bansil, & Uygungil, 2015).

How Is Technology Affecting the Student's Brain?

Students today are surrounded by technology: cell phones, smartphones, multiple televisions, MP3 players, movies, computers, video games, iPads, e-mail, and social media sites. In a 2015 survey of more than 2,600 8- to 18-year-olds, tweens 8 to 12 years old averaged 6 hours of daily media use, while teens 13 to 18 years old averaged 9 hours of media use per day (Common Sense Media, 2015).

In other words, teens spend more time using media than they do sleeping or interacting with their teachers and parents. Technology has become the dominant factor in their lives, and because of neuroplasticity, it is rewiring their brains.

Effect on Attention. The multimedia environment divides their attention. Even newscasts are different. In the past, only the reporter's face was on the screen. Now, the TV screen is loaded with information. Three people are reporting in from different corners of the world. Additional non-related news is scrolling across the bottom, and the stock market averages are changing in the lower right-hand corner just below the local time and temperature. These tidbits are distracting and are forcing viewers to split their attention into several components. They may miss a reporter's comment because a scrolling item caught their attention. Yet, children have become accustomed to these information-rich and rapidly changing messages. They can shift their attention quickly among several things, but their brains can still focus on only one thing at a time.

> *The brain cannot multitask. It can focus on only one task at a time. Alternating between tasks always incurs a loss.*

The Myth of Multitasking. Sure, we can walk and chew gum at the same time because they are separate physical tasks requiring no measurable cognitive input. However, the brain cannot carry out two cognitive processes simultaneously. Our genetic predisposition for survival directs the brain to focus on just one item at a time to determine whether it poses a threat. If we were able to focus on several items at once, it would dilute our attention and seriously reduce our ability to make the threat determination quickly and accurately.

What we refer to as multitasking is actually *task switching*. It occurs as sequential tasking (attention moves from Item A to Item B to Item C, etc.) or alternate tasking (attention moves between Items A and B). Whenever the brain shifts from focusing on Item A to focusing on Item B and back again to Item A, there is a cognitive loss involved. Figure 1.8 illustrates the process that will unfold in the following example. The solid graph line represents the amount of working memory used to process a homework task, and the dotted graph line represents the amount used to process an incoming phone call. Let us say Jeremy is a high school student who is working on a history assignment and has just spent 15 minutes focusing on understanding the major causes of World War II. The thinking part of his brain (frontal lobe) is working hard, and a significant amount of working memory is processing this information.

Suddenly, the cell phone rings. Caller ID shows him that the call is from his girlfriend, Donna. Now his emotional brain (limbic area) is awakened. As he answers the phone, his brain must disengage from processing history information to recalling the steps to answering and attending to a phone call. Jeremy spends the next six minutes chatting with Donna. During that time, much of the World War II information that Jeremy's working memory was processing begins to fade as it is replaced by information from the phone call. (Working memory has a limited capacity.) When Jeremy returns to the assignment, it is almost like starting all over again. The memory of having worked on the assignment may cause the student to believe that all the information is still in working memory, but much of it is gone. He may even mumble, "OK, where was I?" Task switching incurs a price (Al-Hashimi, Zanto, & Gazzaley, 2015; Dindar & Akbulut, 2016; Monk, Trafton, & Boehm-Davis, 2008). Some studies indicate that a person who is interrupted during a task may take up to 50 percent longer to finish the task and make up to 50 percent more errors (Altmann, Trafton, & Hambrick, 2014; Mansi & Levi, 2013; Medina, 2008).

Figure 1.8 When an assignment is interrupted by a phone call, memory resources dedicated to the assignment (solid line) decline, and resources dealing with information from the phone call (dotted line) increase.

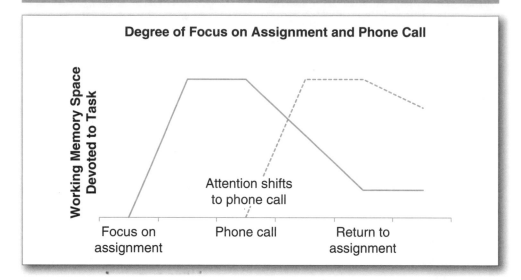

Task Switching and Complex Texts. Living in a world in which task switching is the norm may be affecting students' ability to read and concentrate on complex texts. Results of the 2014 ACT tests, taken by nearly 1.9 million high school students, showed than only 44 percent met the ACT college readiness benchmarks for reading (ACT, 2014). These benchmarks include the ability to comprehend complex texts. These texts usually contain high-level vocabulary and elaborate grammatical structure as well as literal and implied meanings.

Is it possible that high school students have become so adapted to task switching that they have not developed the cognitive discipline necessary to read complex tests? Bauerlein (2011) suggests that successfully reading complex texts demands the following three skills that constantly wired students may not be developing:

1. A willingness to probe an author's writings for literal and implied meanings and to pause and deliberate over the unfolding story. E-texts, on the other hand, are short and move back and forth quickly, habituating students to move quickly over text rather than to slow down and reflect.

2. A capacity for uninterrupted thinking to maintain a train of thought and to hold enough information in working memory to understand the

text. Complex texts are not constructed to allow for quick snippets of attention as they often deal with scenes and ideas not known to today's teenagers. <u>Grasping meaning from complex texts requires single-tasking and constant focus</u>, not the task switching and rapid and constant interaction of digital communications.

3. An openness for deep thinking that involves, for instance, deciding whether to agree or disagree with the author's premise and reflecting on alternatives. Complex texts often cause teenagers to confront the paucity of their knowledge and the limits of their experiences. Instead of being humbled by these revelations and reading deeper, adolescents respond by accepting that the persona they have established on their personal profile pages is self-sufficient.

Bauerlein (2011) suggests that high schools devote at least one hour a day to research assignments that use print matter, require no connection to the Internet, and include complex texts. The key is not to eliminate technology but to control its invasion into the time that should be devoted to deep thinking.

Technology is neither a panacea nor an enemy: It is a tool. Students in the primary and middle school grades still need personal contact and interaction with their teachers and peers. This is an important part of social development, but technology, perhaps to a great extent, is reducing the frequency of these interactions. We should not be providing technology for technology's sake, nor should the technology be an end unto itself. Rather than teaching with the various technologies, teachers should use them to enhance, enrich, and present their content more efficiently. Many Internet sites offer free materials to help teachers expand their lessons with audio and video pieces. See the Resources section at the end of this book for some suggested sites.

Have Schools Changed With the Environment?

Many educators are recognizing the characteristics of the new brain, but they do not always agree on what to do about it. Typical teenagers at home are constantly switching with ease among their MP3 player, cell phone, laptop, video games, and television. Multimedia is all around them. Can we then expect them to sit quietly for 30 to 50 minutes listening to the teacher, filling in a worksheet, or working alone? Granted, teaching methodologies are changing, and teachers are using newer technologies and even introducing pop music and culture to supplement traditional classroom materials. But schools and teaching are not changing fast enough. In high schools, lecturing continues to be the main method of instruction, primarily because of the vast amount of required curriculum material and the pressure of increased accountability and high-stakes testing. Students remark that school is a dull, nonengaging environment that is much less interesting than what is available outside school. Despite the recent efforts of educators to deal with this new brain, many high school students still do not feel challenged. In the 2015 High School Survey of Student Engagement involving 315,000 students, 61 percent of the senior students responded that they were highly challenged to do their best work (National Survey of Student Engagement, 2015).

A 2014 survey of more than 66,000 students in grades 6 to 12 revealed that 43 percent thought "school is boring," while only 44 percent felt that "teachers make school an exciting place to learn" (Quaglia Institute for Student Aspirations, 2014).

The Importance of Exercise. Just think about some of the things we do in schools that run counter to what we know about how the brain learns. One simple but important example is the notion of exercise. Exercise increases blood flow to the brain and throughout the body. The additional blood in the brain is particularly effective in the hippocampus, an area deeply involved in forming long-term memories (van Praag, Fleshner, Schwartz, & Mattson, 2014). Exercise also triggers one of the brain's most powerful chemicals, a tongue twister called brain-derived neurotrophic factor (BDNF). This protein supports the health of young neurons and encourages the growth of new ones. Once again, the brain area that is most sensitive to this activity is the hippocampus. Studies show that increased physical activity in school leads to improved student attention and academic performance (Institute of Medicine, 2013; Taras, 2005). Yet students still sit too much in school, especially in high school, and elementary schools are reducing or eliminating recess to devote more time to preparing for high-stakes testing. In other words, we are cutting out the very activity that could improve cognitive performance on these tests.

> As we continue to develop a more scientifically based understanding about today's novel brain, we must decide how this new knowledge should change what we do in schools and classrooms.

Clearly, we educators have to rethink now, more than ever, how we must adjust schools to accommodate and maintain the interest of this new brain. As we continue to develop a more scientifically based understanding about today's novel brain and how it learns, we must decide how this new knowledge should change what we do in schools and classrooms.

WHAT'S COMING UP?

Now that we have reviewed some basic parts of the brain and discussed how the brain of today's student has become acclimated to novelty, the next step is to look at a model of how the brain processes new information. Why do students remember so little and forget so much? How does the brain decide what to retain and what to discard? The answers to these and other important questions about brain processing will be found in the next chapter.

PRACTITIONER'S CORNER

Fist for a Brain

This activity shows how you can use your fists to represent the human brain. Metaphors are excellent learning and remembering tools. When you are comfortable with the activity, share it with your students. They are often very interested in knowing how their brain is constructed and how it works. This is a good example of novelty.

1. Extend both arms with palms open and facing down and lock your thumbs.

2. Curl your fingers to make two fists.

3. Turn your fists inward until the knuckles touch.

4. While the fists are touching, pull both toward your chest until you are looking down on your knuckles. This is the approximate size of your brain! Not as big as you thought? Remember, it's not the size of the brain that matters; it's the number of connections between the neurons. Those connections form when stimuli result in learning. The thumbs are the front and are crossed to remind us that the left side of the brain controls the right side of the body and that the right side of the brain controls the left side of the body. The knuckles and outside part of the hands represent the *cerebrum* or thinking part of the brain.

5. Spread your palms apart while keeping the knuckles touching. Look at the tips of your fingers, which represent the *limbic* or emotional area. Note how this area is buried deep within the brain and how the fingers are mirror-imaged. This reminds us that most of the structures of the limbic system are duplicated in each hemisphere.

6. The wrists are the *brain stem* where vital body functions (e.g., body temperature, heartbeat, blood pressure) are controlled. Rotating your hands shows how the brain can move on top of the spinal column, which is represented by your forearms.

PRACTITIONER'S CORNER

Arm for a Neuron

This activity shows how the human arm can be used to represent the structure of a neuron in the brain.

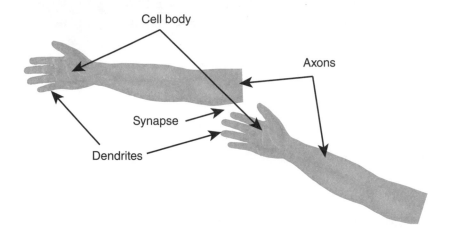

Forearm image: ©iStockphoto.com/Medical Art Inc.

Using the diagrams above, students can point out on their own arms the parts that represent major structures in the neuron. The palm is the cell body, the arm is the axon, and the fingers are the dendrites. The area where the finger on one student's hand almost touches another student's arm represents the synapse.

PRACTITIONER'S CORNER

Review of Brain Area Functions

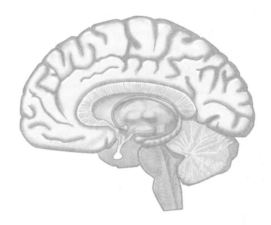

Here is an opportunity to assess your understanding of the major brain areas. Write in the table below your own key words and phrases to describe the functions of each of the eight brain areas. Then draw an arrow to each brain area on the diagram below and label it.

Amygdala:
Brain stem:
Cerebellum:
Cerebrum:
Frontal Lobe:
Hippocampus:
Hypothalamus:
Thalamus:

PRACTITIONER'S CORNER

Using Novelty in Lessons

Using novelty does *not* mean that the teacher needs to be a stand-up comic or the classroom a three-ring circus. It simply means using a varied teaching approach that involves more student activity. Here are a few suggestions for incorporating novelty in your lessons.

- **Humor.** There are many positive benefits that come from using humor in the classroom at all grade levels. See the Practitioner's Corner: Using Humor to Enhance Climate and Promote Retention in Chapter 2, which suggests guidelines and beneficial reasons for using humor.

- **Movement.** When we sit for more than 20 minutes, our blood pools in our seat and in our feet. By getting up and moving, we recirculate that blood. Within a minute, there is about 15 percent more blood in our brain. We do think better on our feet than on our seat! Students sit too much in classrooms, especially in secondary schools. Look for ways to get students up and moving, especially when they are verbally rehearsing what they have learned.

- **Multisensory Instruction.** Today's students are acclimated to a multisensory environment. They are more likely to pay attention if there are interesting, colorful visuals; if they can interact with appropriate technology; and if they can walk around and talk about their learning.

- **Quiz Games.** Have students develop a quiz game or another similar activity to test each other on their knowledge of the concepts taught. This is a common strategy in elementary classrooms but underutilized in secondary schools. Besides being fun, it has the added value of making students rehearse and understand the concepts in order to create the quiz questions and answers.

- **Music.** Although the research is inconclusive, there are some benefits of playing music in the classroom at certain times during the learning episode. See the Practitioner's Corner: Using Music in the Classroom in Chapter 6.

PRACTITIONER'S CORNER

Preparing the Brain for Taking a Test

Taking a test can be a stressful event. Chances are your students will perform better on a test of cognitive or physical performance if you prepare their brains with one of the following:

- **Exercise.** Get the students up to do some exercise for just two minutes. Jumping jacks are good because the students stay in place. Students who may not want to jump up and down can do five brisk round-trip walks along the longest wall of the classroom. The purpose here is to get the blood oxygenated and moving faster.

- **Fruit.** Besides oxygen, brain cells also need glucose for fuel. Fruit is an excellent source of glucose. Students should eat about two ounces (more than 50 grams) of fruit each day. Dried fruit, such as raisins, is convenient. Avoid fruit drinks as they often contain just fructose, a fruit sugar that does not provide immediate energy to cells. The chart below shows how just 50 grams of glucose increased long-term memory recall in a group of young adults by 35 percent and recall from working memory by over 20 percent (Korol & Gold, 1998). Subsequent studies have found similar memory boosts (Smith, Riby, van Eekelen, & Foster, 2011; Scholey et al., 2013; Sünram-Lea et al., 2008).

- **Water.** Wash down the fruit with an eight-ounce glass of water. The water gets the sugar into the bloodstream faster and hydrates the brain.

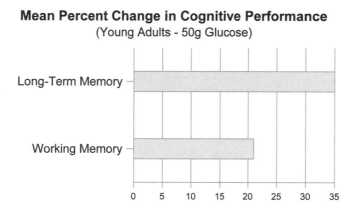

Mean Percent Change in Cognitive Performance
(Young Adults - 50g Glucose)

Wait about five minutes after these steps before giving the test. That should be enough time for the added glucose to fire up the brain cells. The effect lasts for only about 30 minutes, so the steps need to be repeated periodically for longer tests.

CHAPTER 1: BASIC BRAIN FACTS

Key Points to Ponder

Jot down on this page key points, ideas, strategies, and resources you want to consider later. This sheet is your personal journal summary and will help to jog your memory.

_____

_____

_____

_____

_____

_____

_____

_____

_____

_____

_____

2

How the Brain Processes Information

There are probably more differences in human brains than in any other animal partly because the human brain does most of its developing in the outside world.

—Robert Ornstein and Richard Thompson
The Amazing Brain

Chapter Highlights

This chapter presents a modern dynamic model of how the brain deals with information from the senses. It covers the behavior of the two temporary memories, the criteria for long-term storage, and the impact of the self-concept on learning.

Although the brain remains largely a mystery beyond its own understanding, we are slowly uncovering more about its baffling processes. Using scanning technologies, researchers can display in vivid color the differences in brain cell metabolism that occur in response to different types of brain work. A computer constructs a color-coded map indicating what different areas are doing during such activities as learning new words, analyzing tones, doing mathematical calculations, or responding to images. One thing is clear: The brain calls selected areas into play depending on what the individual is doing at the moment. This knowledge encourages us to construct models that explain data and behavior, but models are useful only when they contain some predictability about specific operations. In choosing a model, it is necessary to select those specific operations that can be meaningfully depicted and represented in a way that is consistent with more recent research findings.

THE INFORMATION PROCESSING MODEL

Numerous models exist to explain brain behavior. An Internet search for "information processing model" results in hundreds of examples. Nonetheless, despite their variations in color and design, most of them make use of the same research findings and include the same basic components of memory and information flow. In designing a model for this book, I needed one that would accurately represent the complex research of neuroscientists in such a way as to be understood by educational practitioners. I recognize that a model is just one person's view of reality, and I readily admit that this particular information processing model comes closest to *my* view of how the brain learns. It differs from other models in that it escapes the limits of the computer metaphor and recognizes that learning, storing, and remembering are dynamic and interactive processes. Beyond that, the model incorporates much of the recent findings of research and is sufficiently flexible to adjust to new findings as they are revealed. I have already made several changes in this model since I began working with it more than 30 years ago. My hope is that classroom teachers will be encouraged to reflect on their methodology and decide if there are new insights here that could affect their instruction and improve learning.

Origins of the Model

The precursor of this model was developed by Robert Stahl (1985) of Arizona State University in the early 1980s. Stahl's more complex model synthesized the research from the 1960s and 1970s on cognitive processing and learning. His goal was to convince teacher educators that they should use his model to help prospective teachers understand how and why learning occurs. He also used the model to develop an elaborate and fascinating learning taxonomy designed to promote higher-order thinking skills. Certain components of the model needed to be altered as a result of subsequent discoveries in neuroscience.

Usefulness of the Model

The model discussed here (Figure 2.1) has been updated over the years so that it can be useful to the widest range of teacher educators and practitioners. It uses common objects to represent various stages in the process. Even this revised model does not pretend to include all the ways that researchers believe the human brain deals with information, thought, and behavior. It limits its scope to the major cerebral operations that deal with the collecting, evaluating, storing, and retrieving of information—the parts most useful to educators.

The model starts with information from our environment and shows how the senses reject or accept it for further processing. It then explains the two temporary memories, how they operate, and the factors that determine if a

Figure 2.1 The Information Processing Model represents a simplified explanation of how the brain deals with information from the environment. Information from the senses passes through the sensory register to immediate memory and then on to working memory for conscious processing. If the learner attaches sense and meaning to the learning, it is likely to be stored. The self-concept often determines how much attention the learner will give to new information.

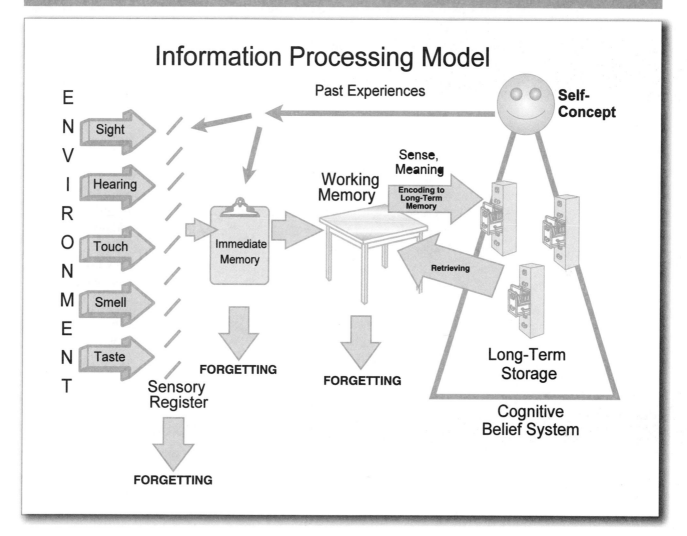

learning is likely to be stored. Finally, it shows the inescapable impact that experiences and self-concept have on present and future learning. The model is simple, but the processes are extraordinarily complex. Knowing how the human brain seems to process information and learn can help teachers plan lessons that students are more likely to understand and remember.

The brain changes its own properties as a result of experience.

Limitations of the Model

Although the explanation of the model will follow items going through the processing system, it is important to note that this linear approach is used solely for simplicity and clarity. Much of the recent evidence on memory supports a model of parallel processing. That is, many items are processed quickly and simultaneously (within limits), taking different paths through and out of the system. Memories are dynamic and dispersed, and the brain has the capacity to change its own properties as the result of experience. Even though the model may seem to represent learning and remembering as a mechanistic process, it must be remembered that we are describing a *biological process*. Nonetheless, I have avoided a detailed discussion of the biochemical changes that occur within and between neurons. That would not contribute to the understanding necessary to convert the fruits of research and this model into successful classroom practice, which is, after all, our goal.

Inadequacy of the Computer Model

The rapid proliferation of computers has encouraged the use of the computer model to explain brain functions. This is indeed tempting, especially as computers become more complex and more integrated into various components of society. Using the analogy of input, processing, and output seems so natural, but there are serious problems with such a model. Certainly, the smallest handheld calculator can out-tally the human brain in solving complex mathematical operations. More powerful computers can play chess, translate one language into another, and correct massive manuscripts for most spelling and grammatical errors in just seconds. The brain performs more slowly because of the time it takes for a nerve impulse to travel along the axon, because of synaptic delays, and because the capacity of its working memory is limited. But computers cannot exercise judgment with the ease of the human brain. Even the most sophisticated computers are closed linear systems limited to binary code, the zeros and ones in linear sequences that are the language of computer operations.

The human brain has no such limitations. It is an open, parallel-processing system continually interacting with the physical and social worlds outside. It analyzes, integrates, and synthesizes information and abstracts generalities from it. Each neuron is alive and altered by its experiences and its environment. As you read these words, neurons are interacting with each other, reforming and dissolving storage sites, and establishing different electrical patterns that correspond to your new learning. Re-reading these words will strengthen the neural connections that make those patterns and increase the depth of your learning.

How the brain stores information is also very different from a computer. The brain stores sequences of patterns, and recalling just one piece of a pattern can activate the whole. We can also identify the same thing in different forms, such as recognizing our best friend from behind or by her walk or voice. Computers cannot yet deal well with such variations. Moreover, emotions play an important role in human processing, comprehension, and creativity. And the ideas generated by the human brain often come from images, not from logical propositions. For these and many other reasons, the computer model is at this time, in my opinion, inadequate and misleading. Of course, it is possible that sometime in the not-too-distant future, computers will be able to mimic many of the qualities, capabilities, and weaknesses possessed by the human brain.

At first glance, the model may seem to perpetuate the traditional approach to teaching and learning—that students repeat newly learned information in quizzes, tests, and reports. On the contrary, the new research is revealing that students are more likely to gain greater understanding of and derive greater pleasure from learning when allowed to *transform* the learning into creative thoughts

> *As you read these words, neurons in your brain are interacting with each other in patterns that correspond to your new learning.*

and products. This model emphasizes the power of transfer during learning and the importance of moving students through higher levels of complexity of thought. This will be explained further in Chapters 4 and 5.

The Senses

Our brain takes in more information from our environment in a single day than the largest computer does in a year. That information is detected by our five senses. (Note: Apart from the five classical senses of sight, hearing, smell, touch, and taste, our body has special sensory receptors that detect internal signals. For example, we have receptors inside the ear and body muscles that detect the body's movement and position in space; sensory hairs in the ear that detect balance and gravity; stretch receptors in muscles that help the brain coordinate muscular contraction; and pain receptors throughout the body. For the purposes of the model, however, I have focused on the traditional five senses because they are the major receptors of *external* stimuli used by the brain to acquire information and skills.)

All sensory stimuli enter the brain as a stream of electrical impulses that result from neurons firing in sequence along the specific sensory pathways. The brain sits in a black box (the skull) and does not see light waves or hear sound waves. Rather, certain specialized modules of neurons process the electrical impulses created by the light and sound waves into what the brain *perceives* as vision and sound.

The senses do not all contribute equally to our learning. Over the course of our lives, sight, hearing, and touch (including kinesthetic experiences) contribute the most. Our senses constantly collect tens of thousands of bits of information from the environment every second, even while we sleep. That number may seem very high, but think about it. The nerve endings on your skin are detecting the clothes you are wearing. Your ears pick up sounds around you, the rods and cones in your eyes are reacting to this print as they move across the page, you may still be tasting recent food or drink, and your nose may be detecting an odor. Put these data together and you see how they can add up. Of course, the stimuli must be strong enough for the senses to detect and record them.

Sensory Register

Imagine if the brain had to give its full attention to all those bits of data at once. We would blow the cerebral equivalent of a fuse! Fortunately, the brain has evolved a system for quickly screening all these data to determine their importance to the individual. This system involves the *thalamus* (located in the limbic system) and a portion of the brain stem known as the *reticular activating system* (RAS). This system, which is also referred to as the *sensory register*, is drawn in the model as the side view of venetian blind slats (see the slashes in Figure 2.1). Like the blinds, the sensory register filters incoming information to determine how important it is.

All incoming sensory information (except smell, which goes directly to the amygdala and other destinations) is sent first to the thalamus, which briefly monitors the strength and nature of the sensory impulses for survival content and, in just milliseconds (a millisecond is one one-thousandth of a second), uses the individual's past experiences to determine the data's degree of importance. Most of the data signals are unimportant, so the sensory register allows them to drop out of the processing system. Have you ever noticed how you can be in a room studying while there is construction noise outside? Eventually, it seems that you no longer hear the noise. Your sensory register is blocking these repetitive stimuli, allowing your conscious brain to focus on more important things. This process is called *perceptual* or *sensory filtering*, and, to a large degree, we are unaware of it.

The sensory register does hold sensory information for a very brief time (usually less than a second). This is referred to as *sensory memory*. Let's say you are intently watching a football game during the final minutes of play. Your spouse comes in and starts talking about an important matter. After a few minutes, your spouse says, "You're not listening to me!" Without batting an eye you say, "Yes, I am," and then proceed to repeat your spouse's last sentence word for word. Fortunately, you captured this sensory memory trace just before it decayed, and you nipped a potential argument in the bud.

Short-Term Memory

As researchers gain greater insight into the brain's memory processes, they have had to devise and revise terms that describe the various stages of memory. *Short-term memory* is used by cognitive neuroscientists to include all of the early steps of temporary memory that will lead to stable long-term memory. Short-term memory is related to *immediate memory* and *working memory* (Cowan, 2009). A conventional distinction describes short-term memory as the storage of information for a limited time, while working memory is a theoretical framework referring to the structures and processes used for manipulating information. However, the terms *short-term memory* and *working memory* are often used interchangeably, and the nature of their relationship is still a matter of debate among researchers. Are they separate entities? Do they have overlapping functions? Does one include the other? Are there differences in their storage capacity, attentional demands, or processing speed? Until neuroscientists reach consensus on this issue, the pragmatic approach now is to focus on the characteristics of working memory because that is where we find substantial research interest as it relates to learning (Aben, Stapert, & Blokland, 2012).

> You cannot recall information that your brain does not retain.

Immediate Memory

Sensory data that are not lost move from the thalamus to the sensory processing areas of the cortex and through the first of two temporary memories, called *immediate memory*. The idea that we seem to have two temporary memories is a way of explaining how the brain deals with large amounts of sensory data and how we can continue to process these stimuli subconsciously for many seconds beyond the sensory register's time limits. Indeed, some neuroscientists equate sensory memory and immediate memory, arguing that separating them is more a convenience than a biological necessity.

For our purposes, we will represent immediate memory in the model as a clipboard, a place where we put information briefly until we make a decision on how to dispose of it. Immediate memory operates subconsciously or consciously and holds data for up to about 30 seconds. (Note: The numbers used in this chapter are averages over time. There are always exceptions to these values as a result of human variations or pathologies.) The individual's experiences determine its importance. If the item is of little or no importance within this time frame, it drops out of the processing system. For example, if you ask a friend for the telephone number of the local pizza parlor, you usually can remember it just long enough to make the call. After that, the number is of no further importance and drops out of immediate memory. Later on, you will have little success in remembering the entire number because you cannot recall information that your brain does not retain.

Examples of Immediate Memory at Work. Here are two other examples to understand how the processing occurs up to this point. Suppose you decide to wear a new pair of shoes to work today. They are snug, so when you put them on, the receptors in your skin send pain impulses to the sensory register. For a short time you feel discomfort. After a while, however, as you get involved with work, you do not notice the discomfort signals anymore. The sensory register is now blocking the impulses from reaching your consciousness. Should you move your foot in a way that causes the shoe to pinch, however, the sensory register will pass this pain stimulus along to your consciousness, and you will become aware of it once again.

Another example: You are sitting in a classroom, and a police car with its siren wailing passes by. Experience reminds you that a siren is an important sound. Signals from the sensory register pass the auditory stimuli over to immediate memory. If over the next few seconds the sound of the siren gets fainter, experience signals the immediate memory that the sound is of no further importance, and the auditory data are blocked and dropped from the system. All this is happening subconsciously while your attention is focused on something else. If asked about the sound 15 minutes later, you will not remember it. You cannot recall what you have not stored.

Suppose, on the other hand, that the siren sound gets louder and suddenly stops, followed by another siren that gets louder and stops. Experience will now signal that the sounds are important because they are nearby, may affect your survival, and therefore require your attention. At this point, the now-important auditory data move rapidly into working memory for conscious processing so that you can decide what action to take.

Threats and Emotions Affect Memory Processing. This last example illustrates another characteristic of brain processing: There is a hierarchy of response to sensory input (see Figure 2.2). Any input that is of higher priority diminishes the processing of data of lower priority. The brain's main job is to help its owner survive. Thus, it will process immediately any data interpreted as posing a threat to the survival of the individual, such as a burning odor, a snarling dog, or someone threatening bodily injury. Upon receiving the stimulus, the reticular activating system sends a rush of adrenaline throughout the brain. This is a reflexive response that shuts down all unnecessary activity and directs the brain's attention to the source of the stimulus.

Emotional data also take high priority. When an individual responds emotionally to a situation, the older limbic system (stimulated by the amygdala) takes a major role, and the complex cerebral processes are suspended. We have all had experiences when anger, fear of the unknown, or joy quickly overcame our rational thoughts. This reflexive override of conscious thought can be strong enough to cause temporary inability to talk ("I was dumbfounded") or move ("I froze"). This happens because the hippocampus is susceptible to stress hormones that can inhibit cognitive functioning and long-term memory.

Under certain conditions, emotions can enhance memory by causing the release of hormones that stimulate the amygdala to signal brain regions to strengthen memory. Strong emotions can shut down conscious processing during the event while enhancing our memory of it. Emotion is a powerful and misunderstood force in learning and memory. Another way of stating the hierarchy illustrated in Figure 2.2 is that before students will turn their attention to cognitive learning (the curriculum), they must feel physically safe and emotionally secure in the school environment.

Over the years, most teacher preparation classes have told prospective teachers to focus on reason, cover the curriculum, and avoid emotions in their lessons. Now, we need to enlighten educators about how emotions consistently affect attention and learning. Districts must ensure that schools are free of weapons and violence. Teachers can then promote emotional security in the classroom by establishing a positive climate that encourages students to take appropriate risks. Students must sense that the teacher *wants* to help them be right rather than catch them being wrong.

Moreover, superintendents and board members need to examine their actions, which set the emotional climate of a district. Is it a place where people want to come to work? Does the district reward or frown on appropriate risk taking?

Students must feel physically safe and emotionally secure before they can focus on the curriculum.

How a person "feels" about a teaching or learning situation determines the amount of attention devoted to it. Emotions interact with reason to support or inhibit learning. To be successful learners and productive citizens, we need to know how to use our emotions intelligently. Thus, we need to explore what and how we teach students about their emotions. For example, we could teach about controlling impulses, delaying gratification, expressing feelings, managing relationships, and reducing

How a person "feels" about a learning situation determines the amount of attention devoted to it.

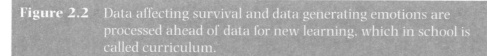

Figure 2.2 Data affecting survival and data generating emotions are processed ahead of data for new learning, which in school is called curriculum.

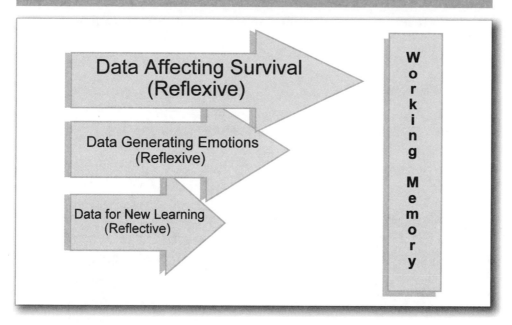

stress. Students should recognize that they can manage their emotions for greater productivity and can develop emotional skills for greater success in life.

Working Memory

Working memory is also a temporary memory and the place where conscious, rather than subconscious, processing occurs. The information processing model represents working memory as a work table, a place of limited capacity where we can build, take apart, or rework ideas for eventual storage somewhere else. When something is in working memory, it generally captures our focus and demands our attention. Information in working memory can come from the sensory/immediate memories or be retrieved from long-term memory. Brain imaging studies show that most of working memory's activity occurs in the frontal lobes, although other parts of the brain are often called into action (e.g., Sato et al., 2013; Shen, Zhang, Yao, & Zhao, 2015).

Capacity of Working Memory. George Miller (1956) discovered years ago that working memory can handle only a few items at once. The capacity of working memory appears to be decreasing for reasons we do not yet understand (see Table 2.1). Not surprisingly, this functional capacity changes with age, in that children have a smaller capacity than adolescents and adults (Cowan et al., 2010; Gilchrist, Cowan, & Naveh-Benjamin, 2009; Zhang, Zhao, Bai, & Tian, 2016). Preschool infants can deal with about two items of information at once. Preadolescents can handle three to seven items, with an average of five. Through adolescence, further cognitive expansion occurs, and the capacity increases to a possible range of five to nine, with an average of seven. For most people, that number remains constant throughout life.

Approximate Age Range in Years	Capacity of Working Memory in Number of Chunks	
	Minimum	Maximum
Younger than 5	1	2
Between 5 and adolescence	3	4
Adults	3	5

Table 2.1 Changes in Capacity of Working Memory With Age

More recent research has raised questions about the exact capacity limit of working memory. Some studies suggest that it now may be three to five chunks for adults. A few others say it is difficult to state an actual number because variables such as interest, mental time delays, and distractions may undermine and invalidate experimental attempts to find a capacity limit (Aben et al., 2012; Cowan, 2010; Oberauer & Hein, 2012). Nonetheless, most of the research evidence to date supports the notion that working memory has a functional limit and that the actual number varies with the learner's age and the type of input (factual information, visual, spatial, etc.; see, e.g., Myers, Stokes, Walther, & Nobre, 2014; Ullman, Almeida, & Klingberg, 2014).

Let's test this notion. Get a pencil and a piece of paper. When ready, stare at the number below for five seconds, then look away and write it down. Ready? Go.

92170

Check the number you wrote down. Chances are you got it right. Let's try it again with the same rules. Stare at the number below for five seconds, then look away and write it down. Ready? Go.

4915082637

Again, check the number you wrote down. Did you get all 10 of the digits in the correct sequence? Probably not. Because the digits were random, you had to treat each digit as a single item, and your working memory just ran out of functional capacity.

This limited capacity explains why we have to memorize a song or a poem in stages. We start with the first group of lines by repeating them frequently (a process called *rehearsal*). Then we memorize the next lines and repeat them with the first group, and so on. It is possible to increase the number of items within the functional capacity of working memory through a process called *chunking*. This process will be explained more fully in the next chapter.

Video: For more information on working memory, see

https://www.youtube.com/watch?v=S9zGpfg0tFw

Why would such a sophisticated structure like the human brain exhibit such severe limitations in working memory capacity? No one knows for sure. One possible explanation is that it is unlikely during the development of the brain thousands of years ago that our ancestors had to process or identify more than one thing at a time. It is also unlikely that they had to make several split-second decisions simultaneously. Even in fight-or-flight situations, there probably was only one enemy or predator at a time. In today's technology-laden environment, however, people are often trying to do several things at once during their workday, making the memory's capacity limits more obvious.

We should not look upon these capacity limitations necessarily as a weakness. Having a relatively small number of items in working memory may allow the items to become more easily associated with each other—that is, chunked—without causing confusion. From one point of view, this could be a distinct cognitive advantage, especially for children. We should also note that, although we have several items in working memory simultaneously, we can really focus on only *one* item at a time (Oberauer & Bialkova, 2009).

> *Keep the number of items in a lesson objective within the capacity limits of students and they are likely to remember more of what they learned. Less is more!*

Implications for Teaching. Can you see the implication this functional capacity has on lesson planning? It means that the elementary teacher who expects students to remember in one lesson the eight rules for using the comma is already in trouble. So is the high school or college teacher who wants students to learn in one lesson the names and locations of the 10 most important rivers in the world. Keeping the number of items in a lesson objective within the age-appropriate capacity limit increases the likelihood that students will remember more of what they learned. Less is more!

We should note here that we have been discussing *cognitive* capacity in working memory and its apparent decrease in processing information. However, there is mounting evidence that the apparent capacity of *visual* working memory is increasing (Cowan, Saults, & Clark, 2015). No one yet has a definite explanation for this finding, but researchers suggest that the increase is due to the growing number of hours that teens spend viewing and interacting with their digital devices.

Time Limits of Working Memory. Working memory is temporary and can deal with items for only a limited time. How long is that time? This intriguing question has been clinically investigated for over a century, starting with the work of Hermann Ebbinghaus (1850–1909) during the 1880s. He concluded that we can process items intently in working memory (he called it short-term memory) for up to 45 minutes before becoming fatigued. Because Ebbinghaus mainly used himself as the subject to measure retention in laboratory conditions, the results are not readily transferable to the average high school classroom.

Any discussion of time limits for processing new information has to include motivation. People who are intensely motivated about a subject can spend hours reading and processing it. They are not likely to quit until they are physically tired. That is because motivation is essentially an emotional response, and we already know that emotions play an important part in attention and learning. Students are not equally motivated in all subjects. Therefore, these time limits are more likely to apply to students who are in learning episodes that they do not find motivating.

Peter Russell (1979) shows this time span to be much shorter and age dependent. More recent studies of the novelty-seeking brain of today are very similar (Medina, 2008; Portrat, Barrouillet, & Camos, 2008). The time span is, for preadolescents, about 5 to 10 minutes, and for adolescents and adults, about 10 to 20 minutes. These are average times, and it is important to understand what the numbers mean. An adolescent (or adult) normally can process an item in working memory *intently* for 10 to 20 minutes before mental fatigue (as opposed to physical fatigue), interference from other items in working memory, or boredom with that item occurs and the individual's focus drifts. For focus to continue, there must be some change in the way the individual is dealing with the item. For example, the person may switch from thinking about it to physically using it or to making different connections to other learnings. If something else is not done with the item, it is likely to fade from working memory.

This is not to say that some items cannot remain in working memory for hours, or perhaps days. Sometimes, we have an item that remains unresolved—a question whose answer we seek or a troublesome family or work decision that must be made. These items can remain in working memory, continually commanding some attention, and, if of sufficient importance, interfere with our accurate processing of other information. This is often referred to as *preoccupation*.

Implications for Teaching. These time limits suggest that packaging lessons into 15- to 20-minute components is likely to result in maintaining greater student interest than one 40-minute lesson. It seems that, with many lessons, shorter is better! We'll talk more about lesson length and memory in Chapter 3.

Criteria for Long-Term Storage

Now comes the most important decision of all: Should the items in working memory be encoded to long-term storage for future recall, or should they drop out of the system? This is an important decision because we cannot recall what we have not stored. Yet teachers teach with the hope that students will retain the learning objective for future use. So, if the learner is ever to recall this information in the future, it has to be stored.

What criteria does the working memory use to make that decision? Figure 2.2 can help us here. Information that has survival value is quickly stored. You don't want to have to learn every day that walking in front of a moving bus or touching a hot stove can injure you. Strong emotional experiences also have a high likelihood of being permanently stored. We tend to remember the best and worst things that happened to us.

But in classrooms, where the survival and emotional elements are minimal or absent, other factors come into play. It seems that the working memory connects with the learner's past experiences and asks just two questions to determine whether an item is saved or rejected: "Does this make *sense*?" and "Does this have *meaning*?" Imagine the many hours that go into planning and teaching lessons, and it all comes down to these two questions! Let's review them.

- **Does this make sense?** This question refers to whether the learner can understand the item on the basis of past experiences. Does it "fit" into what the learner knows about how the world works? When a student says, "I don't understand," it means the student is having a problem making sense of the learning.
- **Does this have meaning?** This question refers to whether the item is *relevant* to the learner. For what purpose should the learner remember it? Meaning, of course, is a very personal thing and is greatly influenced by that person's experiences. The same item can have great meaning for one student and none for another. Questions like "Why do I have to know this?" or "When will I ever use this?" indicate that the student has not, for whatever reason, perceived this learning as relevant.

Here are two examples to explain the difference between sense and meaning. Suppose I tell a 15-year-old student that the minimum age for getting a driver's license in his state is age 16, but it is 17 in a neighboring state. He

> *Information is most likely to get stored if it makes sense and has meaning.*

can understand this information, so it satisfies the sense criterion. But the age in his own state is much more relevant to him because this is where he will apply for his license. Chances are high that he will remember his own state's minimum age (it has both sense *and* meaning) but will forget that of the neighboring state (it has sense but lacks meaning).

Suppose you are a teacher and you read in the newspaper that the average salary for accountants last year was $80,000, whereas the average for teachers was $50,000. Both numbers make sense to you, but the average teacher's salary has more meaning because you are in that profession.

Whenever the learner's working memory perceives that an item does not make sense or have meaning, the probability of it being stored is extremely low (see Figure 2.3). If either sense or meaning is present, the probability of storage increases significantly (assuming, of course, no survival or emotional component). If both sense *and* meaning are present, the likelihood of long-term storage is very high.

Relationship of Sense to Meaning

Sense and meaning are independent of each other. Thus, it is possible to remember an item because it makes sense but has no meaning. If you have ever played *Trivial Pursuit* or similar games, you may have been surprised at some of the answers you knew. If another player asked how you knew that answer, you may have replied, "I don't know. It was just there!" This happens to all of us. During our lifetime, we pick up bits of information that make sense at the time and, although they are trivial and have no meaning, make their way into our long-term memory.

It is also possible to remember an item that makes no sense but has meaning. My sixth-grade teacher once asked the class to memorize Lewis Carroll's nonsense poem "Jabberwocky." It begins, *'Twas brillig, and the slithy toves did gyre and gimble in the wabe.* The poem made no sense to us sixth graders, but when

Figure 2.3   The probability of storing information varies with the degree of sense and meaning that are present.

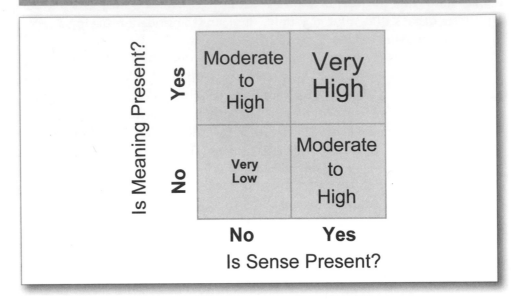

the teacher said that she would call on each of us the next day to recite it before the class, it suddenly had great meaning. Because I didn't want to make a fool of myself in front of my peers, I memorized it and recited it correctly the next day, even though I had no idea what the sense of it was.

Brain scans and other studies have shown that when new learning is readily comprehensible (sense) and can be connected to past experiences (meaning), there is substantially more cerebral activity followed by dramatically improved retention (Bein, Reggev, & Maril, 2014; Poppenk, Köhler, & Moscovitch, 2010; Stern, 2015).

Meaning Is More Significant. Of the two criteria, meaning has the greater impact on the probability that information will be stored. Think of all the television programs you have watched that are *not* stored, even though you spent one or two hours with the program. The show's content or story line made sense to you, but if meaning was absent, you just did not save it. It was *entertainment,* and no learning resulted from it. You might have remembered a summary of the show, or whether it was enjoyable or boring, but not the details. On the other hand, if the story reminded you of a personal experience, then meaning was present, and you were more likely to remember more details of the program.

Test Question No. 2: Learners who can perform a new learning task well are likely to retain it. True or false?

Answer: False. We cannot presume that because a learner performs a new learning task well it will be permanently stored. Sense and/or meaning must be present in some degree for storage to occur.

Implications for Teaching. Now think of this process in the classroom. Every day, students listen to things that make sense but lack meaning. They may diligently follow the teacher's instructions to perform a task repeatedly, and may even get the correct answers, but if they have not found meaning after the learning episode, there is little likelihood of long-term storage. Mathematics teachers are often frustrated by this. They see students using a certain formula to solve problems correctly one day, but they cannot remember how to do it the next day. If the process was not stored, the information is treated as brand new again!

Sometimes, when students ask why they need to know something, the teacher's response is "Because it's going to be on the test." This response adds little meaning to a learning, unless the student is highly motivated by test scores. Students resort to writing the learning in a notebook so that it is preserved in writing but not in memory. We wonder the next day why they forgot the lesson.

Teachers spend most of their planning time devising lessons so that students will *understand* the learning objective (i.e., make sense of it). But to convince a learner's brain to persist with that objective, teachers need to be more mindful of helping students establish *meaning*. We should remember that what was meaningful for us when we were children may not be necessarily meaningful for children today.

Past experiences always influence new learning. What we already know acts as a filter, helping us attend to those things that have meaning (i.e., relevance) and discard those that don't. If we expect students to find meaning, we need to be certain that today's curriculum contains connections to *their* past experiences, not just ours. Further, the enormous size and the strict separation of secondary curriculum areas do little to help students find the time to make relevant connections between and among subjects. Helping students to make connections between subject areas by integrating the curriculum increases meaning and retention, especially when students recognize a future use for the new learning. Meaning is so powerful that most states prohibit trial lawyers from using what is dubbed the "golden rule" argument. It asks the jury, "If you were in this person's situation, what would you have done?"

> *Past experiences always influence new learning.*

Long-Term Storage

Storing occurs when the hippocampus encodes information and sends it to one or more long-term storage areas. The encoding process takes time and usually occurs during deep sleep. While learners may *seem* to have acquired the new information or skill in a lesson, there is no guarantee that storage will be permanent after the lesson. How do we know if **retention** has occurred? If the student can accurately recall the learning after a specific period of time has passed, we say that the learning has been retained. Because research on retention shows that the greatest loss of newly acquired information or a skill occurs within the first 18 to 24 hours, the 24-hour period is a reasonable guideline for determining if information was transferred into long-term storage. If a learner cannot recall new learning after 24 hours, there is a high probability that it was not permanently stored and, thus, can never be recalled. This point has implications for how we test students for retention of previously learned material. See the Practitioner's Corner: Testing Whether Information Is in Long-Term Storage at the end of this chapter. Sometimes, we store only the gist of an experience, not the specifics. This may occur after watching a movie or television program. We store a generalization about the plot but few, if any, details.

> **Test Question No. 3:** Reviewing material just before a test is a good practice to determine how much has been retained in long-term storage. True or false?
>
> **Answer:** False. Reviewing material just before a test allows students to enter the material into working (temporary) memory for immediate use. Thus, the test cannot verify that what the learner recalled actually came from long-term storage.

The long-term storage areas are represented in Figure 2.1 as file cabinets—places where information is kept in some type of order. I have resisted the temptation to replace the file cabinets in the model with a more technologically current storage device—such as a computer hard drive or flash drive. As you may recall, I mentioned earlier the inadequacy of comparing brain functions to computer operations, and introducing such a storage device into the model would contradict that comparison.

Although there are three file cabinets in the diagram for simplicity, we do not know how many long-term storage sites actually are in the brain. Memories are not stored as a whole in one place. Different parts of a memory are stored in various sites that reassemble when the memory is recalled. Long-term memory is a dynamic, interactive system that activates storage areas distributed across the brain to retrieve and reconstruct memories.

Long-Term Memory and Long-Term Storage

This is a good place to explain the difference between the terms *long-term memory* and *long-term storage,* as I use them in the model. Long-term memory refers to the process of storing and retrieving information, while long-term storage refers to the areas in the brain where the memories are kept.

The Cognitive Belief System

The total of all that is in our long-term storage areas forms the basis for our view of the world around us and how it works. This information helps us to make sense out of events, to understand the laws of nature, to recognize cause and effect, and to form decisions about abstract ideas such as goodness, truth, and beauty. This total construct of how we see the world is called the *cognitive belief system.* It is shown in the information processing model as a large triangle extending beyond the long-term storage areas (file cabinets). It is drawn this way to remind us that the thoughts and understandings that arise from the long-term storage data are greater than the sum of the individual items. In other words, one marvelous quality of the human brain is its ability to combine individual items in many different ways. As we accumulate more items, the number of possible combinations grows exponentially.

Because no two of us have the same data in our long-term storage (not even identical twins raised in the same environment have identical data sets), no two of us perceive the world in exactly the same way. People can put the same experiences together in many different ways. To be sure, there are areas of agreement: gravity, for example (few rational people would dispute its effects), or inertia, as most people have experienced the lurch forward or backward when a moving vehicle rapidly changes speed. There can be strong disagreement, however, about what makes an object or person beautiful or an act justified. The persistent debates over abortion and capital punishment are testimony to the wide range of perspectives that people have over any issue. These differences reflect the ways individuals use the experiences in their long-term storage areas to interpret the world around them.

Here is a simple example of how people's experiences can cause them to interpret the same information differently. Close your eyes and form the mental image of an "old bat." Go ahead, try it! What picture comes to mind? For some baseball fans, it might be a marred wooden club that has been in too many games. A zoologist, however, might picture an aging fruit bat as it flies haltingly among the trees in search of food. Still others might recall an old hag whose complaining made their lives unpleasant. Here are at least three very different images generated by the same two words, each one formed by individuals whose experiences are different from the others.

> *The cognitive belief system is our view of the world around us and how it works.*

Self-Concept

Deep within the cognitive belief system lies the **self-concept**. While the cognitive belief system portrays the way we see the world, the self-concept describes the way we view *ourselves* in that world. I might conceptualize myself as a good softball player, an above-average student, or a poor mathematician. These and a long list of other descriptions form part of a person's self-concept.

The self-concept is represented in the information processing model (Figure 2.1) as a face and is placed at the apex of the triangle to emphasize its importance. *Self-concept* is used here as a neutral term that can run the gamut from very positive to very negative (see Figure 2.4). The face on the diagram of the model has a smile, indicating a positive self-concept. But for some people, the face might have a frown because they may not see themselves as positive beings in their world. Emotions play an important role in forming a person's self-concept.

Self-Concept and Past Experiences

Our self-concept is shaped by our past experiences. Some of our experiences, such as passing a difficult test or getting recognition for a job well done, raised our self-concept. Other experiences, such as receiving a reprimand or failing to

Figure 2.4 Self-concept describes how we see ourselves in the world. It can range from very negative to very positive and can vary with different learning situations.

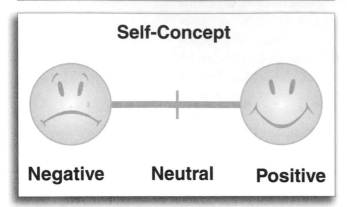

Self-Concept

Negative   Neutral   Positive

accomplish a task, lowered our self-concept. These experiences produced strong emotional reactions that the brain's amygdala encoded and stored with the cognitive event. These emotional cues are so strong that we often re-experience the original emotion each time we recall the event. Over time, new positive and negative experiences moderate the self-concept and alter how we see ourselves in our world.

Self-Concept and Mindset

One of the major components of our self-concept is *mindset.* Mindsets affect our cognitive processing (Schroder, Moran, Donnellan, & Moser, 2014). They develop at a very early age and are the results of interactions with our parents, friends, and elements of our specific culture. These experiences influence us in many ways, including our beliefs about how well we can learn and achieve. Psychologist Carol Dweck has been studying mindsets for years and suggests that they fall into these two basic types: fixed and growth (Dweck, 2006). Individuals with a fixed mindset believe that success comes from one's innate ability. A person either has that ability in a certain domain or does not, and not much can be done about it. You hear a fixed mindset at work when a student says, "I can't do math, and no one in my family can." Students with a fixed mindset avoid challenges for fear of failing, and they give up easily because they do not believe that effort pays off. These behaviors have an impact on their self-concept. On the other hand, students with a growth mindset believe that their success comes from their efforts and persistence. They accept that there may be certain genetic influences, but they rely more on hard work and resilience than on ability for their achievement. These students tend to be more intrinsically motivated to study and learn (Yan, Thai, & Bjork, 2014). The good news is that teachers can play a significant role in helping students with a fixed mindset develop a growth mindset.

Accepting or Rejecting New Learning

Remember that the sensory register and temporary memory systems use past experiences as the guide for determining the importance of incoming stimuli to the individual. Thus, if an individual is in a new learning situation and past experience signals the sensory register that prior encounters with this information were successful, then the information is very likely to pass along to working memory. The learner now consciously recognizes that there were successes with this information and focuses on it for further processing. But if past experiences produced failure, then the sensory register is likely to block the incoming data, just as venetian blinds are closed to block light. The learner resists being part of the unwanted learning experience and resorts to some other cerebral activity, internal or external, to avoid the situation. In effect, the learner's self-concept has closed off the receptivity to the new information. As mentioned earlier in the discussion of the hierarchy of data processing, when a curriculum concept struggles with an emotion, the emotion almost always wins. Of course, it is possible for the rational system (frontal lobe) to override the emotions, but that usually takes time and conscious effort.

Let us use an example to explain this important phenomenon. Someone who was a very successful student in mathematics remembers how that success boosted self-concept. As a result, the individual now feels confident when faced with basic mathematical problems. On the other hand, for someone who was a poor mathematics student, lack of success would lower his or her self-concept. Consequently, such an individual will avoid dealing with mathematical problems whenever possible—a condition known as *math anxiety*. People will participate in learning activities that have yielded success for them and avoid those that have produced failure.

Implications for Teaching. Students who experience self-concept shutdown in the classroom often give signs of their withdrawal—folding their arms, losing themselves in other work, attending to a digital device, or causing distraction. Too often, teachers deal with this withdrawal by reteaching the material, usually slower and louder. But they are attacking the problem from the front end of the information processing system, and this is rarely successful. It is the equivalent of putting a brighter light outside the closed venetian blinds, hoping the light will penetrate. If the blinds are fully closed and effective, no light will get through, regardless of how bright it may be. In other words, the learner's decision to ignore the material is successful.

The better intervention is to deal with the learner's emotions and convince the learner to allow the perceptual register to open the blinds and pass the information along. But because the self-concept controls the blinds, the learner must believe that participating in the learning situation will produce new successes rather than repeat past failures. When teachers provide these successes, they encourage students to open the sensory register and, ultimately, to participate and achieve in the once-avoided learning process. In short, the self-concept controls the feedback loop and determines how the individual will respond to almost any new learning situation. Recognizing this connection gives teachers new insight on how to deal with reluctant learners.

> *People will participate in learning activities that have yielded success for them and avoid those that have produced failure.*

Variations in Processing With Age

The components and dynamics of the processing system remain basically the same throughout our lives. However, there are some variations in students as their brains go through different stages of development and encounter new experiences. Children in preschool and the primary grades have had relatively few experiences that would cause their emerging self-concept to block incoming information. Therefore, these children tend to be open to all types of learning. They see themselves as creative beings exploring a largely unknown environment. Their brains process almost everything in an effort to establish neural networks that will help their owners survive and make sense of the world around them.

Adolescence is a busy time for the brain. In addition to monitoring physical changes, it needs to manage a rapidly growing collection of neural networks. Some of these networks are having an impact on the developing self-concept. Together with the emotional (limbic) brain, they begin to exert their influence in accepting or resisting new learnings. In the midst of all this activity, the social brain is emerging and directing more of the brain's attention resources to social needs than to course content. Meanwhile, learning preferences are developing and affecting how information will be processed.

Learning Profiles (Styles)

Experienced teachers have recognized for years that students learn in different ways. Several decades ago, psychologists and educators began to talk about "learning style" models that could describe the preferences that students had while learning. Rita and Kenneth Dunn (1993) developed one popular model in the 1970s that was organized around five categories: environmental, emotional, sociological, physiological, and psychological preferences. The Dunns suggested that students could achieve more if teachers tailored their instructional strategies to a student's individual learning style. Over the years, several more models emerged, and learning style was also used to describe other variables involved in learning, such as intelligence preferences and cultural influences (Gardner, 1993). Because of the proliferation of these models and the inclusion of other factors, the term *learning style* itself suffered from a vagueness that challenged researchers who wanted to determine whether its components really had an impact on student achievement.

In the late 1990s, Carol Ann Tomlinson (1999) proposed the broader term *learning profile* that included four elements of how individuals process, remember, and use what they learn: learning styles, intelligence preferences, culture, and gender. Despite this broader definition, the whole area of learning preferences remains the subject of considerable debate among researchers and educators. There is little argument that people have various internal and environmental preferences when they are learning. Hundreds of books and articles have been written, both supporting and questioning the notion of learning styles. What is not yet resolved is whether these preferences really matter and whether teachers need to consider them when selecting classroom instructional strategies or when working with individual students. Some researchers argue that teachers should not be using up valuable time assessing students' learning style, but should be using that time to design instruction so that it addresses all styles (e.g., Cuevas, 2015; Omar, Mohamad, & Paimin, 2015; Truong, 2016).

> Teachers tend to teach the way they learn.

One component of learning styles that educators have discussed for years is sensory or modality preferences. You hear comments such as "I learn best when I can see it" or "I need to get involved in my learning through hands-on activities." These are expressions of sensory preferences. Because teachers tend to teach the way they learn, it might be useful for teachers to know their own sensory preferences.

Sensory Preferences

Although we use all five of the common senses to collect information from our environment, they may not contribute equally to our knowledge base. Most people do not use sight, hearing, and touch equally during learning. Just as most people develop a left- or right-handed preference, they also develop preferences for certain senses as they gather information from their environment. Some people have a preference for learning by seeing, for example. They are called visual learners. Others who use hearing as the preferred sense are known as auditory learners. Still others who prefer touch or whole-body involvement in their learning are called kinesthetic/tactile learners. These sensory preferences are an important component of an individual's learning profile.

No one knows exactly why we have these sensory preferences, but most people acknowledge them on a self-assessment instrument. One possibility is that certain genetic factors combine to enhance the neural networks that process one sense's information better or faster than another's. There could also be an organic reason. For example, studies have revealed an astonishing 77 percent jump in hearing loss among 12- to 19-year-olds in 2006 compared to the same age group in the mid-1990s (Shargorodsky, Curhan, Curhan, & Eavey, 2010). Later studies show this percentage to be increasing (Kenna, 2015). Researchers attribute this loss—at least in part—to the loud music that adolescents listen to for long periods through their earphones, in their cars, and at pop concerts. Given its plasticity and recuperative powers, it is possible that the brain strengthens other sensory networks—visual processing, for example—to compensate for the reduction in its auditory capabilities.

Here, too, cognitive neuroscientists caution that teachers should not interpret the notion of sensory preferences to imply that teaching a student predominantly in that student's preferred sense will improve learning or retention. In fact, there is little research evidence at this time to support that notion. Rather, the evidence suggests that using *multisensory* activities that promote student engagement during a learning episode improves student learning and retention (e.g., Tomlinson, 2015). Nonetheless, the existence of sensory preferences means that teachers should consider the following:

- Realize that these sensory preferences are just that—preferences, *not* exclusivities. It is nonsensical to say that a typical student is "just a visual learner." We learn best when many senses are involved.
- Understand that students with different sensory preferences will behave differently during learning.
- Recognize that they tend to teach the way they learn. A teacher who is a strong auditory learner will most likely use a lot of lecture when teaching. Students who also are strong auditory learners will feel comfortable with this teacher's methods, but visual learners may have difficulty maintaining focus. They will doodle or look at other materials to satisfy their visual craving. Note, similarly, that students with auditory preferences want to talk about their learning and can become frustrated with teachers who use *primarily* visual strategies. Strong kinesthetic learners require movement while learning, or they become

restless—tapping their pencils, squirming in their seats, or walking around the room.

- Avoid misinterpreting these variations in learning profile behavior as inattention or as intentional misbehavior. The variations may, in fact, represent the natural responses of learners with different and strong preferences.

- Most important: Understand that a teacher's own learning profile and sensory preferences can affect learning and teaching. Teachers should design lessons that include activities to address all sensory preferences and learning profiles. That way, students not only benefit from instruction that fits their learning preferences, but also get to practice learning with the modalities that are less preferred.

WHAT'S COMING UP?

This completes our trip through the information processing model. Remember that the brain is a parallel processor and deals with many items simultaneously. Even though it rejects much data, it always stores some. The next chapter will examine the nature of memory and the factors that determine and help in the retention of learning.

PRACTITIONER'S CORNER

Walking Through the Brain

Directions: In this activity, students/participants will assume the roles of the different parts of the information processing model.

1. Each participant gets one of the following assignments:

    3–4 persons for the sensory register

    1 person for the immediate memory

    1 person for the working memory

    3–4 persons for the long-term storage

    rest of the group represents incoming information

2. In an open area of the classroom, the participants should arrange themselves in a pattern that approximates the information processing model shown in Figure 2.1.

3. All participants, except those representing incoming information, briefly explain their role and function in the model.

4. The participants representing incoming information then move through the model one at a time, explaining what is happening at each stage.

5. Variations: Replay the activity, demonstrating how information can be accepted or rejected by the sensory register, immediate memory, and working memory. One of the participants representing long-term storage can also represent the feedback loop of past experiences.

6. After demonstrating several different possibilities, discuss how this activity may have enhanced your understanding of the model. Note the positive effect that kinesthetic activities can have on learning new material.

PRACTITIONER'S CORNER

Redesigning the Information Processing Model

This activity gives the students/participants the opportunity to redesign the information processing model explained in this chapter.

Directions: In the area below, redesign the information processing model using a different metaphor (e.g., a sports game, taking a vacation, a cooking recipe). Keep the same metaphor for each of the major parts of the model. Be prepared to explain the metaphor and why you chose it.

PRACTITIONER'S CORNER

Developing Students' Growth Mindset

Teachers can have a significant impact on helping students shift from a fixed mindset to a growth mindset and thus improve their motivation and achievement. Carol Dweck (2006, 2012/2013) suggests that teachers consider the following ideas.

- Determine first your own mindset. To do that, go to http://mindsetonline.com/testyour mindset/step1.php. Look at the results and see if you need to develop a growth mindset before trying to teach it to students. Reflect on how you feel about your students. Do you believe there are some who will never get it? Observe your own practices and ask what you need to do to develop or enhance your growth mindset and your teaching ability.

- Teach the student how the brain changes with learning. Explain that abilities are not fixed. When learning something new, the neurons in the brain make new connections that, over time, can enhance their intellectual abilities. This takes effort and persistence that can make you smarter.

- Be sure to emphasize the importance of effort, not ability, when giving feedback on students' work. Focus on the their efforts and the learning strategies they used, as well as the progress they have made and what they *specifically* need to do in the future to improve.

- Present yourself as a mentor and resource for learning rather than as one who judges a student's intellectual abilities.

- Be aware of negative stereotypes. There are achievement gaps between black and white students and between males and females in mathematics and science. People in those groups often have a fixed mindset about their abilities. They believe they cannot learn something simply because they belong to that group. Remind these students that they can master the necessary skills with the right strategies, the right work ethic, and proper instruction.

- Explain that tests do not measure their potential to achieve in the future.

Determining Your Sensory Preferences

This checklist can reveal your sensory preference(s). It is designed for adults and is one of many that are available. You should not rely on just one checklist for self-assessment. Remember that sensory preferences are usually evident only during prolonged and complex learning tasks.

Directions: For each item, circle "A" if you agree that the statement describes you most of the time. Circle "D" if you disagree that the statement describes you most of the time. Move quickly through the questions. Your first response is usually the more accurate one.

1. I prefer reading a story rather than listening to someone tell it.   A   D

2. I would rather watch television than listen to the radio.   A   D

3. I remember faces better than names.   A   D

4. I like classrooms with lots of posters and pictures around the room.   A   D

5. The appearance of my handwriting is important to me.   A   D

6. I think more often in pictures.   A   D

7. I am distracted by visual disorder or movement.   A   D

8. I have difficulty remembering directions that were told to me.   A   D

9. I would rather watch athletic events than participate in them.   A   D

10. I tend to organize my thoughts by writing them down.   A   D

11. My facial expression is a good indicator of my emotions.   A   D

12. I tend to remember names better than faces.   A   D

13. I would enjoy taking part in dramatic events like plays.   A   D

14. I tend to subvocalize and think in sounds. A D

15. I am easily distracted by sounds. A D

16. I easily forget what I read unless I talk about it. A D

17. I would rather listen to the radio than watch television. A D

18. My handwriting is not very good. A D

19. When faced with a problem, I tend to talk it through. A D

20. I express my emotions verbally. A D

21. I would rather be in a group discussion than read about a topic. A D

22. I prefer talking on the phone rather than writing a letter to someone. A D

23. I would rather participate in athletic events than watch them. A D

24. I prefer going to museums where I can touch the exhibits. A D

25. My handwriting deteriorates when the space becomes smaller. A D

26. My mental pictures are usually accompanied by movement. A D

27. I like being outdoors and doing things like biking, camping, swimming, hiking, etc. A D

28. I remember best what was done rather than what was seen or talked about. A D

29. When faced with a problem, I often select the solution involving the greatest activity. A D

30. I like to make models or other hand-crafted items. A D

31. I would rather do experiments than read about them.   A   D

32. My body language is a good indicator of my emotions.   A   D

33. I have difficulty remembering verbal directions if I have not
    done the activity before.   A   D

Interpreting Your Score

Total the number of "A" responses in items 1–11:   _____

This is your visual score.

Total the number of "A" responses in items 12–22:   _____

This is your auditory score.

Total the number of "A" responses in items 23–33:   _____

This is your tactile/kinesthetic score.

If you scored a lot higher in any one area: This sense is *very probably* your preference during a protracted and complex learning situation.

If you scored a lot lower in any one area: This sense is *not likely* to be your preference in a learning situation.

If you have similar scores in all three areas: You can learn things in almost any way they are presented.

Reflections

A. What was your preferred sense? Were you surprised?

B. How does this preference show up in your daily life?

C. How does this preference show up in your teaching?

PRACTITIONER'S CORNER

Developing a Classroom Climate
Conducive to Learning

Learning occurs more easily in environments free from threat or intimidation. Whenever a student detects a threat, thoughtful processing gives way to emotion or survival reactions. Experienced teachers have seen this in the classroom. Under pressure to give a quick response, the student begins to stumble, stabs at answers, gets frustrated or angry, and may even resort to violence.

There are ways to deal with questions and answers that reduce the fear of giving a wrong answer. The teacher could

- supply the question to which the wrong answer belongs (e.g., "You would be right if I had asked . . .");

- give the student a prompt that leads to the correct answer; or

- ask another student to help.

Threats to students loom continuously in the classroom. The teacher's capacity to humiliate, embarrass, reject, and punish constitutes a perceived threat. Many students even see grading more as a punitive than as a rewarding process. Students perceive threats in varying degrees, but the presence of a threat in *any* significant degree impedes learning. One's thinking and learning functions operate fully only when one feels secure.

Teachers can make their classrooms better learning environments by avoiding threats (even subtle intimidation) and by establishing democratic climates in which students are treated fairly and feel free to express their opinions during discussions. In these environments, students

- develop trust in the teacher;

- exhibit more positive behaviors;

- are less likely to be disruptive;

- show greater support for school policy; and

- sense that thinking is encouraged and nurtured.

FOR FURTHER DISCUSSION

What kinds of emotions in school could interfere with cognitive processing (i.e., have a negative effect on learning)?

_____

_____

_____

What strategies and structures can schools and teachers use to limit the threat and negative effects of these emotions?

_____

_____

_____

What factors in schools can foster emotions in students that promote learning (i.e., have a positive effect)?

_____

_____

_____

What strategies have you used to encourage the positive emotions that promote learning?

_____

_____

_____

PRACTITIONER'S CORNER

Using Humor to Enhance Climate and Promote Retention

Research shows that humor has many benefits when used frequently and appropriately in the classroom and other school settings (e.g., Jeder, 2015).

Physiological Benefits

- **Provides more oxygen.** Brain cells need oxygen and glucose for fuel. When we laugh, we get more oxygen into the bloodstream, so the brain is better fueled.
- **Causes an endorphin surge.** Laughter causes the release of *endorphins* in the blood. Endorphins are the body's natural painkillers, and they also give the person a feeling of euphoria. In other words, the person enjoys the moment in body as well as in mind. Endorphins also stimulate the brain's frontal lobes, thereby increasing the degree of focus and amount of attention time.
- **Moderates body functions.** Scientists have found that humor decreases stress, modulates pain, decreases blood pressure, relaxes muscle tension, and boosts immune defenses. These are all desirable outcomes.

Psychological, Sociological, and Educational Benefits

- **Gets attention.** The first thing a teacher has to do when starting a lesson is to get the students' attention or focus. Because the normal human brain loves to laugh, starting with a humorous tale (such as a joke, pun, or story) gets the learner's attention. Self-deprecating humor ("You won't believe what happened to me this weekend") is particularly effective with teens.
- **Creates a positive climate.** Students are going to be together in a classroom for about 180 days. We need to find ways to help this increasingly diverse student population get along. When people laugh together, they bond and a community spirit emerges—all positive forces for a climate conducive to learning.
- **Increases retention and recall.** We know that emotions enhance retention, so the positive feelings that result from laughter increase the probability that students will remember what they learned and be able to recall it later (e.g., Saraa-Zawyah, Badli, & Dzulkifli, 2013).
- **Improves everyone's mental health.** Schools and all their occupants are under more stress than ever. Taking time to laugh can relieve that stress and give the staff and students better mental attitude with which to accomplish their tasks. Let's take our work seriously but ourselves lightly.
- **Provides an effective discipline tool.** Good-natured humor (not teasing or sarcasm) can be an effective way of reminding students of the rules without raising tension in the classroom. Laughter also dampens hostility and aggression. Teachers who use appropriate humor are more likable, and students have a more positive feeling toward them. Discipline problems, therefore, are less likely to occur.

Using Humor as Part of Lessons. Humor should not be limited to an opening joke or story. Because of its value as an attention-getter and retention strategy, look for ways to use humor within the context of the learning objective. Textbooks often lack humor, so use humorous examples and video clips from the Internet that relate to the learning. Include humorous assignments in homework to maintain student interest. Several books on the market give many helpful suggestions on how to get students to use humor in lessons.

Administrators and Humor. Administrators also need to remember the value of humor in their relationships with staff, students, and parents. As leaders, they set the example. In meetings and other settings, they can show that humor and laughter are acceptable in schools and classrooms. Studies show a principal's sense of humor can motivate teachers (e.g., Akyol & Gündüz, 2014)

Some Barriers to Humor in Classrooms

- **"I'm not funny."** Some teachers want to use humor in the classroom but don't perceive themselves as jokesters. They'll say, "I'm just not funny" or "I can't tell a joke." But the teacher doesn't have to be funny, just the material—and there's plenty of it. Books on humor are available in local stores, as well as video clips on YouTube, and don't forget that students themselves often provide humor by their responses in class and answers on tests. Be certain that you use this material appropriately, ensure anonymity, and avoid teasing or sarcasm.

- **"Students won't enjoy it."** Secondary teachers, particularly, believe that students won't find humor in corny jokes or that they are too sophisticated to laugh. But everyone likes to laugh (or groan) at humor. I suggest starting each class period with humor for three weeks, then stopping. I'm certain that students will say, "Hey, where's the joke?"— evidence that they *were* listening.

- **"It takes too much time."** This is a common concern. Secondary teachers often feel so pressured to cover curriculum material that they are reluctant to give time to what may seem like a frivolous activity. On the other hand, humor is an *efficient* as well as effective way to gain students' attention and improve retention of learning. It really is a useful investment of time.

Avoiding sarcasm. All of the wonderful benefits mentioned above are the result of using wholesome humor that everyone can enjoy and not sarcasm, which is inevitably destructive to someone. (Did you know that the word *sarcasm* comes from the Greek "to bite flesh"?) Some well-intentioned teachers say, "Oh, I know my students very well, so they can take sarcasm." More than ever, today's students are coming to school looking for emotional support. Sarcasm is one of the factors that can undermine that support and turn students against their peers, the teacher, and the school. When a student who is the object of sarcasm smiles, you really do not know if the student thinks the comment is humorous or is, instead, plotting revenge. Besides, there are plenty of sources of good classroom humor without sarcasm.

PRACTITIONER'S CORNER

Increasing Processing Time
Through Motivation

Working memory is a temporary memory, so items have a limited time for processing. But the longer an item is processed (or rehearsed), the greater the probability that sense and meaning may be found and, therefore, that retention will occur. One way to increase processing time is through motivation, which is essentially an emotional response. Not surprisingly, recent research has validated long-standing beliefs that motivation is a key to the amount of attention devoted to a learning situation.

Motivation can come from within the individual, called *intrinsic motivation,* when an activity is related to a person's needs, values, interests, and attitudes. People spend hours on their hobbies because intrinsic motivation brings them joy and satisfaction. These internal attributes are so deeply rooted that they are difficult to change. But they can change over time.

Motivation that comes from the environment, such as rewards and punishment, is called *extrinsic motivation.* External motivators are used to control and reward behavior. Grades, stars, and praise are examples of external motivators used in schools. Although these incentives serve a purpose, they have little relationship to the internal process of learning. It's no secret that focus and learning occur best when the learner is intrinsically motivated. External motivators can be of value by getting students started on a topic so that they can move toward intrinsic rewards.

Here are a few ideas about motivation for teachers to consider (Anderman & Gray, 2015; DePasque & Tricomi, 2015; Jovanovic & Matejevic, 2014):

- **Generate interest.** If the learner is interested in the item, then the processing time can be extended significantly because the learner is dealing with the item in different ways and making new connections with past learnings that once were also of interest. The working memory is seeking ways to use this new learning to enhance the usefulness of the past learning. We all know students who won't give us five minutes of their undivided attention in class but who spend hours working on a stamp collection, playing video games, or repairing a carburetor.

Teachers can identify these interests by having their students complete interest inventories at the beginning of the school year. The information gathered from these surveys can help teachers design lessons that include references to student interests as often as possible. Guidance counselors can provide information on the types and sources of interest inventories.

Today's novelty-seeking brain wants to get actively involved in the learning process. Active learning involves choices and actions that the learner finds pleasurable and effective for developing an understanding of the big picture as well as the relationship between and among the components of the learning objective. This approach stimulates intrinsic motivation and interest. Teachers, then, should

- make clear what the students should be able to do when the lesson objective is accomplished;

- include provocative ideas and challenging activities;

— involve the students in developing the criteria that will be used to assess their competency (e.g., assessment rubrics);

— demonstrate how closely the content is connected to the real world; and

— give students choices in selecting activities and questions to pursue.

- **Establish accountability.** When learners believe they will be held accountable for new learning, processing time increases. High school students have little difficulty staying on task in driver education classes. Not only do they have interest, but they also know they will be legally accountable for their knowledge and skills long after they complete the license tests.

- **Provide feedback.** Research studies clearly show that when students get prompt, specific, and corrective feedback on the results of their thinking, they are more likely to continue processing, make corrections, and persist until successful completion (Hattie, 2012). Formative assessments, such as frequent brief quizzes that are carefully corrected and returned promptly, are much more valuable and effective learning tools than summative assessment, such as the unit test, and are more likely to help students be successful. This success will improve self-concept and encourage them to try more difficult tasks. Computers and similar technology are motivating because they provide immediate and objective feedback and allow students to evaluate their progress and understand their level of competence.

Another effective strategy suggested by Hunter (2004) for increasing processing time through motivation is called *level of concern.* This refers to how much the student cares about the learning. We used to think that if the students had anxiety about learning, then little or no learning occurred. But there is helpful anxiety (desire to do well), and there is harmful anxiety (feeling threatened). Having anxiety about your job performance will usually get you to put forth more effort to obtain positive results. When you are concerned about being more effective (helpful anxiety), you are likely to learn and try new strategies. This is an example of how emotions can increase learning.

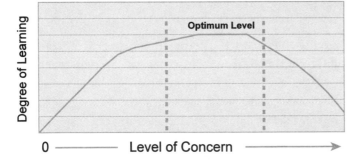

Level of Concern vs. Degree of Learning

The graph shows that as the level of concern increases, so does the degree of learning. If the stress level gets too high, our focus shifts to the emotions and the consequences generated by the stress, and learning fades. Students need a certain level of concern to stimulate their efforts to learn. When there is no concern, there is little or no learning. But if there is too much concern, anxiety shuts down the learning process, and adverse emotions take over. The teacher then has to seek the level of concern that produces the optimum processing time and learning. Hunter (2004) offers four ways to raise or lower the level of concern in a lesson:

- **Consequences.** Teachers raise the level of concern when they say, "This is going to be on the test," and lower it with "Knowing this will help you learn the next set of skills more easily."
- **Visibility.** Standing next to a student who is off task will raise that student's concern; moving away from an anxious student will lower concern. Telling students their work will be displayed can also raise concern. Use this strategy with care.
- **Amount of time.** Giving students only a little time to complete a learning task will raise concern; extending the time will lower it.
- **Amount of help.** If students have little or no help while completing a learning task, concern rises. On the other hand, if they have quick access to help, concern lowers. This can be a problem, however. If students can always get immediate help, either from a person or by "Googling," they may become dependent on those sources and never learn to solve problems for themselves. There comes a time when the teacher needs to reduce the help and tell the students to use what they have learned to solve the problem on their own.

Reflections

A. What types of class activities increase the level of concern beyond the optimum level?

B. What strategies lower the level of concern raised by the activities in your answers to A above?

PRACTITIONER'S CORNER

Creating Meaning in New Learning

Meaning refers to the relevance that students attach to new learning. Meaning is not inherent in content; rather, it is the result of how the students relate the content to their past learnings and experiences. Questions like "Why do I need to know this?" reveal a learner who is having difficulty determining the relevance of the new topic. Here are a few ways teachers can help students attach meaning to new learning.

- **Modeling.** Models are examples of the new learning that the learner can perceive in the classroom rather than relying on experience. Models can be concrete (an engine) or symbolic (a map). The Internet can be a valuable source of models when a real one is impractical. To be effective, a model should do all of the following:

  - Accurately and unambiguously highlight the critical attribute(s) of new learning. A dog is a better example of a mammal than is a whale.

  - Be given first by the teacher to ensure that it is correct during this period of prime time when retention is highest.

  - Avoid controversial issues that can evoke strong emotions and redirect the learner's attention.

- **Using examples from students' experience.** These allow students to bring previous knowledge into working memory to accelerate making sense of and attaching meaning to the new learning. Make sure that the example is clearly relevant to the new learning. This is not easy to do on the spot, so examples should be thought out in advance when planning the lesson.

- **Creating artificial meaning.** When it is not possible to identify exemplary elements from student experience to develop meaning, we can resort to other methods. **Mnemonic** devices help students associate material so they can remember it. Examples are HOMES to remember the Great Lakes and "Every good boy does fine" for the musical notes *e, g, b, d,* and *f* (see Chapter 3).

PRACTITIONER'S CORNER

Using Closure to Enhance Sense and Meaning

Closure describes the covert process whereby the learner's working memory summarizes for itself its perception of what has been learned. It is during closure that a student often completes the rehearsal process and attaches sense and meaning to the new learning, thereby increasing the probability that it will be retained in long-term storage.

- **Initiating closure.** The teacher gives directions that focus the student on the new learning, such as "I'm going to give you about two minutes to think of the three causes of the Civil War that we learned today. Be prepared to discuss them briefly." In this statement, the teacher told the students how much quiet time they have for the cerebral summarizing to occur and identified the overt activity (discussion) that will be used for student accountability. During the discussion, the teacher can assess the quality and accuracy of what occurred during closure and make any necessary adjustments in teaching.

- **Closure is different from review.** In review, the teacher does most of the work, repeating key concepts made during the lesson and rechecking student understanding. In closure, the student does most of the work by mentally rehearsing and summarizing those concepts and deciding whether they make sense and have meaning.

- **When to use closure.** Closure can occur at various times in a lesson.

  - It can start a lesson: "Think of the two causes of the Civil War we talked about yesterday and be prepared to discuss them."

  - It can occur during the lesson (called *procedural closure*) when the teacher moves from one sublearning to the next: "Review those two rules in your mind before we learn the third rule."

  - It should also take place at the end of the lesson (called *terminal closure*) to tie all the sublearnings together.

Closure is an investment that can pay off dramatically in increased retention of learning.

PRACTITIONER'S CORNER

Testing Whether Information
Is in Long-Term Storage

Information that the learner processes during a lesson remains in working memory where it eventually will be dropped out or saved for long-term storage. Just because students act as if they have learned the new information or skill doesn't mean it will be transferred to long-term storage. Extensive research on retention indicates that 70 to 90 percent of new learning is forgotten within 18 to 24 hours after the lesson. Consequently, if the new learning survives this time intact, it is probably destined for long-term storage during sleep, and will not deteriorate further (e.g., Ruch et al., 2012; Schiff & Vakil, 2015).

This time requirement confirms that the processing and transferring between working memory and long-term storage needs adequate time for the encoding and consolidation of the new information into the storage networks. Thus, tomorrow is the earliest reliable time we can confirm that what was learned today has likely been retained.

How to Test. If teachers want to test whether information actually has been transferred to long-term storage, the test needs to

- be given no sooner than 24 hours after the learning;

- test precisely what should have been retained; and

- come as a surprise to the learner, with no warning or preparation time.

Rationale. If the learners have warning about the test, they are likely to review the material just before the test. In this case, the test may determine the amount of information the learners were able to cram and hold in working memory and not what they have recalled from long-term storage. While testing without warning may seem insensitive, it is the only way teachers can be sure that long-term storage was the source of the test information that the learners provided. Unannounced quizzes, then, are formative assessments that should help students assess what they have remembered, rather than be a classroom management device to get students back on task.

Misuse of Tests. Some teachers use unannounced tests as punishment to get students back on task. This is a misuse of a valuable tool. Another approach is for teachers to

- establish sense and meaning to increase the probability that retention will occur;

- explain to students that unannounced tests help them see what as well as how much they have retained and learned over a given period; and

- ensure that the test or quiz matches the rehearsal when it was first taught. If the learning required essentially rote rehearsal, give a rote type of test. If it required elaborate rehearsal, use a test that allows the students more flexibility in their responses.

Using the Test Results. It is important that teachers

- analyze immediately the results of the test to determine what areas need to be retaught or practiced. If some students forgot parts, consider forming cooperative learning groups that focus on reteaching the forgotten areas.

- record the grades of only a small portion of these unannounced assessments. Rather, ask students to share their results and discuss in a think-pair-share format what strategies the students used to remember their correct responses. In this way, students talk about their memory processes and have a better understanding of how they learn and remember.

- decide whether memory strategies such as concept maps, mnemonics, or chunking (see the following chapters) can help in retention.

The analysis might also reveal areas of the curriculum to be reworked or updated for relevance, or it might show that the lesson should be retaught in a different way. A task analysis on a failed lesson is a good way to detect false assumptions about learning that the teacher may have made, and it recasts the lesson into a new presentation that can be more successful for both students and teacher.

Using tests, especially formative assessments, as tools to help students to be right, rather than to catch them being wrong, will create a supportive learning climate that results in improved student performance.

PRACTITIONER'S CORNER

Using Synergy to Enhance Learning

Synergy describes how the joint actions of people working together increase each other's effectiveness. This strategy gets students moving and talking while learning. It is effective because it is novel, is multisensory, uses active participation, is emotionally stimulating, and encourages socialization. Each participant ends up having a better understanding as a result of this interaction (synergy). It can be used from the primary grades to graduate school. Here are the guidelines:

- **Provide adequate time for reflection.** After teaching a concept, ask students to quietly review their notes and be prepared to explain what they have learned to someone else. Be sure to allow sufficient time for this mental rehearsal to occur (usually one to three minutes, depending on the complexity of the topic).

- **Model the activity.** Working with a student, show the students how you want them to behave and interact during the activity.

- **Get students to stand, move, and deliver.** Ask students to walk across the room and pair up with someone they do not usually work with or know very well. They stand face to face and take turns explaining what they have learned. They add to their notes anything their partners have said that they do not have. When done, all students end up with more information and ideas than they would have had if they worked alone. If they cannot agree or don't understand something, they are to ask the teacher about it when the activity is over. (Note: Make sure students stand face to face—rather than just looking at each other's notes—so that they must talk to their partners. Allow pairs only—one trio, if you have an uneven number of students.)

- **Keep in motion.** Move around the room using your proximity to help students stay on task. Answer questions to get them back on track, but avoid reteaching the lesson. Otherwise, students will become dependent on your reteaching rather than on each other's explanations.

- **Provide enough time and adjust as needed.** Allow adequate time for this process to be effective. Start with a few minutes, adding more time if they are still on task and reducing the time when you sense they are done.

- **Ensure accountability.** To help keep students on task, tell them that you will call on several students at random when the activity is over to explain what they discussed.

- **Clarify any misunderstandings.** Ask if there were any misunderstandings or items that need further explanation, and clarify them. An inviting statement would be "Is there anything I need to clarify?" rather than "Is there anything you didn't understand?"

- **Use variety for the pairing.** You can pair students by birth week or month, hair or eye color, height, musical cues, similar first names, and so on. Aim for random pairing as much as practicable to enhance socialization (because students tend to work more with their friends) and to avoid monotony.

Some Potential Barriers to Using Synergy

- **"The teacher should be talking."** The long-standing practice of the teachers being the "deliverers" of information is tough to overcome. For that reason, some teachers are uncomfortable with this activity because they are not "working" (read "talking"). But one of the reasons this activity can be so effective is because it shifts the work to the students' brains, increasing the likelihood that they will find sense and meaning in the new learning.

- **"It takes too much time."** The question is, "What would the teacher be doing otherwise? More talking?" This is a useful investment of time because the students are talking about the lesson, thereby enhancing learning and retention.

- **"The students will get off task."** This is a common and realistic concern. However, off-task behavior can be reduced significantly if the teacher continually moves around the room, listens in and asks questions of the student pairs, and holds them accountable for the learning at the end of the activity.

PRACTITIONER'S CORNER

NeuroBingo

Directions: In this activity, the entire group gets up and moves around. Each person tries to find someone who can answer one of the questions in a box. The person who answers the question initials the box. The object is to get a bingo pattern (horizontally, vertically, or diagonally). No person may initial the same sheet twice. Time limit: 15 to 20 minutes, depending on the size and age of the group.

Find a person who is able to

Explain the function of the sensory register	Explain the importance of sense and meaning to learning	Define "windows of opportunity"	Explain how the brain prioritizes incoming information	Explain the functions of the frontal lobes
State the two functions of the hippocampus	Tell you the function of immediate memory	Explain the function of the amygdala	Explain what is meant by the "novel" brain	Provide an example of how self-concept affects learning
Relate the cognitive belief system to learning	Tell you the functions of the cerebellum	Tell you the functions of the cerebrum	Describe the time limits of working memory	Explain synapses
Explain the meaning of sensory preferences	Describe the capacity limits of working memory	Explain what is meant by emotional control	Explain the function of neurotransmitters	Explain the function of long-term memory
Explain the value of humor in learning	Name the five senses	Describe the sources of brain research	Explain closure	Describe a neuron

CHAPTER 2: HOW THE BRAIN PROCESSES INFORMATION

Key Points to Ponder

Jot down on this page key points, ideas, strategies, and resources you want to consider later. This sheet is your personal journal summary and will help to jog your memory.

3

Memory, Retention, and Learning

The memory should be specially taxed in youth, since it is then that it is strongest and most tenacious. But in choosing the things that should be committed to memory, the utmost care and forethought must be exercised; as lessons well learned in youth are never forgotten.

—Arthur Schopenhauer, philosopher
1788–1860

Chapter Highlights

This chapter probes the nature of memory. It explains why our ability to retain information varies within a learning episode and with the teaching method used. It also discusses the value and pitfalls of practice, as well as techniques for increasing the capacity of working memory.

Memory gives us a past and a record of who we are and is essential to human individuality. Without memory, life would be a series of meaningless encounters that have no link to the past and no use for the future. Memory allows individuals to draw on experience and use the power of prediction to decide how they will respond to future events.

For all practical purposes, the capacity of the brain to store information is unlimited. That is, with about 100 billion neurons, each with thousands of dendrites, the number of potential neural pathways is incomprehensible. The brain will hardly run out of space to store all that an individual learns in a lifetime. Learning is the process by which we *acquire* new knowledge and skills; memory is the process by which we *retain* the knowledge and skills for the future. Most of what makes up our cognitive belief system we have learned. Investigations into the neural mechanisms required for different types of learning are revealing more about the interactions between learning new information, memory, and changes in brain structure. Just as muscles improve with exercise, the brain seems to improve with use. Although learning does not increase the number of brain cells significantly, it does increase their size, their branches, and their ability to form more complex networks.

The brain goes through physical and chemical changes when it stores new information as the result of learning. Storing gives rise to new neural pathways and strengthens existing pathways. Thus, every time we learn something, our long-term storage areas undergo anatomical changes that, together with our unique genetic makeup, constitute the expression of our individuality—further proof that teachers are, indeed, brain changers!

A discussion of memory involves looking at seven different operations, as shown in Figure 3.1. The brain attention system selects the appropriate input and processes it. With subsequent rehearsal and practice, it encodes the

> *The brain goes through physical and chemical changes each time it learns.*

information or skill into long-term memory where it is stored. Later, the memory can be retrieved, and the brain decides how to act. Information can eventually be lost through the process of forgetting. Let's start with the first four steps.

Figure 3.1 The diagram illustrates the seven operations involved in memory formation and retrieval.

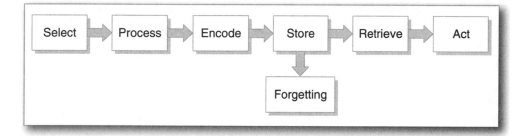

HOW MEMORY FORMS

What is a memory? Is it actually located in a piece of the brain at a specific spot? Are memories permanent? How does the brain manage to store a lifetime of memories in an organ the size of a melon? Is forgetting actually losing the memory or just access to it? The definitive explanation for memory is still elusive. Nevertheless, neuroscientists have discovered numerous mechanisms that occur in the brain that, taken together, define a workable hypothesis about memory formation (encoding), storage, and recall.

Video: For a general overview of how memories form, see

https://www.youtube.com/watch?v=yOgAbKJGrTA

The Temporary Stimulus

You will recall from Chapter 1 that a stimulus (say, the color red, a whiff of perfume, or a musical note) causes nerve impulses to travel down the axon to the gap, or synapse, where neurotransmitter chemicals are released. These chemicals cross the synapse to the dendrite of the adjacent neuron. As the chemical messages enter the neighboring neuron, they spark a series of electrochemical reactions that cause this second neuron to generate a signal, or "fire." The reaction continues and causes more receptor sites on other neurons to fire as well. This sequence forms a pattern of neuronal connections firing together.

The firing may last only for a brief time, after which the memory decays and is lost. If the second neuron is not stimulated again, it will stay in a state of readiness for hours, or days. What is created here is a perception, and even recognition, of an outside stimulus that quickly passes. We are bombarded with thousands of such events each day. The ability for these events to decay quickly means that our brain does not get cluttered with useless memories.

Forming the Memory

On the other hand, if the pattern is repeated during this standby period (through rehearsal and practice), the tendency for the associated group to fire together is increased. The faster a neuron fires, the greater the electrical charge it generates and the more likely it is to set off its neighbors. As the neighbors fire, the surfaces of their dendrites change to make them more sensitive to stimulation. This process of synaptic awareness and sensitivity is called *long-term potentiation* or LTP. Eventually, repeated firing of the pattern binds the neurons together so that if one fires, they all fire, ultimately forming a new memory trace, or *engram* (see Figure 3.2). These individual traces associate and form networks so that whenever one is triggered, the whole network is strengthened, thereby consolidating the memory and making it more easily retrievable (Sara, 2015). Researchers have actually recorded the neuron consolidation process as it was occurring in the human brain (Ison, Quiroga, & Fried, 2015).

Memories are not stored intact. Instead, they are stored in pieces and distributed in sites throughout the cerebrum. The shape, color, and smell of an orange, for example, are categorized and stored in different sets of neurons. Activating these sites simultaneously brings together a recollection of our thoughts and experiences involving an orange. There is also evidence that the brain stores an extended experience in more than one network. Which storage sites to select could be determined by the number of associations that the brain makes between new and past learnings. The more connections that are made, the more understanding and meaning the learner can attach to the new learning, and the more likely it is that it will be stored in different networks. This process now gives the learner multiple opportunities to retrieve the new learning.

Students Seeking Smart Drugs to Enhance Memory

Drugs are now available that appear to enhance the ability of the neurons to form and recall engrams. Most of these drugs, called *nootropics*, are designed to deal with medical problems that affect attention and memory, such as Attention Deficit/Hyperactivity Disorder and Alzheimer's disease, as well as dopamine deficiency problems that result in Parkinson's disease. Pharmaceutical companies continue to work on so-called smart drugs. Although researchers are

Figure 3.2 Memories are formed when a group of neurons fires together when activated. (1) Neuron A receives a stimulus, which causes it to set off neuron B. (2) If neuron A fires again soon, a link is established. Later, neuron A can just fire weakly to set off neuron B. (3) The firing of neurons A and B may set off neighboring neurons C and D. If this happens repeatedly, the four cells become a network and will fire together in the future—forming a memory.

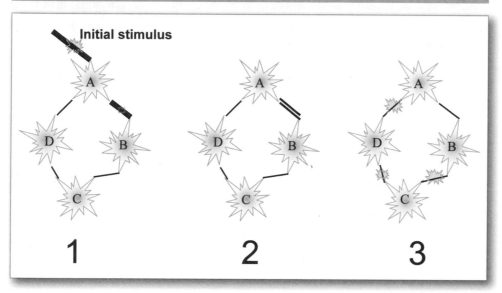

aiming to develop drugs that will help patients with memory disorders, these same drugs seem to help normal people perform memory tasks, such as test taking, with greater success (Ilieva, Hook, & Farah, 2015; Spencer, Devilbiss, & Berridge, 2015). This prospect will pose some interesting ethical questions for classroom teachers. How do we deal with a student who takes a legal smart drug just before we give a test? There is substantial evidence that high school and college students are already misusing such drugs, particularly those pre-scribed for Attention Deficit/Hyperactivity Disorder, to enhance their academic performance (e.g., Clemow & Walker, 2014). The consequences of frequent and long-term use of these drugs are not known.

A disturbing development regarding smart drugs in recent years has been the appearance of over-the-counter products in drugstores and on the Internet that claim to enhance memory. Despite their claims, there is little reliable research evidence that these substances improve cognitive function in normal people. Many of these substances affect neu-rotransmitters and the central nervous system, and their long-term effects are unknown. Furthermore, the safety of these substances, as well as their possible interactions with other substances an individual might be taking, is unknown. It will likely still be some time before a well-tested, safe, and clinically approved smart drug designed to enhance cogni-tive performance in a normal brain is available.

The more sense and meaning the learner can attach to the new learning, the more likely it is that it will be stored in different networks. This process now gives the learner multiple opportunities to retrieve the new learning.

STAGES AND TYPES OF MEMORY

Scientists have been debating for decades how best to classify forms of memory. Numerous case studies of people experiencing memory loss, the results of experiments designed to test memory, and analysis of brain scans all suggest that memories exist in different forms. The problem is getting neuroscientists to agree on a set taxonomy that defines the stages and types of human memory. Furthermore, as new research results emerge, the taxonomy and nomenclature change accordingly. I have attempted here to present what most active researchers seem to accept as a workable model for describing memory systems at the time of publication.

Stages of Memory

The stages of memory are the following: sensory/immediate, working, and long-term. In Chapter 2, we looked at the nature of sensory/immediate and working memories, which you will recall are temporary memories. Some stimuli that are processed in these temporary memories are eventually transferred to long-term memory sites where they actually change the structure of the neurons so they can last a lifetime.

Types of Memory

Although neuroscientists are still not in total agreement with psychologists as to all of the characteristics of long-term memory, there is considerable agreement on some of their types, and their description is important to understand before setting out to design learning activities accordingly. Long-term memory can be divided into two major types, declarative memory and nondeclarative memory. Figure 3.3 shows the stages of memory and the various types of long-term memory.

Figure 3.3 The hypothesized structure of human memory showing the relationship among different forms of memory.

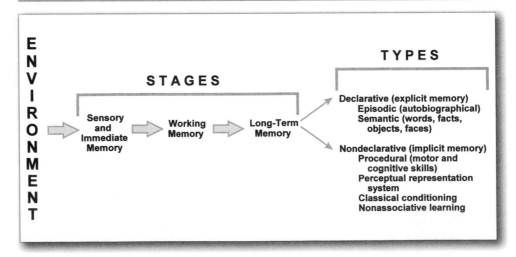

Declarative Memory

Declarative memory (also called *conscious* or *explicit* memory) describes the remembering of names, facts, music, and objects (e.g., where you live and the kind of car you own) and is processed by the hippocampus and cerebrum. Think for a moment about a person who is now important in your life. Try to recall that person's image, voice, and mannerisms. Then think of an important event you both attended, one with an emotional connection, such as a concert, wedding, or funeral. Once you have the context in mind, note how easily other components of the memory come together. This is declarative memory in its most common form—a conscious and almost effortless recall. Declarative memory can be further divided into **episodic memory** and **semantic memory**.

Episodic Memory. Episodic memory refers to the conscious memory of events in our own life history, such as our sixteenth birthday party, falling off a new bicycle, or what we had for breakfast this morning. It helps us identify the time and place when an event happened and gives us a sense of self. Episodic memory is the memory of *remembering.*

Semantic Memory. Semantic memory is knowledge of facts and data that may not be related to any event. It is knowing that the Eiffel Tower is in Paris, how to tell time, how to multiply two numbers, and who the fortieth president was. Semantic memory is the memory of *knowing.* A veteran knowing that there was a Vietnam War in the 1970s is using semantic memory; remembering his experiences in that war is episodic memory.

Recent brain scans show that although recalling episodic and semantic memories activate brain regions that largely overlap, there are some differences in the contributions of the hippocampus and nearby regions (Kim, 2016). Other studies have found that episodic memory is much more susceptible than semantic memory to the effects of Alzheimer's disease (e.g., El Haj, Antoine, & Kapogiannis, 2015). These findings continue to support the model that recognizes episodic and semantic memories as different constructs.

Nondeclarative Memory

Nondeclarative memory (sometimes called *implicit* memory) describes all memories that are *not* declarative memories—that is, memories that can be used for things that cannot be declared or explained in any straightforward manner. For example, you use declarative memory to recall your Social Security number (specific numbers in a certain order) but nondeclarative memory to remember how to ride a bicycle. Because nondeclarative memories do not require the intentional recall of experiences, they have been of particular interest to researchers (e.g., Marsolek, 2015; Reber, 2013). As a result, the descriptions and names of the categories of nondeclarative memories have changed over the last decade in light of new research. To date, the generally accepted categories of nondeclarative memory include *procedural memory, perceptual representation system, classical conditioning,* and *nonassociative learning.*

Procedural Memory. Procedural memory refers to the learning of motor and cognitive skills, and remembering *how* to do something, like riding a bicycle, driving a car, swinging a tennis racket, and tying a shoelace. As **practice** of the skills continues, these memories become more efficient and can be performed with little conscious thought or recall. The brain process shifts from *reflective* to *reflexive*. For example, you may remember the first time you drove an automobile by yourself. No doubt you gave a lot of conscious attention to your speed, maneuvering the vehicle, putting your foot on the correct pedal, and observing surrounding traffic (reflective thought). However, as you continued to practice this routine, the skills were stored in procedural memory and became more automatic (reflexive activity). Now, aren't you sometimes amazed at how you can drive from home to work and not even recall what happened on the road? "Did I really stop at that stop sign back there?" "What was that thump I heard a while ago?" Procedural memory was driving the car while working memory was planning your day.

Much of what we do during the course of a day involves the performance of skills. We go through the morning grooming and breakfast rituals, read the newspaper, get to work, and shake the hand of a new acquaintance. We do all of these tasks without realizing that we have learned them and without being aware that we are using our memory. Although learning a new skill involves conscious attention, skill performance later becomes unconscious and relies essentially on nondeclarative memory.

We also learn *cognitive skills,* such as reading, discriminating colors, identifying tones in music, and figuring out a *procedure* for solving a problem. Cognitive skills are different from cognitive concept building in that cognitive skills are performed automatically and rely on procedural memory rather than declarative memory. Perceptual and cognitive skill acquisition involve some different brain processes and memory sites from cognitive concept learning. If they are learned differently, should they be taught differently?

Perceptual Representation System (PRS). The perceptual representation system (PRS) refers to the structure and form of words and objects in memory that can be prompted by prior experience, without explicit recall. The PRS used to be included as part of procedural memory. But recent studies have identified unique characteristics of this recall system that merit it a separate category. Essentially, the PRS describes our ability to complete fragments of words or tell whether objects in drawings could exist in the real world. For example, can you quickly determine the meaning of the following sentence?

E__ry clo_d h_s a s__v_r li_i_g.

Not surprisingly, our success at completing these tasks is much improved if we have seen the entire combination of words or pictures on a previous occasion, even if we only glimpsed at the words or pictures and did not have time to study them intently. This is a form of implicit (nondeclarative) memory because no explicit processing of the words or pictures is involved (Navawongse & Eichenbaum, 2013).

Classical Conditioning. Classical conditioning (also called Pavlovian conditioning) occurs when a conditioned stimulus to an organism prompts an unconditioned response from that organism. Remember Pavlov ringing a bell as he fed his dogs and watched them salivate? Because the response gets associated with the stimulus, this form of learning is called *associative learning*. Experienced teachers know exactly how to respond in school when the fire alarm bell sounds. They have learned to associate the sound of the fire alarm with the procedures needed to safely evacuate the building.

Nonassociative Learning. Nonassociative learning occurs in two forms. *Habituation* helps us to learn not to respond to things that don't require conscious attention and to accustom ourselves to the environment. Thus, we can become accustomed to the clothes we wear, the daily noisy traffic outside the school, a ticking clock in the den, or the sounds of construction. This adjustment to the environment allows the brain to screen out unimportant stimuli so it can focus on those that matter. In *sensitization*, we increase our response to a particularly noxious or threatening stimulus. For example, Californians who have been through an earthquake respond quickly and vigorously to any weak noise or vibration thereafter, even though it may be unrelated to an earthquake.

It seems that procedural and declarative memories are stored differently. Studies of victims with brain damage and Alzheimer's disease show that they may still be perfectly capable of riding a bicycle (procedural) without remembering the word *bicycle* or when they learned to ride (declarative). Procedural and declarative memories seem to be stored in different regions of the brain, and declarative memory can be lost while procedural is spared (Finn et al., 2016; Hamrick, 2015).

> *Procedural memory helps us to learn things that don't require conscious attention and to habituate ourselves to the environment.*

Emotional Memory

Earlier taxonomies of memory systems usually listed *emotional memory* as a form of nondeclarative memory. But in refining their memory categories, scientists have identified situations requiring explicit (i.e., declarative) learning and memory. So emotional memories can be both implicit and explicit. In either case, the amygdala of the **limbic area** is heavily involved in processing emotional learning and memory. For example, sometimes, an experience is stored merely as an emotional *gist* or summary of the event—that is, we remember whether we liked it or not. A year after seeing a movie, for example, we might be able to recall only bits of the story line (declarative memory) and perhaps its mood and our reaction (nondeclarative memory). Students often can remember whether they liked a particular topic but cannot recall many details about it.

Emotional Memory and Learning

In Chapter 2, we learned how emotions can positively or negatively affect the acquisition of new learning. Emotion drives attention, and attention drives learning and memory. Emotions are always present in the school and classroom, but rarely do we purposely pay attention to them. Generally, teachers only deal with emotions when there is student misbehavior. Secondary school teachers, particularly, tend to focus much more on delivering cognitive content than on discussing or even acknowledging emotion in the classroom. But the reality is that emotions affect learning in two distinct ways. One is the emotional climate in which the learning occurs. The other is the degree to which emotions are associated with the learning content. Figure 3.4 illustrates two ways that emotions directly affect learning.

The Learning Climate. Emotions that students associate with a learning experience (but not the content) become part of the nondeclarative memory system. Emotional climate is directly related to classroom climate, which is regulated by the teacher. Students ask, "Do I have a good rapport with the teacher?" "Is my opinion respected?" "Does the teacher make me feel dumb when I ask for help?" "Am I the butt of sarcastic remarks?" "Does the teacher care whether I succeed?" The answers to these questions generate emotions that determine how students *feel* about the learning situation. These unconscious responses can turn them toward or away from their teachers and future learning experiences.

When students feel positive about their learning environment, endorphins are released in the brain. Endorphins are "feel good" chemicals. They produce a feeling of euphoria and stimulate the frontal lobes, thereby making the learning experience more pleasurable and successful. Conversely, if students are stressed and have a negative feeling about the learning environment, cortisol is released. Cortisol is a hormone that travels throughout the brain and body and activates defense behaviors, such as fight or flight. Frontal lobe activity is reduced by focusing on the cause of the stress and how to deal with it. Little attention is given to the learning task. Cortisol appears to interfere especially with the recall of emotional memories (Bos, van Goethem, Beckers, & Kindt, 2014). However, increased cortisol levels improve our ability to recognize faces—most likely a primordial survival mechanism allowing us to quickly distinguish friend from foe (McCullough, Ritchey, Ranganath, & Yonelinas, 2015).

Simply discussing an upcoming test can provoke strong emotions in some students, generally anxiety. In this case, the student's amygdala is highly activated and anxiety levels can provoke a flight response ("I'll be absent that day"), a fight response ("I'll argue that it's too soon for a test"), a freeze response ("I'm just going to disengage from the learning"), or a fear response ("I don't know enough to pass this test"). In all these possibilities, the cortisol levels are high and the student's feelings about the class and content will likely be negative. However, the teacher can greatly reduce such strong emotions by regularly using formative assessments along the way to provide students with an accurate record of how well they are doing in working toward achieving the lesson objectives. In this approach, prospective test items come as no surprise, and students feel confident about what they have already learned.

Connect Content to Emotions. Research on memory, then, strongly suggests that students are much more likely to remember curriculum content in which they have made an emotional investment. For this to happen, teachers often need to use strategies that get students emotionally involved with the learning content. For example, I once sat in a high school classroom where students had been asked to create some original material that showed how their study of the U.S. Civil War had affected them emotionally.

Figure 3.4 The chart shows the two ways that emotions affect learning. One way is the emotional climate of the environment in which the learning takes place. The other deals with the emotions that the learner experiences while processing the content of the learning.

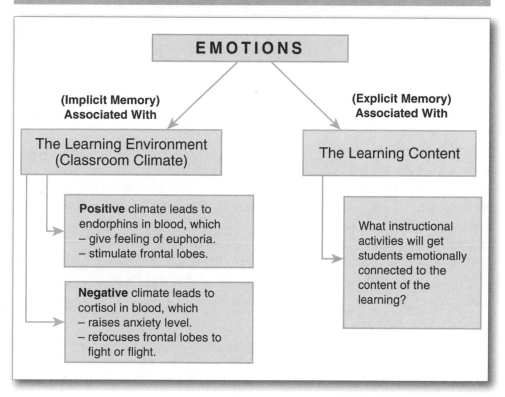

Taking turns, the students sang songs, recited poems, displayed sketches and watercolors depicting battle scenes, and acted out skits of major Civil War events. Some mentioned how the ramifications of the war are still present in today's society. I suspect that more students will remember the causes and results of that war for many years to come. Simulations, role-playing, journal writing, and real-world experiences are all examples of strategies that teachers can use to help students connect emotions to content.(See the Practitioner's Corner: Guidelines for Teaching the Emotional Brain at the end of this chapter.)

Flashbulb Memories

A powerful emotional experience can cause an instantaneous and long-lasting memory of an event, called a *flashbulb memory*. An example is remembering where you were and what you were doing when the *Challenger* space shuttle exploded or when the World Trade Center was attacked. Although these memories are not always accurate, they do attest to the brain's ability to quickly record and recall emotionally significant experiences. This ability most likely results from the stimulation of the amygdala and the release throughout the body of emotion-arousing substances, such as adrenaline. This process puts vivid memory tags on emotionally charged events. As a result, confidence in the recollection is high, although flashbulb memories seem to be no more accurate than the recall of memories of everyday experiences. Researchers are still debating whether flashbulb memories are a separate memory mechanism or just a variation of emotional memory processing (e.g., Cubelli & Della Sala, 2013; Curci & Conway, 2013).

Implications for Teaching

How the learner processes new information presented in school has a great impact on the quality of what is learned and is a major factor in determining whether and how it will be retained. Memories, of course, are more than just information. They represent fluctuating patterns of associations and connections across the brain from which the individual extracts order and meaning. Teachers with a greater understanding of the types of memory and how they form can select strategies that are more likely to improve the retention and retrieval of learning. It is also important for teachers to recognize the power that emotions have in the acquisition and retention of learning. How the student *feels* about being in that classroom and about the lesson content itself can make all the difference between mental withdrawal or active participation and achievement.

LEARNING AND RETENTION

Have you ever noticed how students who did well on a unit test have great difficulty recalling that information just a few months later? Why is that? Learning and retention are different. Learning involves the brain, the nervous system, and the environment, and the process by which their interplay acquires information and skills. Sometimes, we need information for just a short period of time, like the telephone number for a pizza delivery, and then the information decays in just a few seconds. Thus, learning does not always involve long-term retention.

A good portion of the teaching done in schools centers on delivering facts and information to build concepts that explain a body of knowledge. We teach numbers, arithmetic operations, ratios, and theorems to explain mathematics. We teach about atoms, momentum, gravity, and cells to explain science. We talk about countries, famous leaders, and their trials and battles to explain history, and so on. Students may hold on to this information in working memory just long enough to take a test, after which it readily decays and is lost. (See the Practitioner's Corner: Testing Whether Information Is in Long-Term Storage in Chapter 2.) Retention, however, requires that the learner not only give conscious attention but also build conceptual frameworks that have sense and meaning for eventual consolidation into the long-term storage networks.

> *Learning and retention are different. We can learn something for just a few minutes and then lose it forever.*

FACTORS AFFECTING RETENTION OF LEARNING

Retention refers to the process whereby long-term memory preserves learning in such a way that it can locate, identify, and retrieve it accurately in the future. As explained earlier, this is an inexact process influenced by many factors including the degree of student focus, the length and type of rehearsal that occurred, the critical attributes that may have been identified, the student's learning profile, and, of course, the inescapable influence of prior learnings.

The information processing model in Chapter 2 (Figure 2.1) identifies some of these factors and sets the stage for finding ways to transfer what we know into daily classroom practice. Let us look more specifically at the way the brain processes and retains information during a learning episode, how the nature of that processing affects the degree of retention, and how the degree of retention varies with the length of the episode.

Rehearsal

The assignment of sense and meaning to new learning can occur only if the learner has adequate time to process and reprocess it. This continuing reprocessing of information is called *rehearsal*, and it is a critical component in the transference of information from working memory to long-term storage. Rehearsal is somewhat different from practice in that rehearsal deals with the repetition and processing of information whereas practice, for our purposes, refers to the repetition of motor skills.

The concept of rehearsal is not new. Even the Greek scholars of 400 BC knew its value. They wrote,

> *Repeat again what you hear; for by often hearing and saying the same things, what you have learned comes complete into your memory.*
> —from the *Dialexeis*

Two major factors should be considered in evaluating rehearsal: the amount of time devoted to it, which determines whether there is both initial and secondary rehearsal, and the type of rehearsal carried out, which can be rote or elaborative.

Rehearsal deals with the repetition and processing of information whereas practice generally refers to the repetition of motor skills.

Time for Initial and Secondary Rehearsal

Time is a critical component of rehearsal. Initial rehearsal occurs when the information first enters working memory. If the learner cannot attach sense or meaning, and if there is no time for further processing, then the new information is likely to be lost. Providing sufficient time to go beyond the initial processing to secondary rehearsal allows the learner to review the information, to make sense of it, to elaborate on the details, and to assign value and relevance, thus increasing significantly the chance of long-term storage. When done at the end of a learning episode, this rehearsal is called *closure* (see Chapter 2).

Scanning studies indicate that the frontal lobe is very much involved during the rehearsal process and, ultimately, in long-term memory formation. This makes sense because working memory is also located in the frontal lobe. Several studies using fMRI scans of humans showed that during longer rehearsals the amount of activity in the frontal lobe determined whether items were stored or forgotten. Students carry out initial and secondary rehearsal at different rates of speed and in different ways, depending on the type of information in the new learning and their learning styles. As the learning task changes, learners automatically shift to different patterns of rehearsal (e.g., Bayliss, Bogdanovs, & Jarrold, 2015; Fegen, Buchsbaum, & D'Esposito, 2015).

Rote and Elaborative Rehearsal

Rote Rehearsal. This type of rehearsal is used when the learner needs to remember and store information exactly as it is entered into working memory. This is not a complex strategy, but it is necessary to learn information or a cognitive skill in a specific form or sequence. We use rote rehearsal to remember a poem, the lyrics and melody of a song, multiplication tables, telephone numbers, and steps in a procedure.

Elaborative Rehearsal. This type of rehearsal is used when it is not necessary to store information exactly as learned, but when it is more important to associate the new learnings with prior learnings to detect relationships. This is a more complex thinking process in that the learner reprocesses the information several times to make connections to previous learnings and assign meaning. Students use rote rehearsal to memorize a poem, but elaborative rehearsal to interpret its message.

When students get very little time for, or training in, elaborative rehearsal, they resort more frequently to rote rehearsal for nearly all processing. Consequently, they fail to make the associations or discover the relationships that only elaborative rehearsal can provide. Also, they continue to believe that learning is merely the recalling of information as learned rather than recognize its value for generating new ideas, concepts, and solutions.

Rote rehearsal is valuable for certain limited learning objectives. Nearly all of us learned the alphabet and the multiplication tables through rote rehearsal. But rote rehearsal simply allows us to acquire information in a certain sequence. It doesn't mean we understand the information or can apply it to new situations. Too often, students use rote rehearsal to memorize important terms and facts in a lesson, but they are unable to use the information to solve problems. They will probably do fine on a true-false or fill-in-the-blank test. But they will find difficulty answering higher-order questions that require them to apply their knowledge to new situations.

The goal of learning is not just to acquire knowledge, but to be able to use that knowledge in a variety of different settings. To do this, students need a deeper understanding of the concepts involved in the learning. For example, we could teach students the various types of government, such as monarchy, parliamentary, republic, totalitarian state, dictatorship, and theocracy. On a test, we could ask them to write and define the types of government and even to name a country as an example of each type. All this could be accomplished through rote rehearsal. But if we want students to understand why people are willing to die to change their type of government, or to make predictions about how different governments will react to a crisis, then they must have a much deeper grasp of the concepts of government and governing. That requires elaborative rehearsal. Perhaps one reason students are bored in school is that they spend too much time memorizing but not understanding.

When deciding on how to use rehearsal in a lesson, teachers need to consider the time available as well as the type of rehearsal appropriate for the specific learning objective. Keep in mind that rehearsal only contributes to, but does not guarantee that information will transfer into, long-term storage. However, there is almost no long-term retention *without* rehearsal.

> *There is almost no long-term retention of cognitive concepts without rehearsal.*

Test Question No. 4: Increased time on task increases retention of new learning. True or false?

Answer: False. Simply increasing a student's time on a learning task does not guarantee retention if the student is not allowed the time and help to personally interact with the content through rehearsal.

Retention During a Learning Episode

When an individual is processing new information, the amount of information retained depends, among other things, on *when* it is presented during the learning episode. At certain time intervals during the learning, we will remember more than at other intervals. Let's try a simple activity to illustrate this point. You will need a pencil and a timer. Set the timer to go off in 12 seconds. When you start the timer, look at the list of 10 words. When the timer sounds, cover the list and write as many of the 10 words as you remember on the lines to the right of the list. Write each word on the line that represents its position on the list (the first word on line 1, etc.). Thus, if you cannot remember the eighth word, but you remember the ninth, write it on line 9.

Ready? Start the timer and stare at the word list for 12 seconds. Now cover the list and write the words you remember on the lines to the right. Don't worry if you do not remember all the words.

KEF	1.	_____
LAK	2.	_____
MIL	3.	_____
NIR	4.	_____

(Continued)

(Continued)

VEK	5.	_____
LUN	6.	_____
NEM	7.	_____
BEB	8.	_____
SAR	9.	_____
FIF	10.	_____

Turn to your list again and circle the words that are correct. To be correct, they must be spelled correctly and be in the proper position on the list. Look at the circled words. Chances are you remembered the first three to five words (lines 1–5) and the last one to two words (lines 9 and 10), but had difficulty with the middle words (lines 6–8). Read on to find out why.

Primacy-Recency Effect

Your pattern in remembering the word list is a common phenomenon that is referred to as the *primacy-recency effect* (also known as the *serial position effect*). In a learning episode, we tend to remember best that which comes first and remember second best that which comes last. We tend to remember least that which comes just past the middle of the episode. This is not a new discovery. German researcher Hermann Ebbinghaus published the first studies on this effect in the 1880s.

More recent studies help to explain why this is so. The first items of new information are within the working memory's functional capacity, so they command our attention and are likely to be retained in semantic memory. The later information, however, exceeds the capacity and is lost. As the learning episode concludes, items in working memory are sorted or chunked to allow for additional processing of the arriving final items, which are likely held in working memory and will decay unless further rehearsed (Botto, Basso, Ferrari, & Palladino, 2014; Stephane et al., 2010; Terry, 2005).

Figure 3.5 shows how the primacy-recency effect influences retention during a 40-minute learning episode (Averell & Heathcote, 2011). The times are approximate and averages. Note that it is a bimodal curve, with each mode representing the degree of greatest retention during that time. For future reference, I will label the first or primacy mode *prime-time-1* and the second or recency mode *prime-time-2*. Between these two modes is the time period in which retention during the lesson is least. I will refer to that area as the *down-time*. This is not a time when the student is off task or when no retention takes place but a time when it is most difficult for retention to occur.

Prime-time-1 represents the interval during which the student focuses on the new learning. After several minutes, working memory is filling up and, assuming no rehearsal, forgetting begins, attention drifts, and retention drops. This experience may be even more pronounced these days because students are so accustomed to shifting from one screen to another in just seconds on their digital devices. During the down-time, chunking may occur and the learner's brain refocuses on the new learning to acquire more information. That refocusing describes prime-time-2 and results in an increase in retention. Both working memory capacity and the rate of forgetting depend on several factors such as the complexity of the new learning, how it is presented, and whether the learner is finding sense and meaning in it. Any of these factors can alter the time spent in the prime times and in the down-time (Dong, Reder, Yao, Liu, & Chen, 2015).

> *During a learning episode, we remember best that which comes first, second best that which comes last, and least that which comes just past the middle.*

Implications for Teaching

Teach New Material First

There are important implications of the primacy-recency effect for teaching a lesson. The learning episode begins when the learner focuses on the teacher with intent to learn (indicated by "0" in Figure 3.5). New information or a new skill should be taught first, during prime-time-1, because it is most likely to be remembered. Keep in mind that the students will remember almost any information coming forth at this time. It is important, then, that only *correct* information be presented. This is not the time to be searching for what students may know about something. I remember watching a teacher of English start a class with "Today, we are going to learn about a new literary form called *onomatopoeia.* Does anyone have any idea what that is?" After several wrong guesses, the teacher finally defined it. Regrettably, those same wrong guesses appeared in the follow-up test. And why not? They were mentioned during the most powerful retention position, prime-time-1.

The new lesson material should be followed by practice or review during the down-time. At this point, the information is no longer new, and the practice helps the learner organize it for further processing. Closure should take place during prime-time-2 because this is the second most powerful learning position and an important opportunity for the learner to determine sense and meaning. Adding these activities to Figure 3.6 shows how we can take advantage of research on retention to design a more effective lesson.

Figure 3.5 The degree of retention varies during a learning episode. We remember best that which comes first (prime-time-1) and last (prime-time-2). We remember least that which comes just past the middle.

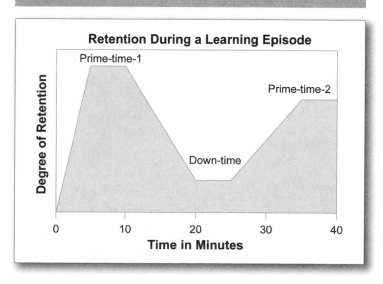

Misuse of Prime-Time

Even with the best of intentions, teachers with little knowledge of the primacy-recency effect can do the following: After getting focus by telling the class the day's lesson objective, the teacher takes attendance, distributes the

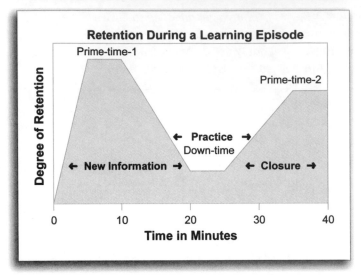

Retention During a Learning Episode

When you have the students' focus, teach the new information. Don't let prime-time get contaminated with wrong information.

previous day's homework, collects that day's homework, requests notes from students who were absent, and reads an announcement about a club meeting after school. By the time the teacher gets to the new learning, the students are already at the down-time. As a finale, the teacher tells the students that they were so well-behaved during the lesson that they can do anything they want during the last five minutes of class (i.e., during prime-time-2) as long as they are quiet. I have observed this scenario, and I can attest that the next day those students remembered who was absent and why, which club met after school, and what they did at the end of the period. The new learning, however, was difficult to remember because it was presented at the time of least retention. See the Practitioner's Corner: Using the Primacy-Recency Effect in the Classroom at the end of this chapter.

Retention Varies With Length of Teaching Episode

Another fascinating characteristic of the primacy-recency effect is that the proportion of prime-time to down-time changes with the length of the teaching episode. Look at Figure 3.7. Note that during a 40-minute lesson, the two prime-times total about 30 minutes, or 75 percent of the teaching time. The down-time is about 10 minutes, or 25 percent of the lesson time. If we double the length of the learning episode to 80 minutes, the down-time increases to 30 minutes, or 38 percent of the total time.

As the lesson time lengthens, the percentage of down-time increases faster than the percentage of prime-times. The information is entering working memory faster than it can be sorted or checked, and it accumulates. This cluttering interferes with the sorting and chunking processes and reduces the learner's ability to attach sense and meaning, thereby decreasing retention and increasing forgetting over time (Elliott, Isaac, & Muhlert, 2014). Think back to some of those college classes that lasted for two hours or more. After about the first 20 minutes, didn't you find yourself concentrating more on taking notes than on consciously processing and learning what was being presented?

Figure 3.7 also shows what happens when we shorten the learning time to 20 minutes. The down-time is about 2 minutes, or 10 percent of the total lesson time. As we shorten the learning episode, the down-time decreases faster than the prime-times. This finding indicates that there is a higher probability of effective learning taking place if we can keep the learning episodes short and, of course, meaningful. Thus, teaching two 20-minute lessons provides 20 percent more prime-time (approximately 36 minutes) than one 40-minute

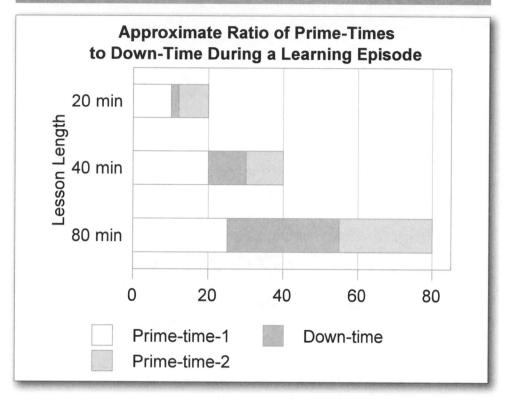

lesson (approximately 30 minutes). Note, however, that a time period shorter than 20 minutes may not give the learner sufficient time to determine the pattern and organization of the new learning and is thus of little benefit.

Table 3.1 summarizes the approximate number of minutes in the prime-times and down-times of the learning cycle for episodes of 20, 40, and 80 minutes. Remember that the times are averages over many episodes and vary among individuals. Nonetheless, these data confirm what we may have long suspected: More retention occurs when lessons are shorter and meaningful.

Table 3.1 Average Approximate Prime-Time and Down-Time in Learning Episodes

Episode Time	Prime-Times		Down-Time	
	Total Number of Minutes	Percentage of Total Time	Number of Minutes	Percentage of Total Time
20 minutes	18	90	2	10
40 minutes	30	75	10	25
80 minutes	50	62	30	38

Shorter Is Better: Impact on Block Scheduling

Because today's students are accustomed to quick change and novelty in their environment, mainly because of their digital devices, many find it difficult to concentrate on the same topic for long periods of time. They fidget, drift, send text messages to each other, and get into off-task conversations. This is particularly true if the teacher is doing most of the work, such as lecturing. The primacy-recency effect has a particularly important impact on block scheduling, in which a learning episode of 80 or more minutes can be a blessing or a disaster, depending on how the time is used. Figure 3.8 shows that a block containing four 20-minute segments will often be much more productive than one continuous lesson. Further, only one or two of the four-block segments should be teacher directed. (See the Practitioner's Corner: Strategies for Block Scheduling at the end of this chapter.)

Figure 3.8   When each learning episode is divided into 20-minute segments, there is proportionately more prime-time to down-time.

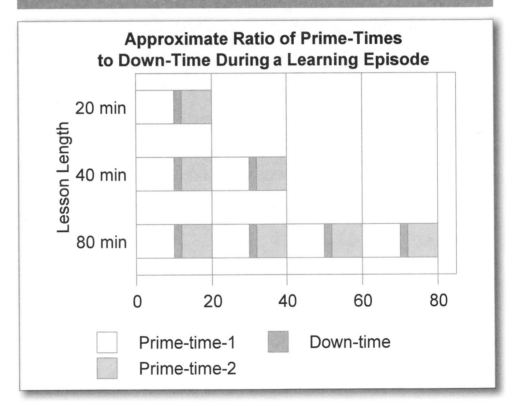

Rest Between Block Lesson Segments

Most teachers believe that staying on task throughout the learning period is best. During my time as an adjunct professor at Seton Hall University, I asked secondary teachers in my graduate classes to conduct **action research** projects in their block schedule classrooms to determine whether going off task between lesson segments (e.g., telling a joke or story, playing music, taking a quiet rest break, or getting students up and moving around) resulted in more, less, or the same amount of attending (measured by the speed with which the students returned to task) than if they had stayed continuously on task.

Figure 3.9 is the compilation of their results, which are similar to Tony Buzan's (1989) findings in the 1980s. The graph suggests that teachers are more likely to keep students focused *during* the lesson segments if they go off task *between* the segments. Granted, this is not a scientifically controlled study, but the results are not surprising given the higher novelty-seeking behavior of today's students. Teachers in non-block classes (i.e., 40 to 45 minutes in length) who take an off-task break about halfway through the period have reported similar results.

Figure 3.9 Compilation of 18 action research studies in secondary school classrooms comparing the degree of attending (focus) to on-task and off-task behavior between lesson segments of a block period.

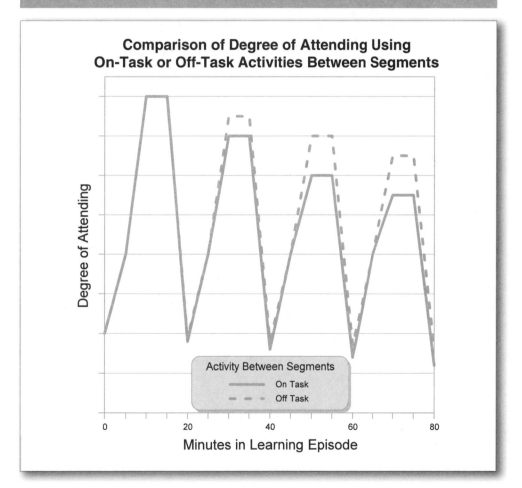

Retention Varies With Teaching Method

The learner's ability to retain information is also dependent on the type of teaching method used. Some methods result in more retention of learning than others do. Furthermore, because of differences in learning profiles, a particular teaching method could result in high retention in one student but low retention in another. Let's look at some current teaching methods and their potential for helping students retain what was taught.

Lecture/Direct Instruction. Lecture continues to be the most prevalent teaching method in secondary and higher education. In a survey of about 3,400 high school students, 55 percent said that their teachers lectured from one-half to three-quarters of the classroom period, mainly in the basic subject areas of history, mathematics, science, and English language arts (Wiggins, 2015). Numerous studies have shown that teacher lecture often results in the lowest student retention compared to other instructional methods. For example, studies show that retention after three days from lecturing is the least compared to other teaching methods (e.g., DiPiro, 2009; Freeman et al., 2014; Leight, Saunders, Calkins, & Withers, 2012). These findings are not surprising because lecture involves verbal processing with little student active participation or mental rehearsal. In this format, the teacher is telling and the students are listening just enough to convert the teacher's auditory output into written or typed notes. Rote rehearsal predominates as auditory information moves onto the notebook paper or into a digital device. Elaborative rehearsal is minimal or nonexistent. Despite the impressive amount of evidence about how little students retain from lecture, it continues to be the most prevalent method of teaching, especially in secondary and higher education. No one doubts that the lecture method allows a lot of information to be presented in a short time. However, the question is not what is presented, but what is learned.

On the other hand, direct instruction can be effective with students who have learning disabilities, especially in mathematics and science, provided it is not the only technique used (Kaldenberg, Watt, & Therrien, 2015; Shillingsburg, Bowen, Peterman, & Gayman, 2015; Zheng, Flynn, & Swanson, 2013). Direct instruction can also be useful for helping students put their new learning in context, for telling stories, or for modeling a particular thought process. Recently, a modification of the lecture format, called *interactive lecture and direct teaching*, has been shown to be effective. In this method, the teacher provides information and direction, but the students have periodic opportunities during the lesson to give feedback on what they have learned. This feedback can be through sharing with a partner, giving hand signals, or using electronic clickers, all of which give the teacher important information on how student learning is progressing.

- **Visual Material.** Adding visual material substantially increases the chances of retention. This is because the brain's visual memory system has an enormous capacity for storage and remarkable availability for recall (Magnussen, 2015).
- **Verbal and Visual Information.** Verbal and visual processing allow students to become more involved in the learning process, and retention increases. This occurs because working memory has both verbal and visual components. Each selects, organizes, and processes its respective information before sending it to the frontal lobe for integration and interpretation (see Figure 3.10). In essence, the learner creates both a verbally based model and a visually based model of the new learning.

These models are then integrated in the prefrontal cortex and connected to information already stored in the learner's memory. Such sensory-rich integration helps the learner find sense and meaning in the new learning, significantly increasing the chances it will be remembered.

- **Learn by Doing/Practice.** A great deal of research shows that getting immediately involved in new learning—that is, practicing it—enhances the memory of that learning. Very often, practice involves kinesthetic and tactile activities, thereby obtaining more sensory input. Learning by doing also encourages problem-based learning, whereby students get a real-world problem to solve that requires using their new information and skills. The problem-based approach has the added advantage of boosting student motivation when compared to lecture-based instruction because students see how the learning can be used to directly address meaningful problems. This is one major reason why video games are so popular with students. They present a challenge, offer immediate feedback, gradually increase the level of difficulty, and are intensely multimodal.

- **Practice and Teaching Others.** We have known for a long time that the best way to learn something well is to prepare to teach it. In other words, whoever explains, learns. This is one of the major components of cooperative learning groups and helps to explain the effectiveness of this instructional technique.

Figure 3.10 The diagram shows how auditory processing in the temporal lobe and visual processing in the occipital lobe are sent on to working memory and then to the prefrontal cortex for integration.

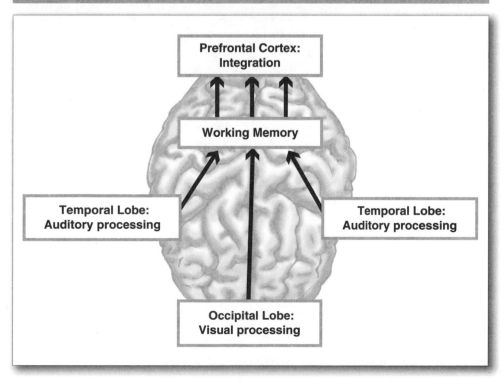

Whoever explains, learns!

Lecture continues to be the most prevalent teaching method in secondary and higher education, despite evidence that it produces the lowest degree of retention for most learners.

No One Teaching Method Is Best. No one teaching method exists that is best for all students all the time. Sometimes, lecture is the appropriate method when a lot of information needs to be given in a short period of time. But neither lecture nor any other method, for that matter, should be used almost all the time. Successful teachers use a variety of methods, keeping in mind that students are more likely to retain and achieve whenever they are actively engaged in the learning.

LEARNING MOTOR SKILLS

Scanning studies show that a person uses the frontal lobe, motor cortex, and cerebellum while learning a new physical skill. Learning a motor skill involves following a set of procedures and can be eventually carried out largely without conscious attention. In fact, too much conscious attention directed to a motor skill while performing it can diminish the quality of its execution. Think of the first time you typed on a keyboard. You had to map out the location of each key and concentrate on that location so you could reach it correctly when needed. However, after considerable practice, you no longer have to think about where the keys are; your fingers just strike them as needed. Stopping to consciously think about where the letters are will actually slow down your performance.

Brain Activity During Motor Skill Acquisition

When first learning the skill, attention and awareness are obviously required. The frontal lobe is engaged because working memory is needed, and the motor cortex of the cerebrum (a thin strip located across the top of the brain) interacts with the cerebellum to control muscle movement. As practice continues, the activated areas of the motor cortex become larger as nearby neurons are recruited into the new skill network. However, the memory of the skill is not established (i.e., stored) until after practice stops. It takes several hours for this consolidation to take place in the cerebellum, depending on the complexity of the skill, and most of it occurs during deep sleep (Doyon, Albouy, Vahdat, & King, 2015; Witt, Margraf, Bieber, Born, & Deuschl, 2010). Consolidation occurs among the key cells needed to perform the new motor task. Other neurons that were originally recruited to assist in the task, but are no longer needed, are less coordinated and are eventually released for other work (see Figure 3.11). Once the skill is mastered, brain activity shifts to the cerebellum, which organizes and coordinates the movements and the timing to perform the task. Procedural memory is the mechanism, and the brain no longer needs to use its higher-order processes because the performance of the skill becomes automatic (Hirano, Kubota, Tanabe, Koizume, & Funase, 2015; Upson, 2014).

Figure 3.11 The diagrams show how a new motor skill gets consolidated into memory. When first learning and practicing a new motor skill (left diagram), many neurons are activated. During sleep (center diagram), the key cells associated with the skill fire together, strengthening their network, while other neurons are less associated, and their connections weaken. As the learner masters the skill (right diagram), only the key cells fire to perform the action, and the other cells are available for learning new tasks (Upson, 2014).

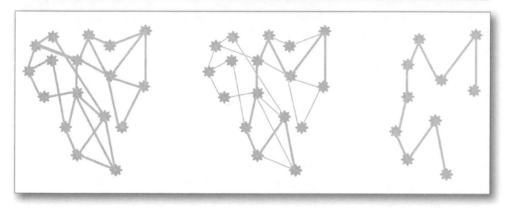

Continued practice of the skill changes the brain structurally, and the younger the learner is, the easier it is for these changes to occur (Wymbs, Bastian, & Celnik, 2016). Most music and sports prodigies began practicing their skills very early in life. Because their brains were most sensitive to the structural changes needed to acquire the skills, they can perform them masterfully. These skills become so much a part of the individual that they are difficult to change later in life. In the 1990s, Michael Jordan tried to become a major league baseball player at the age of 31 after a stellar career as a lead basketball scorer for the Chicago Bulls. Despite much effort, his attempt at baseball failed. Jordan had started playing basketball at the age of 8 and had developed a finely tuned set of specific motor skills in procedural memory that allowed him to be an expert basketball player. Trying to learn a new set of complex motor and perceptual skills to be a successful baseball player in a short period of time was just not possible.

A few minutes of aerobic exercise before learning a new motor skill can enhance the learning of that skill.

One question of research interest is whether any form of exercise before learning a new motor skill could enhance the speed at which one learns that skill. Apparently, the answer is yes. A recent study found that those in a group who had a few minutes of aerobic exercise followed by new motor skill training acquired the new motor skill better than the group without the preliminary exercise (Singh, Neva, & Staines, 2016). The belief here is that aerobic exercise induces greater plasticity in the brain areas responsible for motor skill learning, making it easier for the new motor learning to occur. Here is further evidence of the importance of exercise in school: it can enhance the learning of motor skills as well as cognitive objectives.

The Problem of Learning Two Similar Skills

A surprising finding from studies of motor skill learning was that if the person practiced a very similar skill during the 4- to 12-hour down-time, the second skill interfered with the consolidation and mastery of the first skill—and vice versa. Consequently, the person was not able to perform either skill well (Oberauer & Kliegl, 2004; Witney, 2004). This appears to be evidence that negative transfer—a form of learning interference (see Chapter 4)—can occur during the learning of motor skills as well as during the learning of cognitive concepts. One possible explanation for this phenomenon is that the learning of similar motor tasks recruits the same or overlapping neural networks, and this competition results in the inadequate learning of both tasks (Cantarero, Tang, O'Malley, Salas, & Celnik, 2013; Ranganathan, Wieser, Mosier, Mussa-Ivaldi, & Scheidt, 2014; Rémy, Wenderoth, Lipkens, & Swinnen, 2010). Think of the implications that this has for teaching, wherein similarity is one of the major criteria we use to decide the sequence for presenting information and skills. The key is to ensure that the first skill is well practiced and enough time passes for it to be fully consolidated in memory. At that point, the first skill can actually facilitate the learning of the second similar skill—a form of positive transfer (Panzer & Shea, 2008; Stevens, Anderson, O'Dwyer, & Williams, 2012). See the Practitioner's Corner: Avoid Teaching Two Very Similar Motor Skills at the end of this chapter to review how similarity can interfere with new motor skill learning.

> *Learning two skills that are too similar at the same time causes memory interference so that the student learns neither skill well.*

Test Question No. 5: Two very similar concepts or motor skills should be taught at the same time. True or false?

Answer: False. Teaching two very similar concepts or skills at the same time can cause interference so that the student learns neither.

Does Practice Make Perfect?

Practice refers to learners repeating a skill over time. It begins with the rehearsal of the new skill in working memory, the motor cortex, and the cerebellum. Later, the skill memory is recalled and additional practice follows. The quality of the practice and the learner's knowledge base will largely determine the outcome of each practice session.

Over the long term, repeated and extended practice causes the brain to assign extra neurons to the task, much as a computer assigns more memory for a complex program. The assignment of these additional neurons is more or less on a permanent basis. Professional keyboard and string musicians, for example, have larger portions of the motor cortex devoted to controlling finger and hand movements. Furthermore, the earlier their training started, the bigger the motor cortex (Schlaug, 2015). If practice is stopped altogether, the neurons that are no longer being used are eventually assigned to other tasks, and skill mastery will decline. In other words, use it or lose it!

The old adage that "practice makes perfect" is rarely true. It is very possible to practice the same skill repeatedly with no increase in achievement or accuracy of application. Think of the people you know who have been driving, cooking, or even teaching for many years with no improvement in their skills. I am a self-taught bowler, and although I have been bowling for 30 years, I do not improve. My bowling scores are embarrassingly low and remain there despite years of repeated bowling. Why is this? The answer ahead.

How is it possible for one to continuously practice a skill with no resulting improvement in performance? Clearly other factors are at play. Researchers at Princeton University reviewed more than 150 studies connecting the total time spent practicing to one's ability in music, sports, education, and other fields (Hambrick, Macnamara, Campitelli, Ullén, & Mosing, 2016). They found that the amount of time individuals practiced a skill accounted for only about 12 percent of their variation in performance. The biggest effect of practice was on games such as chess, which accounted for 26 percent of the differences in performance. Although researchers were not sure what other factors besides practice attributed to improved performance, they suggested that general intelligence, natural abilities, and working memory efficiency are important considerations.

> *Practice does not make perfect. Practice makes permanent.*

Conditions for Successful Practice

For practice to *improve* performance, four conditions must be met (Hunter, 2004):

1. The learner must be sufficiently motivated to want to improve performance.

2. The learner must have all the knowledge necessary to understand the different ways that the new knowledge or skill can be applied.

3. The learner must understand how to apply the knowledge to deal with a particular situation.

4. The learner must be able to analyze the results of that application and know what needs to be changed to improve performance in the future.

Teachers help learners meet these conditions when they do the following:

- Start by selecting the smallest amount of material that will have maximum meaning for the learner.
- Model the application process step by step. Studies show that the brain also uses observation as a means for determining the spatial learning needed to master a motor skill (Petrosini et al., 2003).
- Insist that the practice occur in the teacher's presence over a short period of time while the student is focused on the learning.
- Watch the practice and provide the students with prompt and specific feedback on what variable needs to be altered to correct and enhance the performance. Feedback seems to be particularly important during the learning of complex motor skills (Sidaway, Bates, Occhiogrosso, Schlagenhaufer, & Wilkes, 2012; Wilkinson et al., 2015).

Guided Practice, Independent Practice, and Feedback

Practice does make permanent, thereby aiding in the retention of learning. Consequently, we want to ensure that students practice the new learning correctly from the beginning. This early practice (referred to as *guided practice*), then, is done in the presence of the teacher, who can now offer corrective feedback to help students analyze and improve their practice. When the practice is correct, the teacher can then assign *independent practice*, in which the students can rehearse the skill on their own to enhance retention.

This strategy leads to perfect practice, and, as Vince Lombardi said, "Perfect practice makes perfect." In my case, I go bowling every few months to be with the same close friends, who are very busy professionals. Our bowling is noncompetitive and is simply the means that allows us to catch up on our lives, so our scores are of little importance. Thus, I have no *motivation* to improve—and, believe me, I don't.

Teachers should avoid giving students independent practice before guided practice. Because practice makes permanent, allowing students to rehearse something for the first time while away from the teacher is very risky. If they unknowingly practice the skill incorrectly, then they will learn the incorrect method well! This will present serious problems for both the teacher and the learner later on because it is very difficult to change a skill that has been practiced and remembered, even if it is not correct.

Unlearning and Relearning a Skill. If a learner practices a skill incorrectly but well, unlearning and relearning that skill correctly is very difficult. The degree to which the unlearning and relearning processes are successful will depend on the following:

- Age of the learner (i.e., the younger the learner, the easier to relearn because of more efficient neuroplasticity)
- Length of time the skill has been practiced incorrectly (i.e., the longer the practice period, the more difficult to change because networks are more strongly consolidated)
- Degree of motivation to relearn (i.e., the greater the desire for change, the more effort learner is willing to use to bring about change)

> *Avoid giving students independent practice before guided practice.*

Sometimes, students who are young, and who have practiced the skill wrong for only a brief time, are so annoyed at having wasted their time with the incorrect practice that they lose motivation to learn the skill correctly.

Practice and Rehearsal Over Time Increases Retention

Hunter (2004) suggested that teachers use two different types of practice over time, massed and distributed. (Here, Hunter uses *practice* to include rehearsal.) Practicing new learning during time periods that are very close together is called *massed practice*. This produces fast learning, as when you may mentally rehearse a new telephone number if you are unable to write it down. Immediate memory is involved here, and the information can fade in seconds if it is not rehearsed quickly.

Teachers provide massed practice when they allow students to try different examples of applying new learning in a short period of time. Cramming for an exam is an example of massed practice. Material can be quickly chunked into working memory but can also be quickly dropped or forgotten if more sustained practice does not follow soon. This happens because the material has no further meaning, and thus the need for long-term retention disappears. Sustained practice over time, called *distributed practice* or the *spacing effect*, is the key to retention. If you want to remember that new telephone number later on, you will need to use it repeatedly over time. Thus, practice that is distributed over longer periods of time sustains meaning and consolidates the learnings into long-term storage in a form that will ensure accurate recall and applications in the future. It is important to note that the distributed practice is effective only if the learner is directly processing and focused on the learning, rather than just casually repeating it (Greene, 2008). Figure 3.12 shows that recall after periodic review improves over time. This is the rationale behind the idea of the spiral curriculum, whereby critical information and skills are reviewed at regular intervals within and over several grade levels. A great idea supported by research. Whatever happened to it?

Long-standing as well as recent studies have demonstrated the power of distributed practice (e.g., Gerbier & Toppino, 2015; Kang, 2016; Soderstrom & Bjork, 2015). One study found that 5-year-old children benefited from distributed practice in their phonics lessons (Seabrook, Brown, & Solity, 2005). Another study using distributed practice over a six-week period found a significant improvement in the performance of middle school students compared to those in the control group (Metcalfe, Kornell, & Son, 2007). Researchers also found that spacing out practice boosted eighth-grade students' recall of the material in their U.S. history course when tested nine months after the final exposure (Carpenter, Pashler, & Cepeda, 2009). Third-grade students taught mathematics through distributed practice showed significantly higher fluency with mathematical facts than those taught through massed practice (Schutte et al., 2015). Using an intervention that included distributed practice helped eight-grade students with disabilities significantly improve their reading comprehension and social studies knowledge, compared to students taught without the intervention (Swanson, Wanzek, Vaughn, Roberts, & Fall, 2015).

Effective practice, then, starts with massed practice for fast learning and proceeds to distributed practice later for retention. As a result, the student is continually practicing previously learned skills throughout the year(s). Each test should not only test new material but also allow students to practice important older learnings. This method not only helps in retention but also reminds students that the learnings will be useful for the future, not just for the time when they were first learned and tested.

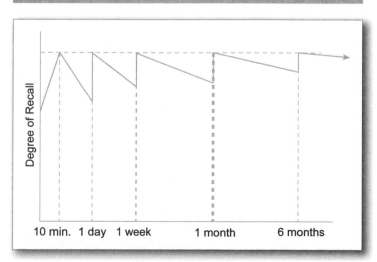

Figure 3.12 Practicing learnings over time (distributed practice) increases their degree of recall.

The Gradual Release Model for Rehearsal and Practice

The Gradual Release of Responsibility (GRR) model was proposed in 1983 as a strategy to help students learn to read (Pearson & Gallagher, 1983). Used appropriately, it continues to be effective in improving literacy achievement, mainly because students eventually become capable thinkers and accountable for their depth of learning and achievement. This occurs because the model encompasses direct instruction, rehearsal, and practice in a way that gradually shifts responsibility in a learning episode from the teacher to the student. A common version of the model has the four major steps shown in Figure 3.13 (Fisher & Frey, 2008):

- **Focused instruction, or "I do it; you watch."** The teacher explains, demonstrates, and models the learning objective, while explaining the thinking processes involved. Focused instruction includes using analogies to link the new learning to prior knowledge, demonstrating how the new learning is completed, and discussing the errors the learners should avoid.

- **Guided instruction, or "We do it."** The goal in this phase of guided practice is to steer the students so they can use the newly presented skills, procedures, or information independently. Using formative assessments, the teacher can directly work with specific students who need more help in acquiring the objective.

- **Collaborative learning, or "You do it together."** This stage gives students the opportunities for deeper understanding by discussing, solving problems, negotiating, and thinking in groups. They interact with their peers by rehearsing, practicing, and applying what they have learned in a collaborative setting. In addition to the group goal, each student must have a specific task to ensure engagement and individual accountability. Closure can also be an important component of this stage.

Figure 3.13   The diagram illustrates the four steps in the Gradual Release of Responsibility model (adapted from Fisher & Frey, 2008).

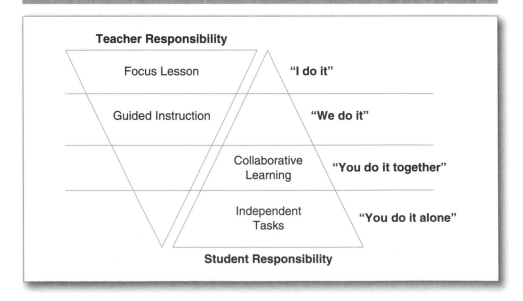

- **Independent tasks, or "You do it alone."** The last step is independent practice and is aimed at fulfilling the goal of all instruction, namely, that students are able to apply what they have learned to new situations in various contexts. To consolidate students' learning, teacher assignments should challenge the students to synthesize information and skills, transform their ideas, evaluate options, and solve problems.

Video: For an example of GRR in the classroom, see

https://www.teachingchannel.org/videos/improving-teacher-practice

This model is but one strategy that teachers can use to foster rehearsal and practice leading to the students accepting more responsibility for their depth of learning. Strategies like GRR also enhance student interest and motivation as they become more engaged in their learning and more responsible for their achievement.

DAILY BIOLOGICAL RHYTHMS AFFECT TEACHING AND LEARNING

Circadian Rhythms

Many of our body functions and their components, such as temperature, breathing, digestion, hormone concentrations, and so on, go through daily cycles of peaks and valleys. These daily cycles are called *circadian rhythms* (from the Latin for "about a day"). The timing of these cycles is determined by the brain's exposure to daylight. Thus, some of the rhythms are related to the sleep-wake cycle and are controlled by a pair of small clusters of just 10,000 neurons in a tiny region of the brain located in the front part of the limbic area. These clusters are called the *suprachiasmatic nuclei* because they sit immediately above (supra) the optic chiasm—the area where the optic nerves from the left and right eye meet on their way to the brain.

One of these circadian rhythms regulates our ability to focus on incoming information with intent to learn. It can be referred to as the *psychological-cognitive cycle*. In recent years, this cycle has drawn the attention of researchers to the awake-and-asleep cycles of students (Carskadon, Acebo, Wolfson, Tzischinsky, & Darley, 1997; Harbard, Allen, Trinder, & Bei, 2016; Killgore, 2010). The findings show that the cognitive rhythm is about the same for a preadolescent and an adult, but starts later in an adolescent. This is because the onset of puberty shifts this particular cycle roughly an hour later than in the preadolescent. It returns to its previous level when the adolescent enters adulthood around the age of 22 to 24 years.

Figure 3.14 shows a comparison of the pre/postadolescent and adolescent cycles. Note the trough that occurs for both groups just past the middle of the day. This is a low point of focus. Learning can still occur during this approximate 20- to 60-minute period, but it will require more *effort*. I refer to the trough as the "dark hole of learning." Some cultures refer to it as the "siesta," having recognized long ago how difficult it is to accomplish much learning or work during this time.

Note that the adolescent cycle has shifted and that these students do not reach their peak until about an hour later. Note, too, that the second peak is flatter than for the other groups. This graph explains why adolescents are sleepier in the morning and tend to stay up later at night than preadolescents and adults.

What Are the Implications? The different rhythms among preadolescents, adolescents, and their teachers have several implications. For example,

- How do the start times at elementary and secondary schools compare to the times when the students they serve are at their cognitive peak?
- Can the performance of students on standardized tests be affected when we test the whole K–12 population of students at the same time—usually in the morning?
- Can classroom climate in high schools be affected in the early afternoon when the teacher is in the trough and the students are still at their peak?
- Can starting high schools later in the morning when students are more apt to be attentive result in lowering the dropout rate?
- Would alternative high schools be more successful if they started in the afternoon?

See the Practitioner's Corner: Impact of Circadian Rhythms on Schools and Classrooms at the end of this chapter.

The Importance of Sleep in Learning and Memory

The encoding of information into the long-term memory sites occurs during sleep, more specifically, during the rapid-eye movement (REM) stage. This is a slow process that can flow more easily when the brain is not preoccupied with external stimuli. Consequently, the brain blocks external sensory input during REM sleep. (The brain also blocks motor output to prevent us from physically acting out our dreams.) When we sleep, the brain reviews the events and tasks of the day, storing them more securely than at the time we originally processed them. What we think and talk about while awake very likely influences the nature and shape of the memory consolidation that occurs during sleep (Tuma, 2005). Will knowing that a test is coming improve the chances of consolidation into long-term memory? Apparently, yes.

Video: For an overview on the importance of sleep and memory, see

https://www.youtube.com/watch?v=gedoSfZvBgE

In a series of interesting experiments, Wilhelm and his colleagues (2011) found that merely expecting that a memory will be needed for a future test determined whether or not sleep significantly benefitted the consolidation of that memory. The researchers told one group of participants that they would be tested 10 hours later on the material they were learning, but the control group was later given a surprise test. Sleep improved retention only in the first group. EEGs showed that the participants in the first group spent more time in deep REM sleep and had more bursts of the electrical activity associated with memory storage than the group not expecting the test.

You may recall from Chapter 1 that neurogenesis—the birth of new neurons—occurs in the hippocampus. It is likely that this process is accelerated during REM sleep. Consequently, prolonged sleep loss can hamper the development of new neuronal growth. Why not share all this information with students?

Adequate sleep is vital to the memory storage process, especially for young learners. Sleep not only consolidates memories so they will not be forgotten, it also makes them more accessible when one is awake (Dumay, 2016). Most teenagers need about nine hours of sleep each night. Yet, many teenagers are not getting enough sleep. Several factors are responsible for eroding sleep time. In the morning, high schools start earlier, teens spend more time grooming, and some travel long distances to school. At the end of the day, there are athletic and social events, part-time jobs, homework, television, video games, and social media. Another contributing factor is that adolescents are consuming increasing amounts of caffeine, a stimulant that delays the sleep cycle. One study of about 200 high school students found that 95 percent of participants regularly used caffeine—most often in soda—and the first use was usually in the evening (Ludden & Wolfson, 2010). Add to all this the normal shift in teens' body clocks that tends to keep them up later, and the average sleep time is more like five to six hours.

> *Teenagers are not getting enough sleep. This sleep deprivation affects their ability to store information, increases irritability, and leads to fatigue, which can cause accidents.*

Figure 3.14 A comparison of the typical pre/postadolescent and adolescent cognitive cycles during the day. Note the trough that develops just past the middle of the day. This is a time when teaching and learning require more effort.

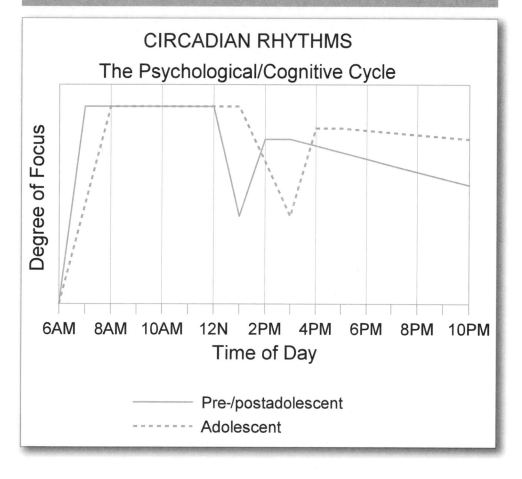

Delayed Sleep Phase Syndrome

Lack of sleep is becoming so prevalent in middle and high school students that some neuroscientists and psychiatrists are convinced that it is a chronic syndrome of the adolescent population. Called *delayed sleep-phase syndrome (DSPS)*, it is characterized by a persistent pattern that includes difficulty falling asleep at night and getting up in the morning, fatigue during the day, and alertness at night. Caused mainly by the shift in the adolescent's circadian rhythm (Figure 3.14), DSPS is aggravated by other conditions.

Figure 3.15 shows the stages and cycles of sleep for teenagers and adults. Most of the encoding of information and skills into long-term storage is believed to occur during the REM phases. During the normal sleep time of eight to nine hours, five REM cycles occur. Adolescents getting just five to six hours of sleep lose out on the last two REM cycles, thereby reducing the amount of time the brain has to consolidate information and skills for long-term storage. This sleep deprivation not only disturbs the memory storage process but can lead to other problems as well. Students may nod off in class or become irritable. Worse, their decreased alertness due to fatigue can lead to accidents in school and in their cars (e.g., Meldrum & Restivo, 2014; Rossa, Smith, Allan, & Sullivan, 2014).

Some studies show that students who get less sleep are more likely to get poorer grades in school than students who sleep longer. Sleep-deprived students

Figure 3.15   The chart shows the cycles of sleep from Waking through Stage 1 (Transitional), Stage 2 (Light Sleep), and Stages 3 to 4 (Deep Sleep). Long-term storage occurs during the rapid-eye movement (REM) phase.

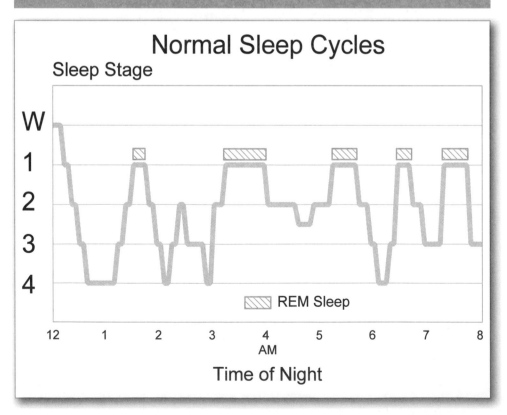

also have more daytime sleepiness and depressed moods. Furthermore, their performance of complex and abstract tasks that involve higher-order brain functions declines more strongly after sleep deprivation than their performance of simple memory tasks (Kopasz et al., 2010; Kreutzmann et al., 2015). It is important to remind students of the significance of sleep to their mental and physical health and to encourage them to reexamine their daily activities to provide for adequate sleep. It should be noted that REM sleep is not required for all memory consolidation. Subsequent memory consolidation can occur when awake, especially the encoding of declarative memories, which seem to be less dependent on REM sleep. Clinical studies show that short-term treatment with melatonin—the sleep-regulating hormone—can help adolescents with DSPS sleep longer and thus improve their performance in school (Gradisar, Smits, & Bjorvatn, 2014).

INTELLIGENCE AND RETRIEVAL

Intelligence

Our modern notion of what constitutes human intelligence is growing in complexity. At the very least, it represents a combination of varied abilities and skills, such as the ability to learn from one's experiences, solve different types of problems, and apply knowledge and adapt to new situations. For many years psychologists referred to a general mental ability, called *the* g *factor,* originally proposed by Charles Spearman in the early 1900s (Spearman, 1904). People who scored high on tests of general mental ability (i.e., IQ tests) were smarter than those who scored lower. The study of human intelligence took a major leap in the 1980s when psychologists Howard Gardner and Robert Sternberg proposed separate models of different types and patterns of intelligence. Their work changed our concept of intelligence from a singular entity to a multifaceted aptitude that varies even within the same person. Many educators have been using the ideas of Gardner and Sternberg in their curriculum, teaching, and school organization.

Different Views of Intelligence

Howard Gardner. In 1983, Howard Gardner defined intelligence as an individual's ability to use a learned skill, create products, or solve problems in a way that is valued by the society of that individual. This approach expands our understanding of intelligence to include divergent thinking and interpersonal expertise. Gardner differentiated between the terms *intelligence* and *creativity* and suggested that in everyday life, people can display intelligent originality in any of seven (now eight) intelligences. They are musical, logical-mathematical, spatial, bodily-kinesthetic, linguistic, interpersonal, intrapersonal, and naturalist (Gardner, 1993).

Gardner (1993) made clear that intelligence is not just how a person thinks, but it also includes the materials and the values of the situation where and when the thinking occurs. The availability of appropriate materials and the values of any particular context or culture will thus have a significant impact on the degree to which specific intelligences will be activated, developed, or discouraged. A person's combined intellectual capability, then, is the result of innate tendencies (the genetic contribution) and the society in which that individual develops (the environmental contribution).

This theory suggests that at the core of each intelligence is an information processing system (similar perhaps to that in Chapter 2) unique to that intelligence. The intelligence of an athlete is different from that of a musician or a physicist. Gardner (1993) also suggests that each intelligence is semiautonomous. A person who has abilities in athletics but who does poorly in music has enhanced athletic intelligence. The presence or absence of music capabilities exists separately from the individual's athletic prowess.

Robert Sternberg. Two years after Gardner's work appeared, Robert Sternberg (1985) at Yale proposed a theory that distinguishes three patterns of intelligence: analytical, creative, and practical. People with analytical intelligence (the analyzers) have abilities in analyzing, critiquing, and evaluating. Those who are creatively intelligent (the creators) are particularly good at discovering, inventing, and creating. By contrast, the practically intelligent (the practitioners) excel at applying, utilizing, and implementing.

In this model, intelligence is defined by these three patterns of behavior, and intelligence refers to the ability to perform the skills in one or more of these areas with accuracy and efficiency. According to Sternberg (1985), various combinations of these three areas produce different patterns of intelligence. This concept was tested in several studies conducted by Sternberg and his colleagues. Students were assessed for their memory as well as their analytical, creative, and practical achievement. The results showed that those students who were taught in ways that best matched their achievement patterns outperformed those whose method of instruction was not a good fit for their pattern of abilities (Sternberg, Ferrari, Clinkenbeard, & Grigorenko, 1996; Sternberg et al., 2000).

Jeff Hawkins. In 2004, Jeff Hawkins, the inventor of the Palm Pilot and a major researcher in artificial intelligence, described human intelligence as being measured by the capacity to remember and predict patterns in the world, including mathematics, language, social situations, and the properties of objects. The brain receives patterns from the outside world through experience, stores them as memories, and makes predictions by comparing what it has seen before to what is happening now. In other words, to Hawkins, prediction, not behavior, is the proof of intelligence (Hawkins & Blakeslee, 2004).

Children's environments may have a much greater impact on the development of intelligence than does their genetic code.

It is clear that no agreement exists about what intelligence is. However, there is general agreement that, contrary to past beliefs, heredity contributes only a fraction to intelligence. Genes may set upper limits on an individual's cognitive abilities, but these limits may be overcome to some degree by the brain's plasticity. Thus, a child's environment probably has a much greater impact on the development of intelligence than does his or her genetic code.

In any event, major efforts to define intelligence are not likely to be advanced significantly by brain imaging anytime in the near future. PET scans and fMRIs do show some localization of brain activity for certain tasks. However, there is no scientific basis for equating the task with a particular type or pattern of intelligence. For example, visual stimuli are processed first in the visual cortex at the rear of the brain, and then in other parts of the brain for spatial perception and recognition. If anything, recent brain scans and case studies are revealing how remarkably integrated brain activity is when performing even the simplest task. Although most neuroscientists agree that there are areas specialized for certain tasks, such as language, areas rarely, if ever, work in isolation in the normal brain (see more about brain specialization in Chapter 5). Some researchers suggest that it is better to think of the brain as having a number of cerebral systems that are primarily responsible for processing the specific content associated with each intelligence. For example, the motor cortex and cerebellum would take the lead in processing new skills associated with the bodily-kinesthetic area.

One interesting discovery is that general intelligence (that *g* factor) is closely linked to the amount of gray matter in key areas of the frontal lobe cortex (Figure 3.16). People with more gray matter in their frontal lobes tend to score higher on tests of intelligence (Haier, Jung, Yeo, Head, & Alkire, 2004). The unanswered chicken-and-egg question is this: Does the early development of more gray matter make a person more intelligent, or do challenging learning experiences result in the production of more gray matter? No one knows.

Recently, however, researchers have found a gene linking intelligence to the thickness of the gray matter that comprises the brain's cortex. The research team analyzed DNA samples and brain scans from nearly 1,600 14-year-old students to whom they had administered tests of verbal and nonverbal intelligence (Desrivières et al., 2015). After analyzing more than 54,000 gene variations involved in brain development, the team found that students with a particular variant had a thinner cortex on the left side of their brains. These students also had lower scores on the tests for intellectual ability. Researchers stressed that they did not discover the gene for intelligence, noting that overall intelligence is greatly influenced by numerous genetic and environmental factors.

Neural Efficiency. PET scans and EEGs also depict that people who score high on tests of reasoning and intelligence show less cerebral activity than people who score lower. These results imply that intelligence may be primarily a matter of *neural efficiency*, whereby the brain eventually learns to use fewer neurons or networks to accomplish a repetitive task, such as is illustrated in Figure 3.11 (Nussbaumer, Grabner, & Stern, 2015). Think of the implications this concept has for altering the way we allocate learning time as well as design and deliver lessons. It suggests, at the very least, that we should vary learning time to accommodate

Figure 3.16 This composite MRI shows the key areas in the frontal lobes and left hemisphere where people with higher IQ scores had more gray matter than those with lower scores (adapted from Haier et al., 2004).

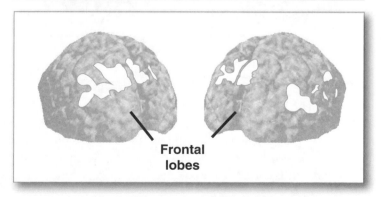

Frontal lobes

the task at hand and move learners to intensive practice as soon as comprehension is established. This approach is one of the basic components of differentiated instruction.

Further evidence of neural efficiency exists in PET scans taken of the brain while playing a computer game. When first learning the game there is a large amount of neural activity. As the player masters the game, the amount of brain activity diminishes significantly (see Figure 3.17). Further, the higher the IQ of the player, the more quickly the neural activity drops while he or she is learning the game (e.g., Hamari et al., 2016). Future research may describe these systems in greater detail and provide a neurological framework for better interpreting how data from the neurosciences support the notion of multiple intelligences.

Fluid Intelligence. While pursuing the elusive relationships between intelligence and brain structure and function, neuroscientists have begun to focus mainly on *fluid intelligence.* This type of intelligence is associated with one's ability to analyze complex relationships, to infer and deduce, and to use knowledge and skills to solve novel problems. It is more about how individuals *use* their knowledge and skills than about how they *acquire* them.

For now, these current notions continue to move us away from the traditional model of intelligence as a singular entity, fixed at birth and best measured by vocabulary and reading. They help us understand that the environment can have significant impact on intelligence, and that human beings can be smart in different ways.

Perhaps the next step is to realize that each of the intelligences described by Gardner (1993), Sternberg (1985), and others has many skills contained within it, and thus, there are *innumerable* ways that each brain can manipulate information and skills during the learning process. Expanding our view beyond separate intelligences to an integrated wealth of intelligences is supported by neuroscience, and it also reduces the chances that we will label kids as "word smart" or "music dumb." Rather, we can accept that the best teaching and learning occurs when we use the greatest variety of techniques, thereby making it more likely that all learners will succeed.

Figure 3.17 These PET images show the level of brain activity while playing a computer game. With the light colored areas indicating high levels of activity, the scans indicate that the expert player (right) uses significantly less energy than the novice player (left) does, an example of increased neural efficiency.

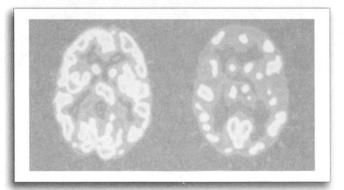

It is clear that no agreement exists about what intelligence is, and major efforts to define intelligence are not likely to be advanced significantly by brain imaging anytime in the near future.

Retrieval

Without retrieval, a stored memory would have no useful purpose. It takes less than 50 milliseconds (a millisecond is one thousandth of a second) to retrieve an item from working memory. Retrieving a memory from long-term storage, however, can be complicated and comparatively time-consuming. One curious finding in recent years is that encoding information into memory involves the left hemisphere more than the right, and retrieval involves the right hemisphere more than the left. Although both processes involve the frontal lobes, it appears that encoding and retrieval activate separate neural systems. Recently, researchers were surprised to discover that the parietal lobe, usually associated with sensory and motor processing, also plays a role in processing retrieved information (Gilmore, Nelson, & McDermott, 2015; Olson & Berryhill, 2009). This discovery indicates that more brain areas are involved in processing retrieved memories than previously thought.

The brain uses two methods to retrieve information from the long-term storage sites, *recognition* and *recall.* Recognition matches an outside stimulus with stored information. For example, the questions on a multiple-choice test involve recognizing the correct answer (assuming the learner stored it originally) among the choices. This method helps explain why even poor students almost always do better than expected on multiple-choice tests. Recall is quite different and more difficult. It describes the process whereby cues or hints are sent to long-term memory, which must search and retrieve information from multiple long-term storage sites, then consolidate and decode it back into working memory.

Both methods require the firing of neurons along the neural pathways to the storage site(s) and back again to working memory. The more frequently we access a pathway, the less likely it is to be obscured by other pathways. Information we use frequently, such as our name and telephone number, is quickly retrieved because the neural impulses to and from those storage sites keep the pathways clear. When the information is moved into working memory, we reprocess it to determine its validity and, in effect, relearn it. However, a word of caution is in order. Whenever a previously consolidated memory is recalled into working memory, it is vulnerable to alteration by any information already in working memory. The new information may add to and strengthen the original memory, or significantly modify it. As the old and new information is reprocessed, what returns to long-term storage may be slightly or considerably different from the original memory. This process is called *reconsolidation* and has neuroscientists wondering if any long-term memories are truly stable (Balderas, Rodriguez-Ortiz, & Bermudez-Rattoni, 2015; Bonin & De Koninck, 2015). What implication does this have for teaching? At the very least, it suggests that whenever teachers ask students to recall old learning, it should relate to what the students are currently processing in working memory.

> *Whenever we retrieve something from long-term storage into working memory, we relearn it. It also becomes vulnerable to alteration.*

Factors Affecting Retrieval

The rate at which the retrieval occurs depends on a number of factors.

- **Adequacy of the Cues.** The cue used to stimulate the retrieval of a memory may prompt a fully accurate recall or an ambiguous one. Because memory is not a digital recorder, the rememberer must reconstruct the memory based on the information retrieved by that cue. Having a strong memory does not seem to be as important as the retrieval cues (Smith & Moynan, 2008; Uzer, 2016).

- **Mood and Beliefs of the Retriever.** Studies show that people in a sad mood more easily remember negative experiences, while those in a happy mood tend to recall pleasant experiences (Christodoulou & Burke, 2016; Lewis, Critchley, Smith, & Dolan, 2005). People also tend to assign positive features to choices they have made in the past and negative features to choices they have rejected (Henkel & Mather, 2007). This may explain why it is so difficult to get individuals to view in a positive and unbiased light those choices they refused to accept in the past.

- **Context of the Retrieval.** Accurate recall is more likely to occur if the context during retrieval is very similar to the context of the period during which information was learned (Hockley & Bancroft, 2015). This is known as *context-dependent memory.* Thus, testing students for information in the same location in which they learned it is likely to result in better retrieval.

- **System of Storage.** Declarative memories get stored across brain structures, most likely in the areas that perceive and process incoming stimuli. Thus, the interests and past experiences of the learner will influence the type of cerebral networks that are constructed to contain the memory.

Students store the same item of information in different networks, depending on how they link the information to their past learnings. These storage decisions affect the amount of time it will take to retrieve the information later. This explains why some students need more time than others to retrieve the same information. When teachers call on those whose hands go up first, they inadvertently signal to the slower retrievers to stop the retrieval process. This is an unfortunate strategy for three reasons: First, the slower-retrieving students feel that they are not getting teacher recognition, thereby lowering their self-concept. Second, by not retrieving the information into working memory, they miss an opportunity to relearn it. Third, it gives students the false impression that fast retrievers are smarter than slower retrievers.

> *Calling on those whose hands go up first signals the slower retrievers to stop the retrieval process.*

Rates of Learning and Retrieval

It is no secret that some people learn a particular item faster or slower than others do. The amount of time it takes someone to learn cognitive information with sufficient confidence that it will be consolidated into long-term memory is called the *rate of learning.* The rate of learning can vary within the same individual because it can be affected by motivation, emotional mood, degree of focus, and the context in which the learning occurs.

In the information processing model in Chapter 2 (Figure 2.1), the rate of learning is represented by the data arrows flowing from left to right, from the senses through the sensory register to immediate memory and into working memory. The *rate of retrieval* is represented by the recall arrow moving information from right to left, from long-term storage to working memory. *These two rates are independent of each other.* This notion is quite different from classic doctrine, which holds that the retrieval rate is strongly related to the rate of learning and, thus, anchored in genetic inheritance (Uzer, 2016). The doctrine is further fueled in our society by timed tests and quiz programs that use the speed of retrieving answers as the main criterion for judging success and intelligence. The disclosure that the rate of retrieval is linked to the nature of the learner's storage method—a learned skill—rather than to the rate of learning is indeed significant. Because it is a *learned* skill, it can be taught. There is now great promise that techniques can be developed for helping us refine our long-term storage methods for faster and more accurate retrieval. (See the Practitioner's Corner: Using Rehearsal to Enhance Retention and Practitioner's Corner: Using Chunking to Enhance Retention at the end of this chapter.)

Because the rate of learning and the rate of retrieval are independent, individuals can be fast or slow learners, fast or slow retrievers, and every combination between. Although most people tend to fall midrange, some are at the extremes. Actually, not only have we had experience with learners possessing the extreme combinations of these two rates, but we have also (perhaps unwittingly) made up labels to describe them. An individual who is a fast learner and a fast retriever we call *gifted* or a *genius*. Such students retrieve answers quickly. Their hands go up first. Their responses are almost always correct, and they get reputations as "brains." Teachers call on them when they want to keep the lesson moving.

A student who is a fast learner but slow retriever we call an *underachiever*. Teachers say to these students, "Come on, John, I know you know this . . . keep trying." We often run out of patience and admonish them for not studying enough. A slow learner and fast retriever we call an *overachiever*. These students respond quickly, but their answers may be incorrect. Teachers sometimes mistakenly view them as trying too hard to learn something that may be beyond them.

For the student who is a slow learner and slow retriever, we have a whole list of uncomplimentary labels. More regrettable is that too often we interpret *slow learner* to mean "unable to learn." What being a slow learner really means is that the student is unable to learn something in the amount of time we have arbitrarily assigned for that learning. All these labels are unfortunate because they perpetuate the mistaken notion that the major factors promoting successful learning are beyond the control of the learner and teacher.

Teachers can help students improve their rate of retrieval by using instructional strategies that assist the learners' brain in deciding how and where to consolidate the new learning in long-term memory. One strategy deals with chunking and is the next topic of discussion. The other involves identifying the critical attributes and is discussed in Chapter 4.

> *Too often we interpret slow learner to mean "unable to learn."*

> *The rate of learning and the rate of retrieval are independent of each other.*

> **Test Question No. 6:** The rate at which a learner retrieves information from memory is closely related to intelligence. True or false?
>
> **Answer:** False. The rate of retrieval is independent of intelligence. It is more closely tied to how and where the information was stored originally.

Chunking

There are three limits to our power of reasoning and thinking: our limited attention span, our working memory, and our long-term memory. Is it possible to consciously increase the number of items that working memory can handle at one time? The answer is yes, through a process called *chunking* (also referred to as *compression*). Chunking occurs when working memory perceives a set of data as a single item, much as we perceive *information* as one word (and, therefore, one item) even though it is composed of 11 separate letters. The ability to chunk appears to be an innate human characteristic, most likely related to the brain's hardwired survival ability to seek out patterns in our environment. Even infants have shown the ability to chunk (Kibbe & Feigenson, 2016).

Video: For simple examples of chunking, see

https://www.youtube.com/watch?v=SlvOnQF55BA and https://www.youtube.com/watch?v=KhZrQQeZOWA

Going back to the number exercise in Chapter 2, some people may have indeed remembered all 10 digits in the right sequence. These may be people who spend a lot of time on the telephone. When they see a 10-digit number, their experience helps them to group it by area code, prefix, and extension. Thus, they see the second number, 4915082637, as (491) 508–2637, which is now three chunks, not 10. Because three are within the working memory's functional capacity, the digits can be remembered accurately (Brady, Konkle, & Alvarez, 2009). Chunking can also occur with spatial items, a skill vital to chess masters (Campitelli, Gobet, Head, Buckley, & Parker, 2007; Sargent, Dopkins, Philbeck, & Chichka, 2010).

Studies suggest that chunking occurs in two ways. In one situation, chunking is a deliberate, goal-oriented process initiated and controlled by the learner. For example, in learning a poem, we are likely to rehearse the first line, then the first two lines, then three lines, and so on, gradually increasing the size of the chunk until we know the whole poem. The other mechanism is more subtle, automatic, continuous, and linked to perceptual processes. This occurs, for instance, when we learn to read. The brain gradually expands the number of words it processes at one time from a single word to two words, to a phrase, and so on. During this process, fMRIs show increased activity in the frontal lobes as working memory encodes the learning content into higher-capacity chunks (Bor, Duncan, Wiseman, & Owen, 2003).

Chunking allows us to deal with a few large blocks of information rather than many small fragments. Problem solving involves the ability to access large amounts of relevant knowledge from long-term memory for use in working memory. The key to that skill is chunking. The more a person is able to chunk in a particular area, the more expert the person becomes. These experts have the ability to use their experiences to group or chunk all kinds of information into discernable patterns. Chunking is also a valuable strategy when learning a complicated procedure, especially if the learners are reading aloud the procedures while carrying them out (Solopchuk, Alamia, Oliver, & Zénon, 2016).

This ability to chunk is much more a reflection of how the expert's knowledge base is organized than a superior perceptual ability. Experience has changed the experts' brains so that they can encode relevant information in greater detail and more fully than the nonexperts. As they gain experience, more patterns are chunked and linked, and the expertise becomes less conscious and more intuitive. Here are some examples:

- An experienced physician takes much less time to diagnose a medical condition than an intern does.
- Expert waiters remember meal combinations rather than single menu items.
- Expert musicians recall long passages, not single notes.
- Chess masters recall board layouts as functional clusters rather than separate pieces.
- Expert readers take in phrases, not individual words.

Test Question No. 7: The amount of information a learner can deal with at one time is genetically linked. True or false?

Answer: False. The amount of information a learner can deal with at one time is linked to the learner's ability to add more items to the chunks in working memory—a learned skill.

Effect of Past Experiences on Chunking

Let's show how past experiences affect chunking. First, look at the following sentence:

Grandma is buying an apple.

This sentence has 22 letters, but only five chunks (or words) of information. Because the sentence is one complete thought, most people treat it as just one item in working memory. In this example, 22 bits of data (letters) become one chunk (complete thought). In addition, visual learners probably form a mental image of a grandmother buying that apple.

Now let's add more information to working memory. Stare at the sentence below for about 10 seconds. Now close your eyes and try recalling the two sentences.

Hte plpae si edr.

Having trouble with the second? That's because the groups of letters make no sense, and working memory is treating each of the 13 letters and three spaces as 16 individual items (plus the first sentence as one item, for a total of 17). The small functional capacity range of working memory is quickly exceeded.

Let's rearrange the letters in each word of the second sentence to read as follows:

The apple is red.

Stare at this sentence for 10 seconds. Now close your eyes again and try to remember the first sentence and this sentence. Most people will remember both sentences because they are now just two items instead of 17, and their meanings are related. Experience, once again, helps the working memory decide how to chunk items.

Here's a frequently used example of how experience can help in chunking information and improving achievement. Get the pencil and paper again. Now stare at the letters below for seven seconds. Then look away from the page and write them down in the correct sequence and groupings. Ready? Go.

DNAN BCT VF BIU SA

Check your results. Did you get all the letters in the correct sequence and groupings? Probably not, but that's OK. Most people do not get 100 percent by staring at the letters in such a short period of time.

Let's try it again. Same rules: Stare at the letters below for seven seconds and write the letters down. Ready? Go.

DNA NBC TV FBI USA

How did you do this time? Most people do much better on this example. Now compare the two examples. Note that the letters in both examples are *identical and in the same sequence!* The only difference is that the letters in the second example are grouped—or chunked—in a way that allows past experience to help working memory process and hold the items. Working memory usually sees the first example as 14 letters plus four spaces (i.e., the grouping is important) or 18 items—much more than its functional capacity. But the second example is quickly seen as only five understandable items (the spaces no longer matter) and, thus, within the limits of working memory's capacity. Some people may even pair NBC with TV, and FBI with USA, so that they actually deal with just three chunks. These examples show the power of past experience in remembering—a principle of learning called *transfer,* which we will discuss in the next chapter.

Chunking is a very effective way of enlarging working memory's capacity. It can be used to memorize a long string of numbers or words. Most of us learned the alphabet in chunks—for some it may have been *abcd, efg, hijk, lmnop, qrs, tuv, wxyz.* Chunking reduced the 26 letters to a smaller number of items that working memory could handle. Even people can be chunked, such as couples (e.g., Romeo and Juliet, Gilbert and Sullivan, Bonnie and

Chunking is an effective way of enlarging working memory's capacity and for helping the learner make associations that establish meaning.

Clyde), in which recalling the name of one immediately suggests the name of the other. Although working memory has a functional capacity limit as to the number of chunks it can process at one time, there appears to be no functional limit to the number of items that can be combined into a chunk. Teaching students (and yourself) how to chunk can greatly increase learning and remembering.

Test Question No. 8: It is usually not possible to increase the amount of information that the working memory can deal with at one time. True or false?

Answer: False. By increasing the number of items in a chunk, we can increase the amount of information that our working memory can process simultaneously.

Cramming Is Chunking

Cramming for a test or an interview is another example of chunking. The learner loads into working memory as many items as can be identified as needed. Varying degrees of temporary associations are made among the items. With sufficient effort and meaning, the items can be carried in working memory, even for days, until needed. If the source of the crammed items was outside the learner—that is, from texts or class notes—then it is possible for none of the crammed items to be transferred to long-term storage. This practice (which many of us have experienced) explains how a learner can be conversant and outwardly competent in the items tested on one day (while the items were in working memory) and have little or no understanding of them several days later because they have since dropped out of working memory into oblivion. We cannot recall later what we have not stored. Is there anything teachers can do about this? (See the Practitioner's Corner: Testing Whether Information Is in Long-Term Storage in Chapter 2.)

Forgetting

Ask teachers how long they want their students to remember what they were taught, and the answer is a resounding "forever." Yet, they know that is not usually the case. Much of what is taught in school is forgotten over time, sometimes within a few days. Forgetting is often viewed as the enemy of learning. But, on the contrary, forgetting plays an important role in promoting learning and facilitating recall.

The human brain processes an enormous amount of incoming information every day. Much of that information remains briefly in temporary memory sites and soon fades. For example, the name of a person whom you have just met may remain in memory for only a few minutes. Yet the name of your best friend is turned into a long-term memory and lasts a lifetime. Why do we forget so much and preserve so little? Forgetting manifests itself in two major ways: the process of discarding newly acquired information and the decay or lack of access that occurs with memories already in long-term storage.

Forgetting New Information

The first major studies on forgetting were conducted by Hermann Ebbinghaus (1850–1909), a German psychologist, whose work led to the development of a forgetting curve. The curve was a mathematical representation of how quickly new experiences were forgotten. Subsequent studies have somewhat modified his findings. When the brain is exposed to new information, the greatest amount of forgetting occurs shortly after the learning task is completed, and continues rapidly throughout the first day. Items that do not make sense to the learner are usually forgotten first. Conversely, traumatic and vivid experiences are rarely forgotten, although what we recall of them may change over time—that reconsolidation thing again. But for most information, forgetting slows down after two weeks when there is not much left to forget.

Forgetting new material can occur as a result of interference from earlier learning. This is a component of a process called *transfer,* which will be discussed in greater detail in Chapter 4. Even *how* one acquires new learning can affect forgetting. For most people, it is easier to forget what is heard than what is read. When listening to new information, extraneous sounds can divert the brain's attention. But reading is a much more focused activity, thereby reducing the effect of distractions (see Figure 3.10). Stress and lack of sleep also contribute to forgetting because the brain is more focused on dealing with stress and insomnia than on using resources to encode seemingly less important information.

Forgetting has some definite advantages. When the brain is presented with a large amount of information, forgetting prevents irrelevant information from interfering with the acquisition, remembering, and recall of relevant information. By screening out the unimportant, the essential data and experiences have a chance to be fully consolidated into long-term memories. Forgetting may be frustrating, but it is most likely a survival adaptation of memory. There is little value in remembering everything that has happened to us. Forgetting the trivial leaves room for the more important and meaningful experiences that shape who we are and establish our individuality.

> *By forgetting the trivial, we leave room for the more important and meaningful experiences that shape who we are and establish our individuality.*

Teachers, of course, believe that all the material they present in class is relevant. Why doesn't the student's brain perceive it that way, too? We already answered that question in Chapter 2. You will recall that sense and meaning (relevance) are key factors affecting whether new information will be remembered or forgotten.

Forgetting Memories

Imagine if the brain remembered everything for a lifetime. Just trying to recall the name of a childhood friend would be a significant challenge. The brain would have to search through thousands of names scattered among the long-term memory sites. At best, the name would take a long time to find; at worst, the result could be confusion, resulting in the recall of the wrong name. By gradually forgetting the names that are not important, the recall process becomes more efficient. Forgetting also helps to update obsolete information. As one changes jobs and relocates, for example, new data, such as addresses and telephone numbers, overwrite the old data. The old data may still reside in long-term memory, but if they are not recalled and rehearsed, they will eventually become less accessible.

Exactly what happens in the brain to old memories over time is still an open question. Some researchers suggest that memory loss of a specific experience can occur if the memory has not been recalled for a long time. They believe that this leads to the slow but steady disassociation of the network of brain cells that form the memory, making retrieval increasingly difficult. Eventually, the integrity of the network fails, and the memory is lost, perhaps forever. Such a process, the researchers say, frees up memory resources so that they become available for new information (Bauer, 2015; Wixted, 2004).

Other researchers contend that old memories remain intact, though other factors somehow block access to them. These factors can include medications, drugs, vivid new experiences, stroke, and Alzheimer's disease. Recent studies have also found that some people can voluntarily block an unwanted past experience with such persistence that it results in what is called *directed forgetting* (Delaney, Goldman, King, & Nelson-Gray, 2015). Does it make any difference whether forgetting is the deterioration of the memory sites or losing the pathways? Is not the result the same, the inability to recall the memory? Sure, the result is the same, but because our understanding of the storage process has changed, so has the method for trying to recall it. We can use a therapy that helps us to find the original pathway, or an alternative pathway, to the memory sites.

Here is an example. Suppose you try to recall the name of the teacher you had when you were in second grade. Unless you have thought recently about that teacher, the pathway to that name has not been used for a long time. It is blocked by newer pathways, and you will have difficulty finding it. The name is still there, but it may take you as long as several days to find it. It will probably come to you when you least expect it.

Another example: Suppose you start thinking about finding an old sweater that you have not seen in several years. If you believe you gave it away, you will not even begin to look for it. That is the same as if you believe that your forgotten memory has been destroyed over time; you will not even try to recall it. On the other hand, if you are convinced that the sweater is somewhere in that big attic, then it is just a matter of time before your hunt pays off and you find it. You'll probably start by thinking of the last time you wore it. This is the same process of memory therapy that is used with brain-damaged individuals. The therapy helps the patient seek other neural connections to find the original or an alternative pathway to the memory sites.

Implications for Teaching. More research is needed before scientists can draw conclusions about the mechanisms that result in the forgetting of old memories. Meanwhile, teachers can take advantage of what *is* known. Namely, important information that students have already learned is more likely to be accurately and firmly consolidated in long-term memory if it is recalled and rehearsed periodically as the students progress through grade levels.

If important information is purposefully revisited throughout a student's entire school experience, then firmly consolidated and robust memories will be available for a long time to come.

Too often, information deemed important is taught just once, and the students are expected to remember it for a lifetime. They may even be tested on it years after they initially learned it. Something worth remembering is worth repeating. If important information is purposefully revisited throughout a student's entire school experience, then firmly consolidated and robust memories will be available for a long time to come.

Confabulation: Telling It Like It Isn't

Have you ever been discussing an experience with someone who had shared it with you and started arguing over some of the details? As described earlier, recall in long-term memory is the process of searching, locating, retrieving, and transferring information from multiple storage sites to working memory. Rote recall, especially of frequently used information, such as your name and address, is actually simple. These pathways are clear, and retrieval time is very short. Retrieving more complex and less frequently used concepts is much more complicated. It requires signaling multiple storage sites through elaborate, cluttered pathways for intermediate consolidation and ultimate decoding into working memory. It is less accurate. First, most of us do not retain 100 percent of elaborate experiences, such as an extensive vacation. Second, we store parts of the experience in many storage sites.

When retrieving such an experience, the long-term memory may not be able to locate all the events being requested, either because of insufficient time or because they were never retained. Moreover, as mentioned earlier, older memories can be modified or distorted by the acquisition of newer information. During the retrieval process, memory can unconsciously fabricate the missing or incomplete information by selecting the next closest item it can recall. This process is called *confabulation* and occurs because the brain is always active and creative, and seems to abhor incompleteness. Confabulation is not unlike the way the brain completes visual patterns that do not exist, as in optical illusions. Take a look at Figure 3.18. Although you may see a white triangle in the diagram, it does not exist. It is the result of confabulation as the brain seeks to make sense of the pattern.

Confabulation is *not* lying because it is an unconscious rather than a deliberate process, and the individual believes the fabricated information to be true. This explains why two people who participated in the same experience will later recall slightly—or even significantly—different versions of the same event. Neither individual stored 100 percent of the experience. If each stored 90 percent, it would not be the *same* 90 percent for both. Their missing and different 10 percent will be fabricated and will cause each to question the accuracy of the other's memory. The less of the experience remembered, the more the brain must fabricate. Over time, the fabricated parts are consolidated into the memory network. As we systematically recall this memory, minor alterations may continue to be made through confabulation. Gradually, the original memory is transformed and encoded into a considerably different one that we believe to be true and accurate. Although we all fall victim to confabulation at one time or another, damage to certain brain areas can cause chronic and extreme confabulation where the recalled memories deviate significantly from reality, or the event being recalled never took place (e.g., Nahum, Bouzerda-Wahlen, Guggisberg, Ptak, & Schnider, 2012).

Implications for Teaching. Confabulation also happens in the classroom. When recalling complex learning, the learner is unaware of which parts are missing and, thus, fabricated. The younger the learner, the more inconsistent the fabricated parts can be because memory has fewer experiences to choose from. The teacher may react by thinking the student is inventing answers intentionally and may discipline accordingly. In another situation, a list of similar words or concepts may induce the confabulation of words or concepts *not* on the list, a common phenomenon. In these cases, the teacher should be aware of confabulation as a possibility, identify the fabricated parts, and provide the feedback needed to help the student correct the inaccurate material. Through practice, the learner will incorporate the corrected material and transfer it to long-term memory.

Figure 3.18 The white triangle you may see does not exist. It is a result of confabulation.

Confabulation has implications for the justice system. This tendency for the brain to fabricate information rather than admit its absence can have serious consequences in court trials where eyewitnesses, under the pressure of testifying, feel compelled to provide complete information. Confabulation also raises questions about the accuracy of witnesses recalling very old memories of unpleasant events, such as a childhood accident or abuse. Experiments have shown how easy it is to distort a person's recollection of even recent events, or to "implant" memories. In the absence of independent verification, it is impossible to decide which events in the recalled "repressed memory" actually occurred and which are the result of confabulation (Patihis, Lilienfeld, Ho, & Loftus, 2014).

> *Our brain fabricates information and experiences that we believe to be true.*

A Word About Brain-Training Programs

There are numerous so-called brain-training programs now available that claim to boost students' attention, working memory, and overall academic performance. Others assert that their programs will protect against attention deficit disorders, brain injury, and dementia. Much of what they claim is not supported by scientific evidence. Some of the companies marketing these programs insist that they have conducted trials proving the effectiveness of their products. However, a 2013 meta-analysis reviewed 23 studies on working-memory training and found that, although there were some improvements, they were not sustained over time (Melby-Lervåg & Hulme, 2013). Furthermore, the improvements did not seem to have any effect on attention control, verbal and nonverbal abilities, word decoding, arithmetic, and general cognitive processing. Other similar studies have had the same results (e.g., Redick et al., 2013).

The U.S. Federal Trade Commission has taken issue with the exaggerated claims of these programs and has levied stiff fines against some of their producers for misleading marketing. Nonetheless, the notion that improving our minds and brains with games has enticed the general public as well as educators who do not have a deep understanding of what "scientific evidence" really means. The good news is that there are some studies suggesting that certain intense and prolonged gaming can improve the cognitive abilities of reasoning and episodic memories. More research is needed. As of now, most neuroscientists will agree that commercial brain-training programs promise much more than they can deliver, and that an effective and proven way to improve general health and brain fitness is through physical exercise.

WHAT'S COMING UP?

One of the most important goals of education is to teach students how to apply what they learn to future situations they will encounter—what is known as the transfer of learning. Transfer affects old learning, new learning, memory, and recall. The nature and power of transfer, as well as how it can help or hinder teaching and learning, are unveiled in the next chapter.

PRACTITIONER'S CORNER

Guidelines for Teaching the Emotional Brain

Emotions play too much of an important part in learning and memory to be ignored in the teaching–learning process. Although teachers are unable to control all the factors that affect the emotional lives of their students, there are some things they can do. Evoking emotions that will help students feel safe in the classroom as well as make connections to the lesson objectives will facilitate deep learning and promote long-term memory.

Here are some guidelines to consider when planning for the emotional brain.

Classroom Climate:

- Ensure a positive classroom climate by (1) promoting positive relationships among the students so they are kind to each other, listen to each other, and respect different viewpoints; (2) cultivating a positive relationship with all your students so they feel you not only care about their academic success but also care about them as individuals; and (3) developing and reinforcing classroom norms and rules that are simple, clear, and provide a physically and emotionally safe learning environment.
- Occasionally interview students individually and ask questions such as whether they feel safe in the class, if students are kind to each other, and do they feel welcomed and included in the class. Use the students' feedback to make any necessary adjustments to improve the climate.

Instruction:

- Use metacognitive activities that ask students to reflect on the motivations of people they encounter in their curriculum, such as famous scientists, explorers, writers, artists, and mathematicians. Encourage them to talk about their own feelings regarding these people and to listen to the feelings of their classmates.
- Consider using statements with emotional connections when asking students to reflect on what they have learned. For instance, ask "How did you feel about this topic when we . . ." and "How do you feel about it now? Why?" After the emotional brain has had its say, move into discussing the cognitive/rational elements of the lesson.
- "Why" questions tend to shift a discussion more to emotions and motivation rather than on bare facts and data. For example, "Why did the French people rise up against King Louis XVI's reign?" is an emotionally loaded question that evokes much more about people's motivation than a "When" or "Where" question.
- Because memories are usually contextual, instructional strategies that draw out emotions provide important cues that will help students recall the information when faced with very similar events in their real world. Such strategies include role-playing, simulations, and cooperative projects.

Remember that the brain first reacts emotionally to new learning before reacting rationally. Thus, any teaching strategy that generates positive emotions about new learning is a valuable tool to help get and keep students engaged and interested.

PRACTITIONER'S CORNER

Avoid Teaching Two Very Similar Motor Skills

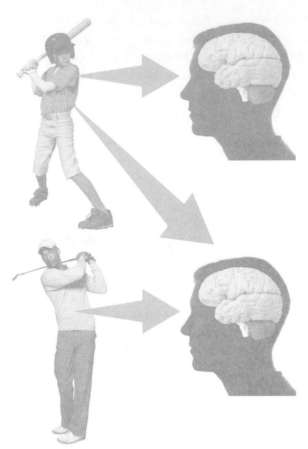

When a learner practices a new skill (in this example, swinging a baseball bat), the motor cortex (across the top of the cerebrum) coordinates with the cerebellum to establish the pathways that will consolidate the movements to perform the skill. After the learner stops the practice, it takes about 4 to 12 hours (down-time) for this consolidation to occur. Further memory pathways are established as the learner sleeps. Practicing the skill the next day will be much easier and more accurate.

If, during the 4- to 12-hour down-time, the learner practices a second skill (in this example, swinging a golf club) that is very similar to the first skill, the pathways for the two skills get confounded. As a result, the learner is able to perform *neither* skill well.

Implications for Practice

- Avoid teaching two motor skills that are very similar to each other in the same day. When in doubt, make a list of their similarities and differences. If the similarities far outweigh the differences, it is best not to teach them together.

- When the time comes to teach the second skill, teach the *differences* first. This ensures that the differences are recognized during prime-time-1, which is the most powerful position for remembering.

PRACTITIONER'S CORNER

Using Rehearsal to Enhance Retention

Rehearsal refers to the learner's reprocessing of new information in an attempt to determine sense and meaning. It occurs in two forms. Some information items have value only if they are remembered *exactly* as presented, such as the letters and sequence of the alphabet, spelling, poetry, telephone numbers, notes and lyrics of a song, and the multiplication tables. This is called *rote rehearsal.* Sense and meaning are established quickly, and the likelihood of long-term retention is high. Most of us can recall poems and telephone numbers that we learned years ago.

More complex concepts require the learner to make connections and to form associations and other relationships in order to establish sense and meaning. Thus, the information may need to be reprocessed several times as new links are found. This is called *elaborative rehearsal.* The more senses that are used in this elaborative rehearsal, the more reliable the associations. Thus, when visual, auditory, and kinesthetic activities assist the learner during this rehearsal, the probability of long-term storage rises dramatically. That is why it is important for students to talk about what they are learning *while* they are learning it, and to have visual models as well.

Rehearsal is teacher initiated and teacher directed. Recognizing that rehearsal is a necessary ingredient for retention of learning, teachers should consider the following when designing and presenting their lessons:

Rote Rehearsal Strategies

- **Simple Repetition.** For remembering short items (telephone numbers, names, and dates), simply say aloud a set of items repeatedly until they can be recalled in correct sequence.

- **Cumulative Repetition.** For longer sets of items (song, poem, list of battles) the learner rehearses the first few items. Then the next set of items in the sequence is added to the first set and rehearsed, and so on. For example, to remember a poem of four stanzas, the learner starts by rehearsing the first stanza, and then rehearses the second stanza alone, followed by the first two stanzas together. With those in place, the learner rehearses the third stanza and then the three stanzas together. The process is repeated by rehearsing the fourth stanza alone and, finally, all four stanzas together.

Elaborative Rehearsal Strategies

- **Paraphrasing.** Students orally restate ideas in their own words, which then become familiar cues for later storage. Using auditory modality helps the learner attach sense, making retention more likely.

- **Selecting and Note Taking.** Students review texts, illustrations, and lectures, deciding which portions are critical and important. They make these decisions based on criteria from the teacher, authors, or other students. Students then paraphrase the idea and write it into their notes. Adding the kinesthetic exercise of writing furthers retention.

- **Predicting.** After studying a section of content, the students predict the material to follow or what questions the teacher might ask about that content. Prediction keeps students focused on the new content, adds interest, and helps them apply prior learnings to new situations, thus aiding retention.

- **Questioning.** After studying content, students generate questions about the content. To be effective, the questions should range from lower-level thinking of recall, comprehension, and application to higher-level thinking of analysis, evaluation, and synthesis (see Bloom's taxonomy in Chapter 7). When designing questions of varying complexity, students engage in deeper cognitive processing, clarify concepts, and predict meaning and associations—all contributors to retention.

- **Summarizing.** Students reflect on and summarize in their heads the important material or skills learned in the lesson. This is often the last and a critical stage where students can attach sense and meaning to the new learning. Summarizing rehearsal is also called *closure* (see the Practitioner's Corner: Using Closure to Enhance Sense and Meaning in Chapter 2 for further explanation).

General Guidelines

If the retention of new information or skills beyond the immediate lesson is an important expectation, then rehearsal must be a crucial part of the learner's processing. The following considerations should be incorporated into decisions about using rehearsal.

- **Teach** students rehearsal activities and strategies. As soon as they recognize the differences between rote and elaborative rehearsal, they can understand the importance of selecting the appropriate type for each learning objective. With practice, they should quickly realize that fact and data acquisition require rote rehearsal, whereas analysis and evaluation of concepts require elaborative rehearsal.

- **Remind** students to continuously practice rehearsal strategies until they become regular parts of their study and learning habits.

- **Keep** rehearsal relevant. Effective elaborative rehearsal relies more on making personally meaningful associations to prior learning than on time-consuming efforts that lack these student-centered connections. Any associations that focus on the teacher's experiences may not be relevant to students.

- **Remember** that time alone is not a trustworthy indicator of the effectiveness of rehearsal. The degree of meaning associated with the new learning is much more significant than the time allotted.

- **Have** learners verbalize their rehearsal to peers or teachers while they are learning new material, as this increases the likelihood of retention.

- **Provide** more visual and contextual clues to make rehearsal meaningful and successful. Students with limited verbal competence will focus on visual and concrete lesson components to assist in their rehearsal. This will be particularly true of students whose first language is not English.

- **Vary** the rehearsal strategies that you initiate to ensure that there is plenty of novelty in the process. Students will bore quickly if the same method of rehearsal (e.g., sharing with the same partner) is used all the time.

PRACTITIONER'S CORNER

Using the Primacy-Recency Effect in the Classroom

The primacy-recency effect describes the phenomenon whereby, during a learning episode, we tend to remember best that which comes first (prime-time-1), second best that which comes last (prime-time-2), and least that which comes just past the middle (down-time). Proper use of this effect can lead to lessons that are more likely to be remembered.

Below is a sketch of two lessons. One is taught by Mr. Blue and the other by Mr. Green. Study their lesson sequences and look for any application of the primacy-recency effect.

Mr. Blue	Lesson Sequence	Mr. Green
"Get ready to tell me the two causes of the Civil War we discussed yesterday." After getting this, he says, "Today we will learn the third and most important cause as we are still living with its aftereffects 140 years later. Before I tell you, let me give back some homework, collect today's homework, collect the notes from Bill and Mary who were absent yesterday, take attendance, and read a brief announcement."	Prime-time-1	"Get ready to tell me the two causes of World War I we discussed yesterday." After getting this, he says, "Today we will learn the third and most important cause as it set the stage for another world war just 30 years later. And here is the third cause!" (He presents the third cause, gives examples, and relates it to yesterday's two causes.)
"Here is the third cause." (He presents the third cause, gives examples, shows a video clip, and relates it to yesterday's two causes.)	Down-time	"Go into your discussion groups and discuss this third cause. Tie it not only to the two causes we learned yesterday but also to other wars we have learned so far. What are the similarities and differences?"
"OK, we've got only 5 minutes to the end of the period. You've listened attentively, so you can do anything you want as long as you are quiet."	Prime-time-2	"Take 2 minutes to review quietly to yourself what you learned about this third cause. Be prepared to share your thoughts with the class."

If these sequences are representative of what happens most of the time in these two teachers' classes, whose students are more likely to remember what they have learned over time? Why? What are some other implications of using the primacy-recency effect in the classroom?

Here are some other considerations for using this effect in the classroom.

- **Teach the new material first** (after getting the students' focus) during prime-time-1. This is the time of greatest retention. Alternatively, this would also be a good time to reteach any concept that students may be having difficulty understanding. This teaching of new information can be done in various ways, such as through direct instruction, an audio-visual presentation, Internet segment, and so on.

- **Avoid asking students** at the beginning of the lesson if they know anything about a *new* topic being introduced. If it is a new topic, the assumption is that most students do not know it. However, there are always some students ready to take a guess—no matter how unrelated. Because this is the time of greatest retention, almost anything that is said, including incorrect information, is likely to be remembered. Give the information and examples yourself to ensure that they are correct.

- **Avoid using precious prime-time** periods for classroom management tasks, such as collecting absence notes or taking attendance. Do these before you get focus or during the down-time.

- **Use the down-time** portion to have students practice the new learning or to discuss it by relating it to past learnings. Remember that retention of learning does occur during the down-time, but it just takes more effort and concentration.

- **Do closure during prime-time-2.** This is the learner's last opportunity to attach sense and meaning to the new learning, to make decisions about it, and to determine where and how it will be transferred to long-term storage. It is important, then, that the student's brain do the work at this time. If you wish to do a review, then do it *before* closure to increase the chances that the closure experience is accurate. Doing review *instead* of closure is of little value to student retention because *you* are doing all the work.

- **Try to package lesson objectives** (or sublearnings) in teaching episodes of about 20 minutes. Link the sublearnings according to the total time available (two 20-minute lessons for a 40-minute teaching period, three for an hour period, and so on).

PRACTITIONER'S CORNER

Strategies for Block Scheduling

More high schools (and some middle schools, too) have converted from the standard 40- to 45-minute daily period to a block schedule consisting of longer teaching periods, usually 80 to 90 minutes. Although there are various formats for the blocks, the main goal of this change is to allow more time for student participation in the learning process.

The benefits of this approach are many: There is less fragmentation to the school day, more time to dig into concepts and allow for transfer to occur, and more time to develop hands-on activities, such as projects. It also allows for more performance-based assessments of student learning, reducing the reliance on paper-and-pencil tests.

The block experience is likely to be more successful if the teacher recognizes the value and need for novelty and resists the temptation to be the focus of the block during the entire time period. Here are some suggestions for a brain-compatible block lesson.

- **Remember the primacy-recency effect.** Teaching a 90-minute episode as one continuous lesson will mean a down-time of about 35 minutes. Plan for four 20-minute learning segments, and your down-time is reduced substantially to about 10 minutes. This down-time can also be productive if the students are engaged in discussions about the new learning.

- **Be in direct control of just one segment.** You may wish to do some direct instruction during one of the lesson segments. If so, use the first segment for this, and then shift the work burden to the students for the other segments. Remember that the brain that does the work is the brain that learns!

- **Go off task between segments.** Figure 3.9 shows how going off task between the lesson segments can increase the degree of focus when the students return to task. This is because of the novelty effect. If you prefer to stay on task, however, then use a joke, story, or cartoon that is related to the learning. You still get the novelty effect without losing focus.

- **Eliminate the unnecessary.** Block scheduling is designed to give students a chance to dig deeper into concepts. To get the time to do this, scrap less important topics that sneak into the curriculum over time. We all know that everything in the curriculum is not of equal importance. Perform this selective abandonment on a regular basis.

- **Work with your colleagues.** Block activities offer an excellent opportunity for teachers to work together in planning the longer lessons. This collegial process can be very productive and interesting, especially when teachers deliver lessons together. Such planning can be within or across subject areas.

- **Vary the blocks.** Novelty means finding ways to make each of the segments different and multisensory. Here are just a few examples of block activities that you can use for the lesson segments:

Teacher talk	Guest speakers
Research	Videos, movies, slides
Cooperative learning groups	Audio recordings
Reading	Reflection time
Student peer coaching	Jigsaw combinations
Laboratory experiences	Discussion groups
Computer/Internet work	Role-playing and simulations
Journal writing	Instructional games and puzzles

- **Vary the assessment techniques.** Block scheduling offers students opportunities to explore content in many different ways. Thus, assessment techniques should also be varied to allow students different methods of showing what they have learned. Here are a few examples of assessment techniques to consider:

Written tests	Interviews
Questionnaires	Journals
Portfolios	Presentations
Exhibitions	Video production
Demonstrations	Dioramas
Modeling	Music and dance

PRACTITIONER'S CORNER

Using Practice Effectively

Practice does not make perfect; it makes *permanent*. Practice allows the learner to use the newly learned skill in a new situation with sufficient accuracy so that the learner will correctly remember it. Before students begin practice, the teacher should model the thinking process involved and guide the class through each step of the new learning's application.

Because practice makes permanent, the teacher should monitor the students' early practice to ensure that it is accurate and to provide timely feedback and correction if it is not. This guided practice helps eliminate initial errors and alerts students to the critical steps in applying new skills. Here are some suggestions by Hunter (2004) for guiding initial practice:

- **Amount of Material to Practice.** Practice should be limited to the smallest amount of material or skill that has the most relevance for the students. This allows for sense and meaning to be consolidated as the learner uses the new learning.

- **Amount of Time to Practice.** Practice should take place in short, intense periods when the student's working memory is running on prime-time. When the practice period is short, students are more likely to be intent on learning what they are practicing.

- **Frequency of Practice.** New learning should be practiced frequently at first so that it is quickly organized. This is called *massed practice.* If we expect students to retain the information in active storage and to remember how to use it accurately, it should continue to be practiced over increasingly longer time intervals. This is called *distributed practice,* and it is the real key to accurate retention and application of information and mastery of skills over time.

- **Accuracy of Practice.** As students perform guided practice, the teacher should give prompt and specific feedback on whether the practice is correct or incorrect and why. This process gives the teacher valuable information about the degree of student understanding and whether it makes sense to move on or reteach portions that may be difficult for some students.

Relearning Through Recall

Every time we recall information from long-term storage into working memory, we relearn it. Therefore, teachers should use classroom strategies that encourage students to recall previously learned information regularly so they will relearn it. One strategy for doing this is to maintain learner participation throughout the lesson. Called *active participation,* this principle of learning attempts to keep the mind of the student consistently focused on what is being learned or recalled through covert and overt activities.

The covert activity involves the teacher asking the students to recall previously learned information and to process it in some way. It could be "Think of the conditions that existed in America just after the Civil War that we learned yesterday, and be prepared to discuss them in a few minutes." This statement informs the students that they will be held accountable for their recall. This accountability increases the likelihood that the students will recall the desired item and, thus, relearn it. It also alleviates the need for the teacher to call on every student to determine if the recall has occurred. After sufficient wait time (see the Practitioner's Corner: Using Wait Time to Increase Student Participation at the end of this chapter), overt activities are used to determine the quality of the covert recall.

Some suggestions follow on how to use active participation strategies effectively:

- **State the question** and allow thinking time *before* calling on a student for response. This holds all students accountable for recalling the answer until you pick your first respondent.

- **Give clear and specific directions** as to what the students should recall. Focus on the lesson objectives and not on the activities unless they were a crucial part of the learning. Repeat the question using different words and phraseology. This increases the number of cues that the learners have during their retrieval search.

- **Avoid predictable patterns** when calling on students, such as alphabetical order, up and down rows, or raised hands. These patterns signal the students *when* they will be held accountable, thereby allowing them to go off task before and after their turns.

PRACTITIONER'S CORNER

Impact of Circadian Rhythms on Schools and Classrooms

This chapter explained the differences in circadian rhythms of adolescents compared to pre/post-adolescents (see Figure 3.14). The adolescent rhythm is about an hour later, and these differences have implications for elementary and secondary schools. For example,

- **Planning Elementary School Lessons.** Remember that both the teacher and elementary school students are in the midday trough together. The tendency here would be for all to just take a nap! That's probably not an option, so we have to decide how to deal with the trough. Here are two things to consider:

  1. Many elementary teachers can decide what time of day to teach certain subjects. Avoid teaching the same subject every day during the trough time. Because of low focus levels, it is boring for the students and tedious for the teacher. Varying the subject taught in the trough provides novelty and interest.

  2. Keep assignments short, and frequently hold the students accountable for what they are learning. For example, instead of assigning 30 minutes of silent reading (a common practice during the trough time), assign just five minutes for the class to read two pages and give a specific assignment related to the reading. You might say, "After five minutes to read pages 12 and 13, decide what other choices the main character could have made and why. I will call on some of you for your answers." Repeating this process results in four or five mini-lessons that will be more productive than trying to attempt a single 30-minute lesson.

- **School Start Times.** Because of this shift in rhythm, teenagers are sleepier in the morning and tend to stay up later at night. They come to school sleep deprived (i.e., many suffer from delayed sleep-phase syndrome) and often with an inadequate breakfast (i.e., lacking glucose, the brain's fuel). Meanwhile, students often face a long bus ride to get to high schools that are starting earlier. District leaders should consider realigning opening times and course schedules more closely with the students' biological rhythms to increase the chances of successful learning. School districts in 43 states that have adopted later starting times for their high schools are reporting positive results. These same positive results apply to elementary schools that start earlier than the traditional time of 9:00 A.M. (Note: For a current list of schools that have delayed start times and their resulting benefits, see http://www.startschoollater.net/success-stories.html)

- **Classroom Lighting.** Adolescents with delayed sleep-phase syndrome have a high amount of melatonin (the hormone that induces sleep) in their bodies. One of the best ways to reduce melatonin levels is with bright light. Keep classroom lights on, open blinds, lift shades, and look for ways to get the students into outdoor light, especially in the morning (Lewy, Emens, Songer, & Rough, 2009).

- **Testing.** School districts usually give standardized tests to all students in the morning. However, high school students tend to perform better on problem-solving and memory tasks later in the day rather than earlier. It is probable that a number of high school students do not do as well on these tests as they could because of the testing times. Some school districts have reported that testing high school students in the later morning and early afternoon improved their performance and scores.

- **Classroom Climate.** Classroom climate problems can arise in high schools if the teacher is in the postnoon trough while the students are still at their pretrough peak. The teacher is likely to be irritable, and minor discipline annoyances can easily escalate into major confrontations. High school administrators in charge of discipline often report a marked rise in student referrals in the early afternoon. One way to deal with this is for high school teachers to plan student-directed activities during this time, such as computer work, simulations, cooperative learning groups, and research projects. These strategies redirect student energy to productive tasks. Meanwhile, the teacher needs to walk around the room, not only to monitor student work but also to overcome the lower energy levels experienced during the trough.

PRACTITIONER'S CORNER

Using Wait Time to Increase Student Participation

Wait time is the period of teacher silence that follows the posing of a question before the first student is called on for a response. Studies first conducted by Mary Budd Rowe (1974) and others indicate that high school teachers had an average wait time of just over one second. Elementary teachers waited an average of three seconds. Although only a few studies have been done in recent years, their findings confirm that these wait times have not increased (Stichter et al., 2009; Sun & van Es, 2015). This may likely be due to the large amount of curriculum content that needs to be covered and the increased emphasis that many schools have placed on preparing for high-stakes tests. If anything, the times now may be even shorter.

One to three seconds is hardly enough time for slower retrievers, many of whom may know the correct answer, to locate that answer in long-term storage and retrieve it into working memory. And as soon as the teacher calls on the first student, the remaining students *stop the retrieval process* and lose the opportunity to relearn the information. Rowe found that the following happened when teachers extended the wait time to at least *five* seconds or more:

- The length and the quality of student responses increased.

- There was greater participation by slower learners.

- Students used more evidence to support inferences.

- There were more higher-order responses.

These results occurred at all grade levels and in all subjects.

Rowe also noted positive changes in the behavior of teachers who consistently used longer wait times. Specifically, she observed that these teachers did the following:

- Used more higher-order questioning

- Demonstrated greater flexibility in evaluating responses

- Improved their expectations for the performance of slower learners

Another effective method for using wait time is think-pair-share. In this strategy, the teacher asks the students to think about a question. After adequate wait time, the students form pairs and exchange the results of their thinking. Some students then share their ideas with the entire class.

PRACTITIONER'S CORNER

Using Chunking to Enhance Retention

Chunking is the process whereby the brain perceives several items of information as a single item. Words are common examples of chunks. *Elephant* is composed of eight letters, but the brain perceives them as one item of information. The more items we can put into a chunk, the more information we can process in working memory and remember at one time. Chunking is a learned skill and, thus, can also be taught. There are different types of chunking.

Pattern Chunking. This is most easily accomplished whenever we can find patterns in the material to be retained.

- Say we wanted to remember the number 3421941621776. Without a pattern, these 13 digits are treated as separate items and exceed working memory's functional capacity. But we could arrange the numbers in groups that have meaning—for example, 342 (my house number), 1941 (when the United States entered World War II), 62 (my father's age), and 1776 (the Declaration of Independence). Now the number is only four chunks with meaning: 342 1941 62 1776.

- The following example, admittedly contrived, shows how chunking can work at different levels. The task is to memorize the following string of words:

   COW   GRASS   FIELD   TENNIS   NET   SODA   DOG   LAKE   FISH

   We need a method to remember the sequence, because nine is more than the typical functional capacity of seven. We can chunk the sequence of items by using a simple story. First, we see a cow eating grass in a field. Also in the field are two people playing tennis. One player hits the ball way over the net. They are drinking soda while their dog runs after the ball that went into the lake. The dog's splashing frightens the fish.

- Learning a step-by-step procedure for tying a shoelace and copying a computer file from a CD-ROM to a hard disk are examples of pattern chunking. We group the items in a sequence and rehearse them mentally until they become one or a few chunks. Practicing the procedure further enhances the formation of chunks, and subsequent performance requires little conscious attention.

Categorical Chunking. This is a more sophisticated chunking process in that the learner establishes various types of categories to help classify large amounts of information. The learner reviews the information looking for criteria that will group complex material into simpler categories or arrays. The different types of categories can include the following:

- **Advantages and Disadvantages.** The information is categorized according to the pros and cons of the concept. Examples include energy use, global warming, genetically altered crops, abortion, and capital punishment.

- **Similarities and Differences.** The learner compares two or more concepts using attributes that make them similar and different. Examples are comparing the Articles of Confederation to the Bill of Rights, mass to weight, mitosis to meiosis, and the U.S. Civil War to the Vietnam War.

- **Structure and Function.** These categories are helpful with concepts that have parts with different functions, such as identifying the parts of an animal cell, a short story, or the human digestive system.

- **Taxonomies.** This system sorts information into hierarchical levels according to certain common characteristics. Examples are biological taxonomies (kingdom, phylum, class, etc.), taxonomies of learning (cognitive, affective, and psychomotor), and governmental bureaucracies.

- **Arrays.** These are less ordered than taxonomies in that the criteria for establishing the array are not always logical, but are more likely based on observable features. Human beings are classified, for example, by learning style and personality type. Dogs can be grouped by size, shape, or fur length. Clothing can be divided by material, season, or gender.

PRACTITIONER'S CORNER

Using Mnemonics to Help Retention

Mnemonics (from the Greek "to remember") are very useful devices for remembering unrelated information, patterns, or rules. They were developed by the ancient Greeks to help them remember dialogue in plays and for passing information to others when writing was impractical. There are many types of mnemonic schemes. The good news is that ordinary people can greatly improve their memory performance with appropriate strategies and practice. Here are two strategies that can be easily used in the classroom. Work with students to develop schemes appropriate for the content.

- **Rhyming Mnemonics.** Rhymes are simple yet effective ways to remember rules and patterns. They work because if you forget part of the rhyme or get part of it wrong, the words lose their rhyme or rhythm and signal the error. To retrieve the missing or incorrect part, you start the rhyme over again, and this helps you to relearn it. Have you ever tried to remember the fifth line of a song or poem without starting at the beginning? It is very difficult to do because each line serves as the auditory cue for the next line.

  Common examples of rhymes we have learned are "I before e, except after c . . . ," "Thirty days hath September . . . ," and "Columbus sailed the ocean blue. . . ." Here are some rhymes that can help students learn information in other areas:

  The Spanish Armada met its fate

  In fifteen hundred and eighty-eight.

  Divorced, beheaded, died;

  Divorced, beheaded, survived.

  (the fate of Henry VIII's six wives, in chronological order)

  The number you are dividing by,

  Turn upside down and multiply.

  (the rule for dividing by fractions)

  This may seem like a clumsy system, but it works. Make up your own rhyme, alone or with the class, to help you and your students remember more information faster.

- **Reduction Mnemonics.** In this scheme, you reduce a large body of information to a shorter form and use a letter to represent each shortened piece. The letters either are combined to form a real or artificial word or are used to construct a simple sentence. For example, the real word HOMES can help us remember the names of the Great Lakes (Huron, Ontario, Michigan, Erie, Superior). BOY FANS gives us the coordinating conjunctions in English (but, or, yet, for, and, nor, so). The name ROY G BIV aids in remembering the seven colors of the spectrum (red, orange, yellow, green, blue, indigo, violet). Here are other examples:

  Please excuse my dear Aunt Sally (the order for solving algebraic equations: parenthesis, exponents, multiplication, division, addition, subtraction).

  Frederick Charles goes down and ends battle (F, C, G, D, A, E, B: the order that sharps are entered in key signatures; reverse the order for flats).

  In Poland, men are tall (the stages of cell division in mitosis: interphase, prophase, metaphase, anaphase, telophase).

  King Phillip came over from Greece sailing vessels (the descending order of zoological classifications: kingdom, phylum, class, order, family, genus, species, variety).

  King Henry doesn't mind drinking cold milk (the descending order of metric prefixes: kilo-, hecto-, deca-, [measure], deci-, centi-, milli-).

  Sober physicists don't find giraffes in kitchens (the order of names for orbital electrons: s, p, d, f, g, i, k).

CHAPTER 3: MEMORY, RETENTION, AND LEARNING

Key Points to Ponder

Jot down on this page key points, ideas, strategies, and resources you want to consider later. This sheet is your personal journal summary and will help to jog your memory.

4
The Power of Transfer

Transfer is the basis of all creativity, problem solving, and the making of satisfying decisions.

—Madeline Hunter
Mastery Teaching

Chapter Highlights

This chapter explains the components of the most powerful principle of learning, transfer. It examines the factors that affect transfer and how teachers can use past learnings effectively to enhance present and future learning.

The brain is a dynamic creation that is constantly organizing and reorganizing itself when it receives new stimuli. More networks are formed as raw items merge into new patterns. Just as musicians in an orchestra join the individual sounds of their instruments in new and melodious ways, the brain unites disconnected ideas with wonderful harmony. We can add beauty and clarity and can forge isolated ideas into spectacular visions.

Transfer is one process that allows this amazing inventiveness to unfold. It encompasses the ability to learn in one situation and then use that learning, possibly in a modified or generalized form, in other situations. Transfer is the core of problem solving, creative thinking, and all other higher mental processes, inventions, and artistic products. It is also one of the ultimate goals of teaching and learning.

WHAT IS TRANSFER?

The principle of learning called *transfer* describes a two-part process:

(1) **Transfer *during* learning.** This refers to the effect that past learning has on the processing and acquisition of new learning.

(2) **Transfer *of* learning.** This refers to the degree to which the learner applies the new learning in future situations. Perkins and Salomon (1988) offered a low-road/high-road theory of transfer of learning. In their model, low-road transfer refers to a learned and nearly automatic transfer of skills when two tasks are very similar to each other. For example, a child who has learned to tie shoelaces on a pair of sneakers can readily transfer that skill to tying shoelaces on his new pair of dress shoes. Like shoelace tying, steering a car and typing on a keyboard are examples of low-road transfer. High-road transfer, on the other hand, involves careful deliberation and study of the task to determine what past knowledge and skills are appropriate for this situation. Thus, high-road transfer requires more time and more mental effort.

Transfer During Learning

The process goes something like this: Whenever new learning moves into working memory, long-term memory (most likely stimulated by a signal from the hippocampus) simultaneously searches the long-term storage sites for any past learnings that are similar to, or associated with, the new learning. If the experiences exist, the memory networks are activated, and the associated memories are reconsolidated in working memory.

How much past learning affects the learner's ability to acquire new knowledge or skills in another context describes one phase of the powerful phenomenon called *transfer*. In other words, the information processing system depends on past learnings to associate with, make sense of, and treat new information. This recycling of past information into the flow not only reinforces and provides additional rehearsal for already stored information but also aids in assigning meaning to new information. The degree of meaning attributed to new learning will determine the connections that are made between it and other information in long-term storage. Consider the following pieces of information:

1. There are seven days in the week.

2. Force = mass × acceleration.

3. The leaders of North Korea are evil people.

4. They also serve who only stand and wait.

5. Jesus is the son of God.

6. There's a sucker born every minute.

In each instance, the meaning of the information depends on the experience, education, and state of mind of the reader. The third and last statements can arouse passionate agreement or disavowal. The second and fourth statements would be meaningless to a second grader, but not the first statement. The fifth could provoke an endless debate among adherents of different religions.

Meaning often depends on context. The transfer process not only provides interpretation of words, but often includes nuances and shadings that can result in very different meanings. "He is a piece of work!" can be either a compliment or a sarcastic comment, depending on tone and context.

These connections and associations give the learner more options to cope with new situations in the future (see Figure 4.1).

> **Figure 4.1** New learning and past learning coming together in working memory is one part of transfer. The learner's understanding of how the combined learning can be used in the future is the other part of transfer.

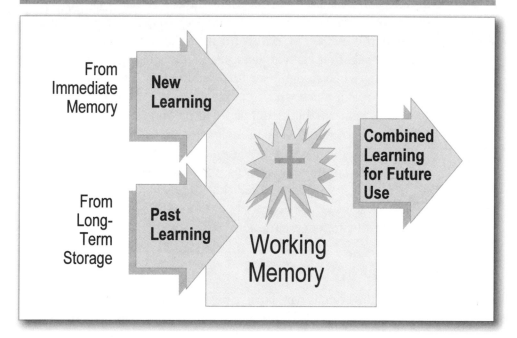

Types of Transfer

Positive Transfer. When past learning *helps* the learner deal with new learning, it is called *positive transfer.* Suppose a violin player and a trombone player both want to learn to play the viola, an instrument similar to the violin. Who will learn the new instrument more easily? The violin player already possesses the skills and knowledge that will help in learning the viola. The trombone player, on the other hand, may be a very accomplished trombonist but possesses few skills that will help to play the viola. Similarly, Michelangelo, da Vinci, and Edison were able to transfer a great deal of their knowledge and skills to create magnificent works of art and invention. Their prior learnings made greater achievement possible.

Negative Transfer. Sometimes past learning *interferes* with the learner's understanding of new learning, resulting in confusion or errors. This process is called *negative transfer.* If, for example, you have been driving cars with only automatic shift, you will have quite a surprise the first time you drive a standard-shift car. You were accustomed to keeping your left foot idle or using it to brake (not recommended). In either case, the left foot has a very different function in a standard-shift car. If it keeps doing its automatic-shift functions (or does nothing), you will have great difficulty driving the standard-shift car. In other words, the skills that the driver's brain assigned to the left foot for the automatic-shift car are not the skills it needs to cope with the standard-shift car. The skill it used before is now interfering with the skill needed in the new situation, an example of negative transfer.

During a lesson, students are dealing continually with transfer as they process and practice new information and skills. Because students' experiences vary, the extent of what transfers also varies. Whether that transfer aids or impedes the acquisition of new learning is a major factor in determining the degree of success each student has in accomplishing the lesson objective.

For example, teachers who teach Romance languages to native English speakers are frequently helped by positive transfer and plagued by negative transfer. Words like *rouge* in French and *mucho* in Spanish help to teach *red* and *much*, respectively, but when students see the French word *librairie* and are told it is a place where books are found, experience prompts them to think that it means "library." It really means "bookstore." (The French word for library is *bibliothèque.*) Never underestimate the power of transfer. Past learning *always* influences the acquisition of new learning.

> Never underestimate the power of transfer. Past learning always influences the acquisition of new learning.

It should be noted that the terms *positive transfer* and *negative transfer* are also used, respectively, to describe the correct and incorrect application of a learning to a new situation.

Transfer of Learning

As a pattern seeker, the brain is wired to use past information and skills to solve new problems. This transfer of learning appears to be controlled, in part, by the striatum, a group of neurons located midbrain, and the hippocampus. In an fMRI study, researchers found that these areas were activated when participants encountered a new learning task that required updating information they had previously learned (Dahlin, Neely, Larsson, Bäckman, & Nyberg, 2008; Gerraty, Davidow, Wimmer, Kahn, & Shohamy, 2014). The striatum is important for updating working memory. Apparently, successful transfer requires the engagement of specific and overlapping brain regions. How does it happen in schools?

A review of any curriculum reveals that transfer is an integral component and expectation of the learning process. Every day, teachers deliberately or intuitively refer to past learning to make new learning more understandable and meaningful. For the long term, students are expected to transfer the knowledge and skills they learn in school to their daily routines, jobs, and ventures outside the school. Writing and speaking skills should help them communicate with others, scientific knowledge should inform their decisions on environmental and health issues, and their understanding of history should guide their responses to contemporary problems at personal, social, and cultural levels. Obviously, the more information students can transfer from their schooling to the context of everyday life, the greater the probability that they will be good communicators, informed citizens, critical thinkers, and successful problem solvers.

Students need to be successful in recognizing how the skills and knowledge they learned in school apply to new situations they encounter in other classes or outside school. Often, students can spontaneously make inferences from one curriculum area to another, but do not make enough inferences to support fully fledged transfer and, thus, for example, have difficulty transferring computational skills they learned in mathematics class to solving problems in science class. One study, for example, showed that high school students rejected the notion that they could apply what they learned about writing in their composition courses to the writing they were expected to do in their other courses (Bergmann & Zepernick, 2007).

The few studies done on transfer suggest that the students' ability to apply knowledge to new situations is limited. Apparently, we are not doing enough in schools to deliberately make the transfer connections to enhance new learning. The more connections that students can make between past learning and new learning, the more likely they are to determine sense and meaning and thus retain the new learning. Moreover, when these connections can be extended across curriculum areas, they establish a framework of associative networks that will be recalled for future problem solving.

Successful transfer can be enhanced by educators who advocate thematic units and an integrated curriculum. This approach provides more stimulating experiences for students, and helps them see the commonalities among diverse topics, while reinforcing understanding and meaning for future applications. Thematic units, for instance, could focus on the environment (global warming, recycling, air quality), history (the U.S. Civil War, exploring the West, Black History Month), science (sources of electrical power, space exploration, ecosystems), or language arts (tall tales, realistic fiction, poetry). Integrated thematic units cut across curriculum areas. The Internet is an excellent source of ideas for integrated units (see "Internet Sites" in the Resources section).

Thematic units and an integrated curriculum enhance the transfer process.

Figure 4.2 is an example of an integrated thematic unit that could be adapted for elementary and secondary grade levels. Beyond restructuring curriculum, the question now becomes this: How can we select teaching that will ensure transfer?

TEACHING FOR TRANSFER

Transfer is more frequently provoked by the environment than done consciously by the learner. Have you ever heard a song that brings back a flood of memories? You could not really control that recall unless something else in the present environment now demanded your immediate attention, such as your crying baby or a ringing fire alarm. So who represents a large portion of the environment for students in school? Yes, the teachers! Teachers are the instruments of transfer for students. If teachers are not aware of that, they can inadvertently provoke negative transfer during learning situations just as easily as they can provoke positive transfer.

> **Test Question No. 9:** Most of the time, the transfer of information from long-term storage is under the conscious control of the learner. True or false?
>
> **Answer:** False. The transfer process is more often provoked by the learner's present environment.

Example of Transfer in a Literature Class. The following anecdote illustrates how transfer can impede or promote a lesson objective. I once observed a senior class in British literature in a large urban high school. It was late April, and as the students entered the class, they were discussing the upcoming final examinations, the prom, and preparations for graduation. After the opening bell rang, the teacher admonished the students to pay attention and said, "Today, we are going to start another play by William Shakespeare." The moans and groans were deafening and abated only after the teacher used every threat short of ripping up their forthcoming diplomas. Judging from their reactions and unsolicited comments, the students' perceptions of past experiences with Shakespeare were hardly positive. Without realizing it, the teacher had provoked negative transfer; getting the students to focus constructively on the new play now would not be easy.

Later that afternoon, I found myself in a different teacher's British literature class. A large television monitor and a videocassette recorder in the front of the classroom got the students' attention as they entered. The teacher asked the students to "watch the television screen and be prepared to discuss what they saw." What unfolded over the next 15 minutes was a cleverly edited collection of scenes from the movie *West Side Story*. There was enough story to get the plot and enough music to maintain interest. The students were captivated; some even sang along. As the showdown between Tony and Maria's brother came on the screen, the teacher stopped the tape. The students complained, wanting to see who won the fight. The teacher noted that this was really an old story set in modern times, and that she had the script of the original play. The characters' names and the location were different, but the plot was the same. While the students were discussing what they had seen, she distributed Shakespeare's *Romeo and Juliet*. Many students eagerly flipped through the pages trying to find the outcome of the fight scene! The teacher's understanding of positive transfer was evident, and she had used it magnificently.

Teachers are frequently the provokers of transfer for their students.

To use transfer effectively, teachers need to purposefully identify factors that facilitate learning (positive transfer) while minimizing or eliminating factors that can cause interference (negative transfer).

Figure 4.2 Here is an example of an integrated thematic unit on water. Students have opportunities to gain a deeper understanding of how water directly affects their daily lives. This approach increases the chances of transfer of learning to future situations.

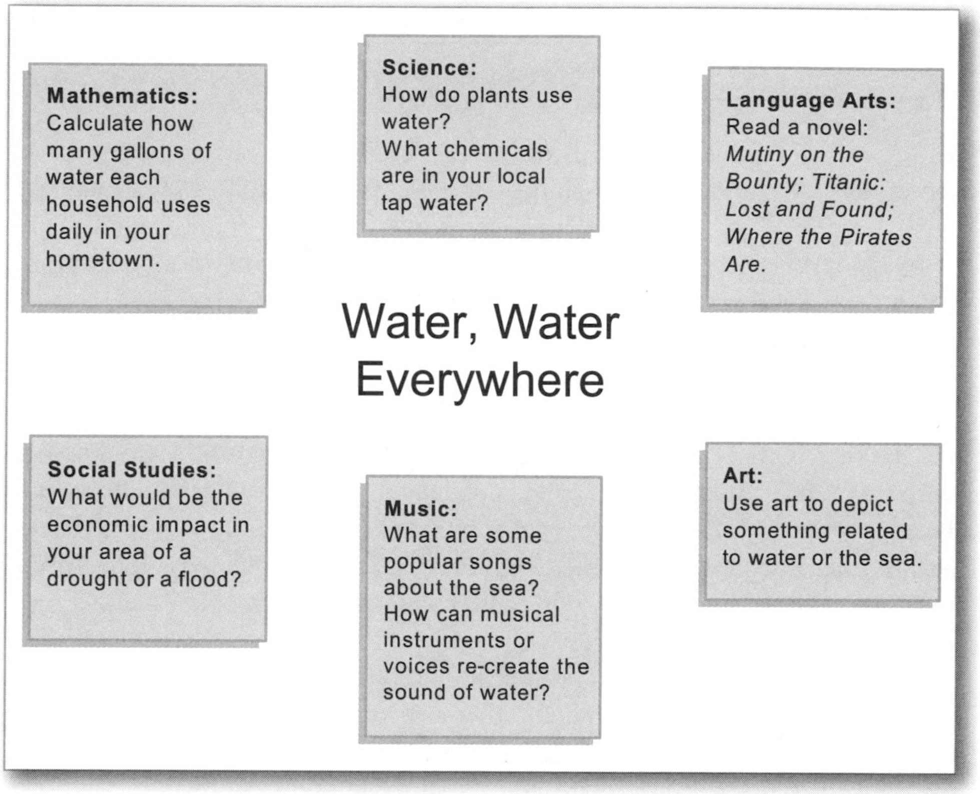

Mathematics:
Calculate how many gallons of water each household uses daily in your hometown.

Science:
How do plants use water?
What chemicals are in your local tap water?

Language Arts:
Read a novel: *Mutiny on the Bounty; Titanic: Lost and Found; Where the Pirates Are.*

Water, Water Everywhere

Social Studies:
What would be the economic impact in your area of a drought or a flood?

Music:
What are some popular songs about the sea?
How can musical instruments or voices re-create the sound of water?

Art:
Use art to depict something related to water or the sea.

Factors Affecting Transfer

How quickly transfer occurs during a learning situation depends on the rate of retrieval. As noted earlier, the rate of retrieval is largely dependent on the storage system that the learner has created and how the learning was originally stored. Designing the filing system in long-term storage is a *learned* skill and can run the gamut from very loose connections to a highly organized series of networks. Working memory uses a cue that it encodes with the material and files in a network containing similar items.

> *Rote learning does not tend to facilitate transfer.*

The cue helps long-term memory locate, identify, and select the material for later retrieval, similar to the way the label on a file folder helps to locate and identify what is in the file. If the learner is recalling a complex concept, information has to come from various storage areas to the frontal lobes for assembly, verification, and decoding into working memory. Many factors in a learning system affect the nature of this transfer process. Researchers have identified the following four of these:

- The context and degree of original learning
- Similarity
- Critical attributes
- Association

No factor is more important than the others, and they often work together (Hunter, 2004).

Context and Degree of Original Learning

The quality of transfer that occurs during new learning is largely dependent on the quality of the original learning. Most of us can recall easily our Social Security number or even a poem we learned in our early school years. If the original learning was well learned and accurate, its influence on new learning will be more constructive and help the student toward greater achievement. Students who did not learn the scientific method well, for example, will not be very effective in laboratory analysis, and they will not be able to transfer this learning to future success.

If something is worth teaching, it is worth teaching well. Rote learning does not tend to facilitate transfer, but learning with understanding does. Thus, trying to learn too many concepts too quickly may hinder transfer because the learner is simply memorizing isolated facts with little opportunity to organize the material in a meaningful fashion, chunk it, and link it to prior related knowledge.

If we teach students to be conscious of both the new learning and the context into which it fits, we are helping them forge strong associations for future recall. When the new learning is too tightly bound to the context, then learners may fail to transfer that knowledge or skill to different contexts. Should the students perceive, for example, that grammatical correctness matters only in English class, then their writing in other classes gets careless.

We discussed in the previous chapter that information is more likely to be remembered if the learner has multiple opportunities to rehearse and use it. But too often, we have time enough only to study a topic until the students reach some low level of mastery, and then we move on to the next topic. But longstanding research on transfer suggests that transfer is improved when students visit important topics often rather than have just one intense exposure.

> Today's learning is tomorrow's transfer. Therefore, if something is worth teaching, it is worth teaching well.

When using transfer, we ask students to bring learnings from their past forward to today. If the past learning was taught well, it should help the students acquire today's learning. What is taught today becomes past learning tomorrow. If it is taught well today, the positive transfer will enhance tomorrow's learning, and so forth. In other words, today's learning is tomorrow's transfer.

Similarity

Transfer can be generated by the similarity of the situation in which something is being learned and the situation to which that learning may transfer. Thus, skills learned in one environment tend to transfer to other environments that are similar. For example, commercial jet pilots are first trained in flight simulators before they sit in the cockpit of the actual plane. All the training and learnings they acquire in the simulator, an exact replica of the actual plane, will transfer to the real flying situation. This positive transfer helps the pilot get accustomed quickly to the actual plane, and it reduces errors. If you have ever rented a car, you realize that it does not take you very long to get accustomed to it and drive away. The environment is similar to your own car, and most of the important components are in familiar places. You may need a few moments, however, to locate the windshield wiper and light switches.

Teachers often use similarity when introducing new material. They may have students learn words with similar spelling patterns, such as *beat, heat, meat,* and *neat.* Students may use their skills at finding locations on a road map to help place ordered numbers on a graph grid. However, as we shall discuss shortly, presenting two items of information at the same time that are *too* similar can cause problems during retention. Other examples of using similarity are fire and tornado drills. Even giving students major tests in the room where they learned the material being tested uses similarity of the environment for positive transfer.

Similarity of sensory modalities is another form of transfer. Using the color red to represent danger can alert us to traffic lights, the location of fire alarm boxes, or hazardous areas. Sensory similarity can also cause error. Students may confuse *there, their,* and *they're* because they sound alike, or they may not be able to pronounce *read* until they know the word's context.

The more specific the cue that working memory attaches to a new learning, the easier it is for long-term memory to identify the item being sought. This process leads to an interesting phenomenon regarding long-term storage and retrieval: We store by similarity, but we retrieve by difference. That is, long-term memory most often stores new learnings into a network that contains learnings with similar characteristics or associations, as perceived by the learner. This network identification is one of the connections made in working memory during rehearsal and closure. To retrieve an item, long-term memory identifies how it is *different* from all the other items in that network (see Figure 4.3).

For example, how would you recognize your best friend in a crowd? It is not because he has two arms, two legs, a head, and a torso. These characteristics make him *similar* to all the others. Rather, it is his more subtle *differences,* such as facial features, walk, and voice, that allow you to distinguish him from everyone else. His unique characteristics are called his *critical attributes.* If your friend is an identical twin, however, you might have difficulty picking him out from his brother if both are in the crowd. Likewise, the high degree of similarity between two concepts, coupled with few differences, makes it difficult for the learner to tell them apart.

The Problem of Items Being Too Similar. Consider the concepts of latitude and longitude. The similarities between these two ideas far outweigh their differences. Both use identical units of measure (degrees and minutes), deal with all four compass points, are imaginary lines, locate points on the Earth's surface, and are similar in sound and spelling. Their only real difference is their orientation in space. Teaching them together can be very difficult because their many similarities obscure their singular difference. The problem of similarity can be pervasive because curriculums are often written with the most alike concepts taught together. In fact, a useful task for a committee rewriting a curriculum is to list those concepts that students find the most difficult. Then determine whether the difficulty is that two very similar concepts or motor skills are taught together, resulting in confusion. See the Practitioner's Corner: Avoid Teaching Concepts That Are Very Similar, at the end of this chapter, for precisely when this can be a problem and how to deal with it.

> *Two concepts that are very similar ordinarily should not be taught at the same time.*

Figure 4.3   We tend to store information in networks by similarity, but we retrieve it into working memory by difference.

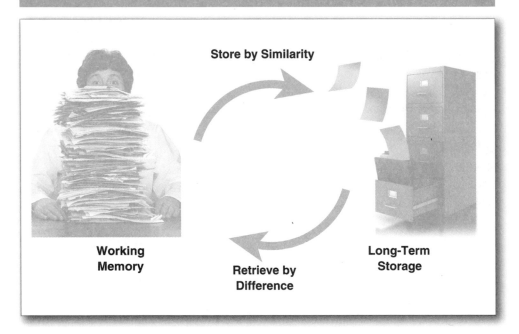

Critical Attributes

Transfer is sometimes generated when a special property, called a *critical attribute*, is recalled. Critical attributes, characteristics that make one idea unique from all others, are the cues of *difference* that learners can use as part of their storage process. Statements like *Amphibians live both on land and in water, Homonyms are words that sound alike but have different spellings and meanings,* and *To produce sound, something must vibrate* are examples of identifying a concept's critical attributes.

Identifying the critical attributes of a concept is a powerful memory tool, but it is not an easy task. We live in a culture driven by a quest for equality for all. This culture places a higher value on similarities than on differences. Thus, our cerebral networks are organized around similarity from an early age, and teachers frequently use similarity in the classroom to introduce new ideas. Successful retrieval from mental storage areas is accomplished by identifying differences among concepts. Consequently, teachers can help learners process new learnings accurately by having them identify the unique characteristics that make one concept different from all others. For example, what are the critical attributes of an explorer? Will these attributes help to separate Vasco da Gama from Napoleon Bonaparte? Students can use critical attributes to sort concepts so that they are stored in logical networks with appropriate cues. This will facilitate long-term memory's searches and increase the probability that students will accurately identify and retrieve the concept they are seeking.

Another useful task for a committee that is updating curriculum is to identify the critical attributes of all the major concepts that will be taught. If the committee members have difficulty agreeing on the critical attributes of a particular topic, imagine the challenge this will pose for the learner (see the Practitioner's Corner: Identifying Critical Attributes for Accurate Transfer at the end of this chapter).

Association

Whenever two events, actions, or feelings are learned together, they are said to be *associated*, or bonded, so that the recall of one prompts the spontaneous recall of the other. The word *Romeo* elicits *Juliet*, and *Batman* gets *Robin*. A song you hear being played at a mall may elicit memories of some event that are associated with that song. The odor of a cologne once worn by a close friend from the past triggers the emotions of that relationship. Trademarks and product symbols, such as McDonald's golden arches, are designed to recall the product. Although there is no similarity between the two items, they were learned together and are, therefore, recalled together.

Here is a simple example of transfer. Look at the words listed below. On the lines to the right, write one or two words that come to mind as you read each word in the list.

Monday	_____	_____
dentist	_____	_____
Mom	_____	_____
vacation	_____	_____
babies	_____	_____
emergency	_____	_____
money	_____	_____
Sunday	_____	_____

What you wrote down represents thoughts that you have associated with each word in the list. Here are some responses that others have written for *Monday:* work, blues, quarterback, beginning. For *Mom*, others have written love, apple pie, caring, important, security, Dad. Were your words anything like these? Maybe they were, or maybe not. Ask your family and friends to complete the list and note their responses. Each of us makes different connections with concepts based on our unique experiences; this activity points out the variety of associations that different people can make with the same thought.

Making associations expands the brain's ability to retain information. New connections are formed between neurons, and new insights are encoded. Much like a tree growing new branches, everything we remember becomes another set of branches to which memories can be attached. The more we learn and retain, the more we *can* learn and retain.

Emotions Associated With Learning. Association is particularly powerful when feelings or emotions are associated with learning. We mentioned earlier that the brain's amygdala encodes emotional messages when they are strong and bonds them to learnings for long-term storage. We also noted that emotions usually have a higher priority than cognitive processing for commanding our attention. Words like *abortion, Holocaust,* and *capital punishment* often evoke strong feelings. Math anxiety is an example of a strong feeling (probably failure) associated with mathematics. Some students will avoid new situations involving learning mathematics mainly to avoid the negative feelings that are recalled with the content. On the other hand, people devote hours to their hobbies because they associate feelings of pleasure and success with these activities. Thus, teachers should strive to bond positive feelings to new learnings so that students feel competent and can enjoy the process. Positive emotions can be associated with learning whenever teachers do the following:

- Use humor (not sarcasm) as an integral part of the lesson.
- Design and tell stories that enhance understanding of the concepts. Studies show that stories engage all parts of the brain because they touch on the learner's experiences, feelings, and actions (Scott-Simmons, Barker, & Cherry, 2003).
- Incorporate real-world examples and activities that have meaning for the learners.
- Demonstrate that they really *care* about their students' success. This means spending less time on the class rules and test schedule and more time on asking, "How do *you* learn? What teaching strategies work best for you?"

The more we learn and retain, the more we can learn and retain.

Learning new concepts is rarely a smooth-flowing linear progression. Rather, it is dynamic with fits and starts, successes generating positive emotions, and failures leading to negative feelings. When learning stalls, the teacher helps the student overcome negative emotions associated with failure by providing the support that leads the student to success—no matter how small that success is.

Teaching Methods

Teachers should not assume that transfer will automatically occur after students acquire a sufficient base of information. Significant and efficient transfer occurs only if we teach to achieve it. Hunter (2004), Mestre (2002), Perkins and Salomon (1988), Wiggins (2012), and others have suggested that when teachers understand the factors that affect transfer, they can plan lessons that use the power of positive transfer to help students learn faster, solve problems, and generate creative and artistic products that enrich the learning experience.

To teach for transfer, we need to consider two major factors: the time sequence and the complexity of the transfer link between the learnings. The time sequence refers to the way the teacher will use time and transfer in the learning situation. Transfer can occur from past to present or from present to future.

Transfer From Past to Present

Past Learning → Helps in → Present Learning

In this strategy, the teacher links something from the learner's past that helps add sense and meaning to the new learning. It is important to select an experience that is clear, unambiguous, and closely relevant (not just related) to the new learning, for example,

- An English teacher uses *West Side Story* to introduce *Romeo and Juliet* so that students transfer their knowledge about street gangs and feuds to help them understand Shakespeare's plot.
- A science teacher asks students to recall what they have learned about plant cells to study the similarities and differences in animal cells.
- A social studies teacher asks students to think of the causes of the U.S. Civil War to see if they can also explain the causes of the Vietnam War.

Transfer From Present to Future

Present Learning → Helps in → Future Learning

The teacher makes the present learning situation as similar as possible to a future situation to which the new learning should transfer. For the transfer to be successful, students must attain a high degree of original (current) learning and be able to recognize the critical attributes and concepts that make the situations similar and different. For example,

- Students learn the critical attributes of fact and opinion so they can transfer that learning in the future when evaluating advertising, news reports, election campaigns, and the like.
- Students learn how to read graphs, pie charts, and tables so that in the future they can evaluate data presented to them for analysis and action.
- Students learn safe personal and interpersonal hygiene practices to protect their health throughout their lives.

Teaching techniques such as *bridging* and *hugging* are designed to help students make transfer links from past to present and from present to future. They can be used in all subject areas and for learning both cognitive concepts and psychomotor skills. Examples of these techniques are found in the Practitioner's Corner exercises at the end of this chapter.

Complexity of the Link Between Learnings

The way that transfer occurs during a learning situation can range from a very superficial similarity to a sophisticated, abstract association. For example, when renting a car, it takes just a few minutes to get accustomed to the model, find the windshield wiper and light controls, and drive off. Interpreting a pie chart in the school budget requires the recall of graph analysis skills from a prior mathematics course. The new learning environments are perceived as being *similar* to others that the learner has practiced, and that similarity automatically triggers the same learned behaviors.

Metaphor, Analogy, and Simile. The transfer connection can also be much more complex, requiring the learner to make an abstract application of knowledge and skills to the new situation. Metaphors, analogies, and similes are useful devices for promoting abstract transfer. The *metaphor* is the application of a word or phrase to an object or concept that it does not literally denote to suggest a comparison with another object or concept. A person may say, "It's raining cats and dogs outside. I'm drowned!" Obviously, it is not raining animals, and the person did not drown. He is speaking figuratively, and the metaphor compares things that are essentially dissimilar. An *analogy* compares partial similarity between two things, such as comparing a heart to a pump. The *simile* compares two unlike things: *She is like a rose.*

Metaphors can often convey meaning of abstract material as well and as rapidly as literal language. Metaphors help to explain complex concepts or processes. A geologist explains the movement of glaciers as flowing like batter on a griddle and that the glacier was like an enormous plow upon the land. Comparing life to taking a long trip also is a metaphor. We ask the learner to reflect on how the situations encountered on the road compare to those encountered in life. How can bumps, detours, road signs, billboards, and places we have visited, passed through, or stayed in for a while all compare to life situations? Complex transfer patterns can reach back to the past: *How does the thinking strategy I used when I encountered a major detour help me to decide what course to choose in life now?* They can also transfer to the future: *The planning I used in preparing for the trip should help me prepare for other major decisions I need to make in my life that require extensive planning.*

> Metaphors can convey the meaning of abstract material as well and as rapidly as literal language.

These strategies are rich in imagery and enhance the thinking process by encouraging students to seek out associations and connections that they would not ordinarily make. They gain insights into relationships among ideas that help to forge a more thorough understanding of new learning. See more on imagery in Chapter 5; see also the Practitioner's Corner: Using Metaphors to Enhance Transfer at the end of this chapter.

Journal Writing for Transfer

Transfer is more likely to occur when students have an opportunity to reflect on their new learning. This reflection time can occur during closure and is more likely to take place if the student is given a specific task. Journal writing—either on paper or in a digital device—is a very useful technique for closure because the specific steps help students to make connections to previous knowledge and organize concepts into networks for eventual storage. The strategy takes but a few minutes, but it can have enormous payback in terms of increased understanding and retention of learning. See the Practitioner's Corner: Using Journal Writing to Promote Transfer and Retention at the end of this chapter for the specific steps that are likely to make this a successful effort.

> *Journal writing is a highly effective strategy for closure and transfer.*

Transfer and Constructivism

The proper and frequent use of transfer greatly enhances the constructivist approach to learning. Constructivist teachers are those who do the following:

- Use student responses to alter their instructional strategies and content
- Foster student dialogue
- Question student understanding before sharing their own
- Encourage students to elaborate on their initial responses
- Allow students time to construct relationships and create metaphors

All these strategies have been discussed here and in previous chapters and are characteristic of teachers who are proficient in using transfer deliberately throughout their lessons.

English Language Learners (ELLs) and Transfer

We discussed earlier in this chapter the influence that transfer has on English language acquisition. Content-area teachers should have a good understanding of the impact of transfer if they are to be successful in teaching English language learners (ELLs). Consider the challenges facing ELLs as they attempt to acquire subject matter content in English-language classrooms. The ELLs' brains are processing two mental dictionaries, one for their native language and one for English (see Figure 4.4). Depending on the ELLs' age and English language exposure, their social vocabulary is likely to be larger than their academic one. The amount of cross-language transfer that occurs depends mainly on the degree of similarity between the writing system and grammar of the ELLs' native language and English. Native Spanish speakers, for instance, will have less of a challenge with English than will native Russian or Chinese speakers whose languages use very different writing systems and rules of grammar.

Regardless of their native tongue, ELLs must acquire and comprehend the academic English they need to translate the content knowledge that they

> **Video:** For a video on how transfer affects second language acquisition, see
>
> https://www.youtube.com/watch?v=UB18y2ZYBiY

already possess in their native language and then acquire new content information so that all of it can be expressed in correct English. This heavy mental burden is both eased and intensified by the impact of transfer. Furthermore, the ELLs' culture plays an important role here. Some cultural values and behaviors will transfer easily to North American society; others will not. ELLs are often uncomfortable outside their culture and are reluctant to mix with their native English-speaking peers who may shun them due to differences in manner, dress, and appearance. They may fear a loss of their cultural identity. Successful teachers of ELLs are aware of which cultural values transfer easily and which ones do not. They integrate multiculturalism into the curriculum to engage, affirm, and accept diversity within the classroom and school environment. For more information and strategies on how to work with ELLs, see Sousa (2011).

Figure 4.4 As ELLs attempt to learn subject matter content in English language classes, cross-language transfer may help or hinder comprehension. Content-area teachers should be alert to these transfer problems and plan lessons for ELLs accordingly (adapted from Sousa, 2011).

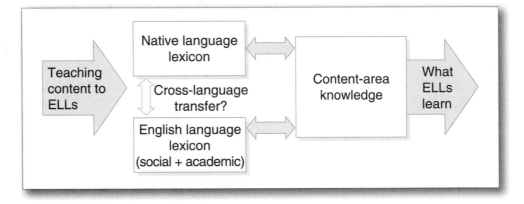

Technology and Transfer

Technology is rapidly changing the classroom environment. Streaming video provides teachers with thousands of video clips that can illustrate curriculum concepts more dramatically than texts. The Internet offers remarkable opportunities for students to share what they are learning with other students and professionals around the world. When students have difficulty understanding how mathematics, for example, is used in the real world, they can communicate with architects, engineers, scientists, and others who can show the practical applications of mathematics in their work. Another transfer-related activity is to share with students in their own and other countries ideas and opinions about global topics, such as climate change, environmental pollution, and overpopulation, in order to understand the views and perspectives of different societies. Such involvement makes the content meaningful and increases the probability that the new learning will be remembered and available for future use.

Using content-related video games in the classroom can often provide the motivation that students need to see connections between what they are learning and the real world. Motivation and interest are key factors that encourage students to better understand their learning and engage in higher-order thinking. Just look at how digital games are designed to incrementally increase the challenge and give rewards at appropriate intervals. The thinking and motor skills that students learn while playing these games can transfer in ways that help them solve the real-world problems they will face in their future.

ADDITIONAL THOUGHTS ABOUT TRANSFER

Transfer can be referred to as the "So what?" phase of learning. The context in which students learn information and skills is often different from the context in which they will apply that learning. If students do not perceive how the information or skill can be used for the future, they will tend to pay little attention and exert even less effort. A 2015 Gallup poll of more than 900,000 middle and high school students found that students became more disengaged as they advanced through middle and high school because their teachers did not make them feel their schoolwork was important (Gallup, 2015). The cognitive research supports the notion that transfer occurs more easily if students have processed the initial learning in ways that promote deep, abstract understanding of the material, rather than emphasizing the rote application of superficial similarities. Teachers help students achieve deep, abstract understandings when they involve students in multiple examples that illustrate the critical attributes in as wide a variety as possible.

Of course, there are times when some rote memorization is needed to facilitate transfer. In fact, we previously noted that research in areas such as reading and early mathematical development suggests that both conceptual learning and rote activities (e.g., decoding skills for reading, number facts for early mathematics) are important.

Teaching strategies mentioned elsewhere in this book can enhance transfer. For example, using music and songs, or performing some physical movements when learning a particular concept, allows students to associate these activities with the concept and assist in recall at some future time.

Transfer and High-Stakes Testing. The continuing attention to accountability and high-stakes testing may actually work against efforts to increase the transfer of learnings. Teaching to the high-stakes test might emphasize rote activities in place of strategies that foster the deep understandings needed for transfer. We need to devise tests that assess transfer of knowledge. Computer programs, for instance, can aid in devising assessments that look at deep conceptual processing. Assessments that focus on preparedness for future learning (e.g., solving a relatively complex novel problem) may be more revealing of transfer than those focused strictly on solving superficial problems in an isolated subject area.

WHAT'S COMING UP?

One of the most interesting discoveries about the brain in the last 40 years is the research evidence showing that some brain areas specialize in performing certain functions. Subsequent studies have given researchers fascinating insights into how the brain is organized and clues about a broad range of cognitive processes. Brain organization has also spawned some myths and stories that endure to this day. What are the facts and fallacies about the left and right sides of the brain? Why is this information so important for teachers and parents? What are some basic understandings about how the brain learns to read and do mathematical calculations? The answers to these and other intriguing questions about brain organization are found in the next chapter.

PRACTITIONER'S CORNER

General Guidelines on Teaching for Transfer

Transfer is essentially the ability for students to apply what they have learned to solve problems in new situations. They should be able to do this without prompting. It is much like a football player running with the ball and viewing which players are around him, what open spaces are available, the distance to the goal line, and then assessing which paths are most likely to get him there to score. Because no two plays are identical, the player must apply all he has learned in practice to every new and changing situation (i.e., play).

Transfer does not occur easily. It requires students to be challenged with solving similar problems in very different contexts. This takes deep learning and understanding and real-world applications that school curriculums do not generally include. As a result, many students do not score well on tests because they fail to see how a test question is related to something they have already learned.

Here are some guidelines to consider when planning to teach for transfer.

- Because the brain is a pattern seeker, present information in a conceptual framework so that students see how the pieces fit together in meaningful ways. Teaching isolated facts or steps in a procedure does not promote transfer when contexts are complex.
- Look for ways to help student see problems at higher levels of complexity of thought, involving analysis and evaluation, and use their creativity to find nontraditional methods for solving the problem. This helps the brain expand the number of networks that connect to the new learning, thereby making future transfer more likely.
- Explain the kinds of situations that students might encounter where they can transfer and apply the new learning. Such explanations aid students in seeing sense and meaning in what they are learning.
- Encourage students to regularly reflect on and monitor their own learning strategies, such as how do they approach problem solving, assess their readiness for a test, and decide what needs improving. Metacognitive practices can increase the likelihood that students will be successful in transferring learning to novel situations.
- Use open-ended questions to provoke divergent thinking, a necessary component when applying past learning to unfamiliar contexts. A question like, "Explain whether we are still living with the consequences of the U.S. Civil War" is much more thought provoking and complex than questions about when the war started and ended and naming the major battles. "What if" questions tend to activate brain networks to higher-order thinking.
- If assigning homework, engage students in the search for examples, analogies, and applications of the new learning to nontypical contexts.
- Remember the power of closure. Using this strategy gives students the opportunity to restate what they have learned in their own words, thereby aiding in making connections to their past learning, enhancing meaning, and seeing possibilities for transfer.

Teaching for transfer is what schools are all about. Students will value what they are learning whenever they see how it applies to their lives and world. Whenever teachers do this, students see meaning in their learning and are likely to be more successful while in school and in life afterward.

PRACTITIONER'S CORNER

Strategies for Connecting to Past Learnings

Transfer helps students make connections between what they already know and the new learning. It is important to remember that the connections are of value only if they are relevant to the *students'* past, not necessarily the teacher's. This process also helps the teacher find out what the students already know about the new material. If students already have knowledge of what is planned for the new lesson, then teachers should make some adjustments and move on. (The curriculum is notably cluttered with too much repetition at every grade level and in every subject area.) This method also alerts the teacher to any prior knowledge that may interfere with new learning (negative transfer). Here are a few suggestions to discover what students already know so that prior learnings can help facilitate new learning (positive transfer). Note that the activities use novelty and shift the task burden to the student. Choose those that are grade-level appropriate.

- **Short Story.** Students write short stories to describe what they already know about a given topic. This can be used in any subject area because writing is a skill that should be continually practiced. (Note: This activity is not journal writing, which serves a different purpose.)

- **Interviews.** In a think-pair-share format, students interview their partners to determine their knowledge levels.

- **Graphic Organizers.** Students select an appropriate graphic organizer to explain and relate their past learning.

- **Mural or Collage.** Students make a mural or collage to communicate their current knowledge.

- **Music Activity.** Students write a song that tells of their prior knowledge.

- **Models.** Students build or draw models to express what they know.

- **Student Ideas.** Students may suggest other ways of showing what they know, such as writing a poem, painting a picture, creating a quiz show, and so on.

PRACTITIONER'S CORNER

Avoid Teaching Concepts
That Are Very Similar

Teachers often use similarity to introduce new topics. They say, "You already learned something about this topic when we . . ." This helps students to use positive transfer by recalling similar items from long-term storage that can assist in learning new information. But as we saw in the Chapter 3 discussion on learning motor skills, similarity can also be a problem.

Whenever two concepts have many more similarities than differences, such as latitude and longitude, mitosis and meiosis, or simile and metaphor, there is a high risk that the learner cannot tell them apart. In effect, the similarities overwhelm the differences, resulting in the learner attaching the same memory retrieval cues to both concepts. Thus, when the learner uses that cue later to retrieve information, it could produce either or both concepts, and the learner may not recognize which is correct.

How to Deal With This Problem. When planning a lesson with two very similar concepts, list their similarities and differences. If the number of similarities and differences is about the same, there is less chance the students will be confused, but if the number of similarities is far greater than the differences, confusion is likely. In that case, try the following:

- **Teach the Two Concepts at Different Times.** Teach the first concept. Make sure that the students thoroughly understand it and can practice it correctly. Then teach a related concept to give the first concept time to be consolidated accurately and fully into long-term memory. Teach the second concept a few weeks later. Now information from the first concept acts for positive transfer in learning the second concept.
- **Teach the Difference(s) First.** Another option is to start by teaching the difference(s) between the two concepts. This works better with older students because they have enough prior learnings to recognize subtle differences. For example, teach that the only real difference between latitude and longitude is their orientation in space and that this can cause confusion when labeling a location. Focusing on and practicing the difference gives learners the warnings and the cues they need to separate the two similar concepts and identify them correctly in the future.

It seems so logical that two concepts that have many similarities should be taught at the same time. And so, for years, teachers have struggled with introducing concepts like the following in the same lesson: latitude and longitude; mitosis and meiosis; simile, analogy, and metaphor; complementary and supplementary angles; monarchy, oligarchy, and plutocracy; writing lowercase *b*, *d*, *p*, and *q*; and many others. But the very fact that they are *so* similar can lead to retrieval problems.

To see how similarity may affect your work, try this activity:

A. Think about and list two or more concepts that are so similar they could cause confusion.

_____

_____

_____

_____

_____

_____

_____

_____

B. How could these concepts be presented to minimize confusion?

_____

_____

_____

_____

_____

_____

_____

PRACTITIONER'S CORNER

Identifying Critical Attributes
for Accurate Transfer

Critical attributes are characteristics that make one concept *unique* among all others. Teachers need to help students identify these attributes so students can use them for eventual and accurate retrieval. Hunter (2004) suggested a five-step process:

1. **Identify the Critical Attributes.** Suppose the learning objective is for the students to understand how mammals are different from all other animals. The two critical attributes of mammals are that (a) they nurse their young through mammary glands and (b) they have hair.

2. **Teacher Gives Simple Examples.** The teacher offers some simple examples, such as the human being, cat, dog, and gerbil, to establish the concept. The teacher gives the examples at this point, not the students. Because this new learning is occurring in prime-time-1 when retention is highest, the examples must be correct. Be sure to match the example to the two critical attributes.

3. **Teacher Gives Complex Examples.** Now the teacher gives more complex examples, such as the porpoise and whale, which, unlike most mammals, live in water. It is important here to show again how the critical attributes apply.

4. **Students Give Examples.** Here the teacher checks for student understanding to ensure that the critical attributes are used correctly and that the concept is firmly in place. The students must also prove that the attributes apply to their examples.

5. **Teach the Limits of the Critical Attributes.** The learner must recognize that critical attributes may have limits and not apply in every instance. In this lesson, these attributes will accurately identify all mammals, but may incorrectly identify some nonmammals. There is a small group of animals called *platypuses* that exhibit not only mammalian characteristics but also those of amphibians and birds. They are in a separate classification.

Take each major concept you teach and use the five-step process above to identify its critical attributes. These attributes help students clearly recognize what makes this concept *different* from all others. These attributes become valuable cues for accuracy and later retrieval.

By identifying the critical attributes, the student learns how one concept is different from all other similar concepts. This leads to clearer understanding, concept attainment, the ability to relate the new concept properly to others, and the likelihood that it will be stored, remembered, and recalled accurately. All subject areas have major concepts whose critical attributes should be clearly identified. Here are a few simple examples:

Social Studies

Law	Rule made by a government entity that is used for the control of behavior, is policed, and carries a penalty if broken.
Culture	The common behavior of a large group of people who can be identified by specific foods, clothing, art, religion, and music.
Democracy	A system of government in which the citizens have power through their elected representatives.

Science

Atom	The smallest part of an element that still retains the properties of that element.
Mammal	An animal that has hair and mammary glands.
Planet	A natural heavenly body that revolves around a star, rotates on its axis, and does not produce its own light.

Mathematics

Triangle	A two-dimensional figure that is closed and three-sided.
Prime	An integer with a value greater than 1 whose only positive factors are itself and 1.
Histogram	A bar graph that shows how many data values fall into a certain interval.

Language Arts

Sonnet	A poem of 14 lines, written in iambic pentameter with a specific rhyming pattern.
Simile	A figure of speech that compares two unlike things.
Hyperbole	An intentional exaggeration not intended to be taken literally.

Try the activity on the next page to help identify the critical attributes of important concepts from your own teaching or learning experiences.

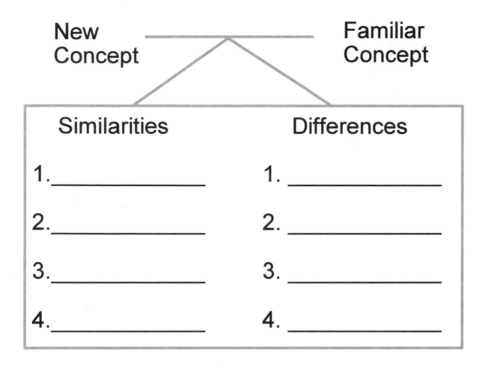

A. Work with a partner to complete the worksheet "Identifying Unique and Unvarying Elements." Begin by using the Analogy Map above to help you decide on the differences between two similar concepts.

B. After completing the worksheet, decide what benefits are provided to the learner by identifying the unique and unvarying elements/critical attributes.

C. List here some concepts in your curriculum that would be good candidates for this strategy.

IDENTIFYING UNIQUE AND
UNVARYING ELEMENTS (CRITICAL ATTRIBUTES)

Identify a major concept and decide on its unique and unvarying elements (critical attributes).

Concept: _____

1. Its unique and unvarying elements (critical attributes) are

    _____
    _____
    _____
    _____

2. Simple examples are

    _____
    _____
    _____
    _____

3. Complex example(s) are

    _____
    _____
    _____
    _____

4. Student examples could be

    _____
    _____
    _____
    _____

5. Limits of the unique and unvarying elements (if any) are

    _____
    _____
    _____
    _____

PRACTITIONER'S CORNER

Teaching for Transfer: Bridging

Perkins and Salomon (1988), among others, have suggested various techniques for teachers to use to achieve positive transfer. In the technique called *bridging,* the teacher invokes transfer by helping students see the connection and abstraction from what the learner knows to other new learnings and contexts. There are many ways this can be accomplished. Here are a few:

- **Brainstorming.** When introducing a new topic, ask students to brainstorm ways this new learning can be applied in other situations. For example, can students use the skills they have just learned in analyzing charts, tables, and graphs? How else can they use their understandings about the law of supply and demand? What future value is there in knowing about nuclear power generation and alternative energy sources?

- **Analogies.** After learning a topic, use an analogy to examine the similarities and differences between one system and another. For example, ask students to make comparisons: How was the post–Vietnam War period in Vietnam similar to and different from the post–U.S. Civil War period in the United States? How is the post–Soviet Union period in Russia today similar to and different from the post–Revolutionary War period in the United States?

- **Metacognition.** When solving problems, ask students to investigate ways of approaching the solutions and discuss the advantages and disadvantages of each. For example, what solutions are there to meet the increased demand for electrical power in a densely populated area? What power sources could be used, and which would be safest, most economical, most practical, and so on? What are the ways in which governments could regionalize to improve their effectiveness and economy of services? What impact might this have on local government and the democratic process? After applying their solutions, the students discuss how well their approaches worked and how they might change their approaches next time to improve their success.

Bridging: Invoking transfer by connecting what the learner knows to other new learning and contexts. Select a concept (e.g., energy, democracy, equilibrium, allegory) and use the strategies below to link that concept to the learner's past knowledge. Look at the Practitioner's Corner: Concept Mapping–General Guidelines in Chapter 5 for help with this task.

www.clipart.com

Brainstorming (applying new learning in other situations):

_____

_____

_____

Analogies (examining similarities and differences):

The Analogy Map could help here (see Practitioner's Corner: Identifying Critical Attributes for Accurate Transfer, above).

_____

_____

_____

Metacognition (solving problems by investigating advantages and disadvantages of alternative solutions):

Advantages	Disadvantages

PRACTITIONER'S CORNER

Teaching for Transfer: Hugging

Hugging, suggested by Perkins and Salomon (1988), uses similarity to make the new learning situation more like future situations to which transfer is desired. This is a lower form of transfer and relies on an almost automatic response from the learner when the new situation is encountered. Teachers should ensure that the similarity of a situation actually involves the student using the skill or knowledge to be transferred. When students use a word search puzzle to identify certain French verbs written forward or backward, this does not mean that they will be able to understand these verbs in written or spoken French. *Hugging* means keeping the new instruction as close as possible to the environment and requirements that the students will encounter in the future. Here are a few ways to design hugging:

- **Simulation Games.** These are useful in helping students practice new roles in diverse situations. Debates, mock trials, and investigating labor disputes are ways that students can experiment with various approaches to solving complex legal and social issues.

- **Mental Practice.** When a student is unable to replicate an upcoming situation, it is very useful for the student to mentally practice what that situation could be like. The student reviews potential variations of the situation and devises mental strategies for dealing with different scenarios. Suppose a student is to interview a political candidate for the school newspaper. In addition to the prepared questions, what other questions could the student ask, depending on the candidate's response? What if the candidate is reticent or changes the course of the questioning?

- **Contingency Learning.** Here the learner asks what other information or skill must be acquired to solve a problem, and then learns it. For example, if the student is building a model to demonstrate gas laws, what else must the student learn in order to design and construct the apparatus at a reasonable cost so that it shows the desired gas relationships effectively?

Hugging: Invoking transfer by making the new learning situation more like future situations to which transfer is desired. Select a concept (or the same one you chose in the bridging activity) and use the strategies that follow to show how the concept can be useful in future circumstances.

www.clipart.com

Simulation games (practicing new roles in diverse situations):

_____

_____

_____

_____

_____

_____

Be prepared to present the simulation to the group.

Mental practice (devising mental strategies for dealing with different scenarios):

_____

_____

_____

_____

_____

_____

Contingency learning (secondary learnings needed to accomplish primary learning):

_____

_____

_____

_____

_____

_____

PRACTITIONER'S CORNER

Using Metaphors to Enhance Transfer

Metaphors can convey meaning as well and as rapidly as literal language. They are usually rich in imagery, are useful bridging strategies, and can apply to both content and skill learnings. West, Farmer, and Wolff (1991) suggest a seven-step process for using metaphors in lesson design:

1. **Select the metaphor.** The criteria for selecting the appropriate metaphor center on goodness of fit (how well the metaphor explains the target concept or process), degree or richness of imagery, familiarity that the students will have with it, and its novelty.

2. **Emphasize the metaphor.** The metaphor must be emphasized consistently throughout the lesson. Students should be alerted to interpret the metaphor figuratively and not literally.

3. **Establish context.** Proper interpretation of the metaphor requires that the teacher establish the context for its use. Metaphors should not be used in isolation, especially if the students lack the background to understand them.

4. **Provide instructions for imagery.** Provide students with the instructions they will need to benefit from the rich imagery usually present in metaphors. "Form a mental picture of this" is good advice (see the Practitioner's Corner: Using Imagery, in Chapter 6).

5. **Emphasize similarities and differences.** Because the metaphor juxtaposes the similarities of one known object or procedure with another, teachers should emphasize the similarities and differences between the metaphor and the new learning.

6. **Provide opportunities for rehearsal.** Use rote and elaborate rehearsal strategies to help students recognize the similarities and differences between the metaphor and the new learning, and to enhance their depth of understanding and types of associations.

7. **Beware mixed metaphors.** Because metaphors are such powerful learning devices, make sure you choose them carefully. Mixed metaphors cause confusion and lead to inaccuracy.

We used metaphors in designing the information processing model (see the Practitioner's Corner: Redesigning the Information Processing Model, in Chapter 2, to help remember the important stages in the process). Now, let's practice it with a different concept.

©iStockphoto.com/procurator

Directions: Working with a partner, select a concept and decide what metaphor(s) would help you or your students remember it.

Concept: _____

Metaphor(s):

_____

_____

_____

_____

_____

_____

_____

_____

_____

_____

_____

PRACTITIONER'S CORNER

Using Journal Writing to Promote Transfer and Retention

Journal writing can be a very effective strategy to promote positive transfer and increase retention. It can be done in nearly all grade levels and subject areas and is particularly effective when used as a closure activity. This activity is more effective if actually done with pencil and paper rather than on a digital device. That is because recent research studies have found that students remember, understand, and can apply more of what they learn when it is written in longhand on paper than when typed into a digital device. That is because writing requires the brain to do more thought processing and summarizing of the content, compared to the mechanical process of typing (Mueller & Oppenheimer, 2014). Students are so accustomed to their digital devices that they may be hesitant about actually writing in longhand. Simply explain what research has found about writing versus typing as well as the benefits to them of remembering more of what they learn.

Teachers may be reluctant to use this technique because they believe it takes up too much class time while adding more papers for them to evaluate. However, this strategy takes just three to five minutes, two or three times a week. That is, the teacher only spot checks journals periodically. The gain in student understanding and retention will be well worth the small amount of time invested. Here are some suggestions for using journal writing for maximum effectiveness:

- Students should keep a different journal for each class or subject area.

- To use this as a closure activity, ask students to write down their responses to these three questions:

  1. **"What did we learn today about** [insert here the *specific* learning objective]*?"* Avoid questions like "Write down what we did today" because younger students are likely to focus on activities rather than on the learning. This question helps to establish *sense.*

  2. **"How does this connect or relate to what we already know about** [insert here some past learning that will help students with positive transfer]?" It is permissible to give hints to guide student thinking. After all, we want to facilitate accuracy. This question can help the learner *chunk* new learning into existing networks.

  3. **"How can this help us, or how can we use this information/skill in the future?"** Give hints if necessary. This question aids in finding *meaning.*

You can use one day's journal entry as a prefocus activity for the following day, provided the new day's lesson is related.

CHAPTER 4: THE POWER OF TRANSFER

Key Points to Ponder

Jot down on this page key points, ideas, strategies, and resources you want to consider later. This sheet is your personal journal summary and will help to jog your memory.

_____

_____

_____

_____

_____

_____

_____

_____

_____

_____

_____

5

Brain Organization and Learning

Despite myriad exceptions, the bulk of split-brain research has revealed an enormous degree of lateralization—that is, specialization in each of the hemispheres.

—Michael Gazzaniga
The Split Brain Revisited

Chapter Highlights

This chapter explores the research on how some regions of the brain are specialized to perform certain tasks. It examines how we learn spoken language, reading, and mathematics, and the implications of this research for classroom instruction, curriculum, and the structure of schools.

It may seem strange at a point this late in the book to introduce another chapter that focuses on brain function—in this case, how brain areas are specialized. But this functional specialization has led to the development of traits that are uniquely human, such as different learning styles and sophisticated spoken and written languages. These remarkable traits rely heavily on memory systems and transfer. Thus, I thought a review of how memory and transfer work was needed first in order to understand better the nature and impact of brain specialization on learning.

BRAIN LATERALIZATION

One of the intriguing characteristics of the human brain is its ability to integrate disparate and seemingly disconnected activities going on in specialized areas of the brain into a unified whole. Brain scans reveal how certain areas of the brain get involved in processing and performing specific tasks. For example, the auditory cortex responds to sound input, the frontal lobe to cognitive rehearsal, and sections of the left hemisphere to spoken language. The ability of certain areas of the brain to perform unique functions is known as cerebral *specialization*. If the activity is mainly limited to one hemisphere, it is called cerebral *lateralization.*

Evidence continues to accumulate regarding specialized brain areas. Even the brains of preterm newborns (less than 30 weeks in utero) show areas of lateralization (Kwon et al., 2015). Consequently, neuroscientists have had to modify their theories of brain organization accordingly. Researchers are now offering the idea that the brain is a set of modular units that carry out specific tasks. According to this modular model, the brain is a collection of units that supports the mind's information processing requirements (a speech module, a numerical computation module, a face recognition module, etc.) and not a singular unit whose every part is capable of any function (e.g., Dwyer et al., 2014; van den Heuvel & Sporns, 2013; Yamaguti & Tsuda, 2015; Yang & Shah, 2014).

The first indications of brain lateralization were discovered long before the development of scanning technologies. During the late 1950s, neurosurgeons decided that the best way to help patients with severe epileptic seizures was to sever the corpus callosum (see Figure 1.2 in Chapter 1), the thick cable of more than 200 million nerve fibers that connects the two cerebral hemispheres. This last-ditch approach isolated the hemispheres so that seizures in the damaged hemisphere would not travel to the other side. The surgery had been tried on monkeys with epilepsy, and the results were encouraging. By the early 1960s, surgeons were ready to try the technique on human beings. One of the pioneers was Dr. Roger Sperry of the California Institute of Technology. Between 1961 and 1969, surgeons Joseph Bogen and Phillip Vogel successfully performed several operations under Sperry's guidance.

Video: For a short video explanation of hemisphere lateralization, see

https://www.youtube.com/watch?v=cqOkYrbJG_M

Although the operations resulted in a substantial reduction or elimination of the seizures, no one was sure what effect cutting this bridge between the hemispheres would have on the "split-brain" patients. Sperry and his student Michael Gazzaniga conducted experiments with these patients and made a remarkable discovery. Splitting the brain seemed to result in two separate domains of awareness. When a pencil was placed in the left hand (controlled by the right hemisphere) of a blindfolded patient, the patient could not name it. When the pencil was shifted to the right hand, however, the patient named it instantly. Neither hemisphere seemed to know what the other was doing, and they acted, as Sperry (1966) said, "each with its own memory and will, competing for control."

As the tests progressed, Sperry (1966) charted the characteristics each hemisphere displayed. He concluded that each hemisphere seems to have its own separate and private sensations, its own perceptions, and its own impulses to act. This research showed that the right and left hemispheres have distinctly different functions that are not readily interchangeable. It also solved the mystery of the corpus callosum. Its purpose is largely to unify awareness and allow the two hemispheres to share memory and learning. Sperry won the 1981 Nobel Prize in medicine in part for this work.

Left and Right Hemisphere Processing (Laterality)

Continued testing of split-brain patients and brain scans of normal (whole-brained) individuals have revealed considerable consistency in the different ways the two halves of the brain store and process information. This cerebral separation of tasks is referred to as *laterality*. The results of numerous studies on laterality continue to provide more insights into the kind of processing done by each hemisphere and expand our understanding of this remarkable division of labor (e.g., Gotts et al., 2013; Wang, Buckner, & Liu, 2014). Figure 5.1 summarizes and Table 5.1 shows more specifically the functions that the hemispheres carry out as they deal with the vast amount of new and past information that must be assessed every second.

Left Hemisphere

The left brain monitors the areas for speech in most right-handed people. Some left-handed people have their speech centers in the right hemisphere (Duffau, Leroy, & Gatignol, 2008). The left hemisphere understands the literal

Figure 5.1 The left and right hemispheres of the brain are specialized and process information differently. However, in complex tasks, both hemispheres are engaged.

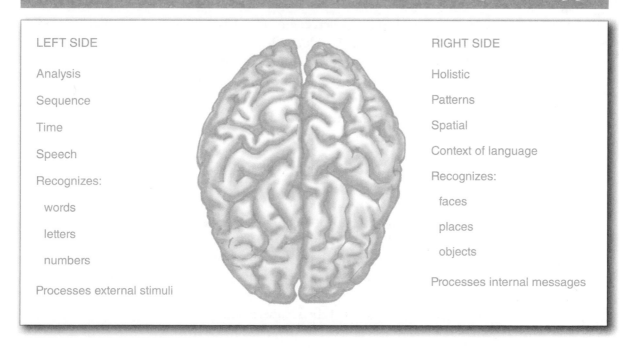

LEFT SIDE	RIGHT SIDE
Analysis	Holistic
Sequence	Patterns
Time	Spatial
Speech	Context of language
Recognizes:	Recognizes:
words	faces
letters	places
numbers	objects
Processes external stimuli	Processes internal messages

Table 5.1 Functions of the Left and Right Cerebral Hemispheres

Left Hemisphere Functions		Right Hemisphere Functions
Connected to right side of the body	C	Connected to the left side of the body
Processes input in a sequential and analytical manner	O R	Processes input more holistically and abstractly
Time-sensitive	P	Space-sensitive
Generates spoken language	U S	Interprets language through gestures, facial movements, emotions, and body language
	C A	
Does invariable and arithmetic operations	L	Does relational and mathematical operations
Specializes in recognizing words and numbers (as words)	L O	Specializes in recognizing faces, places, objects, and music
Active in constructing false memories		More truthful in recall
Seeks explanations for why events occur	S U	Puts events in spatial patterns
Better at arousing attention to deal with outside stimuli	M	Better at internal processing

Sources: Costanzo et al., 2015; Gazzaniga (1998a,1998b); Nagel, Herting, Maxwell, Bruno, & Fair, 2013; Semenza et al., 2006; Stemmer, 2015; Sweeney, 2009.

interpretation of words, and recognizes words, letters, and numbers written as words (Ellis, Ansorge, & Lavidor, 2007; Ossowski & Behrmann, 2015). It is analytical, evaluates factual material in a rational way, perceives the detail in visual processing, and detects time and sequence. It also performs simple arithmetic computations (Zamarian, Ischebeck, & Delazer, 2009). Arousing attention to deal with outside stimuli is another specialty of the left hemisphere, and it appears to process positive emotions such as joy (Hecht, 2010).

Right Hemisphere

The right brain gathers information more from images than from words, and looks for visual patterns. It interprets language through context—body language, emotional content, and tone of voice—rather than through literal meanings (Campbell, 2006). It specializes in spatial perception; recognizes places, faces, and objects; and focuses on relational and mathematical operations, such as geometry and trigonometry (e.g., Ashkenazi, Black, Abrams, Hoeft, & Menon, 2013). This hemisphere also appears to process negative emotions such as sadness and depression (Hecht, 2010).

What Causes Specialization?

No one knows exactly why the brain is specialized, although it does seem that such a capacity enables it to deal with a great amount of sensory data without going on overload. Why would we need two speech centers or face recognition areas? It would seem that as soon as one area of the brain acquired a specialization, there would be no need for it to be duplicated in the other hemisphere. Furthermore, specialization may be what allows us to perform two tasks efficiently at once because different regions of the brains are controlling them (Lust, Geuze, Groothuis, & Bouma, 2011). How it *becomes* specialized is another question. The key to answering this may lie in the brain's structure and wiring. There is general agreement among neuroscientists now that the brain is hardwired for certain functions, such as spoken language, and that this hardwiring is localized.

Another possibility may center around the time it takes for signals to move in the brain. James Ringo and his colleagues (Ringo, Doty, Demeter, & Simard, 1994) used a neural network model that offered a possible explanation for hemispheric specialization. The researchers pointed out that nerve fibers within a hemisphere are shorter than the nerve fibers in the corpus callosum that run between hemispheres. As a result, nerve signals move faster *within* a hemisphere than *between* hemispheres. It would seem, then, that the brain has developed so that each hemisphere can have rapid access to information within itself, but a slower and more limited response to tasks that require communication back and forth across the corpus callosum. The time delays associated with communication between the hemispheres can limit the degree of their cooperation and can encourage the development of hemispheric specialization.

Another factor may be that the left and right hemispheres are physically different. The hemispheres are made up of the cortex (the thin but tough surface) called *gray matter* and the support tissue below it called *white matter*. The left hemisphere has more gray matter, while the right has more white. The left hemisphere's more tightly packed neurons are better able to handle intense, detailed work. The right hemisphere's white matter contains neurons with longer axons that can connect with modules farther away. These long-range connections help the right to come up with broad but rather vague concepts. The information from each hemisphere is then pooled by sending signals across the corpus callosum.

Specialization Does Not Mean Exclusivity

The research data support the notion that each hemisphere has its own set of functions in information processing and thinking. However, these functions are rarely *exclusive* to only one hemisphere, and even in some simple tasks, it is possible for both hemispheres to be involved. Many tasks can be performed by either hemisphere, although one may be better at it than the other.

In a typical individual, the results of the separate processing are exchanged with the opposite hemisphere through the corpus callosum. There is harmony in the goals of each, and they complement one another in almost all activities. Thus, the individual benefits from the integration of the processing done by both hemispheres and is afforded greater comprehension of whatever situation initiated the processing. For example,

- Logic is not confined to the left hemisphere. Some patients with right-brain damage fail to see the lack of logic in their thinking when they propose to take a walk even though they are completely paralyzed.
- Creativity or intuition is not solely in the right hemisphere. Creativity can remain, though diminished, even after extensive right-hemisphere damage.
- Because the two hemispheres do not function independently in a normal brain, it is impossible to educate only one hemisphere.
- Specialization does not mean *exclusivity*. There is no evidence that people are purely left or right brained. One hemisphere may be more active in most people, but only to varying degrees.
- Both hemispheres are capable of synthesis—that is, putting pieces of information together into a meaningful whole.

Examples of Specialization

> *Although each hemisphere has specialized functions, both usually work together when learning.*

Suppose you are right-handed. A pen is on the table just next to your left hand, and someone asks you to pass the pen. Because this is a simple task, you will pick up the pen with your left hand in a smooth motion and pass it. You are not likely to stretch your right hand across your body or twist your torso to hand it over. However, if the person asks you to throw the pen, you will probably use your right hand because this task is more difficult.

During learning, *both* hemispheres are engaged, processing the information or skill according to their specializations and exchanging the results with the opposite hemisphere through the corpus callosum. So if someone were to toss a pen to you, your likelihood of successfully catching it would increase greatly if you used *both* hands, not just your right (dominant) hand.

Knowing the difference between how the left and right hemispheres process information explains why we succeed with some tasks but not with others, especially when we are trying to do them simultaneously. For instance, most of us can carry on a conversation (left-hemisphere activity) while taking a walk (right-hemisphere and cerebellar activity). In this case, each task is controlled by different hemispheres. However, trying to carry on a conversation on the telephone while talking to someone in the room at the same time is very difficult because these are functions mainly of the same (left) hemisphere and can interfere with each other.

Implications of Specialization for Teachers

Brain specialization may be a contributing factor to an individual's learning profile, although there is little neuroscientific research evidence to date to support this notion. The lack of substantial evidence, however, does not negate the observations that experienced teachers have made of the behaviors students display demonstrating the different ways they interpret their learning. When teachers understand these differences, they plan lessons that address all learning preferences. See the Practitioner's Corner: Teaching to the Whole Brain at the end of this chapter.

The Gender Connection

Scientists have known for years that, apart from their different genes, there are structural and developmental as well as performance differences between male and female brains (see Table 5.2). Studies begun in the early 1970s and subsequent studies by other researchers have shown some gender differences in brain characteristics and capabilities. PET scans and fMRIs, for instance, indicate that males and females use different areas of their brains when accomplishing similar tasks (Cahill, 2005; Ruigrok et al., 2014). Let's see what those differences are before we discuss what they mean. Keep in mind that research studies deal with *groups* of males and females. It is not always valid to assign characteristics to a specific person because individuals vary widely from one to another. Furthermore, when there is a difference between two groups (in this case, the genders), we should avoid believing that one group is "better" than the other or that gender is destiny and, thus, the differences cannot be addressed.

Structural and Developmental Differences

- Males have a higher percentage of gray matter (the thin cortex layer containing mostly dendrites) in the left hemisphere than do females. In females, the percentage of gray matter is the same in both hemispheres. However, females have a higher percentage of total gray matter, whereas males have a higher percentage of white matter (mainly myelinated axons below the cortex layer) and cerebral spinal fluid. The corpus callosum (cable connecting the hemispheres) is proportionately larger and thicker in females than in males (Gur et al., 1999; Ingalhalikar et al., 2014). All of these differences could be further evidence to support the idea that female brains are better at communicating between hemispheres and male brains within those hemispheres.

- For most right-handed males and females, the language areas are in the left hemisphere. But females also have an active language processor in the right hemisphere (see Figure 5.2). Females possess a greater density of neurons in the language areas than males (Burman, Bitan, & Booth, 2008; Gazzaniga, Ivry, & Mangun, 2002; Gur et al., 2000; Shaywitz, 2003). These differences may explain why females recover better than males from verbal impairment due to stroke.

- The amygdala (which responds to emotional stimulation), loaded with testosterone receptors, grows more rapidly in teenage boys than in teenage girls, and its final size is larger in men than in women. This is at least a partial explanation of why males tend to demonstrate more overt aggressive behavior than do females. PET scans reveal that during emotional stimulation, females tend to activate the amygdala only in the left hemisphere while males tend to activate the amygdala only in the right hemisphere. Follow-up studies noted that females remembered the details of an emotional event (a typical left-hemisphere function) better than did males, whereas the males remembered better the central aspects, or gist, of the situation (Cahill, 2005; Kreeger, 2002).

- Meanwhile, the hippocampus (responsible for memory formation and consolidation), filled with estrogen receptors, grows more rapidly in girls than in boys during adolescence (Ingalhalikar et al., 2014; Kreeger, 2002). This could explain why preadolescent girls are generally better at language, arithmetic computations, and tasks involving sequence because all these depend on efficient memory processing.

Performance Differences

- There is no significant difference in overall cognitive performance between the sexes. However, on specific skills, more females perform better on tests of perceptual speed, verbal fluency, determining the placement of objects (sequence), identifying specific attributes of objects, precision manual tasks, and arithmetic calculations. More males perform better on spatial tasks, such as mentally rotating three-dimensional objects; at target-directed motor skills; at spotting shapes embedded in complex diagrams; and in mathematical reasoning (Bailey, Littlefield, & Geary, 2012; Cahill, 2005; Gur et al., 2000; Hyde & Linn, 2009; Miller & Halpern, 2014; Neubauer, Grabner, Fink, & Neuper, 2005; Njemanze, 2005).

- When recalling emotions, females use a larger portion of their limbic system than do males. Females are also better at recognizing different types of emotions in others, and that may be due to a more efficient use of mirror neurons (Baron-Cohen, 2003).

  - In face recognition and expression tasks, boys use more of their right brain while girls use more of their left (Everhart, Shucard, Quatrin, & Shucard, 2001; Fine, Semrud-Clikeman, & Zhu, 2009).

Figure 5.2 While processing language, fMRI scans show that male brains (left) use left-hemisphere regions and that female brains (right) activate regions in both hemispheres (white areas).

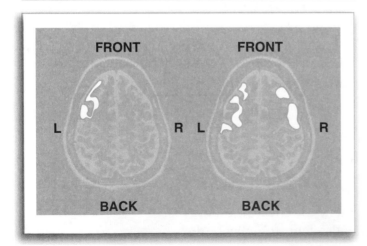

The results of these and other studies further indicate that more females are left-hemisphere preferred and more males are right-hemisphere preferred. Why is this so? To what extent do nature (genetic makeup) and nurture (environment) contribute to these structural and performance differences? Although no one knows for sure, the research evidence suggests that the influence of prenatal hormones, natural selection, and environment could explain these results.

Table 5.2 Structural, Developmental, and Performance Differences Between Female and Male Brains

	Females	Males	Sources
Gray matter	Higher percentage than males, with same amount in both hemispheres.	Lower percentage than females, with more in left hemisphere than right.	Groeschel, Vollmer, King, & Connelly, 2010; Ingalhalikar et al., 2014; Ruigrok et al., 2014; Tang, Jiao, Wang, & Lu, 2013
White matter	Lower percentage than males.	Higher percentage than females, with same amount in both hemispheres.	Chen, Sachdev, Wen, & Anstey, 2007; Ingalhalikar et al., 2014; Ruigrok et al., 2014
Corpus callosum	Larger and thicker than in males.	Smaller and thinner than in females.	Gur et al., 1999; Ingalhalikar et al., 2014
Language areas	Main areas in left hemisphere, with additional processing areas in right hemisphere. Density of neurons in language areas greater than in males.	Located almost exclusively in left hemisphere. Density of neurons in language areas less than in females.	Cahill, 2005; Gur et al., 2000; Lindell & Lum, 2008; Shaywitz, 2003
Amygdala	Grows slower in teenage girls than in boys, and final size is smaller than in males. Only left amygdala activated by emotional stimulation.	Grows faster in teenage boys than in girls, and final size is larger than in females. Only right amygdala activated by emotional stimulation.	Cahill, 2005; Kreeger, 2002
Hippocampus	Grows faster in teenage girls than in boys, and final size is larger than in males.	Grows slower in teenage boys than in girls, and final size is smaller than in females.	Ingalhalikar et al., 2014; Kreeger, 2002
Testing	No different from males in overall cognitive performance, but better than males on tests of perceptual speed, verbal fluency, determining the placement of objects (sequence), identifying specific attributes of objects, precision manual tasks, and arithmetic calculations.	No different from females in overall cognitive performance, but better than females on spatial tasks, such as mentally rotating three-dimensional objects; at target-directed motor skills; at spotting shapes embedded in complex diagrams; and in mathematical reasoning.	Bailey et al., 2012; Cahill, 2005; Gur et al., 2000; Hyde & Linn, 2009; Njemanze, 2005
Facial recognition and expressions	Use more of their left hemisphere.	Use more of their right hemisphere.	Baron-Cohen, 2003; Fine, Semrud-Clikeman, & Zhu, 2009

Possible Causes of Gender Differences

The Structure of Sex Chromosomes. You may recall from biology class that conception results in a fertilized egg containing 23 chromosomes from the mother's egg and 23 from the father's sperm. Two of these are sex chromosomes, which appear in two forms called X and Y. An egg with two X chromosomes develops into a female, while an egg with an X and a Y becomes a male. Thus, the male parent controls sex assignment because only sperm can donate the Y.

The X and Y chromosomes are hardly alike (see Figure 5.3). The X chromosome contains more than 1,000 genes, but the smaller Y has fewer than 100. As a result, females are genetically more complex because they inherit a mix of their mother's and their father's chromosomes. But males' X chromosomes all come from the mother. Furthermore, many of the genes on the X chromosome involve brain function, such as establishing higher cognitive processing and other factors associated with intelligence (Check, 2005; Nguyen & Disteche, 2006). What this means is that if a male's X chromosome is damaged, he has to live with the results. On the other hand, if a female's X is damaged, she can often ignore it because there is a backup X at the ready. This could explain why learning disabilities and mental retardation occur more often in males than in females.

The Effects of Hormones. One possibility is that hormones, such as testosterone and androgen, influence brain development differently in the sexes. As they bathe the fetal brain, these substances direct the wiring and organization of the brain and stimulate the growth and density of neurons in specific areas. Testosterone, for instance, seems to delay the development of the left hemisphere in boys. Thus, girls get a head start in using the left hemisphere; boys are forced to rely more on their right hemisphere (this might also explain why more males are left-handed than are females). The early exposure to these hormones seems to alter other brain functions (such as language acquisition and spatial perception) permanently for the individual. The resurgence of hormones with the onset of puberty may further reconfigure the mental organization of teens, especially as new social pressures emerge with their accompanying emotional shifts (Cahill, 2005; Derntl et al., 2009; Hollier, Maybery, Keelan, Hickey, & Whitehouse, 2104; Lutchmaya, Baron-Cohen, & Raggatt, 2002).

The Effects of Natural Selection. A related explanation is that natural selection affected our brain characteristics as we evolved. For thousands of years, the division of labor between the sexes was distinct. In prehistoric times, men were responsible for hunting large game over long distances, making weapons, and defending the group from predators—animal and otherwise. Women took care of the home and the children, prepared food, and made clothing. Such specialization required different cerebral operations from men and women. Men needed more route-finding and spatial abilities and better

Figure 5.3 This picture of actual X and Y chromosomes shows the difference in their size and shape.

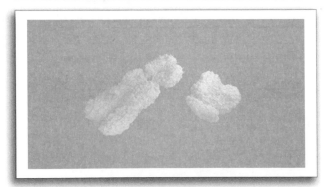

©Firstsignal

targeting skills. Women needed more fine-motor and timing skills to maintain the household and language skills to pass on the native spoken language to their offspring. The individual males and females who could perform their respective tasks well survived long enough to pass their genes on to their children. Moreover, any new genetic combinations eventually led to structural changes in the brain—and other parts of the body—that were specific to each gender and designed to ensure survival.

The Impact of the Environment. Another prevailing explanation looks to a combination of the different ways the sexes develop and interact with their environment. First, studies of infant boys and girls demonstrate that the acuity of senses does not develop identically in both genders. That is, hearing and touch (left-hemisphere controlled) develop more quickly in girls. Spatial vision (right-hemisphere controlled), however, develops more rapidly in boys. Second, parents tend to treat baby boys differently from baby girls. Third, boys and girls between the ages of 6 and 12 typically spend their out-of-school time quite differently as they are growing up. Girls are more likely to spend their free time indoors. In this structured environment, girls are exposed to more language through radio and television, and they are more conscious of time because of clocks, media, and other family members who may be coming home. This environment, psychologists argue, enhances their language development. On the other hand, more boys spend their free time outdoors. In this unstructured environment, boys rely more on space (location) than time, design their own games, use more visual than verbal skills during play, and use language sparingly and only in context to accomplish a task. This behavior enhances the development of visual, spatial, and temporal skills.

The Empathizing Female and Systemizing Male. Simon Baron-Cohen (2003) has summarized the essential laterality differences by proposing that female brains are predominantly wired for empathy, and that male brains are predominantly wired for systemizing—that is, understanding and building systems. According to his intriguing theory, a person (whether female or male) can be one of three brain types. An individual who is stronger at empathizing than at systemizing is Type E. Those who are stronger at systemizing are Type S, and those who are equally strong at both are Type B (for balanced). Baron-Cohen and other researchers (e.g., Frank, Baron-Cohen, & Ganzel, 2015; Lai et al., 2012) believe that the effects of hormones during prenatal and early postnatal development are largely responsible for these sex differences. The researchers, however, admit that genetic traits and the environment also exert their influence.

Baron-Cohen (2003) rightly points out something we should all remember as we study differences in the human brain: Sex does not solely determine how an individual's brain is organized. Some males will have brains organized more like those of females, and some females will have brains organized more like those of males. Individuals of any brain type can be successful in any endeavor.

The evidence suggests that we no longer think in terms of nature versus nurture. Rather, we should see the relationship of these forces as more circular. Genes influence behavior, and behavior can influence how genes function as a child grows and develops. Thus, a combination of nature and nurture factors

During the past decade, technology, such as video games and computers, has had significant impact on how and where children occupy their spare time. It is possible that this impact has already begun to narrow the current differences in brain organization of the genders and will continue to do so in the coming years. The brains of males and females organize differently from very early in their development through their formative years, which may lead to different preferences in learning. More young girls than boys have strong language skills. More young boys than girls have strong visual and spatial skills. The reasons are not as important as our response.

causes the brains of males and females to organize differently from very early in their development through their formative years, leading, among other things, to different preferences in learning and how they interact with their world. One might argue that these gender differences are complementary, thereby increasing the chances that males and females will get together—a scenario that helps perpetuate the species.

Schools and Brain Organization

Recognizing that brain organization is a likely contributor to learning preferences, the question arises as to whether school climate and classroom instruction are designed to embrace different preferences so that all learners can succeed. Is it possible that schools may be designed inadvertently to favor one type of learning preference over another?

Language-Oriented Schools

Take a moment to think about the entire schooling process that takes place from kindergarten through Grade 12. During this mental review, look again at the list of left- and right-hemisphere functions. Is K–12 schooling best described by the characteristics listed for the left hemisphere, the right hemisphere, or both equally? Most educators readily admit that schools are predominantly language-oriented institutions, especially in the elementary grades. Schools are structured environments that run according to time schedules, favor facts and rules over patterns, and offer predominantly verbal instruction, especially at the secondary level. The amount of teacher talk is decreasing due to more use of technology, but at a slow pace.

This means that language-proficient learners (mainly girls) feel more comfortable in this environment. The stronger their language skills, the more successful these learners can be. Conversely, visual- and spatial-proficient learners (mainly boys) are not comfortable; and the stronger these skills are, the more hostile the learning environment seems. This could explain why most teachers admit that they have many more discipline problems with boys than with girls. Maybe what this research is saying is that boys (more accurately, strong visual and spatial learners) are not born with a "mean gene," but they are too often placed in uncomfortable learning environments where they react rebelliously.

Differentiated instruction should recognize that young female and male brains do not mature at the same time. More boys, then, may succeed in schools that recognize different learning styles and individualize instruction accordingly. All students will achieve more when teachers purposefully plan strategies that teach to the whole brain by addressing the strengths and weaknesses of both genders. See the Practitioner's Corner: Strategies for Teaching to the Whole Brain at the end of this chapter.

Most K–12 public schooling tends to favor language-proficient learners.

Impact on Mathematics and Science Programs

Scanning studies show that male and female brains deal differently with numbers and computation (Keller & Menon, 2009). However, numerous recent studies indicate that gender differences in computational processing are more pronounced in preadolescence and become much less important when the brain encounters higher mathematics. In other words, the genetic (nature) component is less significant than we once thought (Lindberg, Hyde, Petersen, & Linn, 2010). It seems more likely that social and cultural forces have had greater influence. Boys in secondary schools are encouraged by their parents and teachers to take more mathematics and science, their experiences in such classes are more compatible with their visual and spatial proficiencies, and they thus score better on tests in these areas. Girls, on the other hand, often encounter a stereotype that presumes females are poor performers in mathematics, and thus less successful in the sciences. Studies have revealed that female performance on mathematics tests was lower than that of males just because of the existence of this stereotype, called *stereotype threat*, and that female performance improved once the stereotype threat was removed (Deemer, Thoman, Chase, & Smith, 2014; Rydell, Van Loo, & Boucher, 2014).

The good news is that the gender gap is narrow. The percentage of girls taking various mathematics and science courses is close to or exceeds that of boys, and girls' test scores on a national average are only a few points lower and not statistically significant (National Center for Education Statistics, 2014). This is an encouraging trend. In part, the explanation for this outcome may be the use of computers and other technology in the classroom. Both boys and girls are on a level playing field. Computer lessons are not closely linked with past successes or failures, representing a new set of skills that both boys and girls are learning at a very early age. Moreover, computers and related technology are patient and fun, contributing to novelty and the fulfillment of expectations of success.

Our job now is to ensure that educators and parents recognize that boys may have some different learning preferences than girls, but both genders have similar *capabilities* to succeed in mathematics and science. To that end, we need to curb the cultural and social forces that would feed past stereotypes about whether students of a certain gender should take only certain subjects. There is plenty of evidence that when girls are encouraged and motivated, they can excel at science and mathematics (e.g., Flore & Wicherts, 2015). It is worth repeating here that scientific studies tell us about averages within groups and nothing about how any particular individual will succeed or fail in any subject area.

SPOKEN LANGUAGE SPECIALIZATION

Many animals have developed ways to communicate with other members of their species. Birds and apes bow and wave appendages; honeybees dance to map out the location of food; and even one-celled animals can signal neighbors by emitting an array of different chemicals. By contrast, human beings have developed an elaborate and complex means of spoken communication that many say is largely responsible for our place as the dominant species on this planet. Spoken language is truly a marvelous accomplishment for many reasons. At the very least, it gives form to our memories and words to express our thoughts. The human voice can pronounce all the vowel and consonant sounds that allow it to speak any of the estimated 6,500 languages (not counting dialects) that exist today. With practice, the voice becomes so fine-tuned that it makes only about one sound error per million sounds and one word error per million words (Pinker, 1994).

Long before the advent of scanning technologies, scientists explained how the brain produced spoken language on the basis of evidence from injured brains. In the 1860s, French surgeon Paul Broca noted that damage to the left frontal lobe induced language difficulties generally known as *aphasia,* wherein patients muttered sounds or lost speech completely. Broca's area (just behind the left temple) is roughly the size of a U.S. quarter-dollar coin. A person with damage to Broca's area (see Figure 5.4) could understand language but could not speak fluently.

Later, in the 1870s, German neurologist Carl Wernicke described a different type of aphasia—one in which patients could not make sense out of words they spoke or heard. These patients had damage in the left temporal lobe. Wernicke's area (above the left ear; see Figure 5.4) is roughly the size of a U.S. silver dollar coin. Those with damage to Wernicke's area could speak fluently,

Figure 5.4   Broca's area and Wernicke's area, located in the left hemisphere, are the two major language processing centers of the brain. The visual cortex across the back of both hemispheres processes visual stimuli, including reading.

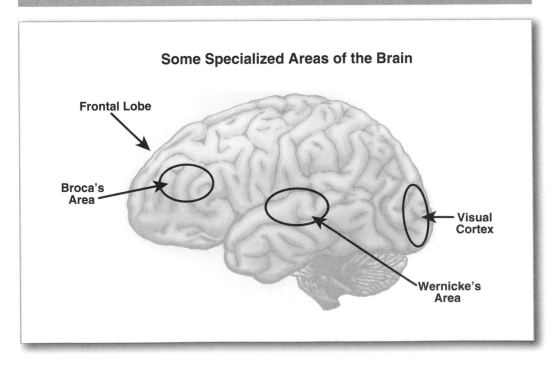

but what they said was quite meaningless. The inferences, then, were that Broca's area processed vocabulary, grammar, and probably syntax of one's native language, while Wernicke's area was the site of native language sense and meaning.

Research, using scanners, indicates that spoken language production is a far more complex process than previously thought. When preparing to produce a spoken sentence, the brain not only uses Broca's and Wernicke's areas but also calls on several other neural networks scattered throughout the left hemisphere. Nouns are processed through one set of patterns; verbs are processed by separate neural networks. The more complex the sentence structure, the more areas that are activated, including the right hemisphere, although more so in females than in males.

Learning Spoken Language

Although early language learning begins in the home, schools are largely responsible for enhancing the spoken language of children and teaching them to read. How quickly and successfully the brain learns to read is greatly influenced by the spoken language competence the child has developed. Therefore, it is important to understand what cognitive neuroscience has revealed about how the brain acquires and processes spoken words. Figure 5.5 presents a general timeline for spoken language development during the first three years of growth. The chart is a rough approximation. Obviously, some children will progress faster or slower than the chart indicates. Nonetheless, it is a useful guide for parents and teachers to show the progression of skills acquired during the process of learning language (National Institute on Deafness and Other Communication Disorders, 2010).

Learning Sounds Called Phonemes

The neurons in a baby's brain are capable of responding to the sounds of all the languages on this planet. At birth (some say even before birth) babies respond first to the *prosody*—the rhythm, cadence, and pitch—of their mother's voice, not the words. Spoken language consists of minimal units of sound, called *phonemes*, which combine to form syllables. For example, in English, the consonant sound /t/ and the vowel sound /o/ are both phonemes that combine to form the syllable *to-* as in *tomato*. Different languages have different numbers of phonemes. It can be as few as 15 in some languages to more than 40 in English. The total number of phonemes in all the world's languages is more than 200, which represents the maximum number of sounds that the human voice apparatus can create, not counting changes in pitch and volume (Sweeney, 2009).

Although the infant's brain can perceive the entire range of phonemes, only those that are repeated get attention, as the particular neurons reacting to the unique sound patterns are continually stimulated and reinforced. The mother helps in this process by speaking in slow, lilting tones with exaggerated emphasis. This precise enunciation is found in all cultures and is called *parentese*. By the age of 10 to 12 months, the toddler's brain has begun to distinguish and remember phonemes of the native language and to ignore foreign sounds.

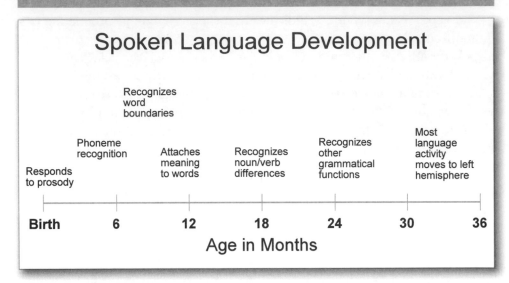

> The neurons in a baby's brain are capable of responding to the sounds of all the languages on this planet.

For example, one study showed that at the age of 6 months, American and Japanese babies are equally good at discriminating between the /l/ and /r/ sounds, even though Japanese has no /l/ sound. However, by age 10 months, Japanese babies have a tougher time making the distinction, while American babies have become much better at it. During this and subsequent periods of growth, the ability to distinguish native sounds improves, while one's ability to distinguish nonnative speech sounds diminishes (Cheour et al., 1998; Yee, 2007).

From Phonemes to Words

The next step for the brain is to detect words from the stream of sounds it is processing. This is not an easy task because people don't pause between words when speaking. Yet the brain has to recognize differences between, say, *green house* and *greenhouse.* Remarkably, babies begin to distinguish word boundaries by the age of 8 months even though they don't know what the words mean (Singh, 2008; Yeung & Werker, 2009). Before they reach the age of 12 months, many babies can learn words in one context and understand them in another (Bergelson & Swingley, 2012). They begin to acquire new vocabulary words at the rate of about 7 to 10 a day. At the same time, memory and Wernicke's area are becoming fully functional, so the child can now attach meaning to words. Of course, learning words is one skill; putting them together to make sense is another, more complex skill.

Learning Grammar

In the 1950s, MIT linguist Noam Chomsky argued that all languages contain some common rules that dictate how sentences are constructed and that the brain has preprogrammed circuits that respond to these rules. Modern linguists think that the brain may not be responding so much to basic language rules as to statistical regularities heard in the flow of the native tongue. They soon discern that some words describe objects while others describe actions. Toddlers detect patterns of word order—person, action, object—so they can soon say, "I want cookie." Other grammar features emerge, such as tense, and by the age of 3 years, over 90 percent of sentences uttered are grammatically correct. Errors are seldom random; they usually result from following perceived rules of grammar. If "I batted the ball" makes sense, why shouldn't "I holded the bat" also make sense? Regrettably, the toddler has yet to learn that nearly 200 of the most commonly used verbs in English are irregularly conjugated (Petersson & Hagoort, 2012; Pinker, 1994).

During subsequent years, practice in speaking and adult correction help the child decode some of the mysteries of grammar's irregularities, and a sophisticated language system emerges from what once was babble. No one knows how much grammar a child learns just by listening or how much is prewired. What is certain is that the more children are exposed to spoken language in the early years, the more quickly they can discriminate between phonemes and recognize word boundaries.

Just letting the toddler sit in front of a television does not seem to accomplish this goal, probably because the child's brain needs live human interaction to attach meaning to the words. Television talk is not the slow, expressive speech that parents use with their infants, which infants like and want to hear. While listening to parentese, toddlers are also watching the movement and shape of the speaker's lips and position of the tongue—clues that will help them when they try to reproduce the sounds to form words. Moreover, the speaker's body language and facial expressions are important hints about the meaning of words and phrases. Television and other media do not provide this critical feedback. Although toddlers may be attracted to the rapidly changing sounds and images on a television, little or no language development is in progress. There is research evidence that prolonged television watching, including so-called educational programs, does not improve a toddler's vocabulary (Alloway, Williams, Jones, & Cochrane, 2014). Other studies have found that habitual television and video viewing is delaying language development in young children by up to 18 months (e.g., Courage & Howe, 2010; Duch et al., 2013).

This is not to say that digital media offer no benefits for youngsters who are acquiring spoken language. Some programs do show promise in helping children with language acquisition, especially those who have language impairments (e.g., Durkin & Conti-Ramsden, 2014). However, care must be taken in selecting and implementing them.

> *Although toddlers may be attracted to the rapidly changing sounds and images on a television, there is little or no language development in progress. Television may actually impair a toddler's brain development.*

Language Delay

Most toddlers begin to speak words around the age of 10 to 12 months. In some children, there is a delay, and they may not speak coherent words and phrases until nearly 2 years of age. There is considerable research evidence that this language delay to 2 years is inherited, and thus it represents a distinct disorder not easily remedied by environmental interventions. This revelation diminishes the claim some people make that it's mainly environmental influences that cause language delay (Burnside et al., 2011; Newbury & Monaco, 2010).

Implications

Given the evidence that the brain's ability to acquire spoken language is at its peak in the early years, parents and preschool teachers should create a rich environment that includes lots of communication activities, such as talking, singing, and reading. In schools, it means addressing any language-learning problems quickly to take advantage of the brain's ability to rapidly rewire improper connections during this important period of growth. It also means that parents and teachers should not assume that children with language-learning problems are going to be limited in cognitive thought processes as well.

Learning a Second Language

The power of a young child's brain to learn spoken languages is so immense that it can learn several languages at one time. But by the age of 10 to 12 months, the brain is already beginning to lose its ability to discriminate sounds between its native language and nonnative languages. The implication here is that if we wish children to acquire a second language, it makes sense to start that acquisition during the early years when the brain is actively creating phonemic sound and syntactic networks. This is particularly true for learning English. There is no reliable one-to-one relationship between how English sounds are pronounced (phonemes) and how they are written (graphemes). And the few rules that do exist have multiple exceptions. Furthermore, English has more vocabulary words than any other language on the planet—more than 250,000—and is filled with idioms, jargon, and slang borrowed from other languages.

> *Proficiency in learning a second language depends not on how long nonnatives have been speaking the language but on how early in life they began learning it.*

Studies show that proficiency in learning a second language depends not on *how long* nonnatives have been speaking the language but on *how early in life* they began learning it (Bloch et al., 2009). This indicates that the window of opportunity (see Chapter 1) for language acquisition slides down in the preteen years so that learning a second language later is certainly possible, but it requires more effort.

Why Is It More Difficult to Learn a Second Language Later?

For most people, the brain areas primarily involved in language acquisition are not very responsive to foreign sounds after the preteen years. Thus, additional areas of the brain must be recruited and programmed to recognize, distinguish, and respond to foreign phonemes. Furthermore, scanning studies using fMRIs show that second languages acquired in adulthood show some spatial separation in the brain from native languages. However, when acquired in the preteen years, native and second languages are represented in the same frontal areas (Broca's area). Hence, younger and older brains react to second language learning very differently (Archila-Suerte, Zevin, & Hernandez, 2015; Dixon et al., 2012; Midgley, Holcomb, & Grainger, 2009).

Although it seems that younger brains are more adept at language learning, this research should not be interpreted to discourage adolescents and adults from pursuing second language study. Nor should it be assumed that youngsters will become fluent solely by studying a second language a few hours a week in the primary grades. Like learning any skill, continuous practice is needed for fluency. Further, the difficulties facing adults learning a second language are very different from those of children. For example, the phonemes, grammar, and syntax rules of the native language are likely to interfere somewhat (an example of negative transfer) with learning those of the second language (Roelofs, Piai, Rodriguez, & Chwilla, 2016). If these difficulties are properly addressed, then learning a second language as an adult can be a rewarding experience, although it may require more focus, more effort, and greater motivation. See Sousa (2011) and the Practitioner's Corner: Acquiring Another Language at the end of this chapter.

> *Although young brains are naturally adept at language learning, this research should not be interpreted to discourage adolescents and adults from pursuing second language study.*

LEARNING TO READ

Let's take a little time now to discuss the one area where neuroscience has made its most important contribution to teaching and learning to date—understanding how the brain learns to read. The more scientists learn about the neural systems required for successful reading, the more they realize how complicated the process is and how much can go wrong. My purpose here is to present a quick description of how we believe the brain learns to read and to mention a few common reading problems. For a much more extensive discussion on reading and teaching strategies, see Sousa (2014) and Shaywitz (2003).

Is Reading a Natural Ability?

Not really. The brain's ability to acquire spoken language with amazing speed and accuracy is the result of genetic hardwiring and specialized cerebral areas that focus on this task. But there are no areas of the brain that specialize in reading. In fact, reading is probably the most difficult task we ask the young brain to undertake. Reading is a relatively new phenomenon in the development of humans. As far as we know, the genes have not incorporated reading into their coded structure, probably because reading—unlike spoken language—has not emerged over time as a survival skill.

Many cultures (but not all) do emphasize reading as an important form of communication and insist it be taught to their children. And so the struggle begins. To get that brain to read, here's what we are saying, for example, to the English-speaking child: "That language you have been speaking quite correctly for the past few years can be represented by abstract symbols we invented called letters of the alphabet. We are going to disrupt that sophisticated spoken language network you have already developed and ask you to reorganize it to accommodate these letters, which, by the way, are not very reliable. You see, although it takes more than about 44 different sounds to speak English, we have only 26 letters to represent them. That means some sounds have more than one letter and some letters stand for more than one sound. Seem like fun? Plus, there are lots of exceptions, but you'll just have to adjust." Female brains are already relishing the adventure, while male brains are wondering how they ever got into this mess.

Once exposed to formal instruction, about 50 percent of children make the transition from spoken language to reading with relative ease. For the other 50 percent, reading is a much more formidable task, and for about 20 to 30 percent, it definitely becomes the most difficult cognitive task they will ever undertake in their young lives.

> *There are no areas of the brain that specialize in reading. Reading is probably the most difficult task we ask the young brain to undertake.*

Learning to read successfully requires three neural systems and the development of specific skills that will work together to help the brain decode abstract symbols into meaningful language. We will first look at the neural systems involved because that will help clarify what skills an individual needs to develop to learn to read.

Neural Systems Involved in Reading

Researchers using fMRIs are getting a clearer picture of the cerebral processes involved in reading. For successful reading to occur, three neural systems are required to work together. Figure 5.6 illustrates those systems. Visual processing begins when the eyes scan the letters of the printed word (in this example, *d-o-g*), and the visual signals travel to the visual cortex located in the occipital lobes at the rear of the brain (see also Figure 5.2). The word's signals are decoded in an area on the left side of the brain called the *angular gyrus*, which separates it into its basic sounds, or phonemes. This process activates the language areas of the brain located in the left hemisphere near and in the temporal lobe, where auditory processing also occurs. The auditory processing system sounds out the phonemes in the head, *duh-awh-guh.* Broca's and Wernicke's areas supply information about the word from their mental dictionaries, and the frontal lobe integrates all the information to provide meaning—a furry animal that barks.

The three systems can prompt each other for more information (represented by the double arrows). For instance, if auditory processing is having difficulty sounding out the word, it might prompt the visual system to rescan the print to ensure that it read the letters correctly. Similarly, the frontal lobe may prompt another visual scan or auditory rehearsal if it is having difficulty attaching meaning to the information. All this occurs in a fraction of a second. The actual process is a little more complicated than described here, but this is essentially what neuroscientists believe happens.

Although the process outlined in Figure 5.6 appears linear and singular, it is really bidirectional and parallel, with many phonemes being processed at the same time. That the brain learns to read at all attests to its remarkable ability to

Figure 5.6 Three neural systems are involved in reading. The visual processing system scans the printed word, the auditory processing system sounds it out in the head, and the frontal lobe integrates the information to produce meaning. The angular gyrus helps decode the visual word recognition signals for further processing in the left hemisphere's language centers (Broca's and Wernicke's areas).

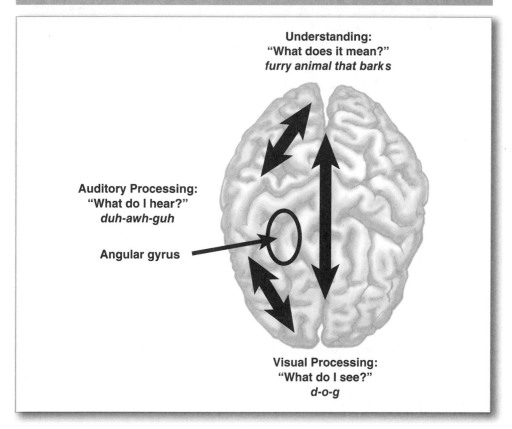

sift through seemingly confusing input and establish patterns and systems. For a few children, this process comes naturally, but most have to be taught.

Skills Involved in Reading

In order for this complex integration of neural systems to result in successful reading, an individual must develop specific skills and possess certain information. Specifically,

- **Phonological and phonemic awareness.** *Phonological awareness* is the recognition that oral language can be divided into smaller components, such as sentences into words, words into syllables, and, ultimately, syllables into individual sounds. This recognition includes identifying and manipulating onsets and rimes as well as having an awareness of alliteration, rhyming, syllabication, and intonation. Being phonologically aware means hearing the difference between *bat* and *pat* and between *bat* and *bet*. Before tackling the printed word, children need to be able to recognize that words are made up of individual sounds (phonemes) and that these sounds can be manipulated to create new words. This skill is called *phonemic awareness* (a subdivision of phonological awareness) and includes the ability to isolate a phoneme (first, middle, or last) from the rest of the word, to segment words into their component phonemes, and to delete a specific phoneme from a word.

- **Alphabetic principle and phonics.** The *alphabetic principle* describes the understanding that spoken words are made up of phonemes and that the phonemes are represented in written text as letters. This system of using letters to represent phonemes is very efficient in that a small number of letters can be used to write a very large number of words. Matching just a few letters on a page to their sounds in speech enables the reader to recognize many printed words. *Phonics* is an instructional approach that builds on the alphabetic principle and associates letters and sounds with written symbols. To demonstrate phonics knowledge, a child tells the teacher which letter is needed to change *cat* to *can.* Simply learning letter-sound relationships during phonics instruction does not necessarily lead to phonemic awareness.

- **Vocabulary.** Readers must usually possess a word in their mental dictionary in order to recognize it in print. Children learn the meanings of most words indirectly, through everyday experiences with oral and written language. These experiences include conversations with other people, listening to adults read to them, and reading on their own. They learn vocabulary words directly when they are explicitly taught individual words and word-learning strategies. Some vocabulary should be taught directly. Direct instruction is particularly effective for teaching difficult words representing complex concepts that are not part of the children's everyday experiences.

- **Fluency.** Fluency is the ability to read a text orally with speed, accuracy, and proper expression. Children who lack fluency read slowly and laboriously, often making it difficult for them to remember what has been read (recall the limited capacity of working memory) and to relate the ideas expressed in the text to their own experiences. Frequent practice in reading is one of the main contributors to developing fluency. Fluency bridges the gap between word recognition and comprehension. Because fluent readers do not need to spend much time decoding words, they can focus their attention on the meaning of the text. With practice, word recognition and comprehension occur almost simultaneously.

- **Text comprehension.** Comprehension is a complex interactive process that begins with identifying words by using knowledge outside the text, accessing word meaning in context, recognizing grammatical structures, drawing inferences, and monitoring oneself to ensure that the text is making sense. When confronted with several meanings for a word in a sentence, the brain needs to select the one that makes sense in context. Many English words have dozens of meanings, depending on their context. Thus, developing the ability to quickly block irrelevant meanings becomes a necessity for reading fluency and comprehension.

Some of these skills may begin to develop at home during the preschool years as parents read to their children and expose them to print materials. This allows them to hear word sounds, to practice pronunciation and speak more fluently, and to learn new words and their meanings. Thus, the degree to which children experience literacy at home will determine largely whether they begin school not just *able* to learn to read, but are also *ready* to learn to read. Children from low-income families are not often exposed to print materials and reading at home. Yet, studies show that when parents and school districts make the extra effort to provide these experiences, the acquisition of language and phonological skills for low-income preschool children is greatly enhanced (Preston et al., 2016; Sparks & Reese, 2013).

> *The degree to which children experience literacy at home determines whether they begin school not just able to learn to read but also ready to learn to read.*

Phases of Learning to Read

As the three neural circuits involved in learning to read develop their capabilities and interconnections, researchers suggest that beginning readers go through three phases (Dehaene, 2010).

- First phase: This is the pictorial stage, when the child's brain photographs words and visually adjusts to the shape of the alphabet's letters.
- Second phase: In this phonological stage, the brain begins to decode the letters (graphemes) into sounds (phonemes).
- Third phase: This is the orthographic stage, when the child is able to recognize words quickly and accurately.

All of these phases activate different brain circuits which, over time and with regular practice, eventually consolidate in a specialized area of the left hemisphere. This region is known as the visual word form area. The consolidation process is complex and occurs at different rates in different students.

Given the recent emphasis on improving the basic cognitive skills of children, pressure is growing to start reading instruction sooner than ever before. In many schools, reading instruction begins in kindergarten. Researchers do not identify a definite age at which the brain can begin to learn to read. Much more important than chronological age is the pace and degree of brain development, both of which vary widely among children of the same age. For some children, the transition from spoken language to learning to read is a relatively easy one once they are exposed to formal instruction. But for others, the transition can be a much more daunting task.

Problems in Learning to Read

Reading is so complex that any little problem along the way can slow or interrupt the process. It is small wonder that children have more problems with reading than any other skill we ask them to learn. In recent years, researchers have made significant progress using fMRI scans to understand how the brain reads. Yet, despite these advancements, fMRI scans are not a practical tool at present for diagnosing reading problems in a single individual. That is because the results of fMRI studies are usually reported for groups rather than for individuals. Researchers have found some variations in the activated areas of the brain among individuals within both poor readers and control groups. More research is needed to clarify these differences before fMRI or any other imaging techniques can be used confidently for diagnostic purposes. Until that time, however, researchers can use the information gained from imaging studies to develop other kinds of diagnostic tests that more closely align with our new understanding of reading and reading problems.

For the moment, critical observation of a child's progress in learning to speak, and eventually in learning to read, remains our most effective tool for spotting potential problems. Most difficulties associated with reading do not go away with time. Therefore, the earlier that parents and teachers can detect reading problems in children, the better.

Many research studies on reading have focused primarily on developmental reading problems that scientists refer to as *developmental dyslexia.* In developmental dyslexia, the child experiences unexpected difficulty in learning to read despite adequate intelligence, sufficient environment, and normal senses. It is a spectrum disorder, varying from mild to severe. Neuroimaging studies have established that there are significant differences in the way normal and dyslexic brains respond to specific spoken and written language tasks. Furthermore, there is now strong evidence that these differences may weaken with appropriate instructional interventions (e.g., Sahari & Johari, 2012; Zhao, de Schotten, Altarelli, Dubis, & Ramus, 2016).

Scientists have long been searching for the causes of reading problems. This has not been an easy task because of the large number of sensory, motor, and cognitive systems that are involved in reading. Struggling readers may have impairments in any one or more of these systems, but not all struggling readers have dyslexia. Specifically, dyslexia seems to be caused by deficits in the neural regions responsible for language and phonological processing or by problems in nonlinguistic areas of the brain.

The following is a brief description of some of the causes of difficulties when learning to read (Sousa, 2014). Most reading problems can be divided into three categories, (1) inadequate reading instruction, (2) social and cultural problems, and (3) physical causes, both linguistic and nonlinguistic. Parents and teachers should consult other resources such as those found in the Resources section of this book, for an in-depth discussion of these problems and how to deal with them.

Inadequate Reading Instruction

Some children have reading problems because they did not get adequate beginning instruction in the skills needed for decoding, such as concepts about the nature of print, recognizing letters, and the alphabetic principle. They may not have had sufficient opportunities for systematic and focused practice in decoding real words. Consequently, they failed to develop a rich mental lexicon, which is essential for promoting reading fluency and comprehension. To successfully understand a language, children need to develop a rich vocabulary and an appreciation for semantics, and combine that understanding with what they know about the real world. They also need to have a good understanding of the mechanics of language (syntax) and they need to be attuned to the phonology of the language so that they do not confuse similar sounding words, such as *fair* and *fear.*

None of these areas can be described as social, cultural, or physical problems that lead to reading difficulties. These deficits are not inherent in the child, but are due to the classroom and to the school system that has not provided the appropriate instructional environment. Schools situated in high-poverty areas are often competing for limited materials and resources. Conscientious but inadequately trained teachers may be using outdated programs and methodologies. This unfortunate combination can be the cause of some children's reading difficulties. Children in this situation do not have dyslexia. Their problem is that they were never fully taught the skills needed to learn how to read. To be successful in teaching all children, teachers should be extremely knowledgeable about effective strategies as well as diagnostic in their approach to reading instruction.

We do not expect beginning readers to acquire the alphabetic principle on their own. Likewise, we cannot expect prospective teachers of reading to independently acquire the knowledge and skills they will need to recognize and implement research-based strategies. They need to be exposed to the latest research on how the brain learns and, specifically, how it learns to read. This information should be presented in their college courses as well as during continuing in-service professional development programs to keep their knowledge base up to date.

Social and Cultural Causes of Reading Problems

A large number of Black and Hispanic children performing below White children in reading display no signs of specific learning impairments. Clearly other factors are at work. Multiple studies have identified social conditions that have an impact on the achievement of children in inner-city schools. Limited teacher training, large class sizes, the absence of literature in the home, and poor parental support for schools have all been cited as causes for lack of student progress. Although these conditions cannot be ignored, schools need to focus more on the direct connections between what we are learning about how the brain learns to read and the *linguistic* barriers interfering with that learning.

Some researchers believe that these children are performing poorly on reading tests because their home language differs substantially from the language used in reading instruction. Others noted that Black children were being immersed in a language dialect that has become known as African American Vernacular English (AAVE). Residential desegregation has increased the impact of AAVE, as has the rapidly escalating popularity of hip hop and rap music (e.g., Rickford et al., 2015). Meanwhile, as Spanish-speaking populations increase, children are faced with learning to read English in school while speaking Spanish at home and in their communities.

Consequently, some of the causes of poor performance by Black and Hispanic children can be attributed to impediments resulting from linguistic differences. That is, their native dialect or language is different in significant ways from what is being taught in school. They come to school with a mental dictionary whose word representations often do not match what they are trying to decode on the printed page in English. Learning to read involves determining which words are present in their mental dictionary, what they represent, and whether they can be comprehended in context. This is not a physiological deficit; it is a social and cultural problem. For these children, we should not be looking at what is wrong with them but how we can alter instruction to make them more successful in learning to read. Such alterations can be made when teachers of reading are properly trained to recognize when a child's reading problems are the result of linguistic clashes and not a pathology. Furthermore, that training should also help teachers understand how they can use some of the linguistic attributes of AAVE and Spanish to help children pronounce, decode, and understand conversational and academic English.

Physical Causes of Reading Problems

Long ago, nature fashioned complex neural networks to process spoken language and, in doing so, helped our species survive. But decoding written text is an artificial creation that makes demands of neural areas devoted to other tasks. Reading is such a complex undertaking that any problem along the way can slow or interrupt the process. Physical causes of reading difficulties are generally divided into types: linguistic and nonlinguistic.

Linguistic Causes. Several potential linguistic cause of reading problems and developmental dyslexia have been identified in research studies. They include phonological deficits, differences in auditory and visual processing speeds, structural differences in the brain, phonologic memory deficits, genetics, and lesions in the visual word form area. Several of these causes may be related to each other and can coexist in the same individual.

- **Phonological deficits.** The readers have difficulty sounding out the sounds of the phonemes in their heads. The exact causes of this impairment are not clear because the results of fMRI studies are not conclusive (e.g., van Ermingen-Marbach, Grande, Pape-Neumann, Sass, & Heim, 2013).
- **Differences in auditory and visual processing speeds.** When learning to read, the visual and auditory processing systems work at similar speeds to decode letters into sounds. Research studies of poor readers have revealed that some of them have a slower than normal auditory processing speed (e.g., Moll, Hasko, Groth, Bartling, & Schulte-Körne, 2016; Schulte-Körne & Bruder, 2010). Consequently, the visual system may already be processing the third letter of a word while the auditory system is still processing the first letter's sound. As a result, the brain incorrectly associates the sound of the first letter with the symbol of the third letter. For example, in reading the word *dog,* the visual system may already be processing the *g,* but the slower

auditory system is still processing the *duh* sound associated with the letter *d.* This reader's brain, then, mistakenly associates the letter *g* with the sound *duh.*

- **Structural differences in the brain.** MRI studies have found that the brains of people diagnosed with dyslexia are structurally different from nondyslexic brains. These differences could contribute to the deficits associated with dyslexia (e.g., Steinbrink et al., 2008). A common research finding is the reduced level of activity in the visual word form area as well as reduced connectivity to other language processing areas (e.g., van der Mark et al., 2011). One study found that children at risk for developmental dyslexia showed signs of atypical structural connectivity in the white matter in infants as young as 7 to 18 months old (Langer et al., 2015). It seems, too, that most children with developmental dyslexia have visual analysis and phonological decoding regions of the brain that are not sufficiently active and dysfunctional.

- **Phonological memory deficits.** Some poor readers have difficulty retaining phonemes in working memory and are thus unable to remember a sequence of words long enough to generate a sentence (e.g., Carretti, Borella, Cornoldi, & De Beni, 2009; Lu et al., 2016).

- **Genetics and gender.** There is a strong association between dyslexia and genetic mutations in twins and families. To date, more than 10 susceptible genes have been associated with developmental dyslexia (e.g., Bishop, 2015; Darki, Peyrard-Janvid, Matsson, Kere, & Klingberg, 2014). Studies consistently show that more boys are diagnosed with developmental dyslexia than girls (e.g., Quinn & Wagner, 2015). Researchers offer various reasons for the gender discrepancy. Some say boys are genetically more vulnerable than girls to reading impairment. Others cite studies showing that boys are more likely to act out their frustration with their reading difficulties by exhibiting disruptive behavior. Thus, they are more likely than girls to be noticed and referred for evaluation. This explanation suggests that boys are overidentified as having reading problems, while females are often underidentified.

- **Brain lesions in the visual word form area.** fMRI scans have shown that some people with developmental dyslexia have lesions in the areas on the left side of the brain in the visual word form area (e.g., Huang, Baskin, & Fung, 2016). You will recall that this area is responsible for processing and decoding written words. However, in another example of the brain's incredible plasticity, other studies show that when a lesion occurs in the visual word form area during childhood, an area exactly symmetrical to it, located in the right hemisphere, can take over its functions, albeit not as efficiently (Cohen et al., 2004).

Nonlinguistic Causes. Some people who are not otherwise impaired still experience great difficulty in reading because of deficits in auditory and visual processing not related to linguistic systems. In other words, they have the ability to process language, but they have problems with decoding auditory and visual signals or with other executive functions. Here are some of the nonlinguistic causes.

- **Perception of sequential sounds.** Some poor readers are unable to detect and discriminate sounds presented in rapid succession. This deficit is related to auditory processing in general, not just to distinguishing phonemes as part of phonological processing. Being able to hear words accurately when reading or from a stream of rapid conversation is crucial to comprehension (Wright, Bowen, & Zecker, 2000).

- **Sound-frequency discrimination.** Some individuals with reading disorders are impaired in their ability to hear differences in sound frequency. This auditory defect can affect the ability to discriminate tone and pitch in speech. A longitudinal study found that children with pitch discrimination problems as newborns had more difficulties than typical children when learning to read. This was particularly evident in families with a history of dyslexia (Leppänen et al., 2010).

- **Detection of target sounds in noise.** The inability to detect tones within noise is another nonlinguistic impairment affecting one's learning to read. The individuals have difficulty hearing the differences between tones and noise. This makes reading very challenging because the reader's brain cannot distinguish phonemic tones from all the other incoming auditory information (e.g., Dole, Meunier, & Hoen, 2014). When added to the findings in the two deficits mentioned just above, this evidence suggests that auditory functions may play a much greater role in reading disorders than previously thought.

- **Motor coordination and the cerebellum.** Several imaging studies show that many dyslexic readers have processing deficits in the cerebellum of the brain (e.g., Stoodley, 2016). The cerebellum is located at the rear of the brain just below the occipital lobe. It is mainly responsible for coordinating learned motor skills. Deficiencies in this part of the brain could result, according to researchers, in problems with reading, writing, and spelling.

- **Attention deficit/hyperactivity disorder (ADHD).** Attention deficit/hyperactivity disorder (ADHD) is a developmental disorder characterized by difficulty in focusing and sustaining attention. Children with ADHD are often assumed to also have developmental reading problems. But that is not usually the case. ADHD and developmental dyslexia are separate disorders, although some brain regions may be affected by both. Estimating the percentage of ADHD children who also have dyslexia is difficult because of the inconsistency of criteria used for diagnosis.

Implications for Teaching Reading

Teaching children to read is no easy task, especially in primary classrooms where teachers welcome children from an ever-increasing variety of home situations, cultures, and native languages. Given these variables, successful teachers of reading are flexible rather than rigid in their approach, and they know through experience what they need to do to make learning to read exciting and meaningful. They also acknowledge that the findings of scientific studies are clear: Effective reading programs must contain components that support phonemic awareness, the alphabetic principle, vocabulary building, comprehension, and fluency. Developmentally appropriate literature complements this process to provide relevant and enjoyable reading experiences. See the Practitioner's Corner: Considerations for Teaching Reading at the end of this book.

LEARNING MATHEMATICS

Researchers in cognitive neuroscience have learned a great deal in recent years about how the human brain processes mathematical operations. My purpose here is to present a short explanation of how we believe the brain learns mathematics and the problems that can develop during that process. For a much more extensive discussion, see Dehaene (2010) and Sousa (2015a).

Number Sense

Of major interest to educators is the understanding that we have an innate talent known as *number sense*. First introduced in the 1950s, it describes the ability to determine the number of objects in a small collection, to count, and to perform simple addition and subtraction, all without direct instruction. Brain scans have found that the human brain is more sensitive to changes in numbers than to changes in other visual properties (e.g., Park, Dewind, Woldorff, & Brannon, 2016). Number sense became an innate ability most likely because it contributed to our survival. When our hunting ancestors went searching for food, they had to determine quickly whether the number of animals they spotted represented a danger or an opportunity. Were they too big to capture, or too far away, or moving too fast? A mistake in these calculations could be fatal. Consequently, individuals who were good at making these determinations survived and contributed to strengthening our species' genetic capabilities in number sense. Other animals, such as birds, lions, and chimpanzees, also possess number sense at various levels of sophistication.

> *Humans developed an innate number sense because it contributed to their survival.*

How Number Sense Develops

The development of number sense seems to be critical to one's future success in learning mathematics. Studies have shown that the number sense possessed by infants as young as 6 months of age predicts their success in learning mathematics in the elementary grades (e.g., Starr, Libertus, & Brannon, 2013). Others studies found a positive correlation between students' number sense and their scores on the mathematics section of the Scholastic Aptitude Test (e.g., Libertus, Odic, & Halberda, 2012).

How can teachers assess a child's understanding of number sense? Here are some stepping-stones that researchers suggest are key indicators of progressive development of number sense in children (e.g., Baroody, Eiland, & Thompson, 2009; Gersten & Chard, 1999; Jordan, Kaplan, Ramineni, & Locuniak, 2009).

Step 1. Children have not yet developed number sense. They have no sense of relative quantity and may not know the difference between "less than" and "more than" or "fewer" and "greater."

Step 2. Children are starting to acquire number sense. They understand terms like "lots of," "five," and "eight," and are beginning to understand the concepts of "less than" and "more than." They also understand lesser or greater amounts but do not yet have basic computation skills.

Step 3. Children fully understand "less than" and "more than." They have a concept of computation and may use their fingers or objects to apply the "count up from one" strategy to solve problems. Errors occur when the child is calculating numbers higher than five because this requires using the fingers of both hands.

Step 4. Children now rely on the "count up" or "counting on" process instead of the "counting all" process they used on the previous step. They understand the conceptual reality of numbers in that they do not have to count to five to know that five exists. Assuming they can count accurately, children on this step are able to solve any problem with digits.

Step 5. Children demonstrate retrieval strategies for solving problems. They have already automated addition facts and are acquiring basic subtraction facts.

To progress through these steps, researchers have suggested a model in which the child relies on three phases, as shown in Figure 5.7 (Griffin, 2002). In the first phase, the visual processing system recognizes objects in a collection. For small collections, the number can be determined without counting, thanks to innate abilities. As the collection increases, the child moves to the second phase and creates number words to communicate to others the exact count. In the third phase, the child realizes that writing number words for large quantities is tiresome, and that these words do not lend themselves to mathematical manipulation. Hence, the child moves to relying on numerical symbols and operational signs. At the beginning, the flow from one phase to another is linear. However, with practice, all three phases interact whenever the child performs mathematical operations. This model has been supported by several research studies (e.g., Grotheer, Ambrus, & Kovács, 2016; Holloway, Price, & Ansari, 2010).

What this model shows is the significant impact that language processing has on mathematical processing. When performing mathematical operations, we silently say what we are doing in our heads. This is particularly true when doing exact arithmetic, such as multiplying a pair of two-digit numbers. One stunning example of the influence that language has over quantitative processes came from a study of the Piraha, a tribe in the Amazon whose language is anumeric, meaning it lacks words for numbers. As a result, they have difficulty performing simple arithmetic tasks. When a missionary used the Piraha language to create number words and taught them to the natives, their quantitative skills improved (Everett & Madora, 2012).

Figure 5.7 This model shows the development of number sense from recognizing real-world quantities to devising words and symbols to represent those quantities (adapted from Griffin, 2002).

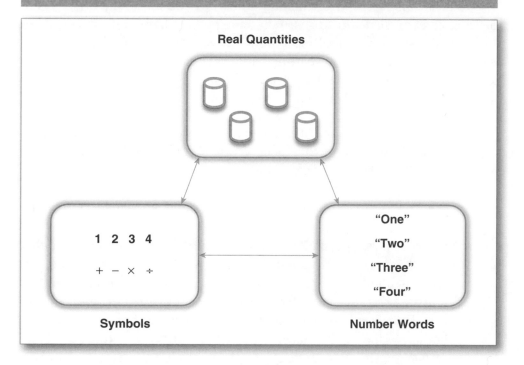

Consequently, children with strong language skills when entering the primary grades tend to do better in mathematics than children with poorer language skills. Numerous research studies support this language-mathematics connection (e.g., Purpura & Reid, 2016; Vukovic & Lesaux, 2013). You can prove this to yourself by trying to multiply a pair of two-digit numbers while reciting the alphabet aloud. This task is difficult to do because speaking demands attention from the same language areas required for mental computation and reasoning. We should note, however, that despite this cooperation between the language and reasoning areas of the brain, they are still distinct and anatomically separate. Case studies show that one area can function normally even when the other is damaged (e.g., Brannon, 2005). Therefore, teachers should not assume that students who have difficulty with language processing will necessarily also have difficulty with arithmetic operations, and vice versa.

Learning to Calculate

Children's first excursion into calculation begins when they add two sets by counting them both on their fingers. Eventually, they learn to add without using their fingers and they recognize the commutativity of addition, that is $a + b$ is always equal to $b + a$. But as the calculations become more difficult, errors arise, even for adults. Why? In our development as a species, nothing prepared our brain for the task of memorizing dozens of multiplication facts or for performing multistep mathematical operations. Our ability to approximate numerical quantities was enough for our survival. Number sense may be genetically directed, but dealing with exact symbolic calculations is not, and learning to do it can be an error-prone nightmare.

To be successful at understanding numerical quantities, the brain has to develop cerebral structures to visually manipulate objects and assign them number words and symbols. Researchers believe that these number structures emerge during the preschool years and are in place by the time the child enters kindergarten (Griffin, 2002; Purpura & Lonigan, 2013). They suggest the following developmental scheme for number structures in young children.

- In 4-year-olds: By this age, children have developed two major structures: global quantity that relies on number sense, and one for counting a small number of objects, mainly through one-to-one correspondence with fingers. They begin to understand counting. They know that each number word occurs in a sequence and can be assigned to only one object in a collection.
- In 6-year-olds: Now children have developed a mental number line that gives them a central conceptual structure for whole numbers. They recognize that numbers higher up in the counting sequence indicate quantities that are larger than numbers lower down. Also, they realize that the numbers themselves have magnitude, in that 8 is bigger than 6. The number line allows them to do simple addition and subtraction without an actual set of objects just by counting forward or backward along the number line.
- In 8-year-olds: By the time they reach age 8, children can manipulate numbers along two number lines that are loosely coordinated. They understand place value and can mentally solve double-digit addition problems, knowing which of the two double-digit numbers is smaller or larger. Furthermore, the double number line structure permits them to read the hours and minutes on a clock and to solve money problems involving dollars and cents.
- In 10-year-olds: At this age, children have expanded the double number line structure to easily handle two quantities or to include a third quantitative variable. They can solve problems with three-digit numbers and can translate from hours to minutes to determine which of two time periods is longer.

Keep in mind that these stages represent *average* rate of development. The rate in individual children will vary, depending on the strength of their innate number sense, the degree of their exposure to numeracy, and other factors.

Teaching Brain-Friendly Mathematics

As research reveals more about the workings of the human brain and how it learns, we need to consider whether the instructional strategies we are using to teach mathematics are consistent with the research findings. Do our strategies in the primary grades take advantage of the children's innate number sense and extend their understandings to numerical manipulation and concept development? Are we emphasizing memorization at the expense of understanding? Do teachers of mathematics have adequate professional development opportunities that expose them to the newer research and to decide what instructional approaches are more likely to be successful with today's students? Let's look at some of the major instructional ideas that educators might consider at different grade levels regarding mathematics instruction.

Primary Grades

Not surprisingly, studies show that the kind of mathematics instruction students experience in preschool and kindergarten is strongly associated with their mathematics achievement in middle and high school (e.g., Watts, Duncan, Siegler, & Davis-Kean, 2014). Early mathematics instruction should build on the children's innate number sense and help them develop the cerebral structures they need to successfully manipulate numbers and understand conceptual schema. To do that, early childhood researchers and mathematics educators agree that preschoolers and kindergartners should be exposed to the following areas and skills (e.g., Clarke, Doabler, Nelson, & Shanley, 2015; Doabler & Fien, 2013; Dyson, Jordan, & Glutting, 2013).

- **Numbers.** Children learn about numbers by counting objects and talking about their results. "You gave Mary three cards. How many does Billy need?" Children count spaces on board games. "You are now on space two. How many more spaces do you need to go to get to space six?" They count the days until their birthdays. The teacher might say, "Yesterday there were eight days until your birthday. How many days are there now?" Children read counting books and recite nursery rhymes with numbers.
- **Geometry and spatial relations.** Children practice constructing various shapes and discussing their properties. They can see thin triangles, fat triangles, and upside-down triangles and gradually realize that they are all still triangles.
- **Measurement.** Children compare the height of a block tower with the height of a chair or table. They measure each other's height and the distance from the desk to a wall. They learn that a block is too short or too long to complete a project.
- **Patterns/geometry.** Children become aware of patterns in their environment. They learn to recognize patterns of different colors and sizes in beads, blocks, and their clothes. They practice reproducing simple patterns by stringing beads and copying designs with colored blocks.
- **Analyzing data.** Children sort objects by color, size, and shape; count them; and record the data on graphs and charts. These charts might reflect how many bean plants have sprouted, the class pet's growth, the number of rainy days in March, or the number of children with a birthday in January.

Learning these areas and skills will give young children the background they need to feel comfortable with the nature of number system and with handling numerical calculations.

Intermediate Grades

As the young brain continues to develop, it becomes a formidable pattern seeker, trying to make sense of the new information it is encountering in school and elsewhere. Any new information that helps the brain determine a pattern is likely to be understood and have meaning—the fundamental criteria that lead to long-term storage.

> To develop meaning, teachers should show students why they are performing certain arithmetic operations.

From Memorization to Meaning. Mathematics instruction in the intermediate grades often focuses mainly on memorizing procedures, with little attention given to meaning. However, meaning affords the learner the opportunity to change procedures as the nature of the problem changes. Without meaning, students memorize the procedures without understanding how and why they work. They end up confused about when to use which procedure. This confusion leads to frustration that can create negative attitudes toward mathematics.

Why is this instructional approach so common? Could it be because that is how most teachers learned arithmetic themselves? Could this explain why arithmetic instruction in the primary and intermediate grades has not changed very much over the years? We teach students a procedure for solving computation problems, which they then repeatedly practice (procedural memory). But the practice does not result in computational fluency because we rarely talk about how and why the procedure works. Consequently, when we give the students a problem to solve, they reflexively draw on their knowledge of the practiced procedure and apply that procedure quickly and efficiently but with little understanding of the mathematical concepts involved. Of course, students need to learn some basic procedural activities, such as memorizing some version of the multiplication tables along with a few number facts. But the emphasis should be on showing students (at the earliest possible age) *why* they are performing certain arithmetic operations. The more arithmetic we can teach through declarative processes involving understanding and meaning, the more likely students will succeed and actually enjoy mathematics.

Using a Declarative Approach. In a declarative approach to instruction, teachers emphasize not only arithmetic facts but how they are related to each other and connected to other concepts the students have already learned. They use elaborative rehearsal and provide for cognitive closure. Furthermore, a declarative approach focuses on capitalizing on the students' innate number sense, intuitive notions of counting by finger manipulation, and an understanding of a base-10 model for expressing quantities. It includes allowing students to create their own procedures for arithmetic computations so that they truly understand the algorithms involved. Researchers have long recognized, and recent studies confirm, that students in the primary grades are capable of constructing their own methods of computation (e.g., Guerrero & Palomaa, 2012).

Understanding the development of mathematical thinking in young students allows teachers to anticipate procedures that students are apt to invent and to find ways to support students as they progress through their understanding of arithmetic operations and relationships. When teachers encourage students to invent alternative problem-solving strategies, the learning objectives are different from those that result from instruction using standard memorization procedures. The emphasis is on making sense and finding meaning in the methods that students create and successfully use.

Mathematical Reasoning. One question that teachers and parents of children in the primary/intermediate grades ask is whether the brains of these children have developed sufficiently to carry out reasoning skills. The answer: yes, but it depends on which reasoning skill. By the age of 6, most students can demonstrate deductive reasoning using concrete objects. Abstract reasoning, on the other hand, is possible but more difficult, and it becomes easier in the early teen years and over the course of adolescence as the brain's frontal lobes mature. Teachers of preadolescents can find many activities in books and on the Web designed to enhance reasoning skills. Using activities that move students from concrete to abstract reasoning in effect also moves them from arithmetic thinking to algebraic thinking (Hewitt, 2012).

Advantages of Technology. Teachers in the intermediate grades are sometimes reluctant to use much technology in mathematical investigations because of concerns about undermining students' computational skills. Research studies show that, particularly in middle-grade mathematics, technology, including online peer tutoring, can have positive effects on students' attitudes toward learning, on their confidence in their abilities to do mathematics, and on their motivation and time on task. Furthermore, technology use can help students make significant gains in mathematical achievement and conceptual understanding (e.g., Burns, Kanive, & DeGrande, 2012; Schacter & Jo, 2016; Tsuei, 2012).

Research studies also suggest that using technology for nonroutine (i.e., novel) applications, such as exploring number concepts and solving complex problems, leads students to greater conceptual understanding and higher achievement, whereas using technology for routine calculations does not. Students often perceive calculators as simply computational tools. But when they engage in mathematical exploration and problem solving with calculators and other technologies, they broaden their perspective and see these instruments as tools that can enhance their learning and understanding of mathematics (Gibson et al., 2014).

Technology cannot replace the instructional strategies teachers use to deepen a students' understanding of mathematical concepts or their problem-solving skills. However, when used appropriately, it can extend their ability to make sense of mathematics, broaden their mathematical reasoning, improve their computational fluency, and gain access to additional content not available in the classroom. It is equally important for professional development programs to continually update teachers' knowledge of various technologies and their practical application in the teaching-learning process.

High School Grades

As the adolescent brain develops, working memory and attention span increase as well as the brain's pattern-making capabilities and interest in novelty. Teachers ultimately decide whether mathematics is full or devoid of novelty. If adolescents have already mastered a mathematical operation but we continue to give them more of the same assignments, they see no purpose in completing repetitive practice. They lose interest, they see mathematics as boring and hum-drum work, their motivation drops, and their grades slump. Rather, the teacher should find different and meaningful applications of the mathematical operation or concept to maintain interest and attention, key components of motivation. Moreover, the teacher should recognize how much practice each student needs to show mastery and no more.

Novelty and motivation are also undermined by a mathematics curriculum that focuses mainly on a strict formal approach, heavy in memorizing abstract axioms and theorems. This model from the 1970s was based on the brain-computer metaphor—the notion that cognitive processing in the human brain is similar to that in a computer. But neuroscience reveals that the differences between the brain's operations and those of a computer's are far greater than their similarities. An adolescent's brain, unlike that of a computer, is a structured entity that requires facts only insofar as they can be integrated into prior knowledge to elucidate new situations. It is adapted to represent continuous quantities and to mentally manipulate them in analogical form. Conversely, it is not innately prepared to handle vast arrays of axioms or symbolic algorithms. For most people, to do so requires heavy doses of motivation, interest, and novelty.

The *Common Core State Standards for Mathematics* (National Governors Association Center for Best Practices & Council of Chief State School Officers, 2010) shift away from a heavy emphasis on memorization to deep understanding of fewer key concepts and applying that understanding to solve problems in real-world situations. Word problems can be anathema to high school students if their content deals with meaningless topics that have little relevance to their world. Topics in word problems that catch the interest of adolescents include the following:

- probability (does gambling pay off?)
- calculating financial deals (financing the purchase of a car)
- broader social issues (calculating population growth)
- personal issues (determining the best cell phone plan, deciding whether it is best to work by the hour or for a fixed salary)

Recall that meaning is one of the major criteria that the brain uses to determine whether new learning gets encoded into long-term memory. Mathematical experiences that are connected to real teenage-world issues will likely help high school students be successful in their mathematics achievement.

DIFFICULTIES IN LEARNING MATHEMATICS

Why are some children so adept at mathematical calculations, while others struggle despite motivation and considerable effort? The answer to this question is complicated by at least two considerations:

1. We need to distinguish whether the poor achievement is due to inadequate instruction or some other environmental factor, or whether it is due to an actual cognitive disability.

2. Exactly how is mathematics being taught? Instructional approaches can determine whether a cognitive deficit is really a disability at all. For example, one instructional approach emphasizes conceptual understanding while deemphasizing the learning of procedures and mathematical facts. Another approach places heavy emphasis on procedures and facts. A student with a deficit in retrieving arithmetic facts might not be considered as having a learning disability in the first approach because of the deemphasis on memory-based information. However, that deficit would be a serious disability in the second approach. Recognizing this dichotomy, the *Common Core State Standards for Mathematics* (National Governors Association Center for Best Practices & Council of Chief State School Officers, 2010) have focused more on conceptual understanding than on memorization.

Standardized testing is not a reliable means of detecting the *cause* of mathematical difficulties. They include many types of items, and it is possible for students to demonstrate average performance in some areas of mathematics and show deficits in others. Recent research into identifying the factors that may cause students to have difficulties with mathematics can be sorted into two categories: environmental and neurological.

Environmental Factors

Student Attitudes About Mathematics. In modern American society, reading and writing have become the main measures of a good student. Mathematics ability has been regarded more as a specialized function than as a general indicator of intelligence. Consequently, the stigma of not being able to do mathematics was reduced and became socially acceptable. Just hearing their parent say, "I wasn't very good at math" allowed children to embrace the social attitudes that regard mathematics failure as acceptable and routine.

Despite the high-stakes testing and heavy emphasis that schools have placed in recent years on raising standards, student attitudes about mathematics have not improved much. Students (including those who like mathematics) find making nonmathematical mistakes much more embarrassing than making mathematical mistakes. Furthermore, regardless of the efforts toward gender equity, female high school students still rate themselves as less confident in mathematics than their male peers (Martinez & Guzman, 2013). Apparently, many students do not view competence in mathematics as a basic skill. Until this view changes, students will have little incentive to master mathematics.

Fear of Mathematics (Math Anxiety). Anxiety about learning and doing mathematics (commonly referred to as *math anxiety*) has been around a long time. It can be described as a feeling of tension that interferes with the manipulations of numbers and the solving of mathematical problems in academic and ordinary life situations. Students at all grade levels often develop a fear (or phobia) of mathematics because of negative experiences in their past or current mathematics class, or they have a simple lack of self-confidence with numbers. It appears to be more prevalent in girls than in boys (Devine, Fawcett, Szucs, & Dowker, 2012; Smetackova, 2015). Math anxiety conjures up fear of some type. Perhaps it is the fear that one won't be able to do the calculations, or the fear that it's too difficult, or the fear of failure that often stems from having a lack of confidence. In people with math anxiety, the fear of failure often causes their minds to draw a blank, leading to more frustration and more blanks. Added pressure of having time limits on mathematics tests also raises the levels of anxiety for many students.

Typically, students with this phobia have a limited understanding of mathematical concepts. They may rely mainly on memorizing procedures, rules, and routines without much conceptual understanding, so panic soon sets in. Mathematics phobia can be as challenging as any learning disability, but it is important to remember that these students have neurological systems for computation that are normal. They need help primarily in replacing the memory of failure with the possibility of success. As we shall see later, students with mathematical disorders, on the other hand, have a neurological deficit that results in persistent difficulty in processing numbers.

Regardless of the source, the most prevalent consequences of this anxiety are poor achievement and poor grades in mathematics. One reason for the poor performance is biological. Anxiety of any type causes the body to release the hormone cortisol into the bloodstream. Cortisol's main function is to refocus the brain on the source of the anxiety and to determine what action to take to relieve the stress. Heart rate increases and other physical indicators of worry appear. Meanwhile, the frontal lobe is no longer interested in learning or processing mathematical operations because it has to deal with what appears to be a threat to the individual's safety. As a result, the student cannot focus on the learning task at hand and has to cope with the frustration of inattention. Furthermore, the anxious feelings disrupt the working memory's ability to manipulate and retain numbers and numerical expressions (Trezise & Reeve, 2014; Vukovic, Kieffer, Bailey, & Harari, 2013).

Alleviating Math Anxiety. Here are five areas that research studies suggest can lessen math anxiety and improve student achievement in mathematics (Beilock & Maloney, 2015; Finlayson, 2014; Geist, 2010; Powell, 2015).

- **Teacher Attitudes.** Teacher attitude appears to be the most dominant factor in molding student attitudes about mathematics. Teachers can maintain a positive attitude in themselves and their students when they show mathematics as a great human invention and how it contributes to other disciplines as well as society; promote student curiosity by assigning interesting and relevant tasks; focus on goals and process rather than finding the correct answer; and create opportunities for success.

- **Curriculum.** Studies of mathematics curriculum in kindergarten through Grade 8 show much repetition of subject matter. One comprehensive study of 183 mathematics topics taught in kindergarten through Grade 8 by more than 7,000 teachers in 27 states showed a considerable amount of redundancy (Polikoff, 2012). From 70 to 80 percent of instructional time from Grade 3 through middle school repeated material taught in the previous grade. Thus, only 20 to 30 percent of time was devoted to new topics. The study also noted that the *Common Core State Standards for Mathematics* have even more redundancy in the early grades but much less repetition in middle school. Math anxiety emerges as students move into the intermediate and secondary grades because the curriculum shifts from concrete applications to increasing degrees of abstractness. Teachers can help in this transition by devoting more time in elementary school to new material, discovery, and application; pruning the mathematics curriculum to eliminate less important items and working toward a deeper understanding of major topics; and providing activities that constantly encourage students to apply their knowledge to new ideas.

- **Instructional Strategies.** Another important factor in how well students learn mathematics is the quality of the teaching. Studies show that student achievement in mathematics is strongly linked to the teacher's expertise in mathematics. Students of a teacher expert in mathematics perform better on achievement tests than students of a teacher with limited training or a lower level of competence in mathematics (e.g., Henry et al., 2013). Teaching techniques that center on "explain-practice-memorize" are among the main sources of math anxiety because the focus is on memorization rather than on understanding the concepts and reasoning involved. Students taught with this approach do not have the skills to successfully deal with material that goes beyond memorization. Students are more successful in mathematics classes when teachers possess a mathematics skill level that goes beyond basic understanding; understand student confusion and frustration; limit the frequency of memorizing, doing rote practice, searching for one right answer, and making calculations that can be performed by computers and calculators; develop meaning by showing practical applications that are related to students' lives; and encourage students to investigate and formulate questions involving mathematical relationships.

- **Classroom Culture.** Classroom culture can be defined as the norms and behaviors that regularly guide classroom interactions. Structured, rigid classes in which there is little opportunity for debate can become a source of math anxiety. If the culture includes that inevitable search for the one right answer, then students feel there is no recognition or reward for the cognitive processes involved. The culture may also place a strong emphasis on answering quickly and on timed tests. Placing a strong emphasis on speed does not encourage students to reflect on their thinking processes or to analyze their results. Math anxiety is likely to be lower in classrooms in which teachers create a culture where students can ask questions, discover learning, and explore ideas; provide an environment where students can feel secure in taking risks and not feel embarrassed for giving wrong answers; discourage valuing speed over time for reflection; and encourage students to make sense of what they are learning rather than just memorize steps or procedures.

- **Assessment.** Tests can be the primary source of students' anxiety in any subject. But the anxiety may be greater in those subjects, such as mathematics, that are the basis for the high-stakes tests that have emerged since the adoption of curriculum standards and minimum competencies. Tests often diminish the students' confidence because they have no flexibility in the testing process, and as a result, the tests do not stir their curiosity or inventiveness. Furthermore, tests are often used to determine which students will enter classes of advanced mathematics. One can question whether poor assessment techniques should be used to determine how students advance in the mathematics curriculum, especially since these decisions can affect their post–high school choices. Teachers can alleviate the math anxiety caused by testing when they limit class tests and do not time them, because timed tests increase the pressure on students, which disrupts processing in both working and long-term memories; reduce the weight given to tests in determining grades, ranking students, or measuring isolated skills; include multiple methods of assessment such as oral, written, or demonstration formats; and provide feedback that focuses on a lack of effort rather than a lack of ability, so that students remain confident in their ability to improve.

Neurological Factors

One major problem facing researchers in the field of mathematics disabilities is distinguishing those factors that *cause* difficulties with mathematics from those that are the *consequences* of these factors. Because students with moderate mathematical difficulties are often of average or higher intelligence and possess good reading skills, the brain regions involved in mathematics difficulties are likely localized or modular. In other words, the neurological causes of mathematics difficulties can be limited and not affect other cognitive areas, such as reading.

Dyscalculia. The condition that causes persistent problems with processing numerical calculations is referred to as *dyscalculia* (pronounced dis-kal-KOOL-ee-ah), from the Greek meaning "counting badly." Dyscalculia is a difficulty in conceptualizing numbers, number relationships, outcomes of numerical operations, and estimation, that is, what to expect as an outcome of an operation. If the condition is present from birth, it is called *developmental dyscalculia*. Genetic studies of twins reveal that developmental dyscalculia is moderately inheritable (Tosto, Malykh, Voronin, Plomin, & Kovas, 2013). If the condition results from an injury to the brain after birth, it is called *acquired dyscalculia*. Whether developmental or acquired, for most individuals, this disorder is the result of specific disabilities in basic numerical processing and is not necessarily the consequence of deficits in other cognitive abilities (Kucian, 2016; Landerl, Göbel, & Moll, 2013).

Possible Causes. The difficulty that individuals with developmental dyscalculia have may be due to deficits in the number processing regions of the brain. Several fMRI studies have found that the parts of the brain responsible for making the approximations necessary for number sense are much less activated in children with developmental dyscalculia than in typical children. However, brain activation during exact calculations was similar for both groups (e.g., Cappelletti & Price, 2014).

Individuals with visual processing weaknesses almost always display difficulties with mathematics. This is probably because success in mathematics requires one to visualize numbers and mathematical situations, especially in algebra and geometry. Students with sequencing difficulties also may have dyscalculia because they cannot remember the order of mathematical operations or the specific formulas needed to complete a set of computations.

> *The neurological basis of developmental dyscalculia is an impairment in the person's innate number sense capabilities.*

Genetic factors also seem to play a significant role. Studies of identical twins reveal close mathematics scores. Children from families with a history of mathematical giftedness or learning disorders show common aptitudes with other family members. Girls born with Turner's syndrome (a condition caused by the partial or complete absence of one of the two X chromosomes normally found in females) usually display dyscalculia, among other learning problems (Mazzocco & Hanich, 2010).

Dyscalculia and Reading Disorders. Students with dyscalculia can also have developmental reading difficulties or dyslexia. Although these disorders do not appear to be genetically linked, nearly 50 percent of children with mathematics difficulties also have reading difficulties (Ashkenazi et al., 2013). No one knows for sure why these conditions appear simultaneously in so many children. Some research suggests this comorbidity may be because both reading and mathematics share cerebral regions responsible for working memory, processing speed, and verbal comprehension (Willcutt et al., 2013). It is also possible that students with both disorders are less successful in solving mathematics problems than those who have only dyscalculia because they have difficulty translating word problems into mathematical expressions.

Dyscalculia and Attention Deficit/Hyperactivity Disorder (ADHD). Because many children with ADHD have difficulty with mathematics, some researchers wondered whether these two conditions had related genetic components, increasing the possibility that they would be inherited together. But studies show that these two disorders are transmitted independently and are connected to distinctly different genetic regions (Hart et al., 2010). These findings underscore the need for separate identification and treatment strategies for children with both conditions.

MATHEMATICS FOR ENGLISH LANGUAGE LEARNERS

English language learners (ELLs) are the fastest growing population in the U.S. public schools, the largest portion being native Spanish speakers. ELLs have difficulty learning mathematics, as evidenced by their scores in Grades 4 and 8 on the National Assessment of Educational Progress over recent years (National Center for Education Statistics, 2013). They are consistently lower than non-ELL students. Clearly, there is an achievement gap in mathematics that educators need to address.

Language is a major concern in mathematics teaching because most of the content is conveyed through oral language, as teachers tend to do the majority of the talking in mathematics classes. ELL students do not derive a significant portion of their learning from reading mathematics textbooks. The language issue becomes more significant now because the *Common Core State Standards for Mathematics* curriculum shifts instruction in mathematics from more emphasis on numbers to more emphasis on word problems (National Governors Association Center for Best Practices & Council of Chief State School Officers, 2010). Consequently, to understand and be successful in mathematics, students need to be able to read, solve problems, and communicate using technical language in a specialized context—and to properly discuss and explain mathematics content, teachers must use technical language. Students lacking proficiency in the English language and in the specialized language of mathematics understandably frustrate teachers who are faced with an increasing number of ELL students in their classrooms.

Cognitive processing is closely tied to language processing. Consequently, mathematics teachers of ELL students need to determine whether the students have mastered a concept even if they have difficulty expressing their understanding in English. One effective method for dealing with this issue and assisting students in solving mathematics problems is called *reciprocal teaching*. In reciprocal teaching, students read in small groups, using cognitive strategies to comprehend the text. One successful approach is to teach ELL students how to use four cognitive strategies to help them deal with the language challenge: (1) clarifying the meaning of words and phrases so the students know the basic components of the problem, (2) questioning extensively to identify the key elements of the problem, (3) summarizing to each other the purpose of the problem, and (4) devising a plan to solve the problem. Frequent use of this strategy improves ELL performance in mathematics.

Whatever success ELL students have in learning mathematics comes down, as always, to individual teachers. Teachers should have the information and strategies they need to be effective in conveying mathematics concepts to these students, understand how to implement them, and have the necessary professional development and administrative support to carry it out.

WHAT'S COMING UP?

In too many schools, budget constraints and anxiety over high-stakes testing are reducing the amount of time that students are exposed to the arts and physical education. Yet, scientific evidence continues to accumulate about the positive impact that music, visual arts, and movement have on brain growth and development. The next chapter discusses some of that evidence and argues why we must preserve the arts and physical education if schools are to be truly brain compatible.

PRACTITIONER'S CORNER

Teaching to the Whole Brain—General Guidelines

Although the two hemispheres process information differently, we learn best when both are fully engaged in learning. Just as we would catch more balls with both hands, we catch more information with both hemispheres processing and integrating the learning. Teachers should design lessons so that students can integrate the new learning into a meaningful whole. In doing so, students get opportunities to develop both their strong and their weak learning preferences. Here are some ways to do that in daily planning:

- **Deal With Concepts Verbally *and* Visually.** When teaching new concepts, alternate discussion with visual models. Write key words on the board that represent the critical attributes of the concept, then use a simple diagram to show relationships among the key ideas within and between concepts. This helps students attach both auditory and visual cues to the information, increasing the likelihood that sense and meaning will emerge and that they will be able to accurately retrieve the information later. When using a video presentation, show the *smallest* segment with *maximum* meaning, then stop the video and have students discuss what was shown.

- **Design Effective Visual Aids.** How we position information on a visual aid (e.g., overhead transparency, board, easel pad, video screen) indicates the relationships of concepts and ideas. Vertical positioning implies a step or time sequence or a hierarchy. Thus, writing

    Delaware

    Pennsylvania

    New Jersey

is appropriate to indicate the order of these states' admission into the Union (chronology).

    Writing them horizontally

    Delaware, Pennsylvania, New Jersey

implies a parallel relationship that is appropriate to identify any three populous eastern states. Avoid writing information in visual aids in a haphazard way whenever a parallel or a hierarchical relationship among the elements is important for students to remember.

- **Discuss Concepts Logically and Intuitively.** Concepts should be presented to students from different perspectives. For example, if you are teaching about the U.S. Civil War, talk about the factual (logical) events, such as major causes, battles, and the economic and political impacts. When the students understand these, move on to more thought-provoking (intuitive) activities, such as asking what might have happened if Lincoln had not been assassinated, or what our country might be like now if the Confederate states had won the war.

  After teaching basic concepts in arithmetic, ask students to design a number system to a base other than 10. This is a simple and interesting process that helps students understand the scheme of our decimal number system. In literature, after reading part of a story or play, ask students to write a plausible ending using the facts already presented. In science, after giving some facts about the structure of the periodic table of the elements, ask students to explain how they would experiment with a new element to determine its place in the table.

- **Avoid Conflicting Messages.** Make sure that your words, tone, and pacing match your gestures, facial expressions, and body language. The left hemisphere interprets words literally, but the right hemisphere evaluates body language, tone, and content. If the two hemispheric interpretations are inconsistent, a conflicting message is generated. As a result, the student withdraws internally to resolve the conflict and is no longer focused on the learning.

- **Design Activities and Assessments for Different Learning Preferences.** Students with different learning preferences express themselves in different ways. Give students options in testing and in completing assignments so they can select the option best suited to their learning preferences. For example, after completing a major unit on the U.S. Civil War, students could write term papers on particular aspects of the war; draw pictures; create and present plays or write songs of important events; or construct models that represent battles, the surrender at Appomattox, and so on. Simulations, role-playing, designing computer programs, and building models are all effective assessment tools in addition to the traditional paper-and-pencil tests.

PRACTITIONER'S CORNER

Strategies for Teaching to the Whole Brain

Students learn best when teachers use strategies that engage the whole brain. Although current research shows that both hemispheres work together in many processing activities, it is still useful to know teaching strategies that involve the skills inherent in—but not necessarily limited to—each hemisphere. *Remember that we cannot educate just one hemisphere.* Rather, we are ensuring that our daily instruction includes activities that stimulate the whole brain. Here are some teaching strategies to consider:

- **Efficient Classroom Organization.** Have an efficient work area. Distribute the talkers around the room as they will spark discussions when needed.

- **Relevant Bulletin Boards.** Organize bulletin boards to be relevant to the current content and easily understood. Encourage students to bring in their own appropriate additions to the board.

- **Clean the Board.** Make clean erasures on the board. This reduces the chance that previous and unrelated word cues will become inadvertently associated with the new topic under discussion.

- **Use a Multisensory Approach.** Let students read, write, draw, act out, and compute often in all subject areas.

- **Use Metaphors.** Create and analyze metaphors to enhance meaning and encourage higher-order thinking.

- **Encourage Punctuality.** Stress the importance of being on time. Encourage students to carry agendas.

- **Encourage Goal Setting.** Teach students to set study goals for themselves, stick to their goals, and reward themselves when they achieve them.

- **Stimulate Logical Thinking.** Ask "What if?" questions to encourage logical thinking as students consider all possibilities for solving problems. Suggest sites on the Internet where they can find challenging problems related to what they are studying.

- **Give Students Some Options.** For example, allow them to do oral or written reports. Oral reports help students piece concepts together while requiring fewer mechanics than written work. Some students may prefer to present a short play or skit.

- **Use Visual Representations.** Use the board and video screens to show illustrations, cartoons, charts, timelines, and graphs that encourage students to visually organize information and relationships. Have students use appropriate Internet sites to create or collect their own visual representations of the new concepts.

- **Help Students Make Connections.** Tying lessons together and using proper closure (see Chapter 3) allow the brain to compare new information to what has already been learned.

- **Encourage Direct Experiences.** Facilitate direct experiences with new learning through solving authentic problems and involvement in real-world situations.

- **Allow for Student-to-Student Interaction.** Students need time to interact with each other as they discuss the new learnings. Remember, whoever explains, learns.

- **Teach for Transfer.** Teach students to use generalities and perceptions. Have them use metaphors and similes to make connections between unlike items. This is an important function for future transfer of learning.

- **Incorporate Hands-On Learning.** Provide frequent opportunities for experiential and hands-on learning. Students need to realize that they must discover and order relationships in the real world.

PRACTITIONER'S CORNER

Concept Mapping—General Guidelines

Concept mapping consists of extracting ideas and terms from curriculum content and plotting them visually to show and name the relationships among them. The learner establishes a visual representation of relations between concepts that might have been presented only verbally. Integrating visual and verbal activities enhances understanding of concepts whether they are abstract, concrete, verbal, or nonverbal. The key to concept mapping is the clear indication of the relationship that one item has to another. West et al. (1991) summarize nine types of cognitive relationships:

Name	Relationship	Example
1. Classification	A is an example of B	A cat is a mammal.
2. Defining/subsuming	A is a property of B	All mammals have hair.
3. Equivalence	A is identical to B	$2(a + b) = 2(b + a)$
4. Similarity	A is similar to B	A donkey is like a mule.
5. Difference	A is unlike B	A spider is not an insect.
6. Quantity	A is greater/less than B	A right angle is greater than an acute angle.
7. Time sequence	A occurs before/after B	In mitosis, prophase occurs before metaphase.
8. Causal	A causes B	Combustion produces heat.
9. Enabling	A enables/allows B	A person must be at least 18 years old to vote.

Concept mapping uses graphic diagrams to organize and represent the relationships between and among the components. These diagrams are also called *graphic* and *visual organizers.* Studies show that graphic organizers are particularly effective with students who have learning disabilities (Sheriff & Boon, 2014) and with students who are English language learners (Konrad, Joseph, & Itoi, 2011). Students should discuss these different types of relationships and give their own examples before attempting to select a concept map. Numerous sites on the Internet offer dozens of possible organizers. Below are three common types. In each, the relationship between items is written as a legend (for a few examples) or next to the line connecting the items (when there are many examples).

- **Spider maps** best illustrate classification, similarity, and difference relationships.
- **Hierarchy maps** illustrate defining and/or subsuming, equivalence, and quantity relationships.
- **Chain maps** illustrate time sequence, causal, and enabling relationships.

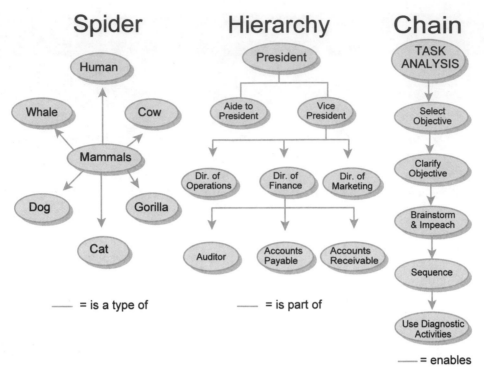

More Types of Concept Maps

- **Story maps** are useful for classifying main ideas with supporting events and information from the story. These are particularly helpful for readers who have difficulty finding the main idea in a piece of writing.
- **Analogy maps** illustrate similarities and differences between new and familiar concepts. This map can help teachers determine whether two concepts are too similar to each other and should, therefore, be taught at different times (see Chapter 4).
- **K-W-L maps** illustrate the degree of new learning that will be needed. The *K* is for what we already *know*; the *W* is for what we *want* to know; and the *L* is for what we *learned.* This map is a useful device for lesson closure (see Chapter 2).

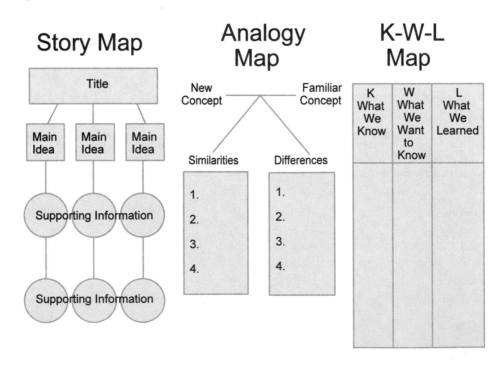

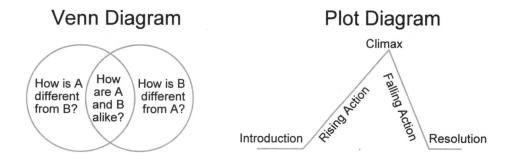

Venn Diagram

Plot Diagram

A Brace Map

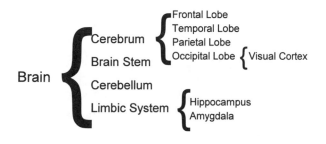

More Types of Concept Maps

- **Venn diagrams** map the similarities and differences between two concepts. Like analogy maps, these help teachers determine if two concepts are too similar to each other to be taught in the same lesson.
- **Plot diagrams** are used to find the major parts of a novel.
- **A brace map** shows subsets of larger items.

Directions: Time for practice. Select a broad curriculum concept, such as energy, time, or forms of government. Draw an appropriate graphic organizer in the box below and fill it in with the major parts of the concept. Present your work to other participants.

PRACTITIONER'S CORNER

Acquiring Another Language

When Should Children Learn Another Language? Although the brain maintains its ability to learn throughout life, it is quite clear from the research described earlier in this text that language learning occurs most easily during the first 10 years or so. We should take advantage of this window of opportunity if we offer additional languages in schools.

Why Learn Another Language? In addition to knowing our native language, we benefit significantly from learning another language. Language instruction should start as soon as possible. Here are some reasons for learning another language at an early age:

- It enriches and enhances a child's mental development.
- It gives students more flexibility in thinking, greater sensitivity to language, and a better ear for listening. (The brain learns to respond to phonemes that are different from the native language.)
- It improves understanding of a child's native language. (Unless a language or hearing difficulty exists, research does not support the claim that learning a second language early will interfere with learning the native language.)
- It gives a child the ability to communicate with people he or she would otherwise not have the chance to know.
- It opens the door to other cultures and helps a child understand and appreciate people from other countries. (This is important as our country becomes increasingly multicultural.)
- It gives a student a head start in language requirements for college.
- It increases job opportunities in many careers where knowing another language is a considerable asset.

What Are the Characteristics of an Effective K–6 Additional Language Program?

- **All students** have access to the program regardless of race/ethnic origin, learning styles, home language, or future academic goals.
- **Program goals** are consistent with the time devoted to additional language instruction. In the primary grades, the main goal is to hear the sounds, flow, and syntax of another language. There are different types of K–6 second language programs that achieve different levels of language proficiency and require different time commitments.
- **Sequence** of language instruction should be available through the K–12 school years. Acquisition of another language requires consistent practice, so a K–12 sequence is crucial to mastery. For this reason, instruction in other languages is often exempted from block scheduling formats that limit classes to one semester per year.
- **Systematic curriculum development** in content of another language is part of the school plan. Look for ways to include these language experiences across the curriculum.
- **Native speakers** must be used for the primary-grade instruction to ensure that the young brain hears authentic language sounds.
- **Connections between language and culture** are made explicit so that the learners understand the development of the additional language in the context of its culture.

Teaching Strategies for Acquiring Another Language

Teaching strategies for instruction in another language vary with the age of the learner who is beginning the study. Primary-grade teaching focus is mainly on recognizing, discriminating, and practicing the phonemes of the other language, as spoken by native speakers. Grammar is not taught, per se, but implied through extensive student conversation. In the intermediate and later grades (including adult levels), the main goal is to develop communication competencies so that the student feels comfortable speaking, writing, and thinking the other language. Thus, teachers of other languages and of English language learners should follow a sequence that begins with young learners. This sequence aims to do the following:

- **Develop Communication Competence.** One of the primary goals of learning another language is to gain competence in communication. This involves acquiring four major competencies, requiring integration of the verbal and nonverbal aspects of language as well as right- and left-hemisphere processing. Teachers should keep these four competencies in mind as they select their instructional strategies:

Grammatical Competence. The degree to which a student has mastered the formal linguistic code of the language including vocabulary, rules of punctuation, word formation, and sentence structure. This entails the analytic and sequential processing of the left hemisphere.

Sociolinguistic Competence. The ability to use grammatical forms appropriately in contexts that range from very informal to very formal styles. It includes varying the choice of verbal and nonverbal language to adapt the speech to a specific person or social context, and this requires sensitivity to individual and sociocultural differences. This is essentially the right hemisphere's ability to contextualize language.

Discourse Competence. The ability to combine form and thought into a coherent expression. It involves knowing how to use conjunctions, adverbs, and transitional phrases to achieve continuity of thought. This requires the integration of both hemispheres: the analytic ability of the left hemisphere to generate the grammatical features and the use of the right hemisphere to synthesize them into meaningful, coherent wholes.

Strategic Competence. The ability to use verbal and nonverbal communication strategies, such as body language and circumlocution, to compensate for the user's imperfect knowledge of the language, and to negotiate meaning.

This research points out the need for teachers to ensure that the nonverbal form of intellect is not neglected in second language acquisition. In planning lessons, teachers should

- not rely heavily on grammar, vocabulary memorization, and mechanical translations, especially during the early stages of instruction;
- do more with contextual language, trial and error, brainstorming of meaning, visual activities, and role-playing; and
- give students the opportunity to establish the contextual networking they need to grasp meaning, nuance, and idiomatic expressions.

When these skills are in place, shift to more work on enlarging students' vocabulary and knowledge of grammar.

PRACTITIONER'S CORNER

Considerations for Teaching Reading

Reading is the result of a complex process that relies heavily on previously acquired spoken language, but also requires the learning of specific skills that are not innate to the human brain. Because of the many steps involved in learning to read, challenges can occur anywhere along the way. Children often devise strategies to overcome problems but may need help in getting to the next step. As with learning any skill, reading requires practice.

The scientific research suggests that reading instruction include a balance between the development of phonemic awareness and the use of enriched texts to help learners with syntax and semantics. Here are some basic points to consider when teaching reading.

Basic Guidelines for a Balanced Approach

- **No one reading program is best for all children.** Successful teachers of reading have developed activities that differentiate among their students according to their current level of readiness to read.
- **Developing phonemic awareness.** The brain reads by breaking words into sounds. Children first need to be taught the 44+ basic sounds (phonemes) in the English language and be able to manipulate these sounds successfully. This is known as phonemic-awareness training. The more difficulty a learner has in beginning reading, the more likely the need for concentrated practice on phonemic awareness.
- **Mastering the Alphabetic Principle (decoding).** Beginning readers need to be able to recognize the sounds represented by the letters of the alphabet. The better that a learner can *sound out* words, the faster the brain learns to match what it sees to what it hears. Therefore, readers should be taught to discern the individual sounds within words as they read them, and to say them aloud. *Dog* is "duh-awh-guh," and *bat* is "bah-ah-tuh." This practice helps the brain remember the decoding process of sight-to-sound so crucial to accurate and fast reading. However, problems develop when the reader's eyes move faster than the sound processing system can decode the phonemes. In this case, slow down the visual speed by having the student move a finger under each letter (grapheme). This also ensures that readers keep their eyes moving across the page, not fixating them into a stare, which also retards the reading process.
- **Phonics Is Important.** Phonics is the instructional approach that helps students master the alphabetic principle. It is an important component of learning to read but should not be taught as a separate unit through drill and rote memorization. Students lose interest and motivation to read. It is more effective to teach phonics as a means of developing spelling strategies and word analysis skills.
- **Practice for Comprehension.** Once the alphabetic principle is learned, practice in reading aloud is needed to develop speed and accuracy so that learners can comprehend what they are reading and get a sense of the language's syntax. This also helps teachers hear how accurately the student has matched the visual grapheme with the auditory phoneme.
- **Read With the Learners.** Teachers should read aloud as learners follow along in the text. This helps students with prosody—hearing the flow, rhythm, and tonal changes of the language. Have students move a finger under the words to show that they are correctly matching what they hear the teacher say with what they see on paper.

- **Read to the Learners.** Read literature slightly advanced for the learner while students listen, even with their eyes closed, to absorb the richness, rhythm, imagery, sound, and feeling of language in different contexts.
- **Introduce Literature.** Move on to interesting books and other forms of literature for practice and motivation to read. At this point, it is important to emphasize the contextual nature of the English language. Most meaning and pronunciation comes from *how* words are used in relation to all other words in the sentence (the context). Compare, for example, "The boy picked up the *lead* weight" to "The boy had a *lead* part in the school play."
- **Avoid** asking new readers to guess the sounds of words if they have not had phonemic-awareness training. Without the training, they have no clue how the word should sound, and mispronouncing the word will only reinforce the incorrect association between the grapheme and the phoneme. Remember that practice makes permanent, not necessarily perfect.

The chart on the next page is a reasonable hierarchy to be considered for teaching reading based on a deeper scientific understanding of the complexity of how the brain reads. In this hierarchy, emphasis is placed on ensuring accurate phonemic awareness at the very beginning of reading instruction. More evidence is emerging from brain scans of children reading that problems arise when there is poor phonemic awareness, thus confusing the decoding system.

EXAMPLE OF A HIERARCHY FOR TEACHING READING	
Note: This procedure for teaching reading reflects the research on how the brain learns to read. It balances the early need for solid phonemic awareness with the later introduction of literary samples illustrating the more complex semantic and syntactic elements of language.	
Semantic Level: The learners recognize that the meaning of words can change in different contexts. The teacher selects a variety of literature examples to illustrate contextual variations of language.	Students are likely to master these skills with literary texts that are rich with writing that contains syntactic and semantic variations.
Syntax Level: The learners create more complex sentences with correct grammatical structure. The teacher reads stories aloud to help learners develop a sense of syntax by listening to the phrasing and word positions in sentences. They recognize that in the sentences "The dog chased the boy" and "The boy was chased by the dog," the syntax has changed but not the meaning. Having students read aloud allows the teacher to check pronunciation.	
Discourse Level: The learners construct and connect simple sentences in a logical sequence. Their spoken language has already developed some sentence patterns intuitively, such as subject-predicate-object, as in "I want a cookie" or "He throws the ball." Prefixes and suffixes are introduced and practiced.	Students are likely to master these skills faster if they use texts with the words that contain the phonemes being taught. These are called decoded texts.
START HERE: **Phonological Level:** This level focuses on developing phonological awareness and mastering the alphabetic principle. Learners are processing the basic sound elements of language. Students read aloud to ensure that the correct connections are made between the 44 English phoneme sounds and the 26 letters of the alphabet. Then practice with rhyming, word recognition, and meaning.	

PRACTITIONER'S CORNER

Reading Guidelines for All Teachers

To some extent, all teachers are teachers of reading. Beyond the primary grades, students read to learn, and teachers place heavy reliance on their students' ability to acquire information through reading. Because this reliance increases substantially in the upper grades, reading ability is a major determinant of student success in high school. Reading in all subject areas is likely to be more successful when teachers help students use reading skills efficiently and effectively. Here are some strategies to consider (Sousa, 2014):

- **Use direct instruction** to clearly identify important concepts in the reading and explain why we are learning them. Ask students to summarize the main points you just made. This helps the students determine sense and meaning. The amount of reading assigned should be just enough to accomplish the task. Don't overwhelm students with nonessential reading, especially in subject areas where they lack confidence.
- **Conquer vocabulary** by defining any new words or words used in an unfamiliar context. This should be done *before* assigning the reading.
- **Help with comprehension** by advising students to scan for key words and phrases that aid in comprehension, and to ask themselves questions like the following: How much do I need to read in this sitting? Why am I reading this? What's the main point? Why is it important? What else is this like that I've already learned? Can I summarize in my own words what I just read?
- **Talk, Talk, and Talk Some More.** You will remember that talk is a very powerful learning and memory tool. When working together, students should ask each other questions about the text they are reading, summarize main points, and clarify anything they did not understand. Cooperative learning groups is an effective strategy to accomplish this sharing, especially in classes that have a wide range of student abilities, including reading.
- **Use Graphic Organizers.** Have students use or design their own graphic organizers and concept maps to help understand the major points in their reading. This is particularly useful in textbooks and nonfiction reading that is full of detail.
- **Add Novelty.** Add novelty (Chapter 3) so that students don't see reading as drudgery. For example, get students to speculate on what might happen next in a story, or have them write their own plausible endings. Consider giving them the option to write a song or a poem or a skit to illustrate some of the story's main events or characters. Let them create their own stories, plays, or publications, which they can read or perform for other students.
- **Incorporate supplemental textbooks** that cover the same material as the course text but are written at a lower reading level. This may require several books because it is unlikely that one book will cover all the course content.
- **Establish in-class vertical files**, on both paper and discs, of magazine and newspaper articles about subjects found in the course text. Update the files periodically and encourage students to contribute to the files when they come across an appropriate article.
- **Use audiovisual aids.** These are a great help to students who have reading problems. Many students have become acclimated to a multimedia environment. Whenever possible, use video clips, audio resources, computer programs, television, interactive whiteboards, and other technology to supplement and accompany direct instruction.

PRACTITIONER'S CORNER

Instructional Considerations for Teaching PreK–12 Mathematics

Based on current cognitive neuroscience, a reasonable model for teaching mathematics to children and adolescents would proceed through four major steps. The first step would be to build on young children's intuitions about number sense, quantitative manipulations, and counting. These innate talents are strongly rooted in developing neural networks and should be cultivated with concrete activities rather than stunted with paper worksheets. Activities and instruction should play to these students' natural curiosity with amusing number puzzles and problems.

The next step is to introduce symbolic notation in mathematics, emphasizing how it offers a powerful and convenient shortcut when manipulating quantities. It is important at this point to continue to tie the symbolic knowledge once again to the quantitative intuitions. In this way, the symbolic representations become part of the intuitive network instead of being memorized as a separate and unrelated language.

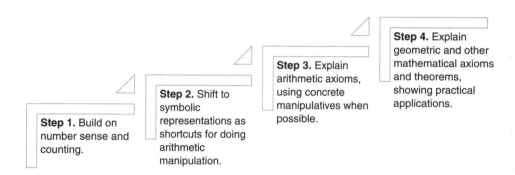

In Step 3, introduce the preadolescent brain to arithmetic axioms. Appropriate concrete manipulatives should be used here as much as possible because we are moving into that critical time when students can be turned off by the increasingly abstract nature of symbolic mathematics. Later, as adolescents, their brain's frontal lobe becomes more adept at higher-order thinking and logic. So in Step 4, introduce and explain mathematical and geometric axioms and theorems. But it is still necessary to show practical applications whenever possible. Remember, when students understand and recognize practical uses for what they are learning, they can attach meaning and thus increase their chances of retention.

I certainly recognize that this model may be simplistic. On the other hand, one reason that students get turned off mathematics is that we often do not try hard enough to keep relating what they are experiencing in the classroom to concrete and practical applications. There are few school subjects in which teachers hear the lament, "Why do I have to know this?" more than in mathematics. That observation alone should be ample warning that we have to work harder at helping students find meaning in mathematics.

CHAPTER 5: BRAIN ORGANIZATION AND LEARNING

Key Points to Ponder

Jot down on this page key points, ideas, strategies, and resources you want to consider later. This sheet is your personal journal summary and will help to jog your memory.

_____

_____

.

_____

_____

_____

_____

_____

_____

_____

_____

_____

_____

6

The Brain
and the Arts

The quality of civilization can be measured through its music, dance, drama, architecture, visual art, and literature. We must give our children knowledge and understanding of civilization's most profound works.

—Ernest L. Boyer

Chapter Highlights

This chapter discusses how recent brain imaging studies are helping us understand the role and importance of music, the visual arts, and movement in brain growth and cognitive function. It suggests ways to incorporate artistic activities into lessons at all grade levels and in all subject areas.

We have never discovered a culture on this planet, past or present, that doesn't have art. Yet there are a number of cultures—even today—that don't have reading and writing. Why is that? A very likely explanation is that the activities represented by the arts—dance, music, drama, and visual arts—are basic to the human experience and necessary for survival. If they weren't, why would they have been part of every civilization from the Cro-Magnon cave dwellers to the urban citizens of the 21st century?

Readers who are wondering why this chapter is even in this book should read the preceding paragraph at least one more time. Some non-arts-related subject matter teachers in secondary and higher education have questioned the need for this chapter in a basic book about how the brain learns. I try to gently remind them that the arts were part of our ancient cultures long before there was science or mathematics or written history. We survived as a species because of our innate creativity—our ability to solve problems in our primeval environment so we could feed, clothe, shelter, and defend ourselves. And the arts were how we communicated with each other.

Our students come to our schools full of curiosity, eager to explore, and with their own creative ideas about how the world works. But something happens along the way. By the time they reach high school, only a small percentage of students rate themselves as creative. I will leave it to others to speculate on why students seem to feel less creative as they move from elementary to secondary school. My concern here is that we should ensure that all grade level and subject area teachers use instructional strategies that support rather than dampen students' creativity. And that is exactly what art-related activities do when properly implemented.

THE ARTS ARE BASIC TO THE HUMAN EXPERIENCE

As we learn more about the brain, we continue to find clues as to why the activities required for the arts are so fundamental to brain function. Music: It seems that certain structures in the auditory cortex respond only to musical tones. Dance: A portion of the cerebrum and most of the cerebellum are devoted to initiating and coordinating all kinds of movement, from intense running to the delicate sway of the arms. Drama: Specialized areas of the cerebrum focus on spoken language acquisition and call on the limbic system to provide the emotional component. Visual arts: The internal visual processing system can recall reality or create fantasy with the same ease.

These cerebral talents did not develop by accident. They are the result of many centuries of interaction between humans and their environment, and the continued existence of these talents must indicate they contribute in some way to our survival. In those cultures that do not have reading and writing, the arts are the media through which that culture's history, mores, and values are transmitted to the younger generations and perpetuated. They also transmit more basic information necessary for the culture's survival, such as how and what to hunt for food and how to defend the village from predators.

Consequently, art is an important force behind group survival. For example, more than 800 of the nearly 7,000 languages on this planet are spoken in just one place—New Guinea! Each language is totally unrelated to any other known language in New Guinea (or elsewhere) and is spoken by a tribe of just a few thousand people living within a 10-mile radius. Even more astonishing is that each tribe has its own music, visual arts, and dance (Pereltsvaig, 2011).

In modern cultures, the arts are thought of rarely as survival skills, but rather as frills—the esthetic product of a wealthy society with lots of time to spare. In fact, people pay high ticket prices to see the arts performed professionally, leading to the belief that the arts are highly valued. This cultural support is often seen in high schools, which have their choruses, their bands, their drama classes, and an occasional dance troupe.

Yet seldom do public elementary schools enjoy this continuous support, precisely when the young brain is most adept at refining the skills needed to develop artistic talent and creativity (several private school initiatives have been the exception, most notably the Montessori schools and the Waldorf schools). Furthermore, when school budgets get tight, elementary-grade art and music programs are among the first to be reduced or eliminated. Consistent pressure to raise standards and improve reading and mathematics achievement is prompting elementary schools to trade instruction in the arts for more classroom preparation for high-stakes testing. It seems that state testing programs consider it much more important for students to know the letters that make up words and sentences than to know the notes of the scale that produce a melody. Yet our brain has developed elaborate neural networks to process both language and music as different forms of communication. Why would that be if both were not biologically important?

> *We have never discovered a culture on this planet—past or present—that doesn't have music, art, and dance.*

WHY TEACH THE ARTS?

The basic arguments I make here are these:

Video: For a brief video on the importance of arts in education, see

https://www.youtube.com/watch?v=41nVnLm7EZU

- The arts play an important role in human development, enhancing the growth of cognitive, emotional, and psychomotor pathways.
- Schools have an obligation to expose children to the arts at the earliest possible time and to consider the arts as a fundamental—not an optional—curriculum area.
- Learning the arts provides a higher quality of human experience throughout a person's lifetime.
- The skills that the arts develop are creativity, problem solving, critical thinking, communications, self-direction, initiative, and collaboration. All these skills—which align with what many educators now refer to as "21st-century skills"—will be needed by every student in order to survive successfully as an adult in an increasingly complex world.

The Arts and the Young Brain

In Chapter 1, we discuss the explosive growth of dendrites and synaptic connections during the brain's early years. Much of what young children do as play—singing, drawing, dancing—are natural forms of art. These activities engage all the senses and help wire the brain for successful learning. When children enter school, these art activities need to be continued and enhanced. The cognitive areas are developed as the child learns songs and rhymes and creates drawings and finger paintings. The dancing and movements during play develop gross motor skills, and the sum of these activities enhances emotional well-being.

The arts also contribute to the education of young children by helping them realize the breadth of human experience, see the different ways humans express sentiments and convey meaning, and develop subtle and complex forms of thinking (Eisner, 2002b).

The Arts Develop Cognitive Growth

Although the arts are often thought of as separate subjects, like chemistry or algebra, they really are a collection of skills and thought processes that transcend all areas of human engagement. Whether separately or integrated with other subjects, when the arts are taught well, they develop cognitive competencies that benefit learners in every aspect of their education and prepare them for the demands of the 21st century. Here is a list of competencies that young people learn from studying the arts and arts-integrated subjects (Eisner, 2002a; Phillips, 2013):

- **Creativity and the perception of relationships.** Creating a work in music, words, or any other art discipline helps students practice thinking creatively and recognize how parts of a work influence each other and interact. For example, this is the kind of skill that enables an executive to appreciate the way a particular system affects every other subsystem in an organization.

- **Sustained focus.** In the age when digital devices are constantly demanding and dividing our attention, being able to focus for an extended time period is an important skill. This skill is developed through ensemble work. When working with others to create a project, keeping a balance between listening and contributing involves a great deal of concentration and focus. Participants must not only think about their roles, but how their roles contribute to the overall plan of what they are creating.

- **An attention to nuance and nonverbal communication.** The arts teach students that small differences can have large effects. Great amounts of visual reasoning go into decisions about nuance, form, and color to make an art work satisfying. In writing, similarly, great attention to detail in use of language is needed to employ allusion, innuendo, and metaphor. Through their experiences in theater and dance, students learn to breakdown the mechanics of body language. They encounter different ways of moving and learn how those movements communicate different emotions.

- **The perspective that problems can have multiple solutions and questions can have multiple answers.** Artistic creations are the result of constant problem solving. How many ways can I portray a particular emotion through dance, music, or a painting? Good things can be done in different ways. Schools often emphasize learning focused on a single correct answer. In business and in life, most difficult problems require looking at multiple options with differing priorities. This continuing practice in solving problems develops students' understanding and reasoning skills.

- **The ability to shift goals in process.** Work in the arts helps students recognize and pursue goals that were not thought of at the beginning. Too often in schools, the relationship of means to ends is oversimplified. Arts help us see that ends can shift in process.
- **The permission to make decisions in the absence of a rule.** Arithmetic has rules and measurable results, but many other things lack that kind of rule-governed specificity. In the absence of rules, it is personal judgment that allows one to assess what feels right and to decide when a task is well done.
- **The development of perseverance.** When students start playing a musical instrument for the first time, they know that playing Beethoven right away is not possible. However, with continued practice, the students learn the skills and techniques, and their performance improves. Perseverance is a key to skill mastery. As students move into an increasingly competitive world, where people are being asked to continually develop new skills, perseverance will be essential for their success.
- **The use of imagination as the source of content.** Arts enhance the ability to visualize situations and use the mind's eye to determine the rightness of a planned action.
- **The acceptance of operating within constraints.** No system, whether linguistic, numerical, visual, or auditory, covers every purpose. Arts give students a chance to use the constraints of a medium to invent ways to exploit those constraints productively.
- **The ability to see the world from an aesthetic perspective.** Arts help students frame the world in fresh ways—like seeing the Golden Gate Bridge from a design or poetic angle.
- **The development of collaborative skills.** Whether in art or in arts-integrated subject areas, collaboration is almost always needed for a successful outcome. Students learn to work together, share responsibility, and compromise with others to achieve a common goal. They understand that their contribution is needed for the group's success.
- **The gaining of confidence.** Through theater, students learn how to convincingly deliver a message and build the confidence they need to take command of the stage. Theater training gives students the opportunity to move out of their comfort zone and allows them to make mistakes and learn from them in rehearsal. As a result, students gain the confidence to perform in front of large audiences.
- **Receiving constructive feedback.** Constructive feedback about an artistic endeavor is an accepted part of working in the arts. It is important for students to learn that constructive feedback is a valuable part of learning that can help them improve their skills and outcomes.

In recent years, neuroscientists have been developing theories about ways in which art develops cognition. One common element of the current theories is that each art form involves different brain networks, as shown in Figure 6.1 (Posner, Rothbart, Sheese, & Kieras, 2008). Visual arts are processed mainly in the occipital and temporal lobes. The linguistic arts (e.g., prose writing and poetry) involve Broca's and Wernicke's areas (the dotted-line ovals in Figure 6.1)—which you may recall are the primary language areas of the brain. Movement arts are processed through the motor cortex, a thin strip across the top of the brain, indicated by the dotted lines. Music is processed by the auditory cortex, located in the temporal lobes just behind the ears.

Using electroencephalography techniques with children, the researchers discovered that arts training required them to focus and that this concentrated attention and improved cognition. Thus, children who begin participating in arts training at an early age get the benefit of improving their cognitive growth while their brain is still developing. In addition, the arts often involve powerful emotions, and we have already discussed how such emotions enhance cognitive processing and memory.

Figure 6.1 The diagram shows the different brain areas involved in the performance of art forms (adapted from Posner et al., 2008).

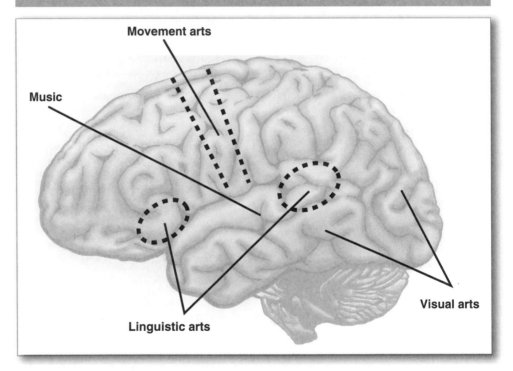

The Arts and Creativity

Several definitions of creativity exist, but most seem to include the notion that creativity is, as the saying goes, thinking outside the box. It includes the ability to use divergent thinking to probe deeply, and to find alternative solutions to a problem that were not previously considered. Although creativity comes naturally to some individuals, there is growing realization that creativity can be taught. It means, however, putting limits on the common instructional approach in today's classrooms that revolves predominantly around convergent thinking—that is, finding the one correct solution to a problem—and where memorization prevails over deep understanding. Schools should be dedicated more to helping students think, rather than just know.

Neuroscientists who are exploring the nature of creativity suggest that creative thinking involves communication among brain regions that do not normally interact with each other during noncreative thinking. Most creative activities involve the brain's frontal lobe, although researchers agree that there is not one single brain area responsible for creativity. EEG and brain scanning studies reveal that more brain areas are stimulated and interacting when performing creative activities than during conventional activities, especially in areas involved in working memory, cognition, and emotion (e.g., Mayseless, Aharon-Peretz, & Shamay-Tsoory, 2014; Saggar et al., 2015).

Video: For an amusing and compelling talk by Sir Ken Robinson on the importance of fostering creativity in schools, see

https://www.youtube.com/watch?v=iG9CE55wbtY

A key revelation regarding the nature of creativity comes from fMRI studies that explored regions of the brain associated with inhibition. One study compared the brain activity of professional jazz pianists as they played the music they memorized to their brain activity as they played spontaneous improvisational jazz. The fMRIs taken during the improvisation revealed that the areas of the brain responsible for inhibition and self-regulation were much less activated than during the memorized performance, but activity increased in the brain areas associated with individuality and self-expression (Limb & Braun, 2008). Apparently, turning off the brain areas involving inhibition and self-regulation leads to less focused attention and spontaneous and creative behavior.

Participation in the arts can foster spontaneity and self-expression, moderate the limiting effects of inhibition, and lead to creative results. It can develop the attentional control needed for persistence to overcome the fear, frustration, and failure that can accompany creative endeavors. Artistic activities also enhance imaging skills and introspection because they often require one to create and manipulate mental images of a task before doing it and to self-evaluate the quality of one's performance.

These research findings alone should justify teaching the arts for the arts' sake, and one should not have to suggest that we teach the arts only because they enhance the learning of other academic subjects. Nonetheless, it may be necessary to document any spillover effects that learning the arts can have on learning other subjects. That is because of the risk that the arts will fall by the wayside as schools are held more accountable for improving achievement in language arts and mathematics, despite strong public support for arts programs.

Video: For examples of integrating science and the arts, see

https://www.youtube.com/watch?v=uDfVMvbCusY and

https://www.youtube.com/watch?v=vYN-anlXcBs

It is encouraging that more states have recently promoted the arts in their curriculum through policies such as including the arts as part of high school graduation requirements, standards, and assessments. Although the extent of commitment varies, some states have developed more extensive programs in the arts for schools and created partnerships with state arts councils and local arts organizations. We must be cautious, however, not to accept the notion that arts education is only for those students who want to be artists. To do so would imply that we should teach history only to those students who want to be historians and science only to those who want to be physicists, chemists, or biologists.

The Sciences Need the Arts

Few people will argue against studying the natural sciences in the elementary and middle schools, and support remains strong for the sciences—including Advanced Placement courses—in high schools. When budgets get tight, some people even view music and other arts courses as a drain on the funds needed to preserve science and mathematics courses. Others often see science and the arts as polar opposites. The sciences are thought of as objective, logical, analytical, reproducible, and useful; the arts are supposed to be subjective, intuitive, sensual, unique, and frivolous. In the competition between the arts and sciences in U.S. society, the arts have frequently lost. Typically, more public and private funds are given to any single technical or scientific discipline than all the arts combined.

But scientists and mathematicians know that the arts are vital to their success and use skills borrowed from the arts as scientific tools. These include the ability to observe accurately, to think spatially (how does an object appear when I rotate it in my head?), and perceive kinesthetically (how does it move?). These skills are not usually taught as part of the science curriculum but are at home in writing, drama, painting, and music.

Indeed, the arts often inform the sciences (e.g., Beal, 2013; Root-Bernstein, 1997). For example,

- Buckminster Fuller's geodesic domes can describe soccer balls and architectural buildings as well as the structure of viruses and some recently discovered complex and enormous molecules.
- NASA employs artists to design displays that present satellite data accurately, yet understandably.
- A biochemist looks at the fiber folds in her weaving cloth as another way of explaining protein folding.
- Computer engineers code messages to the frequencies of a specific song to prevent interception or blocking of the message, unless the decoder knows the song.
- Genetic researchers convert complex data into musical notation to facilitate analysis of the data as, for example, decoding the sequence of genes in a chromosome.

Thus, playing the piano, writing a poem, or creating a painting sharpens observations, hones details, and puts things into context. These are the same tools needed by a good scientist. The study of the arts not only allows students to develop skills that will improve the quality of their lives but also sustains the same creative base from which scientists and engineers seek to develop their innovations and breakthroughs of the future.

IMPACT OF THE ARTS ON STUDENT LEARNING AND BEHAVIOR

Arts Education and Arts Integration

Numerous research studies show that well-designed arts experiences produce positive academic and social effects as well as assist in the development of critical academic skills, basic and advanced literacy, and numeracy. The studies look at both stand-alone arts programs and programs that integrate concepts and skills from the arts into the many areas of study, such as science, technology, engineering, and mathematics, the so-call STEM subjects. One intriguing and important revelation of these studies is that the most powerful effects are found in programs that *integrate* the arts with subjects in the core curriculum.

Researchers speculate that arts integration causes both students and teachers to rethink how they view the arts and generates conditions that educational researchers and cognitive scientists say are ideal for learning. The arts are not just expressive and affective; they are deeply cognitive. They develop essential thinking tools: pattern recognition and development; mental representations of what is observed or imagined; symbolic, allegorical, and metaphorical representations; careful observation of the world; and abstraction from complexity (Rinne, Gregory, Yarmolinskaya, & Hardiman, 2011). Studies repeatedly show the following in schools where arts are integrated into the core curriculum (e.g., Park et al., 2015; Rabkin & Redmond, 2004):

- Students have a greater emotional investment in their classes.
- Students work more diligently and learn from each other.
- Cooperative learning groups turn classrooms into learning communities.
- Parents become more involved.
- Teachers collaborate more.
- Art and music teachers become the center of multiclass projects.
- Learning in all subjects becomes attainable through the arts.
- Curriculum becomes more authentic, hands-on, and project based.
- Assessment is more thoughtful and varied.
- Teachers' expectations for their students rise.

All of the above outcomes can lead to impressive gains in student engagement and motivation. When teachers give students opportunities to be purposefully creative in their work, regardless of the subject matter, focus, collaboration, and achievement are very likely to increase (Wang & Holcombe, 2010).

STEM to STEAM

In 2006, the U.S. National Academies of Sciences raised the alarm about the declining state of education in the United States in science, technology, engineering, and mathematics (STEM). In response, Congress passed the

Video: For one example of how scientists use art to stimulate student motivation in STEM subjects, see

https://www.youtube.com/watch?v=OrAbylCphUk

America COMPETES Act in 2007, which authorized funding for STEM initiatives from kindergarten through graduate school. Numerous school districts have since participated in some form of increased teaching time for the STEM subjects.

Despite the funding already spent on STEM, progress has indeed been slow. Test results from the 2015 National Assessment of Educational Progress (NAEP) show no significant improvement in the Grade 8 average achievement scores in mathematics between 2005 and 2015 (National Center for Education Statistics, 2015). Grade 8 science scores moved up slightly in 2011, the latest data available at the time of printing (National Center for Education Statistics, 2012). Clearly, something is not working as planned. We need to ask ourselves what types of activities would raise motivation, increase student engagement, focus on relevant issues, and increase creativity? Isn't that what the arts do? Integrating arts-related skills and activities into STEM courses could be one very effective way to enhance student interest and achievement.

> Ultimately, the main objective of both art and science is discovery.

Ultimately, the main objective of both art and science is discovery. Scientists and artists work creatively toward a product. Now neuroscience adds its research to the mix by revealing that creativity can be taught (e.g., Kaufman et al., 2016; Monroy, 2015). This revelation further supports the integration of arts-related topics into STEM courses as well as STEM topics into arts-centered courses. The focus here is on encouraging collaboration between STEM educators and those in the arts so that STEM adds the *A* for arts to become STEAM.

STEAM: Reports from the Field

A number of public and private schools have enhanced their curriculum by shifting from STEM to STEAM. Many report that implementing STEAM has resulted in improved student engagement and motivation. Here is a list of just a few of the schools implementing STEAM at the time of this printing. They generally welcome inquiries about their program.

- Andover Public Schools, Andover, Massachusetts
- Ann Arbor Public Schools, Ann Arbor, Michigan
- Blue School, New York, New York
- Boise-Eliot/Humboldt STEAM Public School, Portland, Oregon
- Cushman School, Miami, Florida
- DeSoto Independent School District, DeSoto, Texas
- Drew Charter School, Atlanta, Georgia
- Elizabeth Buckley School, Victoria, British Columbia
- Ford Elementary School, Acworth, Georgia
- Hilburn Academy, Raleigh, North Carolina
- Mankato Area Public Schools, Mankato, Minnesota
- Metro High School STEAM Academy, Cedar Rapids Community School District, Cedar Rapids, Iowa
- Middle School 534, Brooklyn, New York

- Schools of the Diocese of Providence, Rhode Island
- Taylor Elementary School, Arlington, Virginia
- University Place Elementary School, Tuscaloosa, Alabama

As STEAM programs multiply, increased student engagement using creative approaches to solving real-world problems should contribute to an increase in student achievement in the STEM subjects.

Other Areas of Impact

Disaffected and Disadvantaged Students. "Boring!" is the most common way that many dropouts describe school. The arts reach students who are not otherwise being reached. The arts sometimes provide the only reason that certain students stay in touch with school. Without the arts, these young people would be left with no access to a community of learners. Here are some research findings:

- A 10-year ongoing study in the Chicago public schools shows test scores of sixth graders in arts-integrated schools rising faster on the Iowa Test of Basic Skills reading section than a matched population (for neighborhood, family income, and academic performance) of sixth graders in the regular schools (Rabkin & Redmond, 2004). Shortly after this study, the Chicago Arts Partnerships in Education (CAPE) began integrating afterschool programs in the Chicago public schools. Research studies from 2006 through 2010 in Grades 4, 5, and 6 examined the effects of arts integration and demonstrated a clear positive relationship between arts integration in schools and improved standardized test scores (CAPE, 2016).
- A longitudinal study of nearly 175,000 Grade 9 students found that those with cumulative credits in the arts were consistently less likely to drop out of school than their peers who were not taking arts-related courses (Thomas, Singh, & Klopfenstein, 2015).
- A study of nearly 70 at-risk middle school students in Florida showed that participating in arts programs assisted them in decreasing delinquency, fostering academic competence, maintaining control, and feeling a closer relationship with their school (Respress & Lutfi, 2006).
- A program called the YouthARTS Development Project, a partnership involving the National Endowment for the Arts and the U.S. Justice Department, engaged at-risk youth in art programs. After two years, the participants had improved their ability to work on tasks from start to finish, were better able to communicate effectively, had a better attitude toward school, and decreased their frequency of delinquent behavior and court referrals (Clawson & Coolbaugh, 2001). Because of the success of this initial study, the program has remained available for other school districts to implement. For more information, see http://youtharts.artsusa.org.
- A study of more than 3,800 students in Arkansas found that students who participated in arts programs had stronger critical thinking skills

than their peers who did not participate. Moreover, the effects were larger for students from disadvantaged backgrounds (Bowen, Greene, & Kisida, 2014).

- Several studies have found that at-risk students introduced to arts education in the primary grades demonstrated higher achievement than those who did not get this instruction (Brown, Benedett, & Armistead, 2010). Similar results were found in longitudinal studies of at-risk high school students (Catterall, Dumais, & Hampden-Thompson, 2012). The researchers concluded that at-risk children and adolescents with high levels of arts engagement show more positive outcomes in a variety of school-related areas compared to their low-arts-engaged peers.

- A study of more than 200 New York City public schools showed that the schools in the top third in graduation rates offered their students the most access and support to arts education. Schools in the bottom third offered the least access and fewest resources to the arts (Israel, 2009).

Different Learning Preferences. Ample research evidence indicates that students learn in many different ways. This research also notes that some students can become behavioral problems if conventional classroom practices are not engaging them. Success in the arts is often a bridge to successful learning in other areas, thereby raising a student's self-concept. Several studies show that the arts may be particularly helpful for students with learning disabilities (e.g., Darrow, 2014). One two-year study found that engaging in the arts helped students with learning disabilities do the following (Mason, Steedly, & Thormann, 2008):

- Find their voice for expressing what they know through art forms. The arts helped the students find appropriate ways to communicate, including expressing fear, frustration, unhappiness, and confusion. This outlet improved the students' self-esteem and positive attitudes toward school.

- Increase their choices, especially because so much of what they do is scripted by educational policy. Working in the arts allowed the students to make their own choices about what art form to engage in so they could share their thoughts. They also made choices while working in the art form, such as what format of poem to write, what colors to use when painting on canvas, or what to say onstage in a play.

- Have access to parts of the school, curriculum, and challenges they might not otherwise have had. They participated in plays, learned to play musical instruments, and sang songs, all of which led to a deep sense of accomplishment.

A Canadian study reported on the progress of students, aged 9 to 15 years, from low-income communities who participated in community-based youth arts programs (Wright et al., 2006). Over a three-year period, students in the program showed significant gains in social and artistic skills and a significant reduction in emotional problems, compared to the control group.

Personal and Interpersonal Connections. The arts connect students to themselves and each other and help develop their social skills. Creating art is a personal experience, as students draw upon their own resources to produce the result. This is a much deeper involvement than just reading text to get an answer. Studies indicate that the attitudes of young people toward one another improve through their arts learning experiences. For instance, asking students to use drama and act out a concept they are learning requires deeper engagement and understanding. A meta-analysis of 47 studies where students got involved in drama-based instructional strategies showed a significant improvement in student achievement. The improvements were strongest when the innovation lasted more than five lessons and when they were integrated into the English language arts or science curriculum compared to other subject areas (Lee, Patall, Cawthon, & Steingut, 2015).

School and Classroom Climate. The arts transform the environment for learning. Schools become places of discovery when the arts are the focus of the learning environment. Arts change the school culture, break down barriers between curriculum areas, and can even improve the school's physical appearance.

Gifted and Talented Students. The arts provide new challenges for students already considered successful. Students who outgrow their learning environment usually get bored and complacent. The arts offer a chance for unlimited challenge. For instance, older students may teach and mentor younger ones who are learning to play musical instruments, and some advanced students may work with professional artists.

The World of Work. The arts connect learning experiences to the world of everyday work. The adult workplace has changed. The ability to generate ideas, bring ideas to life, and communicate them to others is key to workplace success. Whether in a classroom or in a studio as an artist, the student is learning and practicing future workplace behaviors. Let's take a look at the three major forms of artistic expression—music, visual arts, and dance and drama—and observe what brain research is telling us. What impact will these studies have on student learning and success?

MUSIC

Music exerts a powerful effect on the brain through intellectual and emotional stimulation. It can also affect our body by altering our heart rate, breathing, blood pressure, pain threshold, and muscle movements. These responses result from the activation of neural networks that include the frontal cortex, the amygdala, and other limbic areas involved in motivation and reward.

Is Music Inborn?

Many researchers now believe that the ability to perceive and enjoy music is an inborn human trait. But is there any credible evidence to support this biological basis of music? First of all, any behavior thought to have a biological foundation must be universal. Even though the uses of music may vary across past and current cultures, all cultures do sing and associate certain meanings and emotions with music.

Second, biologically based behaviors should reveal themselves early in life. Researchers have shown that infants of just 3 months old can learn and remember to move an overhead crib mobile when a certain song is played. Thus, infants can use music as a retrieval cue. Babies respond to pitch and harmonics as young as between 3 and 4 months of age (He & Trainor, 2009) and can also differentiate between two adjacent musical tones and recognize a melody when it is played in a different key (Weinberger, 2004). At the age of 7 months, infants can categorize rhythmic and melodic patterns on the basis of underlying meter (Hannon & Johnson, 2005), and can learn to repeatedly discriminate between happy and sad music (Flom & Pick, 2012). Moreover, preschool children spontaneously use music in their communication and play.

Third, if music has a strong biological component, then it should exist in other animals. Monkeys, for example, can form musical abstractions, such as determining harmonic patterns. Although many animals use musical sounds to attract mates and signal danger, only humans have developed a sophisticated and unlimited musical repertoire.

Fourth, if music has biological roots, we might expect the brain to have specialized areas for music—and it does. For example, areas in the auditory cortex are organized to process pitch. Furthermore, the brain's ability to respond emotionally to music is connected to biology and culture. The biological aspect is supported by the fact that the brain has specialized areas that respond primarily to music, and these areas are able to stimulate the limbic system, provoking an emotional response (Daly et al., 2015; Norman-Haignere, Kanwisher, & McDermott, 2015). EEG and PET scans show that the neural areas stimulated depend on the type of music—melodic tunes stimulate areas that evoke pleasant feelings, whereas dissonant sounds activate other limbic areas that produce unpleasant emotions (Chapin, Jantzen, Kelso, Steinberg, & Large, 2010; Menon & Levitin, 2005).

> *Compelling evidence suggests that the brain's response to music is innate and has strong biological roots.*

Effects of Listening to Music Versus Creating Instrumental Music

No one arts area has gained more notoriety in recent years than the impact of music on the brain. Numerous books are on the market touting the so-called Mozart effect and promising that music can do all sorts of things from relieving pain, to increasing a child's IQ, to improving mathematics skills. To what degree are these claims backed by credible scientific evidence? As with most claims of this nature, there is a growing body of scientific data, followed by media attention and a lot of hype. Let's try to sort out what the research in music is saying so that we can reap its benefits while making informed decisions about the validity of the assertions.

Research on the effects of music on the brain and body can be divided into the effects of *listening* to music and the effects of *creating* or *producing* music on an instrument, especially an acoustic rather than an electronic one. The brain and body respond differently in these two situations. Unfortunately, not enough attention has been paid to this crucial distinction. Consequently, people have mistakenly assumed that the results of studies that involved creating music would be repeated when listening to music. If educators want to use the research on the effects of music to benefit students, then it is important that they differentiate the studies on listening from those on creating music.

How the brain responds when listening to music is very different from how it responds when creating music.

How the Brain Listens to Music

The sounds of music are transmitted to the inner ear and are broken down according to the specific frequencies that make up the sounds (see Figure 6.2). Different cells in the *cochlea* respond to different frequencies, and their signals are mapped out in the auditory cortex. The left hemisphere responds to musical rhythm better than the right, but the right hemisphere is where perceptions of pitch, melody, timbre, and harmony emerge. This information is then transmitted to the frontal lobe where the music can be linked to emotion, thoughts, and past experiences. Over time, the auditory cortex is "retuned" by experience so that more cells become sensitive to important sounds and musical tones. This sets the stage for the processing of the more complex music patterns of melody, harmony, and rhythm (Sweeney, 2009).

Each hemisphere of the brain contains areas that respond to both music and language. But, as mentioned in Chapter 5, the left hemisphere also contains

Figure 6.2   Sound entering the ear is converted into nerve impulses in the cochlea. These impulses are transmitted to the auditory cortex in the temporal lobe in which specialized regions, especially in the right hemisphere, analyze pitch and timbre. Information from the auditory cortex is transmitted to the frontal lobe, which associates the sound of music with thought and stimulates emotions and past experiences.

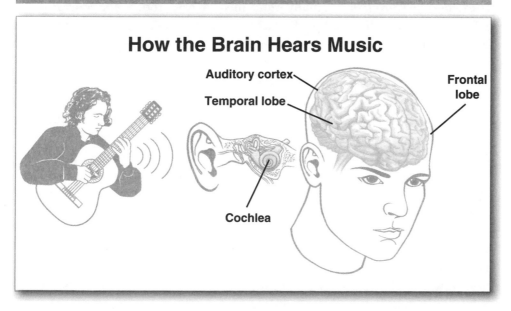

regions of specialization that respond primarily to language, and the right hemisphere has areas devoted primarily to music perception. This explains why some people can be extraordinarily talented in language skills but have difficulty humming a melody. The reverse situation occurs in the brains of individuals with savant syndrome, who are talented musicians despite severe language difficulties.

The discovery that the auditory cortex (located in the temporal lobes) in the right hemisphere has regions that respond primarily to music came from studies comparing patients who have damage to their left or right temporal lobes. Patients with right temporal lobe damage have lost the ability to recognize familiar songs, a condition known as *acquired amusia*. However, only the response to music is affected. The patients can still recognize human voices, traffic sounds, and other auditory information. Researchers estimate that about 4 percent of the U.S. population is born lacking the ability to recognize musical tones or rhythm, a condition known as *congenital amusia* (Wilcox, He, & Derkay, 2015).

Music can also be imagined because people have stored representations of songs and the sounds of musical instruments in their long-term memory. When a song is imagined, the brain cells that are activated are identical to those used when a person actually hears music from the outside world. But when a song is imagined, brain scans show that the visual cortex is also stimulated so that visual patterns are imaged as well. Although the mechanism that triggers musical imagery is not yet fully understood, recent studies indicate that it involves the brain networks associated with perception, memory, emotions, and spontaneous thoughts (Farrugia, Jakubowski, Cusack, & Stewart, 2015). but it is not uncommon for people to have songs running through their heads when they get up in the morning. If a song really gets stuck in your head and goes on and on, it is referred to as an *earworm*, from the German *ohrwurm*, which means *earwig*. Not surprisingly, earworm attacks are more frequent and last longer in musicians and music lovers (Liikkanen, 2012).

The Benefits of Listening to Music

Therapeutic Benefits. For many years, medical researchers and practitioners have reported on the therapeutic effects of music to relieve stress (Trappe, 2010), diminish pain (Klassen, Liang, Tjosvold, Klassen, & Hartling, 2008), and treat other, more severe disabilities, such as mental retardation, Alzheimer's disease (Pavlicevic, O'Neil, Powell, Jones, & Sampathianaki, 2014; Simmons-Stern, Budson, & Ally, 2010), and visual and hearing impairments. Other studies have shown that listening to music can boost immune function in children, and that premature babies exposed to lullabies in the hospital went home earlier and had fewer stress-related problems (Gooding, 2010). Music, including singing, dancing, and creative movement, can improve the social skills of individuals with autism spectrum disorders (Eren, 2015). The sheer volume of studies and positive results attest to music's therapeutic benefits.

How does music work this magic? That is still a mystery, but there are some important hints. Researchers have known for a long time that music can directly influence blood pressure, pulse, and the electric activity of muscles. Newer evidence shows that music may even help build and strengthen connections between brain cells in the cortex. This effect is important, and some doctors are already using music to help rehabilitate stroke patients. Some stroke patients who have lost their ability to speak retain their ability to sing. By singing what they want to say, patients' fluency improves, and therapists can use existing pathways to retrain the speech centers of the brain (Norton, Zipse, Marchina, & Schlaug, 2009).

Educational Benefits. The notion that music could affect cognitive performance catapulted from the research laboratory to the television talk shows in 1993 when Frances Rauscher and Gordon Shaw conducted a study using 84 college students. They reported that the students' spatial-temporal reasoning—the ability to form mental images from physical objects or to see patterns in time and space—improved after listening to Mozart's Sonata for Two Pianos in D Major (K.448) for 10 minutes. But the students' improved abilities faded within an hour (Rauscher, Shaw, & Ky, 1995).

The results of this study, promptly dubbed "the Mozart effect," were widely publicized and soon reinterpreted to incorrectly imply that listening to a Mozart sonata would enhance intelligence by raising IQ. In fact, the study reported that the music improved only spatial-temporal reasoning (one of many components of total IQ) and that the effect quickly faded. But the results did encourage the researchers to go further and test whether *creating* music would have a longer-lasting effect.

Two decades of subsequent studies continue to yield conflicting results. A meta-analysis of nearly 40 studies, involving more than 3,000 participants, found that the enhancement in spatial reasoning attributed to Mozart's music is too small to be statistically significant (Pietschnig, Voracek, & Formann, 2010). One interesting EEG study revealed that listening to Mozart's K448 sonata caused some activation of cognitive networks, but listening to Beethoven's "Für Elise" did not (Verrusio et al., 2015). Some researchers suggest that the spatial task improvement may be due to the music's relaxing effect between pretest and posttest, or to its arousal level and mood, rather than to cognitive priming (Gittler & Fischer, 2011).

Meanwhile, other studies are claiming that Mozart's and other kinds of music enhance cognitive functions. They show, for example, improvement in visual attention (Ho, Mason, & Spence, 2007; Zhu et al., 2008) and enhancement of various types of spatial and temporal reasoning tasks (Jaušovec, Jaušovec, & Gerlič, 2006). If the Mozart effect is real, what causes it? Researchers suspect that the complex rhythms and musical structure of Mozart's music activate the same regions in the brain's right hemisphere that are involved in spatial cognition. Assuming this to be the case, nonmusicians should display greater response to the Mozart effect because they process music primarily in the right hemisphere. Musicians, on the other hand, process music in both hemispheres. One study tested this hypothesis by asking musicians and nonmusicians to perform spatial rotation tasks before and after listening to Mozart's music and in silence (Aheadi, Dixon, & Glover, 2009). Indeed, the performance on these tasks improved only for the nonmusicians after listening to Mozart.

Although studies on the Mozart effect are inconclusive, most researchers agree that passive listening to music appears to stimulate spatial thinking and that neural networks normally associated with one kind of mental activity can readily share the cognitive processes involved in a different activity. Researchers have also found that listening to background music enhances the efficiency of those working with their hands. In a study of surgeons, for example, background music enhanced their alertness, concentration, and performance (Siu, Suh, Mukherjee, Oleynikov, & Stergiou, 2010). This explains why background music in the classroom helps many students stay focused while completing certain learning tasks. However, one must exercise caution in selecting the *type* of background music. Overly stimulating music serves more as a distraction and interferes with cognitive performance. See the Practitioner's Corner: Using Music in the Classroom at the end of this chapter.

> *Although the Mozart effect remains controversial, listening to background music can enhance recall, visual imagery, attention, concentration, and dexterity.*

Creating Music

> **Video:** For an explanation of how creating music helps develop the brain, see
>
> https://www.youtube.com/watch?v=ROJKCYZ8hng

Although passive listening to music does have some therapeutic and short-term educational benefits, the making of music seems to provide many more cerebral advantages. Learning to play a musical instrument challenges the brain in new ways. In addition to being able to discern different tone patterns and groupings, one must learn and coordinate new motor skills in order to play the instrument. These new learnings cause profound and seemingly permanent changes in brain structure. For example, the auditory cortex, the motor cortex, the cerebellum, and the corpus callosum are larger in musicians than in nonmusicians (Angulo-Perkins et al., 2014; Schlaug, 2015).

These differences in brain structures between musicians and nonmusicians raise an interesting question: Are the brains of musicians different because of their training and practice in music, or did these differences exist before they learned music? The answer came when researchers trained nonmusicians to listen for small changes in pitch and similar musical components. In just three weeks, their brains showed increased activation in the auditory cortex. This suggests that the brain differences in highly skilled musicians are more likely the result of training and are not inherited (Restak, 2003). In support of this notion, another study compared 5- to 7-year-olds who were beginning piano or string lessons with a similar group not beginning instrument training. The researchers found no preexisting neural, cognitive, motor, or musical differences between the two groups and no correlations between music perceptual skills or visual-spatial measures. As in previous studies, correlations were found between music perceptual skills and phonemic awareness (Norton et al., 2005). No doubt some genetic traits enhance music learning, but it seems that most musicians are made, not born.

> *No doubt some genetic traits enhance music learning, but it seems that most musicians are made, not born.*

Benefits of Creating Music

The effects of learning to play an instrument can begin at an early age. One leading-edge study involved 78 preschoolers from three California preschools, including one serving mostly poor, inner-city families. The children were divided into four groups. One group (Keyboard) took individual, 12- to 15-minute piano lessons twice a week along with singing instruction. Another group (Singing) took 30-minute singing lessons five days a week, and a third group (Computer) trained on computers. The fourth group received no special instruction. All students took tests before the lessons began to measure different types of spatial-reasoning skills.

After six months, the children who received six months of piano keyboard training had improved their scores by 34 percent on tests measuring spatial-temporal reasoning (see Figure 6.3). On other tasks, there was no difference in scores. Furthermore, the enhancement lasted for days, indicating a substantial change in spatial-temporal function. The other three groups, in comparison, had only slight improvement on all tasks (Rauscher et al., 1997). Subsequent studies continue to show a strong relationship between creating music with keyboards and the enhancement of spatial reasoning in young children (Hetland, 2000; Rauscher & Zupan, 2000).

Why did piano keyboard training improve test performance by 34 percent while the computer keyboard training didn't? Remember that the study measured spatial-temporal improvements only. As this and other studies show, music training seems to specifically influence neural pathways responsible for spatial-temporal reasoning, and that effect is more noticeable in the young brain. This may be due to the combination of tactile input from striking the

piano keys, auditory input from the sounds of the notes, and the visual information of where one's hand is on the keyboard. This is a much more complex interaction than from the computer keyboard. Computers are, of course, very valuable teaching tools, but when it comes to developing the neural pathways responsible for spatial abilities, the piano keyboard is much more effective.

Figure 6.3 The graph shows the results of a spatial-temporal task performed by the preschool students before and after piano keyboard training, group singing, training on the computer, and no lessons. National standard age scores for all ages are 10, showing that these were average children before training.

Creating Music Benefits Memory

Numerous studies have shown that musical training improves verbal memory. Researchers in one study administered memory tests to 90 boys between the ages of 6 and 15. Half belonged to their school's strings program for one to five years, while the other half had no musical training. The musically trained students had better verbal memory, but showed no differences in visual memory. Apparently, musical training improves the ability of the left temporal lobe (where Broca's and Wernicke's areas are located) to handle verbal learning.

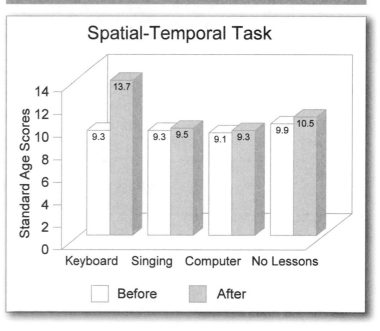

Furthermore, the memory benefits of musical training are long lasting. Students who dropped out of the music training group were tested a year later and found to retain the verbal memory advantage they had gained earlier (Ho, Cheung, & Chan, 2003).

Another study showed that musical training improves working memory. Musicians outperformed nonmusicians in tests of working memory, involving visual, phonological, and executive memory (George & Coch, 2011). Not surprisingly, musicians allocated more neural resources to auditory processing, and updating auditory memory required less mental effort than in nonmusicians. Other studies report similar findings (e.g., Hansen, Wallentin, & Vuust, 2013).

Does Creating Music Affect Ability in Other Subjects?

Research studies continue to look for the impact that music instruction can have on learning in other subject areas. The question here is whether the brain changes that come about as a result of music training also enable an individual to be more successful in other curriculum areas and later as an adult learner (Portowitz, Lichtenstein, Egorova, & Brand, 2009; Skoe & Kraus, 2012). Two subject areas of particular interest are mathematics and reading.

Music and Mathematics

Of all the academic subjects, mathematics seems to be most closely connected to music. Music relies on fractions for tempo and on time divisions for pacing, octaves, and chord intervals. Here are some mathematical concepts that are basic to music:

- **Patterns.** Music is full of patterns of chords, notes, and key changes. Musicians learn to recognize these patterns and use them to vary melodies. Inverting patterns, called counterpoint, helps form different kinds of harmonies.
- **Counting.** Counting is fundamental to music because one must count beats, count rests, and count how long to hold notes.
- **Geometry.** Music students use geometry to remember the correct finger positions for notes or chords. Guitar players' fingers, for example, form triangular shapes on the neck of the guitar.
- **Ratios and Proportions, and Equivalent Fractions.** Reading music requires an understanding of ratios and proportions—that is, a whole note needs to be played twice as long as a half note, and four times as long as a quarter note. Because the amount of time allotted to one beat is a mathematical constant, the duration of all the notes in a musical piece are relative to one another on the basis of that constant. It is also important to understand the rhythmic difference between 3/4 and 4/4 time signatures.
- **Sequences.** Music and mathematics are related through sequences called intervals. A mathematical interval is the difference between two numbers; a musical interval is the ratio of their frequencies. Here's another sequence: Arithmetic progressions in music correspond to geometric progressions in mathematics.

Because of the many common mathematical concepts that underlie music, scientists have long wondered how these two abilities are processed in the brain. Several fMRI studies have shown that musical training activates the same areas of the brain (mainly the left frontal cortex) that are activated during mathematical processing. It may be, then, that early musical training begins to build the very same neural networks that will later be used to complete numerical and mathematical tasks (Schmithhorst & Holland, 2004).

Keyboard Training. Motivated by the studies showing that music improved spatial-temporal reasoning, Gordon Shaw set out to determine whether this enhancement would help young students learn specific mathematics skills. He focused on proportional mathematics, which is particularly difficult for many elementary students, and which is usually taught with ratios, fractions, and comparative ratios. Shaw and his colleagues worked with 136 second-grade students from a low-socioeconomic neighborhood in Los Angeles. One group (Piano-ST) was given four months of piano keyboard training, as well as computer training and time to play with newly designed computer software to teach proportional mathematics. The second group (English-ST) was given computer training in English and time to play with the software; the third group (No Lessons) had neither music nor specific computer lessons, but did play with the computer software.

The Piano-ST group scored 27 percent higher on proportional math and fractions subtests than the English-ST students, and 166 percent higher than the No Lessons group (see Figure 6.4). These findings are significant because proportional mathematics is not usually introduced until fifth or sixth grade, and because a grasp of proportional mathematics is essential to understanding science and mathematics at higher levels (Graziano, Peterson, & Shaw, 1999).

Another piano study of more than 100 second-grade students explored whether piano instruction had an effect on their vocabulary and verbal sequencing skills. About one-half of the students participated in three consecutive years of formal piano instruction while the other group had no exposure to piano instruction, either in school or privately. Figure 6.5 shows that the students receiving piano lessons scored significantly higher than the control group on standardized tests of vocabulary and verbal sequencing.

Strings Training. Begun in 2000, the Newark (New Jersey) Early Strings Program created a partnership with the New Jersey Symphony Orchestra to provide Suzuki-based string instruction to students in Newark's

Figure 6.4 The mean overall and fraction and proportions subtest scores of the group that had piano and computer training with special software (Piano-ST), the group with computer and software (English-ST), and the group with no lessons.

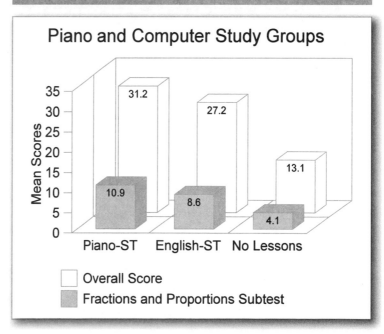

Piano and Computer Study Groups

elementary schools, starting in second grade. Annual assessments show that students in the program in Grades 2 through 4 perform significantly better on standardized tests in language arts and mathematics than their peers. The program has also had a positive effect on the students' self-esteem and self-discipline, and increased parent involvement in the schools (Abeles, 2009).

A recent study in some Chicago elementary schools showed how creating music can make a difference for students with low socioeconomic status. The low-socioeconomic students who took music lessons had a higher attendance rate and scored significantly higher than those low-socioeconomic students who were not involved in music (Kelley & Demorest, 2016).

A subsequent review of studies involving more than 300,000 secondary school students confirmed the strong association between music instruction and achievement in mathematics. Of particular interest is an analysis of six experimental studies that revealed a causal relationship between music and mathematics performance, and that the relationship had grown stronger over the years (Vaughn, 2000).

A study of six school districts in Maryland, involving more than 6,000 adolescents, showed that formal instrumental or choral music instruction significantly improved the algebra test scores of eighth and ninth graders, compared to the scores of their peers who did not receive music instruction (Helmrich, 2010). Instrumental instruction had a greater impact on algebra scores than choral music. Moreover, the greatest difference in scores was between the instrumental and no-music-instruction groups of African Americans. Isn't this something that educators should consider in planning the

Figure 6.5 The chart shows the improvement in vocabulary and verbal sequencing scores of the group of second graders who took three consecutive years of piano lessons compared to the control group who had no in-school or private musical instruction.

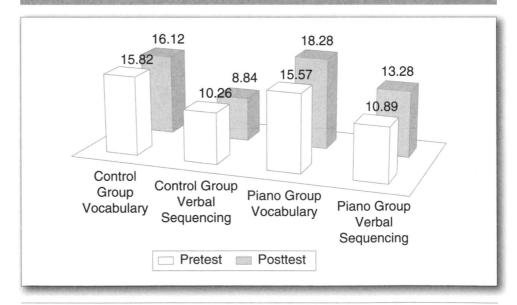

Source: Adapted from Piro & Ortiz, 2009.

core curriculum? If numeracy is so important, perhaps every student should learn to play a musical instrument.

Music and Reading

Several studies confirm a strong association between music instruction and standardized tests of reading ability (e.g., Tierney & Kraus, 2013; Wandell, Dougherty, Ben-Shachar, Deutsch, & Tsang, 2008). One possible explanation for this relationship may lie in brain imaging studies of professional musicians doing three-dimensional mental rotation tasks (Sluming, Brooks, Howard, Downes, & Roberts, 2007). Unlike nonmusicians, musicians recruit Broca's area, one of the brain's language regions, during these tasks. This may be because musicians rely on Broca's area for sight-reading during musical performance. The enhancement of Broca's area needed to develop sight-reading skills may also allow musicians to become better readers in general.

Although we cannot say that this is a causal association (that taking music instruction *causes* improvement in reading ability), this consistent finding in a large group of studies builds confidence that there is a strong relationship (Standley, 2008; Tierney, Krizman, & Kraus, 2015). The relationship may result because of positive transfer occurring between the language and reading neural networks. The rationale is as follows:

- Although music and written language use highly differentiated symbol systems, both involve similar decoding and comprehension reading processes, such as reading from left to right, sequential ordering of content, and so forth.
- There are interesting parallels in the underlying concepts shared between music and language reading skills, such as sensitivity to phonological or tonal distinctions.
- Reading music involves the simultaneous incorporation and reading of written text with music.
- Learning in the context of a highly motivated social context, such as music ensembles, may lead to a greater desire for academic responsibility and performance that enhances reading achievement.
- The rhythmic and melodic flow of music may help develop fluency in reading text.
- Musical lyrics raise awareness of phonemes, syllabification, and rhyming patterns.

Studies done with 4- and 5-year-old children revealed that the more music skills children had, the greater their degree of phonological awareness and reading development. Apparently, music perception taps and enhances auditory areas that are related to reading (Anvari, Trainor, Woodside, & Levy, 2002).

Student Attitudes Toward Music in the Schools

Students seem to like music more outside of school than inside school. That is a major finding of a study of more than 3,000 middle and high school students across the United States (McPherson & Hendricks, 2010). The degree of student interest in music instruction when in school was lower than that for all other subjects. Furthermore, the trend in interest dropped significantly between Grade 6 and Grades 7 through 9, but increased in Grades 10 through 12. For interest in music outside of school, the trend in interest between grade levels was similar to that for interest in school. However, interest in music outside of school was the second highest among school subject areas (after physical education) in Grades 6 and 7 through 9, and moved even higher than physical education in Grades 10 through 12.

The researchers speculated that these results could reflect how students view the role of music as an academic subject compared to a leisure activity. Perhaps schools need to do more to highlight the importance and usefulness of music in school settings. One way would be to integrate music in other academic subjects, such as history and mathematics.

THE VISUAL ARTS

The human brain has the incredible ability to form images and representations of the real world or sheer fantasy within its mind's eye. Solving the mystery of DNA's structure, for example, required Watson and Crick in the early 1950s to imagine numerous three-dimensional models until they hit on the only image that explained the molecule's peculiar behavior—the spiral helix. This was an incredible marriage of visual art and biology that changed the scientific world forever. Exactly how the brain performs the functions of imagination and meditation may be uncertain, but no one doubts the importance of these valuable talents, which have allowed human beings to develop advanced and sophisticated cultures.

Imagery

For most people, the brain's left hemisphere specializes in coding information verbally whereas the right hemisphere codes information visually. Although teachers spend much time talking (and sometimes have their students talk) about the learning objective, little time is given to developing visual cues. This process, called *imagery*, is the mental visualization of objects, events, and arrays related to the new learning and represents a major way of storing information in the brain. Imagery can take place in two ways: *Imaging* is the visualization in the mind's eye of something that the person has actually experienced; *imagining* depicts something the person has not yet experienced and, therefore, has no limits. A mental image is a pictorial representation of something physical or of an experience. The more information an image contains, the richer it is. Some people are more capable of forming rich images than others, but the research evidence is clear: Individuals can be taught to search their minds for images and be guided through the process to select appropriate images that, through hemispheric integration, enhance learning and increase retention. When the brain creates images, the same parts of the visual cortex are activated as when the eyes process real-world input. Thus, the powerful visual processing system is available even when the brain is creating internal pictures in the mind's eye (Brucker, Scheiter, & Gerjets, 2014; Thompson, Slotnick, Burrage, & Kosslyn, 2009).

The human brain's ability to do imagery with such efficiency is likely due to the importance of imagery in survival. Our prehistoric ancestors relied on mental imagery to map out their location during their hunt for food, and to ensure a safe return to their shelter. When we are confronted with a potentially life-threatening event—say, a car speeding toward us in the wrong traffic lane—the brain's visual processing system and the frontal lobes process several potential scenarios in a fraction of a second and initiate a reflex reaction that is most likely to keep us alive. As students today increasingly engage with electronic media that produce images, they are not getting adequate practice in generating their own imaging and imagining, skills that not only affect survival but also increase retention of learning and, through creativity, improve the quality of life.

Mental imagery can be so powerful that learning a skill through imaging it can be almost as effective as actually performing it (Helene & Xavier, 2006). This capability is very likely the result of the activity of the mirror neuron system. You will recall that mirror neurons respond not only to physical activity but also to the mental images of those activities. Training students in imagery encourages them to search long-term memory for appropriate images and to use them more like a movie than a photograph. For example, one recalls the house one lived in for many years. From the center hall with its gleaming chandelier, one mentally turns left and "walks" through the living room to the sunroom beyond. To the right of the hall is the paneled dining room and then the kitchen with the avocado-green appliances and oak cabinets. In the back, one sees the flagstone patio, the manicured lawn, and the garden with its variety of flowers. The richness of the image allows one to focus on just a portion of it and generate additional amounts of detail. In this image, one could mentally stop in any room and visualize the furniture and other decor. Imagery should become a regular part of classroom strategies as early as kindergarten. In the primary grades, the teacher should supply the images to ensure accuracy.

> *Imagery not only affects survival, but increases retention and improves the quality of life.*

Imagery can be used in many classroom activities, including note taking, cooperative learning groups, and alternative assessment options. Mind mapping is a specialized form of imagery that emerged in the 1970s. The process combines language with images to help show relationships between and among concepts, and how they connect to a key idea.

Research on Visual Arts and Learning

A review of the research literature shows that studies examining the impact of visual imagery on learning center primarily on individuals with psychological and physical disorders. Studies looking at connections between visual imagery and learning with typical students are very limited. One reason is the difficulty in determining which aspects of visual arts training (apart from imagery) are at work in programs that integrate visual art into core curriculum subjects.

Most studies in this area relate to imagery in sports. Coaches have known for a long time that athletes who use imagery to mentally rehearse what they intend to do perform better than if they do not use imagery. Studies reveal that the more time and intensity an athlete devotes to imagery, the better the athletic performance (Gee, 2010; Mellalieu, Hanton, & Thomas, 2009; Ridderinkhof & Brass, 2015). Apart from sports, some studies have looked at imagery and creativity. They find that students who used visual imagery while processing information were more creative in their work products than those students who did not (e.g., Palmiero, Nori, & Piccardi, 2016).

Although it is difficult to find studies connecting performance in the visual arts to improvement in academic areas, some researchers suggest that visual arts training can contribute to developing certain habits of mind that are a distinct advantage for students. For instance, Winner and her colleagues observed arts classes and interviewed students about what content and skills they learned (Winner, Hetland, Veenema, Sheridan, & Palmer, 2006). After sorting through videotapes of the classes and the student interviews, the following eight habits of mind emerged:

- **Develop Craft.** Students learn to work in different media and to use and care for tools and materials appropriately.
- **Engage and Persist.** Students learn how to engage themselves in a project and to persist with it even when challenges arise. This includes learning how to stay focused and to resist quitting when frustrated.
- **Envision.** Students learn to use mental imagery to envision what they cannot directly observe and to imagine underlying structures in their drawings and how that structure could be shown.
- **Express.** Students learn to express beyond words through moods, atmosphere, or sounds and to create works that convey a strong personal meaning.
- **Observe.** Students learn to look beyond the obvious, and to examine their own works and those of others for structure, line, color, style, and expression.
- **Reflect.** Students learn to think about their work and to explain their processes, decisions, and intentions when producing it. They also learn how to evaluate their own work and the works of others, to be self-critical, and to reflect on how they could improve.
- **Stretch and Explore.** Students learn to extend beyond what they have created, to explore and see what happens, to take risks with new ventures, and to learn from their mistakes.
- **Understand the Art World.** Students learn about the domain of art and how they relate to it. This includes understanding the art communities of museums, galleries, and curators and to think about how they might fit into these communities.

The researchers further suggest that many of these habits of mind can transfer to other domains of learning. For example, observing and envisioning can be useful habits in the science class, and expressing can be helpful in language arts assignments.

MOVEMENT

The mainstream educational community has often regarded thinking and movement as separate functions, assigning them different priorities. Activities involving movement, such as dance, theater, and occasionally sports, are often reduced or eliminated when school budgets get tight. But as brain studies probe deeper into the relationship between body and mind, the importance of movement to cognitive learning becomes very apparent.

Movement and the Brain

Role of the Cerebellum

In earlier chapters, we discussed the long-known role of the cerebellum in coordinating the performance of learned motor skills such as walking, driving a car, swinging a golf club, and tying a shoelace. For several decades, neuroscientists assumed that the cerebellum carried out its coordinating role by communicating exclusively with the cerebrum's motor cortex. However, this view did not explain why some patients with damage to the cerebellum also showed impaired cognitive function. Recent research using scans centered on the cerebellum shows that its nerve fibers communicate with other areas of the cerebrum as well.

Studies have found that the cerebellum plays an important role in attention, long-term memory, spatial perception, impulse control, social interactions, and the frontal lobe's cognitive functions—the same areas that are stimulated during learning (Bower & Parsons, 2003; Hautzel, Mottaghy, Specht, Müller, & Krause, 2009; Van Overwalle & Mariën, 2016). Now we find that the cerebellum also seems to be involved in verbal working memory, in speech tasks, and even in emotional processing (Durisko & Fiez, 2010; Marvel & Desmond, 2016; Timmann et al., 2010). It seems that the more we study the cerebellum, the more we realize that movement is inescapably linked to learning and memory (see Figure 6.6).

Autism and ADHD. Further evidence of the link between the cerebellum and cognitive function has come from some studies of autism and Attention Deficit/ Hyperactivity Disorder (ADHD). Brain images show that many children with autism have smaller brain stems and cerebellums and fewer cerebellar neurons. This cerebellar deficit may explain the impaired cognitive and motor functions seen in autism (Schroeder, Desrocher, Bebko, & Cappadocia, 2010; Wang, Kloth, & Badura, 2014). Children with ADHD also exhibit deficits in their cerebellum (Mulder et al., 2008).

> *The more we study the role of the cerebellum, the more we realize that movement and learning are inescapably linked.*

Physical Exercise Improves Brain Performance

Many people say they think better on their feet. Even short, moderate physical exercise can improve brain performance. Studies indicate that physical activity increases the number of capillaries in the brain, thus facilitating blood transport. It also increases the amount of oxygen in the blood, which the brain needs for fuel. The concentration of oxygen affects the brain's ability to carry out its

Figure 6.6 Researchers earlier thought that the cerebellum's role was limited to coordinating movement with the motor cortex. Recent studies indicate that the cerebellum also acts to support limbic functions (such as attention and impulse control) and multiple cognitive processes in the frontal lobe.

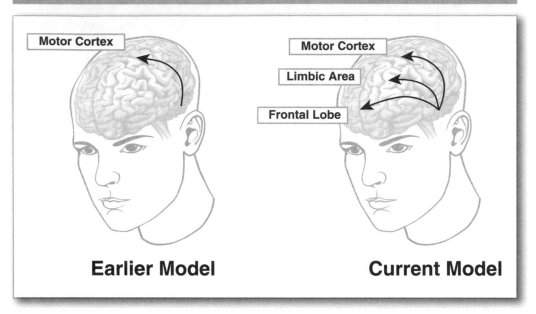

tasks. Studies confirm that higher concentrations of oxygen in the blood significantly enhance cognitive performance in healthy young adults. They are able to recall more words from a list and perform visual and spatial tasks faster. Moreover, their cognitive abilities vary directly with the amount of oxygen in the brain (Chung et al., 2009).

When you take a walk, the cerebellum, the motor cortex in the cerebrum, and the midbrain work together to coordinate the movement of your body. They also coordinate and stimulate the flow of thoughts by triggering neurons to fire signals throughout their networks. Sometimes, creative solutions to complex problems can arise just by taking a walk (Ratey, 2008). Despite the realization that physical activity enhances brain function and learning, secondary students spend most of their classroom time sitting.

Implications for Schools

Armed with the knowledge that movement is connected to cognitive learning, teachers and administrators need to encourage more movement in all classrooms at all grade levels. At some point in every lesson, students should be up and moving about, preferably talking about their new learning. Not only does the movement increase cognitive function, but it also aids in learning motor skills (Singh et al., 2016). Furthermore, movement during class helps students use up some kinesthetic energy—the "wiggles," if you will—so they can settle down and concentrate better later. Mild exercise before a test also makes sense because it can calm anxiety and improve cognitive performance. So does teaching dance to all students in K–8 classrooms. Dance techniques help students become more aware of their physical presence, spatial relationships, breathing, and timing and rhythm in movement.

Whatever Happened to Recess?

Given what we are learning about how movement and exercise stimulate brain activity, it seems counterproductive for so many elementary schools to be reducing or eliminating the time for daily recess. This free playtime not only gives students a much needed boost to blood circulation and oxygen levels, but it provides opportunities for developing communication, social, and gross motor skills as well. Through their social interactions, students also learn to listen, share, and cooperate. Furthermore, one research study, involving more than 11,000 8- to 9-year-olds, found that students who had at least 15 minutes of recess each day had significantly fewer behavior problems in school than those who had no daily recess (Barros, Silver, & Stein, 2009). And let us not forget the increasing number of elementary school students who are overweight and who could benefit from burning calories on the playground.

When I have raised this paradox with building principals, they offer several explanations. First, they say that the current drive for school productivity and accountability demands that students spend more time in class. Recess seems too much like play and is indefensible when so many students are doing so poorly in basic academic subjects. Second, recess time has to be cut to better meet the demands of the high-stakes testing mandates from federal and state agencies. The time that the school would use for recess is devoted instead to additional work in the academic areas being tested. Third, they say that too many altercations happen on the playground that can spill over into classrooms, causing disruptions for students and teachers. Besides, they caution that in this litigious society it may be more prudent to avoid situations like recess where misbehavior could lead to lawsuits.

Although each of these arguments has validity, we can address them all. If productivity, accountability, and scores on high-stakes tests are a major concern, would it not make sense to ensure that students are in the best mind-brain shape they can be in when taking these and other tests? Moreover, the fear of lawsuits could be an excuse for avoiding nearly everything in schools, not just recess. Recess does not have to be an unsupervised melee. Altercations are less likely to happen during recess when the people in charge know how to engage students in play that is constructive and fun.

Summarizing the research on the interplay of motion and the cognitive functions of the brain, Lengel and Kuczala (2010) suggest that teachers should consider using movement activities because they do the following:

- Provide an opportunity to take a break from learning and to refocus attention. Recall from Chapter 2 that working memory has a limited capacity that can be exceeded when too much information is presented at once. Giving students a chance every 10 to 20 minutes (depending on age) to reflect on what they have learned helps them to establish sense and meaning, and a subsequent movement activity gives the brain a chance to tag the information for storage and then to refocus on what comes next.

- Allow for implicit learning beyond the typical explicit learning that occurs through reading, teacher talk, worksheets, and discussion. Implicit learning involves emotions and the deeper thought processes that are stimulated through movement. Activating implicit learning is more likely to result in retention than relying just on explicit learning.

- Improve brain function by providing neurons with more glucose and oxygen to carry out their work, while stimulating the growth of new neurons.

- Meet basic needs, such as belonging, freedom, and fun.

- Improve the students' state of mind and their ability to self-regulate and manage their learning.

- Differentiate instruction by providing kinesthetic learners the movement they need to stay focused, to process new information, and to share what they have learned with their peers.

- Engage the senses. This multimodality approach increases the probability that students will understand what they are learning and generate the cues they need for long-term storage.

- Reduce the stress of the classroom environment because movement and exercise lower the cortisol (that infamous stress hormone) level while raising the endorphin levels in the bloodstream.

- Enhance episodic memory by allowing students to associate movement with their learning, thereby making the information easier to recall.

Teachers can find many ways to weave movement into all lessons: act out a social studies lesson; walk through a map of the world, or plot out a geometric formula on the gymnasium floor; use a dance to show the motion of molecules in the different states of matter or the planets in the solar system. See the Practitioner's Corner: Strategies for Using Movement at the end of this chapter for some additional suggestions.

> *At some point in most lessons, students should be up and moving around, talking about the new learning.*

WHAT'S COMING UP?

Solving the environmental, social, and economic problems of the 21st century will require plenty of creative thinking and imagination. Are schools doing enough to teach students how to analyze problems, judge competing solutions, and create new answers to old problems? Is the strong emphasis on high-stakes testing really advancing the level of thinking, or is it merely stressing the acquisition of more facts? How to foster a classroom that genuinely encourages higher-order thinking, while trying to do everything else, is the subject of the next chapter.

PRACTITIONER'S CORNER

Including the Arts in All Lessons

Including arts activities in any subject and at any grade level can be simple and fun. It doesn't need to be additional work and may substitute for some other activity you usually do.

- **Visual Arts.** Are there components of the lesson that students can draw, sketch, color, or paint? Would a visual arts project be acceptable as an alternative assessment to measure student understanding?

Example: A science teacher has a student draw a chart to illustrate the important steps in an experiment.

- **Music.** Is there an appropriate song or other musical composition that could be incorporated into the lesson or unit? Remember that music is a very effective memory device. Is there a familiar tune that would help students remember important facts about the unit?

Example: A social studies teacher has students put important facts about the Revolutionary War to a familiar melody.

- **Literary Device.** Could students write a poem, limerick, or play to illustrate major points in the unit? Rhyming is also an excellent memory tool: "In fourteen hundred ninety-two, Columbus sailed the ocean blue . . ."

Example: A mathematics teacher has students devise limericks to help them remember the mathematical order of operations.

- **Dance and Theater.** Is there a dance that could help students remember some critical events or information? Can students act out a play that other students wrote?

Example: An English teacher has students write and act out a different but plausible ending to Shakespeare's *Romeo and Juliet*.

- **Community Artists.** Are there community artists who can demonstrate their skills in the classroom? Teachers working with artists receive on-the-job training and learn techniques that they can use later on their own.

PRACTITIONER'S CORNER

Using Music in the Classroom

Listening to music in the classroom can promote student focus and productivity at all grade levels. Remember that no one musical selection, nor the volume at which it is played, will please *everyone*. Just ensure that the music played enhances rather than interferes with the situation or task. Here are a few guidelines to consider when planning to use music:

- **When to Play the Music.** Music can be played at different times during the learning episode. Be sure to choose the appropriate music for the particular activity. Music can be played

  - before class begins (choose music that sets the emotional mood);

  - when students are up and moving about (choose an upbeat tune);

  - when the students are busy doing seat work, either alone or in groups (choose music that facilitates the learning task); or

  - at the end of the class (students leave on a positive note, looking forward to returning).

  It is *not* advisable to play music when you are doing direct instruction (unless the music is part of the lesson) because it can be a distraction.

- **Be Aware of Beats per Minute.** Because music can affect a person's heart rate, blood pressure, and emotional mood, the number of beats per minute in the music is very important. If you are using the music as background to facilitate student work, choose music that plays at about 60 beats per minute (the average heartbeat rate). If the music is accompanying a fast-paced activity, then choose 80 to 90 beats per minute. To calm down a noisy group as, say, in the school cafeteria or commons area, choose music at 40 to 50 beats per minute.

- **With or Without Lyrics?** Using music with or without lyrics depends on the purpose of playing the music. Music played at the beginning or end of class can contain lyrics because the main purpose is to set a mood, not get focus. But if students are working on a learning task, lyrics become a distraction. Some students will try to listen to the lyrics, and others may discuss them—in both instances, they are off the task.

- **Select Familiar or Unfamiliar Music?** Once again, this depends on the music's purpose. Familiar music is fine when setting a mood. However, when working on a specific assignment, you may wish to use music that is unfamiliar. If the students know the background music, some will sing or hum along, causing a distraction. Choose unfamiliar music, such as classical or new age music, and have enough different selections so that each is played infrequently. Avoid the nature sounds selections as background music because they can be the source of much discussion and controversy. Of course, nature sounds could be used to stimulate discussion in appropriate lesson contexts.

- **Student Input.** Students may ask to bring in their own selections. To maintain a positive classroom climate, tell them that they *can* bring in their music, *provided the selections meet the preceding criteria.* Explain to them why this is necessary. Some kinds of student music would be appropriate in certain contexts as, for example, to facilitate a student discussion on interpreting music or another art form. In some cases, music may provide just the amount of meaning needed to enhance learning and retention.

- **Suggestions** (from teachers who have tried these, and reported success):

Beginning and end of class:	Fast-paced activity:
Vivaldi, *The Four Seasons*	Rock
Kenny G, any selection	Disco
Bach, Brandenburg Concertos	Reggae
Yanni, most selections	Hits from the 1970s
The Beach Boys	Hits from the 1980s
Chopin, most selections	Marches (e.g., Sousa)

Reflection or processing activity:

Beethoven, "Moonlight Sonata"

Pachelbel, Canon in D Major

Mozart, piano concertos

Enya (New Age), most selections

Ray Lynch (New Age), any selection

George Winston, *All the Seasons*

Gary Lamb (instrumental), any selection

Happy listening!

PRACTITIONER'S CORNER

Using Imagery

Imagery runs the gamut from simple concrete pictures to complex motor learning and multistep procedures. Because imagery is still not a common instructional strategy, it should be implemented early and gradually. Keep in mind, too, that the digital devices students spend so much time with constantly generate images, so students have had less practice than in the past generating their own mental images. This would be a good time to ask students to put away their digital devices and rely on their own brain as a valuable source of imagery. These guidelines are adapted from Parrott (1986) and West et al. (1991) and are still very effective for using imagery as a powerful aid to understanding and retention:

- **Prompting.** Use prompts for telling students to form mental images of the content being learned. They can be as simple as "Form a picture in your mind of . . ." to more complex directions. Prompts should be specific to the content or task and should be accompanied by relevant photographs, charts, or arrays, especially for younger children.

- **Modeling.** Model imagery by describing your own image to the class and explaining how that image helps your recall and use of the current learning. Also, model a procedure and have the students mentally practice the steps.

- **Interaction.** Strive for rich, vivid images where items interact. The richer the image, the more information it can include. If there are two or more items in the images, they should be visualized as acting on each other. If the recall is a ball and a bat, for example, imagine the bat hitting the ball.

- **Reinforcement.** Have students talk about the images they formed and how it helped their learning. Ensure that they get ample feedback from others on the accuracy and vividness of the images.

- **Add Context.** Whenever possible, add context to the interaction to increase retention and recall. For example, if the task is to recall prefixes and suffixes, the context could be a parade with the prefixes in front urging the suffixes in the rear to catch up.

- **Avoid Overloading the Image.** Although good images are complete representations of what is to be remembered, they should not overload the working memory's capacity in older students of about five to seven items.

PRACTITIONER'S CORNER

Visualized Note Taking

Visualized note taking is a strategy that encourages students to associate language with visual imagery. It combines on paper sequential verbal information with symbols and holistic visual patterns. Teachers should encourage students to link verbal notes with images and symbols that show sequence, patterns, or relationships. Technology can be used to generate and enhance these activities, where appropriate. Here are a few examples:

- **Stickperson.** Use the stickperson symbol to remember information about a person or group of people. The student attaches notes about a person in eight areas to the appropriate spot on the stick figure: ideas to the brain; hopes/vision to the eyes; words to the mouth; actions to the hands; feelings to the heart; movement to the feet; weaknesses to the Achilles' tendon; and strengths to the arm muscle.

- **Expository Visuals.** These take many forms. Use a set of flow boxes to help students collect and visualize the cause-effect interrelationships for an event. Causes are written in the boxes on the left, the event goes in the center box, and effects go in the boxes on the right. Creating different designs to visualize other topics is a valuable imaging activity.

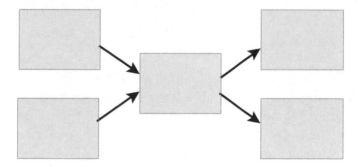

- **Notebook Design.** Even the design of the notebook page can call imagery into play to enhance learning and retention. One variation involves dividing the notebook page into sections for topics, vocabulary, important questions, things to remember, next homework assignment, and next test (see example below). Positioning each area on the page acts as a visual organizer that promotes the use of appropriate symbols.

Topics:	Things to Remember:
Vocabulary:	Next Homework Assignment:
Important Questions:	Next Test:

Notebook Pages

- **Mind Mapping.** Mind maps are powerful visual tools for remembering relationships between and among parts of a key idea. Using a mind map for notes helps the student see relationships unfolding during the note-taking process. The maps also allow students to look beyond the obvious, make inferences, and discover new knowledge not otherwise possible in the traditional lecture note-taking format. See Buzan (1989) and Hyerle (1996, 2004) for lots of ideas on different ways to draw and use mind maps.

PRACTITIONER'S CORNER

Strategies for Using Movement

Incorporating movement activities into lessons is interesting and fun for the teacher and the students. Although moving around in class is common in the primary grades, it drops dramatically at the secondary level. Middle and high school teachers are understandably concerned about having adequate time to cover the enormous amount of material in the curriculum. But because trading a few minutes of teacher talk for a movement activity can actually increase the amount of learning retained, it could be a very worthwhile investment of time.

©iStockphoto.com/syntika

Remember that not many students participate in the physical education program. Yet physical activity is essential to promoting the normal growth of mental function, to generating positive emotions, and in learning and remembering cognitive material. Some suggestions are as follows:

- **Energizers.** Use movement activities to energize students who are at low points in their energy levels (e.g., during early morning periods for high school students or during that down-time just past the middle of the day). For example,

  "Measure the room's length in hand spans."

  "Touch seven objects in the room that are the same color."

  "Go to four different sources of information in this room."

  "In your group, make a poster-sized mind map of this unit."

  "Use ball toss games for review, storytelling, and vocabulary building."

- **Acting Out Key Concepts.** This strategy uses the body in a physical way to learn and remember a difficult concept. If the lesson objective is to learn the continents, try this: Stand in front of a world map. Say the continent and point to the assigned body part (Chapman & King, 2000).

North America = left hand	Europe = forehead
Asia = right hand	Africa = waist
South America = left knee	Australia = right knee
Antarctica = a point on the floor between the feet	

Allow time for practice, then remove the map and repeat the activity.
Is there a difficult concept that you teach that could be acted out?

- **Role-Playing.** Do role-plays on a regular basis. For example, students can organize extemporaneous pantomime or play charades to dramatize major points in a unit. Have them develop and act out short commercials advertising upcoming units or to review previously learned material.

- **Vocabulary Building: Act Out the Word.** Look for vocabulary words that lend themselves to a physical movement. Then do the following:

  a. Say the word.

  b. Read the meaning.

  c. Do the movement (the movement acts out the meaning of the word).

  For example,

  a. oppugn

  b. "to oppose or attack"

  c. make body gestures that indicate "opposing" or "attacking."

  Do the three parts (a, b, and c) three times. This places the information in working memory. Now continue rehearsing the word, and use it in context so that it transfers to long-term memory (Chapman, 1993).

- **Verbal to Physical Tug-of-War.** In this activity, students choose a partner and a topic from the unit they have been learning. Each student forms an opinion about the topic and has 30 seconds to convince a partner why his or her own topic is more important (the verbal tug-of-war). After this debate, the partners separate to opposite sides for a physical tug-of-war with a rope.

CHAPTER 6: THE BRAIN AND THE ARTS

Key Points to Ponder

Jot down on this page key points, ideas, strategies, and resources you want to consider later. This sheet is your personal journal summary and will help to jog your memory.

_____

_____

_____

_____

_____

_____

_____

_____

_____

_____

_____

7

Thinking Skills and Learning

Too often children are given answers to remember rather than problems to solve.

—Robert Lewin

Chapter Highlights

This chapter discusses some of the characteristics and dimensions of human thinking. It examines the revised Bloom's Taxonomy, notes its continuing compatibility with current research on higher-order thinking, and explains its relationship to difficulty, complexity, and intelligence.

How can something as tangible as the human brain create such phantom things as ideas? How does it create Beethoven's symphonies, Michelangelo's sculptures, and Einstein's universe? What processes translate the countless neuron firings into thoughts and then into products of magnificent beauty or weapons of destruction? The human brain collects information about the world and organizes it to form a representation of that world. This representation, or mental model, describes *thinking*, a process that an individual human uses to function in that world.

CHARACTERISTICS OF HUMAN THINKING

Thinking is easier to describe than to define. Its characteristics include the daily routine of reasoning where one is at the moment, where one's destination is, and how to get there. It includes developing concepts, using words, solving problems, abstracting, intuiting, and anticipating the future. Other aspects of thinking include learning, memory, creativity, communication, logic, and generalization. How and when we use these aspects often determine the success or failure of our many interactions with our environment. This chapter discusses thinking, explores strategies that attempt to describe the characteristics of various types of thinking, and suggests how they can be used in the classroom to increase student engagement and promote higher-order thinking and learning.

Video: For some excellent videos on aspects of critical thinking, see

https://www.youtube.com/watch?v=fRmh B3MW6GE&list=PLpbtRdN7xWUcPTOqWBfC52 FubQxcgdgjk

Types of Thinking

Can you answer these questions?

- Who was the second president of the United States?
- What are the similarities and differences between the post–Civil War and post–Vietnam War periods?
- Defend why we should or should not have capital punishment.

Each of these questions requires you to think, but the type of thinking involved is not the same. The first question requires you to simply refer to a listing you have in long-term memory that recalls the sequence of presidents. Dealing with the second question is quite different. You must first recall what you have stored about both wars, separate these items into lists, then analyze them to determine which events were similar and which were different. The third question requires the retrieval and processing of large amounts of information about capital punishment, its impact on society, and its effectiveness as a deterrent to crime. Then you need to form a judgment about whether you believe criminals will be influenced by a capital punishment penalty. These three questions require different and increasingly complex thought processes to arrive at acceptable answers. Thus, some thinking is more complex than other thinking. Brain scans indicate that different parts of the brain, particularly in the frontal cortex, are involved as the problem-solving task becomes more complicated (Cole, Bagic, Kass, & Schneider, 2010; Newman & Green, 2015). This seems to be particularly true when solving mathematical problems (Anderson, Lee, & Fincham, 2014).

Brain scans show that different parts of the brain are involved as the problem-solving task becomes more complicated.

The brain has evolved different mechanisms for dealing with various situations. Logic is one of those. It recognizes, for example, that if A is equal to B, and B is equal to C, then A must be equal to C. There are other mechanisms, too. Rationality, pattern identification, image making, and approximation are all forms of thinking that serve to help the individual deal with a concept, a problem, or a decision.

Thinking as a Representational System

Although the file cabinets and their ordered system are useful metaphors for explaining the operation of long-term storage in the information processing model (see Chapter 2), they do not explain all the situations one encounters when the brain behaves as a representational system. Sometimes we cannot recognize a person's face, but we remember the name and the events that surrounded our first meeting with this person. And just thinking of the word *beach* evokes a complex series of mental events that corresponds to the internal representation we have of all the beaches we have ever encountered. Beaches gleam in the sun, are often hot, create a shoreline, merge with water, are dotted with umbrellas, and recall memories of holiday fun. The word itself is not actually a beach, but it brings forth many associations having to do with beaches. This is an example of a representational system, and it illustrates the diversity of patterns in human thinking. It is this recognition of diversity that has led to the notion of multiple intelligences. That is, an individual's thinking patterns vary when encountering different challenges, and these semiautonomous variations in thinking result in different degrees of success in learning.

Thinking and Emotion

Emotions play an important role in the thinking process. In Chapter 2, we discussed the amygdala's role in encoding emotional messages into long-term memory. We also noted that emotions often take precedence during cerebral processing and can impede or assist cognitive learning. If we like what we are learning, we are more likely to maintain attention and interest and move to higher-level thinking. We tend to probe and ask those "what if?" kinds of questions. When we dislike the learning, we usually spend the least amount of time with it and stay at minimal levels of processing. That's why the classroom's emotional climate is so important.

Students sometimes feel neutral about a new learning topic. Challenging them with activities that require higher-order thinking often sparks an interest that brings forth positive feelings. Recent studies reaffirm that as learners generate positive emotions, their scope of attention broadens and their critical thinking skills are enhanced. Neutral and negative emotions, on the other hand, narrow the scope of attention and thinking (Treur & van Wissen, 2013; Zenasni & Lubart, 2011). When students recognize the power of their own thinking, they use their skills more and solve problems for themselves rather than just waiting to be told the answers.

It is also interesting to note that students who are consistently displeased or angry about their learning (or lack of it) do not always let their emotions take control of their thinking. Studies show that upset individuals have the capacity to override their emotions and cognitively reflect on the factors that caused this negative state (Moons & Mackie, 2007). The implication here is that displeased students are able to figure out why they have these negative emotions toward their learning. If teachers have a personal talk with these students, they may be able to address and ameliorate the conditions that are causing the negative feelings.

Technology May Be Affecting How Students Think

Neuroscientists have recently been looking at whether the explosion of children's exposure to technology is affecting the way they think. Although the results so far are not conclusive, a few important insights are emerging that parents and educators should know. Several studies have found that young children who watch more than one hour of television a day had reduced executive function capacity as well as significant delays in language, cognitive, and motor development (e.g., Christakis, 2011; Lin, Cherng, Chen, Chen, & Yang, 2015).

Another impact of technology is the vast amount of information (and misinformation) available on the Internet. Students can become frustrated or paralyzed by the overwhelming amount of information and surrender, a condition known as *information avoidance*. This outcome, however, does not seem to deter them from spending hours on their digital devices. Their ability to surf through so many media pages seems to have lowered their patience for video delays. One study of the playback habits of millions of Internet users showed that they abandon a video if it takes more than two seconds to start (Krishnan & Sitaraman, 2012). This impatience can carry over into the classroom, suggesting that teachers need to engage students in the lesson objective quickly to increase the likelihood the students will pay attention.

We should recognize, too, that consistent reliance on the Internet for information may diminish the brain's need to be creative and do critical thinking. Frequently, when trying to solve a complex problem, students turn to Google to find out how *other* people solved it, rather than use their *own* creativity and thinking skills to do so. They readily accept other people's opinions and work instead of developing their own. Like any other skill, the less their creative talents are used, the less effective they become. One study looked at the creativity scores on the Torrance Tests of Creative Thinking of more than 270,000 students from kindergarten through Grade 12, from 1990 to 2008. It found that although IQ scores rose, creative thinking scores significantly decreased. The decrease for kindergartners through third grade was the most significant (K. H. Kim, 2011). Students are essentially becoming gatherers and reporters of information rather than becoming original, curious, and critical thinkers. Is this the type of thinking behavior we want our schools to accept?

THE DIMENSIONS OF HUMAN THINKING

Designing Models

Cognitive psychologists have been designing models for decades in an effort to describe the dimensions of thinking and the levels of complexity of human thought. The models have generally divided thinking processes into two categories, *convergent* or lower-order thinking and *divergent* or higher-order thinking. Other multidimensional frameworks have appeared that attempt to describe all aspects of thinking in detail. Of course, a model is only as good as its potential for achieving a desired goal (in this case, encouraging higher-order thinking in students) and the likelihood that teachers feel sufficiently comfortable with the model to make it a regular part of their classroom practice. In examining the models that describe the dimensions of thinking, most include the following major areas:

- **Basic processes** are the tools we use to transform and evaluate information, such as

  o *observing:* includes recognizing and recalling.
  o *finding patterns and generalizing:* includes classifying, comparing and contrasting, and identifying relevant and irrelevant information.
  o *forming conclusions based on patterns:* includes hypothesizing, predicting, inferring, and applying.
  o *assessing conclusions based on observations:* includes checking consistency, identifying biases and stereotypes, identifying unstated assumptions, recognizing over- and under- generalizations, and confirming conclusions with facts.

The consistency with which these basic processes appear in most models results from the recognition that they allow us to make sense of our world by pulling together bits of information into understandable and coherent patterns. Further, these processes support the notion that conclusions should be based on evidence. From these conclusions, we form patterns that help us to hypothesize, infer, and predict.

- **Domain-specific knowledge** refers to the knowledge in a particular content area that one must possess in order to carry out the basic processes described above.
- **Critical thinking** is a complex process that is based on objective standards and consistency. It includes making judgments using objective criteria and offering opinions with reasons.
- **Creative thinking** involves putting together information to arrive at a whole new concept, idea, or understanding. It often involves four stages that include preparation (gathering and examining the needed information), incubation (mulling over the idea and making connections to other experiences), illumination (the "Aha!" when the new idea comes to light), and verification (methods for testing the idea).
- **Metacognition** is the awareness one has of one's own thinking processes. It means that students should know when and why they are using the basic processes, and how these functions relate to the content they are learning. Metacognition consists of two processes occurring simultaneously: monitoring progress *while* learning and making appropriate changes when problems occur *during* learning. This is different from *reflection,* when the looks back *afterward* on the thinking processes that were used during the learning.

Are We Teaching Thinking Skills?

The ordinary experience of thinking about that sunny beach raises intriguing questions about how the brain is organized to think with increasing complexity.

What skills does the human brain need to maneuver through simple and complex thoughts? Can these skills be learned, and if so, how and when should they be taught?

Most humans are born with a brain that has all the sensory components and neural organization necessary to survive successfully in its environment. The neural organization changes dramatically, of course, as the child grows and learns, resulting in the expansion of some networks and the elimination of others. Even the most superficial look at human information processing reveals a vast system of magnificent neural networks that can learn language, recognize one face among thousands, and infer an outcome by rapidly analyzing data. Every bit of evidence available suggests that the human brain is *designed* for a broad range of thinking patterns. So if the brain is capable of higher-order thinking, why do we see so little of it in the normal course of student discussion and performance?

It just may be that the reason our students are not thinking critically is that we have not exposed them consistently to models or situations in school that require them to do so. Schooling, for the most part, still demands little more than several levels of convergent thinking. Its practices and testing focus on content acquisition through rote rehearsal, rather than the processes of thinking for analysis and synthesis. Even those teachers who have worked conscientiously to include activities requiring higher-order thinking are confronted with the realities of preparing students for high-stakes testing that usually focuses on recall and application.

> *We do not teach the brain to think. We can, however, help learners to organize content to facilitate more complex processing.*

Repeating the answer becomes more important than the process used to get the answer. Consequently, students and teachers frequently deal with learning at the lower levels of complexity.

What we are trying to do now is recognize these limitations, rewrite curriculum, retrain teachers, and encourage students to use their innate thinking abilities to process learning at higher levels of complexity. In other words, we need to work harder at teaching them *how to organize content in such a way that it facilitates and promotes higher-order thinking.*

Modeling Thinking Skills in the Classroom

Teachers serve as valuable and authentic role models when they use creative and critical reflection to improve their practice. Students are more likely to learn thinking skills in classrooms where teachers nurture a love for learning and establish a setting that is conducive to creative and critical thought. Such a positive learning climate emerges when teachers do the following:

- Exhibit genuine interest and commitment to learning
- Analyze their own thinking processes and classroom practices and explain what they do
- Change their own positions when the evidence warrants it
- Are willing to admit a mistake
- Allow students to participate in setting rules and making decisions related to learning and assessment

- Encourage students to follow their own thinking and not just repeat the teacher's views
- Allow students to select assignments and activities from a range of appropriate choices
- Prepare and present lessons that require higher-order thinking to achieve learning objectives

Having established a classroom environment that fosters higher-level thinking, the teacher's next task is to select a practical and easily understood model for teaching students the skills they need for creative, critical, and divergent thinking. Of all the current models available, let's look at a very workable and effective design that has stood the test of time—Bloom's Taxonomy.

REVISITING BLOOM'S TAXONOMY OF THE COGNITIVE DOMAIN

What model can teachers use that, when properly implemented, promotes thinking, has been successful in the past, and holds the promise of success for the future? My suggestion is to start with the taxonomy of the cognitive domain developed more than 50 years ago by Benjamin Bloom, and see if we can adapt it to the needs of the modern era. Writing a fifth edition gave me another opportunity to decide what model to present here that is flexible, encourages higher-order thinking, and can adapt to modern curriculum initiatives. Please bear with me to learn why this model may continue to form the basis for successful classroom activities that promote higher-order thinking.

Why do I continue to propose this type of model? In recent years, I have seen the spread of state-adopted curriculum standards, the new mandates of the Every Student Shall Succeed Act, a greater emphasis on state and national testing, and an intense public insistence that school and teacher accountability be measured in test scores. Consequently, teachers who are under pressure to teach to the test are not likely to implement overly complicated, multilevel thinking skills programs. That is why I am comfortable proposing that we reexamine this familiar model and decide how, with some adjustments, it can still serve our needs. My aim is to convince you of its value in aiding less able students experience the excitement of higher-order thinking and the exhilaration of greater achievement. To me, implementing this user-friendly model is more important than ever, given the earlier discussion on the effects technology seems to be having on student thinking.

Why Start With This Model?

One of the more enduring and useful models for enhancing thinking was developed by Benjamin Bloom and his colleagues in the 1950s. Bloom's system of classification, or taxonomy, identifies six levels of complexity of human thought (Bloom, Engelhart, Furst, Hill, & Krathwohl, 1956). I believe that with some revisions, this framework can upgrade the quality of teacher instruction and student learning for the following reasons:

- It is familiar to many prospective and practicing teachers.
- It is user-friendly and simple when compared to other models.
- It provides a common language about learning objectives that cuts across subject matter and grade levels.
- It requires only modest retraining for teachers to understand the relationship between the difficulty and complexity components.
- It helps teachers recognize the difference between difficulty and complexity, so they can help slower learners improve their thinking and achievement significantly.
- It can be implemented in every classroom immediately without waiting for major reform or restructuring.
- It is inexpensive in that teachers need only a few supplementary materials to use with the current curriculum.
- It motivates teachers because they see their students learning better, thinking more profoundly, and showing more interest.
- With revisions, it can reflect the latest research on brain functions.

With revisions, Bloom's Taxonomy can still be a useful tool for moving students, especially slower learners, to higher levels of thinking.

Although Bloom's Taxonomy has been standard fare in preservice and inservice teacher training for many years, the taxonomy's value as a model for moving all students to higher levels of thinking has not been fully explored. Moreover, as we will discuss later, the taxonomy's connection to student ability has been largely misunderstood and misapplied. This situation is regrettable because the model is easy to understand and, when used correctly, can accelerate learning and elevate student interest and achievement, especially for slower learners.

Video: For an amusing illustration of the six levels of Bloom's revised taxonomy, using scenes from Harry Potter movies, see

https://www.youtube.com/watch?v=TI4kZbOvLiY

The Model's Structure and Revision

Bloom's original taxonomy contained six levels: knowledge, comprehension, application, analysis, synthesis, and evaluation (see Figure 7.1). From 1995 through 2000, a group of educators worked to revise the original taxonomy based on more recent understandings about learning, as shown in Figure 7.2 (Anderson et al., 2001).

In the revised taxonomy, the original *Knowledge* level was renamed *Remember* because it more accurately describes the brain's recall process occurring at this level. Also, knowledge can be acquired at *all* levels. *Comprehension* was renamed *Understand* because that is the term most commonly used when teachers discuss this level. *Application, Analysis,* and *Evaluation* were changed to the verbs *Apply, Analyze,* and *Evaluate.*

Figure 7.1 Bloom's original taxonomy had six levels, from knowledge (lowest complexity) to evaluation (highest complexity).

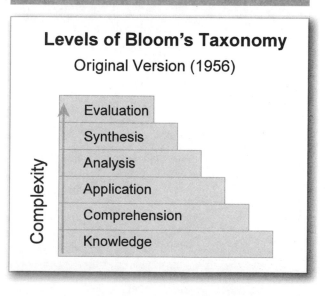

Levels of Bloom's Taxonomy
Original Version (1956)

Complexity

- Evaluation
- Synthesis
- Analysis
- Application
- Comprehension
- Knowledge

Figure 7.2 The revised taxonomy retains the six levels but changes the labels to verb form, renames three levels, and interchanges the top two levels. The dotted outline suggests a more open and fluid model, recognizing that an individual may move among the levels during extended processing.

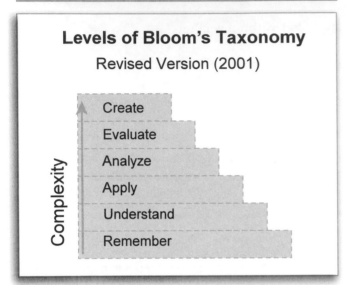

Levels of Bloom's Taxonomy
Revised Version (2001)

Complexity

Create
Evaluate
Analyze
Apply
Understand
Remember

Synthesis changed places with *Evaluation* and was renamed *Create.* This exchange was made because studies in cognitive neuroscience suggest that generating, planning, and producing an original product demands more complex thinking than making judgments based on accepted criteria (see Table 7.1). Although there are still six separate levels, the hierarchy of complexity is not as rigid, and it recognizes that an individual may move easily among the levels during extended processing.

Below is a review of each level using the story "Goldilocks and the Three Bears" and the bombing of Pearl Harbor as examples of how two differing concepts can be taken through the taxonomy.

Remember. Remember refers to the mere rote recall and recognition of previously learned material, from specific facts to a definition or a complete theory. All that is required is bringing it forth from long-term memory in the form in which it was learned. This is recall of semantic memory. It represents the lowest level of learning in the cognitive domain because there is no presumption that the

Table 7.1 Revision of Bloom's Taxonomy of the Cognitive Domain

Below are the levels in decreasing order of complexity with terms and sample activities that illustrate the thought processes at each level.

Level	Terms	Sample Activities
Create	imagine compose design infer	Pretend you were a participant in the Boston Tea Party and write a diary entry that tells what happened. Rewrite "Little Red Riding Hood" as a news story. Design a different way of solving this problem. Formulate a hypothesis that might explain the results of these three experiments.
Evaluate	appraise assess judge critique	Which of the two main characters in the story would you rather have as a friend? Why? Is violence ever justified in correcting injustices? Why or why not? Which of the environments we've studied seems like the best place for you to live? Defend your answer. Critique these two products and defend which one you would recommend to the consumer.
Analyze	analyze contrast distinguish deduce	Which events in the story are fantasy and which really happened? Compare and contrast the post–Civil War period with the post–Vietnam War period. Sort this collection of rocks into three categories. Which of these words are Latin derivatives and which are Greek?
Apply	practice calculate apply execute	Use each vocabulary word in a new sentence. Calculate the area of your classroom. Think of three situations in which we would use this mathematics operation. Use the parts to reassemble this motor correctly.

Level	Terms	Sample Activities
Understand	summarize discuss explain outline	Summarize the paragraph in your own words. Why are symbols used on maps? Write a paragraph explaining the duties of the mayor. Outline the steps for completing this experiment.
Remember	define label recall recognize	What is the definition of a verb? Label the three symbols on this map. What are the three branches of government? Which object in the picture is a xylophone?

Source: Adapted from Anderson et al., 2001.

learner understands what is being recalled. Students in first grade recite the Pledge of Allegiance daily. Do they all comprehend what they are saying? If so, would one fine, patriotic boy have started his pledge with, *I led the pigeons to the flag of the United . . . ?*

Examples: What did Goldilocks do in the three bears' house?

What was the date of the bombing of Pearl Harbor?

Understand. This level describes the ability to make sense of the material. Understanding may occur by converting the material from one form to another (words to numbers), by interpreting the material (summarizing a story), or by estimating future trends (predicting the consequences or effects). The learning goes beyond mere rote recall and represents the lowest level of comprehension. When a student understands the material, rather than merely recalling it, the material becomes available for future use to solve problems and to make decisions. Questions at this level attempt to determine if the students comprehend the information in a sensible way. When this happens, students may say, "Now I get it."

Examples: Why did Goldilocks like the baby bear's things best?

Why did the Japanese bomb Pearl Harbor?

Apply. This level refers to the ability to use learned material in new situations with a minimum of direction. It includes the application of such things as rules, concepts, methods, and theories to solve problems. The learner activates procedural memory and uses convergent thinking to select, transfer, and apply data to complete a new task. Practice is essential at this level.

Examples: If Goldilocks came to your house today, what things might she do?

If you had been responsible for the defense of the Hawaiian Islands, what preparation would you have made against an attack?

Analyze. This is the ability to break material into its component parts so that its structure may be understood. It includes identifying parts, examining the relationships of the parts to each other and to the whole, and recognizing the organizational principles involved. The learner must be able to organize and reorganize information into categories. The brain's frontal lobes are working hard at this level. This stage is more complex because the learner is aware of the thought process in use (metacognition) and understands both the content and structure of the material.

Examples: What things in the Goldilocks story could have really happened?

What lesson did our country learn from Pearl Harbor?

Evaluate. This level deals with the ability to judge the value of material based on specific criteria and standards. The learner may determine the criteria or be given them. The learner examines criteria from several categories and selects those that are the most relevant to the situation. Activities at this level almost always have multiple and equally acceptable solutions. This is a high level of cognitive thought because it contains elements of many other levels, plus conscious judgments based on definite criteria. At this level, learners tend to consolidate their thinking and become more receptive to other points of view.

Examples: Do you think it was right for Goldilocks to go into the bears' house without having been invited? Why or why not?

Do you feel that the bombing of Pearl Harbor has any effect on Japanese-American relations today? Why or why not?

Create. This refers to the ability to put parts together to form a plan that is new to the learner. It may involve the production of a unique communication (essay or speech), a plan of operations (research proposal), or a scheme for classifying information. This level stresses creativity, with major emphasis on forming new patterns or structures. This is the level where learners use divergent thinking to get an Aha! experience. It indicates that being creative requires a great deal of information, understanding, and application to produce a tangible product. Michelangelo could never have created the statues of *David* or the *Pietà* without a thorough comprehension of human anatomy and types of marble, as well as the ability to use polishing compounds and tools with accuracy. His artistry comes from the mastery with which he used his knowledge and skill to carve magnificent pieces. Although most often associated with the arts, this process can occur in all areas of the curriculum (see Chapter 6).

Examples: Retell the story as "Goldilocks and the Three Fishes."

Retell the story of Pearl Harbor, assuming the U.S. armed forces had been ready for the attack.

Test Question No. 10: Bloom's Taxonomy has not changed over the years. True or false?

Answer: False. In 2001, a team of researchers and psychologists published a revision of Bloom's Taxonomy that aligned it more closely with current research and usage.

Important Characteristics of the Revised Model

Several points need to be made here about the revision, especially in light of recent discoveries in how the brain processes information.

Loosening of the Hierarchy

Bloom's original model held that the six levels were cumulative: that is, each level above the lowest required all the skills of lesser complexity. To Bloom, a learner could not comprehend material without mentally possessing it. Similarly, one could not correctly apply a learning to new situations without understanding it. However, because the 2001 revision gives much greater weight to teacher choice and usage, the strict hierarchy has been loosened to allow levels to overlap one another. For example, certain forms of explaining, usually associated with *Understand*, might be more complex than executing, which is associated with *Apply*.

Moreover, this loosening is more consistent with evidence from brain research showing that different brain areas are used to solve different types of problems. Studies using imaging scans and EEG have found different cerebral regions were involved in solving problems of logic and sequence (deductive reasoning) rather than in solving open-ended problems with multiple answers (inductive reasoning; Jauk, Benedek, & Neubauer, 2012; Mihov, Denzler, & Förster, 2010). This evidence tends to weaken Bloom's basic notion that one type of thinking is dependent on the prior activation of lower level thinking. But cognitive psychologists have long suspected that thinking skills at the upper levels were a lot more fluid than Bloom's rigid hierarchy suggested. Nonetheless, the experimental findings support the notion that there are different types of thinking which the revised taxonomy accurately describes.

Other Ways to View the Levels

To align the revised taxonomy more with recent studies on cognitive processing, it is helpful to look at other ways of describing the levels. For example, the lower three levels (*Remember, Understand,* and *Apply*) describe a *convergent* thinking process whereby the learner recalls and focuses what is known and comprehended to solve a problem through application. The upper three levels (*Analyze, Evaluate,* and *Create*) describe a *divergent* thinking process, because the learner's processing results in new insights and discoveries that were not part of the original information. When the learner is thinking at these upper levels, thought flows naturally from one to the other and the level boundaries disappear.

Another approach is to view *Remember* and *Understand* as skills designed to acquire and understand information and *Apply* and *Analyze* as skills for changing and transforming information through deduction and inference. The skills at *Evaluate* and *Create* generate new information by appraising, critiquing, and imagining. Even here, one must remember that the levels are fluid and overlap.

Cognitive and Emotional Thinking

It is important to remember that Bloom's model describes the *cognitive* processing of information that poses no immediate danger to the learner. It is *not* intended to describe *emotional* thinking, which often occurs without cognitive input. For example, when a stranger walks near you on a dark street, the amygdala in your brain immediately evaluates the environmental stimuli to determine if a threat exists. The amygdala reacts to a threatening voice or menacing look, often triggering a fight-or-flight reaction. In this situation, the individual's brain is evaluating without the benefit of conscious thought. There is no time for remembering, understanding, applying, or analyzing. Let's just get out of here! This taxonomy is not appropriate here because it addresses conscious and deliberate cognitive thought, not survival behavior. That said, it should be noted that Bloom and his colleagues also developed a five-level taxonomy of the affective domain, setting up a hierarchy of emotional connections to learning (Bloom, Mesia, & Krathwohl, 1964).

Testing Your Understanding of the Taxonomy

To determine if you understand the revised taxonomy's six different levels, complete the activity below. Then, look at the answers and explanation following the activity.

Directions. Identify the highest level (remember, the levels are cumulative) of the taxonomy indicated in these learning objectives.

1. Given a ruler to measure the room, find how long the room is.

2. What is the Sixth Amendment to the U.S. Constitution?

3. Given copies of the Articles of Confederation and the Bill of Rights, the learner will write a comparison of the two documents and discuss similarities and differences.

4. Identify and write a question for each level of the taxonomy.

5. Use your own words to explain the moral at the end of the fable.

6. Given two ways to solve the problem, the learner will make a choice of which to use and give reasons.

7. Write your own fairy tale including all the characteristics of a fairy tale.

Answers:

1. *Apply.* The learner must know the measuring system, comprehend the meaning of length, and use the ruler correctly.

2. *Remember.* The learner simply recalls that the Sixth Amendment deals with the rights of the accused.

3. *Analyze.* The learner must separate both documents into their component parts and compare and contrast them for relationships that describe their similarities and differences.

4. *Apply.* The learner knows each level, comprehends its definition, and then uses this information to write the question for each level.

5. *Understand.* The learner shows comprehension by explaining the fable's moral.

6. *Evaluate.* The learner chooses between two feasible options and explains the reasons for the choice.

7. *Create.* Using the general characteristics of fairy tales, the learner creates a new one.

The Taxonomy and the Dimensions of Thinking

To what extent does the revision of Bloom's taxonomy address the major areas mentioned earlier that are included within most of the current models describing the dimensions of thinking?

Basic Processes. The six levels of the revised taxonomy cover all the skills included under these processes. *Observing* is contained in the levels of *Remember* and *Understand. Finding patterns* and *generalizing* are skills in the levels of *Remember, Understand,* and *Analyze. Forming conclusions based on patterns* is in *Analyze* and *Create.* Finally, *assessing conclusions* is a characteristic of the taxonomy's *Evaluate* level.

Domain-Specific Knowledge. The revised taxonomy recognizes that the acquisition of knowledge occurs at all levels. It specifically separates this domain into four types of knowledge: factual (names, dates), conceptual (ideas, patterns), procedural (steps, sequences), and metacognitive (reflections on thought processes).

Critical Thinking. The upper levels of the taxonomy require critical thinking in order to analyze, contrast, criticize, and accurately assess information.

Creative Thinking. Students working diligently at the *Create* level are using all the skills associated with creative thinking.

Metacognition. This is the one area that is not explicitly cited in any one of the six levels. Nonetheless, when analyzing or discussing the rationale for selecting from among equally viable choices at the *Evaluate* level, the learner has to reflect on the processes used to arrive at the selection and gather data to defend the choice. This self-awareness of the thinking process used is the essence of metacognition. The other components, such as having a respect for self-monitoring as a valued skill, a positive and personal attitude toward learning, and an attention to learning through introspection and practice, are very likely to result from the accurate, frequent, and systematic use of the taxonomy's upper levels.

The Critical Difference Between Complexity and Difficulty

Complexity and difficulty describe different mental operations, but are often used synonymously. This error, resulting in the two factors being treated as one, limits the use of the taxonomy to enhance the thinking of all students. By recognizing how these concepts are different, the teacher can gain valuable insight into the connection between the taxonomy and student ability. *Complexity* describes the *thought process* that the brain uses to deal with information. In the revision of Bloom's Taxonomy (Table 7.1), it can be described by any of the six words representing the six levels. For example, the question, "What is the capital of Rhode Island?" is at the *Remember* level, while the question, "Tell me in your own words what is meant by a state capital," is at the *Understand* level. The second question is more *complex* than the first because the thought process required is at a higher level in the taxonomy.

Difficulty, on the other hand, refers to the *amount of effort* that the learner must expend *within* a level of complexity to accomplish a learning objective. It is possible for a learning activity to become increasingly difficult without becoming more complex. For example, the task "Name the states of the Union" is at the *Remember* level of complexity because it involves simple recall (semantic memory) for most students. Similarly, the task "Name the states of the Union and their capitals" is also at the *Remember* level, but is more difficult than the prior question because it involves more neural effort to recall additional information. Similarly, the task "Name the states and their capitals in order of their admission to the Union" is still at the *Remember* level, but it is considerably more difficult than the first two. It requires gathering more information and then sequencing it in chronological order.

> Teachers are more likely to increase difficulty, rather than complexity, when attempting to raise student thinking.

These are examples of how students can exert great effort to achieve a learning task while processing at the lowest level of thinking. When seeking to challenge students, classroom teachers are more likely (perhaps unwittingly) to increase difficulty rather than complexity as the challenge mode. This may be because they do not recognize the difference between these concepts or that they believe that difficulty is the method for achieving higher-order thinking (see Figure 7.3).

Connecting Complexity and Difficulty to Ability

When teachers are asked whether complexity or difficulty is more closely linked to student ability, they more often choose complexity. Some explain their belief that only students of higher ability can carry out the processes indicated in the *Analyze, Evaluate,* and *Create* levels. Others say that whenever they have tried to bring slower students up the taxonomy, the lesson got bogged down. But the real connection to ability is difficulty, not complexity.

The mistaken link between complexity and ability is the result of an unintended but very real self-fulfilling prophesy. Here's how it works. Teachers allot a certain amount of *time* for the class to learn a concept, usually based on how long they think it will take the *average* student to learn it (see Figure 7.4). The fast learners learn the concept in less than the allotted time. During the remaining time, their brains often sort the concept's sublearnings into important and unimportant categories; that is, they select the critical attributes for storage and discard what they decide is unimportant. This explains why fast learners are usually fast retrievers: They have not cluttered their memory networks with trivia.

Figure 7.3 Complexity and difficulty are different. Complexity establishes the level of thought while difficulty determines the amount of effort required within each level.

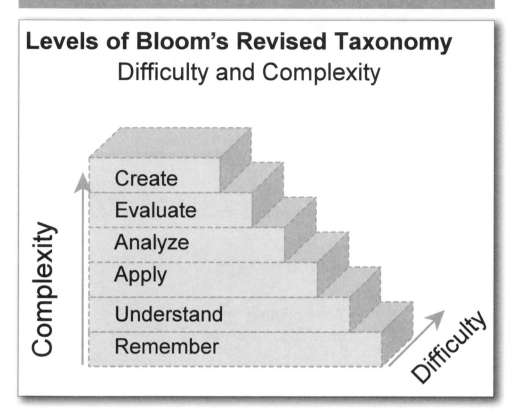

Levels of Bloom's Revised Taxonomy
Difficulty and Complexity

Complexity

Create
Evaluate
Analyze
Apply
Understand
Remember

Difficulty

Meanwhile, the slower learners need more than the allotted time to learn the concept. If that time is not given to them, not only do they lose part of the sublearnings, but they also do not have time to do any sorting. If the teacher attempts to move up the taxonomy, the fast learners have the concept's more important attributes in working memory to use appropriately and successfully at the higher levels of complexity. The slow learners, on the other hand, have not had time to sort, have cluttered their working memory with all the sublearnings (important and unimportant), and do not recognize the parts needed for more complex processing. For them, it is like taking five big suitcases on an overnight trip, whereas the fast learners have taken just a small bag packed with the essentials. As a result, teachers become convinced that higher-order thinking is for the fast learners and that ability is linked to complexity.

Bloom reported on studies that included slower students for whom the unimportant material was not even taught. The curriculum was sorted from the start, and the focus was on critical attributes and other vital information. When the teacher moved up the taxonomy, these students in some cases demonstrated better achievement than the control groups (Bloom, 1976). When teachers differentiate between complexity and difficulty, a new view of Bloom's Taxonomy emerges, one which promises more success for more students. It is important to remember that slow

> *With guidance and practice, slower learners can regularly reach the higher levels of Bloom's revised taxonomy.*

Figure 7.4 The time allotted to learn a concept is usually fixed even though students learn at different rates.

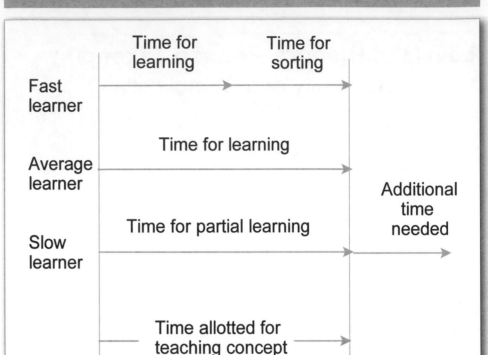

learner means it takes more time for the student to learn something than the typical learner. It does not mean an inability to learn.

The Taxonomy and Constructivism

In their description of the characteristics of constructivist teachers, Brooks and Brooks (1999) noted that these teachers ask open-ended questions and continually encourage students to analyze, evaluate, and create. From this description, it seems evident that teachers who constantly use the upper levels of Bloom's revised taxonomy are demonstrating, among other things, constructivist behaviors.

Curriculum Changes to Accommodate the Taxonomy

The implications from these studies are very significant in that they suggest two important things about using the taxonomy:

- If teachers avoid the self-fulfilling prophecy snare, they can get slower learners to do higher-order thinking successfully and often.
- One way to accomplish this is to review the curriculum and remove the topics of least importance in order to gain the time needed for practice at the higher levels. This is known as *strategic abandonment*. An effective method for doing this pruning is to list all the concepts in a curriculum

in order of most important to least. Delete the least important bottom 20 to 25 percent, and use the time gained by this sorting and paring to move all students up the taxonomy. Finally, take advantage of the power of positive transfer by integrating these concepts with previously taught material and connecting them to appropriate concepts in other curriculum areas.

Higher-Order Thinking
Increases Understanding and Retention

The number of neurons in our brains declines as we age, but our ability to learn, remember, and recall is dependent largely on the number of connections between neurons. The stability and permanency of these connections reflect the nature of the thinking process and the type and degree of rehearsal that occurred during the learning episode.

As mentioned earlier, brain scans show that elaborative rehearsal, involving higher-order thinking skills, engages the brain's frontal lobe. This engagement helps learners make connections between past and new learning, creates new pathways, strengthens existing pathways, and increases the likelihood that the new learning will be consolidated and stored for future retrieval.

Many teachers recognize the need to do more activities that require elaborate thinking rather than just rote rehearsal. They admit that when they move up through higher levels of Bloom's Taxonomy (or any other thinking skills framework) students demonstrate a much greater depth of engagement and understanding. However, they also admit that there are barriers to using this approach regularly because it takes more time. Examples of the barriers they cite are the pressures to cover an ever-expanding curriculum and the tyranny of quick-answer testing of all types. These obstacles will not be overcome easily, but teachers can work toward a compromise—finding ways to engage the novel brain with challenging activities and developing alternative assessment strategies, such as brain-friendly formative assessments (Sousa, 2015b).

> *Our students would make a quantum leap to higher-order thinking if every teacher in every classroom correctly and regularly used a model such as Bloom's revised taxonomy.*

OTHER THINKING SKILLS PROGRAMS

Other thinking skills programs and models exist, and new ones are appearing. Here are a few that I have seen teachers use effectively to deepen student thinking and encourage creativity.

- **Habits of Mind.** Developed by Arthur Costa and Bena Kallick, the Habits of Mind model looks at the characteristics that people demonstrate when trying to solve problems for which there is no immediate and obvious solution (Costa & Kallick, 2009). It suggests these 16 characteristics: persisting; managing impulsivity; listening with empathy; thinking flexibly; thinking about thinking; striving for accuracy; questioning and posing problems; applying past knowledge to new situations; thinking and communicating with clarity and precision; gathering data through the senses; creating, imaging, and innovating; responding with wonderment and awe; taking responsible risks; finding humor; thinking independently; and remaining open to continuous learning.

- **Understanding by Design (UbD).** This framework was originally presented in 1995 by Grant Wiggins and Jay McTighe and is based on two main ideas: focusing on teaching and assessing for deep understanding and for the transfer of learning, and designing curriculum backward from those outcomes (Wiggins & McTighe, 2005). The authors propose six facets of understanding. Explanation to support claims and assertion with evidence; interpretation that draws inferences and generates something new about them; application that uses the knowledge and skills in a new or unexpected situation; perspective for analyzing different points of view about a topic; empathy that demonstrates the ability to walk in another's shoes; and self-knowledge to assess, evaluate, refine, and revise their own thinking.

- **Webb's Depth of Knowledge (DoK).** Norman Webb (1997) suggests a four level model of the complexity of thinking that is essentially a collapsed version of the six levels in Bloom's Revised Taxonomy. Level 1 is Recall and Reproduction, which correlates to Bloom's levels Remember and Understand. Level 2 is Skills and Concepts, which correlates to Bloom's Apply level. Level 3 is Short-term Strategic Thinking, which is closely associated with Bloom's Analyze level. Finally, level 4 is Extended Thinking, which is akin to Bloom's Evaluate and Create levels. Districts that have adopted Webb's DoK model say it can be easier to manage than Bloom's model. Furthermore, they note that the activities at each DoK level look more at the students' products rather than just focusing on Bloom's action verbs.

In reviewing these programs, I have found that many of the thinking skills and characteristics can be associated with at least one level of the revised taxonomy. In most of these programs, the difference is in how the skills are labeled and organized. I am convinced that if every teacher correctly used Bloom's revised taxonomy, or another model if they choose, in every classroom and in every subject area, our students would make a quantum leap forward in their ability to do higher-order thinking and enhance their creativity. And they can do this now while waiting for more comprehensive reform efforts to become reality.

WHAT'S COMING UP?

Now that we have looked at important aspects of how the brain learns and remembers, the next step is to consolidate this information into a workable design for planning lessons. What components should be included in a lesson? What questions should teachers be asking when considering content and strategies for instruction? How do teachers get the support they need in their school to try out new techniques and to keep abreast of what we are learning about learning? The answers to these vital questions are coming up in the next chapter.

PRACTITIONER'S CORNER

Understanding Bloom's Revised Taxonomy

Directions: With a partner, explain verbally what the pictorial view below is all about. Then fill in the chart on the next page, using the explanation of the pictures to describe your thought processing at each level of the taxonomy.

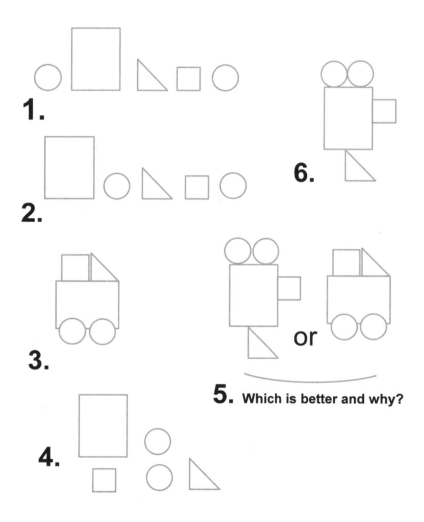

Directions: Write on the lines below the six levels of the revised Bloom's Taxonomy, starting with the least complex at the bottom. Then write a few words next to each level that explain the type of processing that occurs when describing the various pictures on the previous page.

Level	Description of Processing
6.	
5.	
4.	
3.	
2.	
1.	

PRACTITIONER'S CORNER

Take a Concept/Situation Up the Taxonomy!

Directions: Think of a task that you need to accomplish with your own child, parent, colleague, or spouse (e.g., how to use the washing machine with different types of clothes, planning a vacation) and describe questions or activities that move the task up Bloom's revised taxonomy.

©iStockphoto.com/spwidoff   CONCEPT/SITUATION: _____

Create (putting ideas together to form a new whole):

Evaluate (judging material using certain criteria):

Analyze (breaking down a concept and looking for relationships):

Apply (using a concept or principle in a new situation):

Understand (translating the material to achieve comprehension):

START HERE: Remember (rote remembering of information):

PRACTITIONER'S CORNER

Tips on Using Bloom's Revised Taxonomy

- **Watch the Behavior of the Learner.** The learner's behavior reveals the level of complexity where processing is taking place. Whenever the brain has the option of solving a problem at two levels of complexity, it generally chooses the less complex level. Teachers can inadvertently design activities that they believe are at one level of complexity that students actually accomplish at a different (usually lower) level. For example, the teacher may ask students to create (top level) a model that illustrates the concept they are learning. Students who devise models from their own imagination and that is new to them, are genuinely at Bloom's *Create* level. But students who create models based on someone else's work they found on the Internet, are just at the *Understand* level, or possibly at the *Apply* level. In any case, they are not at the *Create* level that the teacher was envisaging.

- **Provide Sufficient Practice at the Lower Levels.** In most instances, students should deal with the new learnings thoroughly and successfully at lower levels before moving to upper levels. It is very difficult to create an original product without a solid knowledge base and sufficient practice in applying the learnings.

- **Beware of Mimicry.** Sometimes students seem to be applying their learning to a new situation (*Apply* level) when they are just mimicking the teacher's behavior. Mimicry is usually the *Remember* level. For students to be really at the *Apply* level, they must understand and explain why they are using a particular process to solve *new* problems.

- **Discuss Core Concepts at the Higher Levels.** Not all topics are suitable for processing at the upper levels. There are some areas in which creativity is not desired (e.g., basic arithmetic, spelling, the rules of grammar), but consider taking to the upper levels every concept that is identified as a core learning. This helps students to attach meaning and make connections to past learnings, thereby significantly increasing retention.

- **Choose Complexity Over Difficulty.** Give novel, multisensory tasks to move students progressively up the taxonomy. Limit the exposure to trivial information and discourage students from memorizing it, a process that many find monotonous and meaningless. Instead, give them divergent activities in *Analyze, Evaluate,* and *Create* that are more interesting and more likely to result in a deeper understanding and retention of the learning objectives. For example, given the persistent concerns over immigration, a discussion of tourists, migrants, and immigrants could ask students to *analyze* these concepts in the context of rights and obligations of nonresidents and noncitizens, *evaluate* proposals for dealing with social problems such as illegal immigrants, and *create* policies that solve specific social problems without causing other problems (e.g., dealing with immigrants without negatively affecting tourism).

PRACTITIONER'S CORNER

Bloom's Taxonomy: Increasing Complexity

Examples become more complex from bottom to top, and more difficult from left to right.

BLOOM'S LEVEL		INCREASING LEVEL OF DIFFICULTY ⟶	
↑ I N C R E A S I N G C O M P L E X I T Y	CREATE	Rewrite the story from the point of view of the dog.	Rewrite the story from the points of view of the dog and of the cat.
	EVALUATE	Compare the two main characters in the story. Which would you rather have as a friend and why?	Compare the four main characters in the story. Which would you rather have as a friend and why?
	ANALYZE	What were the similarities and differences between this story and the one we read about the Civil War hero?	What were the similarities and differences between this story, the one we read about the Civil War hero, and the one about the Great Depression?
	APPLY	Think of another situation that could have caused the main character to behave that way.	Think of at least three other situations that could have caused the main character to behave that way.
	UNDERSTAND	Write a paragraph that describes the childhood of any one of the main characters.	Write a paragraph that describes the childhood of each of the four main characters.
	REMEMBER	Name the major characters in this story.	Name the major characters and the four locations in this story.

PRACTITIONER'S CORNER

Understanding the Difference
Between Complexity and Difficulty

First, let's try a real-life application.

1. Select a partner and decide who is Partner A and who is Partner B.

2. Each partner performs, in turn, the activities for each situation in Table X below.

3. When both partners have completed the three situations, discuss whether complexity or difficulty was changed in each situation when moving from A's to B's activity.

Table X   Deciding Whether Complexity or Difficulty Has Changed

Situation	Partner A's Activity	Partner B's Activity	Complexity or Difficulty Changed? How?
1	Tell your partner the month of your birth and the city and state where you were born.	Tell your partner the make of your current automobile.	
2	Roll a piece of paper into a ball. Stand 10 feet from your partner. Ask your partner to stand and to form his/her arms into a ring in front (as though to hug someone). Now toss the ball five times and try to get all five tosses through the ring formed by your partner's arms.	Repeat what your partner just did, except stand facing away from your partner and toss the paper ball over your head five times, still aiming for your partner's ringed arms.	
3	Fanfold a piece of paper. Then explain to your partner three uses for the folded paper.	After listening to your partner's explanation of the uses, choose one you think is best and explain why.	

Now, let's try a school situation. Examine how each teacher in Table Y below changes Activity A to Activity B. Then decide whether the teacher has increased that activity's level of complexity or difficulty.

Table Y Deciding Whether Complexity or Difficulty Has Increased

Teacher	Activity A	Activity B	Increased Complexity or Difficulty?
1	Make an outline of the story you just read.	Make an outline of the last two stories you read.	
2	Compare and contrast the personalities of Julius Caesar and Macbeth.	After reading three acts of Macbeth, write a plausible ending.	
3	Choose one character in the story you would like to be and explain your choice.	Choose two characters in the story you would like to be and explain why.	
4	Name the three most common chemical elements on Earth.	Describe in your own words what is meant by a "chemical element."	

Reflections:

Is complexity or difficulty more closely related to intelligence?

_____

_____

_____

_____

_____

How will understanding that difference affect my teaching?

_____

_____

_____

_____

_____

Summary: Increasing the *difficulty* of a task adds to the students' efforts without increasing the level of their thinking processes. Think of it as moving *horizontally* within a level of the revised Bloom's Taxonomy. Strategies such as repetition and drill tend to increase difficulty. Jot down below some other strategies that increase difficulty. For what types of learning would it be important to use strategies to increase difficulty?

_____

_____

_____

_____

_____

_____

_____

_____

_____

_____

Increasing the *complexity* of a task causes the students to change the way they mentally process the task. Think of it as moving *vertically* up the taxonomy from one level to a higher one. Strategies that cause students to compare and contrast, or to choose among viable options and defend their choice, are examples of increasing complexity. Jot down below some other strategies that increase complexity. For what types of learning would it be important to use strategies to increase complexity?

_____

_____

_____

_____

_____

_____

_____

_____

_____

PRACTITIONER'S CORNER

Questions to Stimulate Higher-Order Thinking

Incorporate these questions into lesson plans to stimulate higher-order thinking. Be sure to read the guidelines for using the Bloom's revised taxonomy to ensure the maximum effectiveness of these questions. Remember to provide adequate wait time. Students should become accustomed to this type of questioning in every study assignment.

What would you have done? Why do you think this is the best choice?

What are some of the things you wondered about while this was happening?

Could this ever really happen? What might happen next?

What do you think might happen if . . . ? What do you think caused this?

How is it different from . . . ? Can you give an example?

Where do we go next? Where could we go for help on this?

Have we left out anything important?

Can we trust the source of this material?

In what other ways could this be done? How can you test this theory?

How many ways can you think of to use . . . ?

Do you agree with this author/speaker? Why or why not?

Can you isolate the most important idea?

How could you modify this? How would changing the sequence affect the outcome?

How can you tell the difference between . . . and . . . ?

Activities to Stimulate Higher-Order Thinking

The following activities help teachers encourage higher-order thinking in their classrooms:

- Encourage students to use analogies and metaphors when describing and comparing new concepts, theories, and principles.

- Have students attempt to solve real life problems (e.g., energy crisis, environmental pollution) where there is a possibility of more than one adequate solution.

- Ask questions that foster higher-order thinking, such as those with multiple answers or several equally correct answers.

- Involve students in debates and discussions that tackle more than one side of an issue, and require students to support their arguments with evidence.

- Get students in role plays or simulations of historical events where people held conflicting views (e.g., drafting the U.S. Constitution, women's right to vote).

- Supplement regular textbooks with additional materials (including audio/visual content, appropriate Internet sites) that provide a wider variety of perspectives about a particular idea.

- Encourage students to watch television programs, attend community meetings, visit Internet sites, and read newspaper articles that express different viewpoints. Follow this with an analysis of the relative strengths and weaknesses of the arguments, including an analysis of the possible motives underlying the various positions.

- Have students analyze the content of popular media (e.g., television, movies, music, social media) for their accuracy and completeness of its portrayals of everyday life. For example, do commercials glorifying the acquisition of expensive personal goods balance with the existence of poverty in the community. Do the media perpetuate stereotypes?

- Explore with students the methods used to develop knowledge in a particular field. For example, what technologies help us look inside the living human brain?

CHAPTER 7: THINKING SKILLS AND LEARNING

Key Points to Ponder

Jot down on this page key points, ideas, strategies, and resources you want to consider later. This sheet is your personal journal summary and will help to jog your memory.

_____

_____

_____

_____

_____

_____

_____

_____

_____

_____

_____

8

Putting It
All Together

In the world of the future, the new illiterate will be the person who has not learned to learn.

—Alvin Toffler

Chapter Highlights

This chapter focuses on how to use the research presented in this book to plan daily lessons. It suggests guidelines and a format for lesson design and mentions support systems to maintain expertise in the techniques and continuous professional growth.

The preceding chapters discussed some of the major strides that research is making in exploring how the brain processes information and learns. Suggestions are offered in each chapter's Practitioner's Corners on how to translate these new discoveries into practical classroom strategies that can improve the efficacy of teaching and learning. But this information is of value to students only if teachers can incorporate it into their classroom practice so that it becomes part of their daily instructional behavior. The question now is, How do we use this large amount of information when planning our daily lessons?

STUDENTS SHOULD KNOW HOW THEIR BRAINS LEARN

Your success in using the strategies suggested in this book is likely to be greater if your students have some basic knowledge about how their brains learn.

Teachers who have shared this information in their classes have reported great student interest. Students are eager to know what goes on inside their heads while learning something. Here are some suggestions.

- Start with a brain model and explain what each part does. There are numerous videos on the Internet that will help you with that.
- Explain in age-appropriate terms about attention, memory systems, meaning, and retention of learning.
- Encourage the students to use in class words and phrases associated with the brain, such as neurons and working and long-term memories.
- Emphasize the importance of sleep and the many cognitive, emotional, and physical difficulties that can result from lack of sleep. Ask students to keep track of how many hours of sleep they get on school nights, and whether they think that is adequate.
- Explain the physiological reasons for why you regularly get them up, moving, and talking about their learning. Essentially, it is important to increase blood circulation in the frontal lobe while doing cognitive processing, and whoever explains, learns.

Consider regularly adding to your lessons a brief description of one facet of how the brain learns, followed by student discussions. This activity will not only engage the students, but reaffirm that the school is a place where teachers and students are working together to get a deeper understanding of the teaching and learning process.

WHAT ABOUT THE FLIPPED CLASSROOM?

One teaching approach that has emerged into the limelight in recent years is the **flipped classroom** model. It is called flipped because it reverses the traditional teacher-centered model of instruction, whereby the teacher presents new information and skills in the classroom and the students then practice what they have learned outside of school. In the flipped classroom model, instruction is learner centered, whereby the students familiarize themselves with the new learning outside of school by watching teacher-made or commercial videos, digital media, and other resources. When they return to the classroom, they engage in higher-order thinking skills through group discussions about the new learning, analyzing components of new concepts, developing alternative ideas, solving problems related to the lesson objective, and practicing skills through laboratory experiments and hands-on projects.

Video: For videos explaining flipped classrooms, see

https://www.youtube.com/watch?v=G_p63W_2F_4&nohtml5=False and

https://www.youtube.com/watch?v=2H4RkudFzlc

Proponents of the flipped classroom list the following advantages (Fulton, 2012; Herreid & Schiller, 2013):

- Students move through the content at their own pace.
- Teachers can update and customize curriculum.

- Doing the discussions in class gives teachers better insight into their students' learning preferences and difficulties.
- Classroom time can be used more effectively and creatively.
- Students are more engaged and interested and achieve better.
- Use of technology is flexible and appropriate for modern learning.
- Teachers have more time to spend with students on authentic research.
- Model promotes thinking inside and outside the classroom.

There are also a few drawbacks:

- Students new to the method may resist at first because it requires that they learn new content at home rather than be first exposed to it at school. Consequently, they may come unprepared to class and unable to participate in the active learning activities.
- The homework, such as readings and videos, must be carefully tailored in order to prepare the students for the in-class activities. For most teachers, videos are the method of choice for delivering the out-of-class portion of the instruction. However, teachers often report that finding good quality videos is difficult. Thus, they reluctantly resort to making their own, which can be labor intensive and very time-consuming.

Research evidence on the effectiveness of the flipped classroom model is mixed, and most of it has been in higher education courses. Several case studies exist that have found modest increases in middle and high school classes using flipped learning (Yarbro, Arfstrom, McKnight, & McKnight, 2014). Researchers are conducting more studies in the secondary schools, and the initial evidence on the effectiveness of flipped learning is promising.

DAILY PLANNING

General Guidelines

Start by keeping the following general thoughts in mind while planning:

- Learning engages the entire person (cognitive, affective, and psycho-motor domains).
- The human brain seeks patterns in its search for meaning.
- Emotions affect all aspects of learning, retention, and recall.
- Past experience always affects new learning.
- The brain's working (temporary) memory has a limited capacity.
- Lecture usually results in the lowest degree of retention.
- Rehearsal is essential for retention.
- Practice does not make perfect.
- Each brain is unique.

Daily Lesson Design

To use this research in daily planning, we need a lesson plan model as a framework. The type of lesson plan that a teacher uses depends to a large degree on the instructional method the teacher decides to use. The following are examples of some instructional methods:

- **Direct Teaching.** The teacher lectures, does much of the work, and can present a great deal of information in a short period of time. Extent of student participation varies from none to considerable. Still the most common teaching method in secondary schools and higher education. Direct teaching can be to the entire class, to small groups of students, or one on one, as is often done with students with special needs.

- **Demonstration.** Teacher shows something, tells what is happening, and asks the students to discuss the demonstration.

- **Concept Attainment.** Students figure out the attributes of a group or category (provided by the teacher) by comparing and contrasting examples that possess the attributes and examples that do not. Through discussion, students develop a definition or hypothesis about the concept (lesson objective).

- **Socratic Method.** In this lesson, the teacher draws information from students through a series of carefully designed questions that eventually help students achieve the lesson objective.

- **Cooperative Learning.** Students work together in groups to accomplish a specific task. The teacher decides whether the groups are heterogeneous or homogeneous in ability, based on interests, choice, or some other criterion. True cooperative learning is different from just putting students in groups. To achieve their objective, the group's activities and engagement must be linked to five basic conditions that research shows will likely result in the deepest learning (Johnson, Johnson, & Holubec, 2007): (1) positive interdependence, whereby all group members must participate and contribute to complete the objective; (2) all individuals are accountable for their contributions; (3) students successfully use interpersonal skills to work within the group; (4) the entire group processes all ideas needed to achieve the objective; and (5) all communication is face to face. There is a mountain of research over the past four decades attesting to the effectiveness of cooperative learning strategies when used correctly (e.g., Slavin, 2015).

- **Simulations and Games.** The lesson centers around a problem situation that represents reality. Role-playing is used to help students understand the motives and behaviors of people. Educational games involve students in decision-making roles.

- **Individualized Instruction.** These methods include differentiated instruction, mastery learning, and independent study.

- **Drill and Practice.** This lesson specifically targets the recall and improvement of certain skills to enhance accuracy and speed.

No single lesson plan format fully addresses every aspect of every possible teaching method. But I do think one comes very close. The format I propose evolved from Madeline Hunter's (2004) work at UCLA in the 1970s. Hunter was a clinical psychologist and a pioneer in recognizing the need to include strategies from cognitive science in teaching. Despite its age, the format is based on sound principles of brain-compatible learning while being flexible enough to use with a variety of instructional methods.

I have made minor modifications to Hunter's original format by expanding it to include some of the more recent strategies. The nine components of the design are the following:

1. *Anticipatory Set.* This strategy captures the students' focus. Recall what we discussed in an earlier chapter about how digital devices are reducing the amount of time adolescents take in deciding whether to remain with an item or move on. Almost any technique to get their initial attention can be valuable. Vary the initial attention-getter to provide novelty, and remember the power of humor in getting attention and setting a positive emotional climate for the lesson to follow. Once you get their initial attention, the rest of the set is most effective when it

   a. allows students to remember an experience that will help them acquire the new learning (positive transfer from past to present)

   b. involves active student participation (while avoiding "guessing" games during prime-time-1),

   c. is relevant to the learning objective.

2. *Learning Objective.* This is a clear statement of what the students are expected to accomplish during the learning episode, including the levels of difficulty and complexity, and should include

   a. a specific statement of the learning,

   b. the overt behavior that demonstrates whether the learning has occurred, and whether the appropriate level of complexity has been attained.

When the teacher states the learning objective explicitly at the beginning of the lesson, it is called an *expository* lesson—that is, the objective is now "exposed." Of course, there are some learning objectives that require several lessons to accomplish. We can call that the terminal objective. Each separate lesson, however, should have a specific en route objective that is a subset of the terminal objective and that the students need to accomplish during one learning episode. Succeeding en route objectives, then, are linked to the prior ones so the students can see the terminal objective coming together with meaning.

Sometimes we prefer to have the students discover the lesson objective on their own. This is obviously called a *discovery* lesson. Discovery lessons require more careful planning and guidance to ensure that the students actually get to the intended objective. If the learner doesn't know where the lesson is going, *any* place will do.

3. *Purpose.* This states *why* the students should accomplish the learning objective. Whenever possible, it should refer to how the new learning is related to the students' prior and future learnings to facilitate positive transfer and meaning.

4. *Input.* This is the information and the procedures (skills) that students will need to acquire in order to achieve the learning objective. It can take many forms, including reading, lecture, cooperative learning groups, audiovisual presentations, the Internet, and so on.

5. *Modeling.* Clear and correct models help students make sense of the new learning and establish meaning. Models must be given first by the teacher and be accurate, unambiguous, and noncontroversial. Nonexemplars could be included later to show contrast.

6. *Check for Understanding.* This refers to the strategies the teacher will use during the learning episode to verify that the students are accomplishing the learning objective. The check could be in the form of oral discussion, questioning, written quiz, think-pair-share, or any other overt format that yields the necessary data. Depending on the results of these checks, the teacher may decide to provide more opportunities for input, reteach, or move on to new material.

7. *Guided Practice.* During this time, the student is applying the new learning in the presence of the teacher, who provides immediate and specific feedback on the accuracy of the learner's practice. Later, the teacher checks any corrections that the student made as a result of feedback.

8. *Closure.* This is the time when the mind of the learner can summarize for itself its perception of what has been learned. The teacher gives specific directions for what the learner should mentally process and provides adequate time to accomplish it. This is another opportunity the learner has to attach sense and meaning to the new learning, both of which are critical requirements for retention. Daily closure activities can take many forms, such as using synergy strategies or journal writing. Closure activities for the end of a unit might include writing plays, singing songs, reciting poetry, playing quiz games, and so on.

> *Closure is another opportunity the learner has to attach sense and meaning to new learning.*

9. *Independent Practice.* After the teacher believes that the learners have accomplished the objective at the correct level of difficulty and complexity, students try the new learning on their own to enhance retention and develop fluency.

Important Note. Not every lesson needs to include every component. However, the teacher should consider each component and choose those that are relevant to the learning objective and teaching method. For example, when introducing a new major unit of study, the lesson may focus primarily on *objectives* (What do we hope to accomplish?) and *purpose* (Why are we studying this?). On the other hand, a review lesson before a major test might include more ways of *checking for understanding* and for *guided practice.*

> *Not every lesson needs every component. The teacher should consider each component and choose those that are relevant to the learning objective and teaching method.*

Table 8.1 shows the lesson components that could be used with each teaching method. Table 8.2 shows the

Table 8.1 Lesson Components for Different Teaching Methods

	Direct Teaching	Demonstration	Concept Attain	Socratic Method	Coop. Learning	Simul. & Games	Indepen. Instruc.	Drill & Practice
Antic. Set	X	X	X	X	X	X		
Lesson Objective	X	X	X		X	X		X
Purpose	X	X	X		X	X	X	X
Input	X		X	X	X		X	X
Modeling	X	X	X	X	X			X
Check for Under.	X	X	X	X	X	X	X	X
Guided Practice	X		X				X	X
Closure	X	X	X	X	X	X	X	X
Indepen. Practice	X					X	X	X

Table 8.2 Components to Consider in Designing Lessons

Lesson Component	Purpose	Relationship to Research	Example
Anticipatory Set	Focuses students on the learning objective.	Establishes relevance and fosters positive transfer during prime-time-1.	"Think of what we learned yesterday about prefixes and be prepared to discuss them."
Learning Objective	Identifies what is to be learned by the end of the lesson.	Students know what they should learn and how they will know they have learned it.	"Today we will learn about suffixes, and you will make up words with them."
Purpose	Explains why it is important to accomplish this objective.	Knowing the purpose for learning something builds interest and establishes meaning.	"Learning about suffixes will help us understand more vocabulary and give us greater creativity in our writing."
Input	Gives students the information, sources, and skills they will need to accomplish the objective.	Bloom's remember level. Helps identify critical attributes.	"Suffixes are letters placed after words to change their meanings."

Lesson Component	Purpose	Relationship to Research	Example
Modeling	Shows the process or product of what students are learning.	Modeling enhances sense and meaning to help retention.	"Examples are: -less, as in helpless; -able, as in drinkable; and -ful, as in doubtful."
Check for Understanding	Allows instructor to verify if students understand what they are learning.	Bloom's understand level.	"I'll ask some of you to tell me what you learned so far about the meaning and use of suffixes."
Guided Practice	Allows the students to try the new learning under teacher guidance.	Bloom's apply level. Practice provides for fast learning.	"Here are 10 words. Add an appropriate suffix to each and explain their new meanings."
Closure	Allows students time to mentally summarize and internalize the new learning.	Last chance to attach sense and meaning, thus improving retention.	"I'll be quiet now while you think about the attributes and uses of suffixes."
Independent Practice	Students try new learning on their own to develop fluency.	This practice helps make the new learning permanent.	"For homework, add suffixes to the words on page 121 to change their meanings."

lesson components, their purpose, their relationship to the research, and an example from a lesson on teaching the characteristics of suffixes.

Twenty-Two Questions to Ask During Lesson Planning

Table 8.3 contains some important questions that teachers should ask while planning lessons. The questions relate to information and strategies included in previous chapters. Following each question is the rationale for considering it and the chapter number where its main reference can be found.

Table 8.3 Questions to Ask When Planning Lessons

	Question	Rationale	Chapter
1.	What tactics am I using to help students attach meaning to the learning?	Meaning helps retention.	2
2.	How will I use humor in this lesson?	Humor is an excellent focus device and adds novelty.	2
3.	Have I divided the learning episode into mini-lessons of about 20 minutes each?	Short lesson segments have proportionally less down-time than do longer ones.	3

(Continued)

Table 8.3 (Continued)

	Question	Rationale	Chapter
4.	What motivation and novelty strategies am I using?	Motivation and novelty increase interest and accountability.	1 & 2
5.	Which type of rehearsal should be used with this learning, and when?	Rote and elaborative rehearsal serve different purposes.	3
6.	Am I using the prime-times to the best advantage?	Maximum retention occurs during the prime-times.	3
7.	What will the students be doing during down-time?	Minimum retention occurs during down-time.	3
8.	Does my plan allow for enough wait time when asking questions?	Wait time is critical to allow for student recall to occur.	3
9.	What chunking strategies are appropriate for this objective?	Chunking increases the number of items working memory can handle at one time.	3
10.	What related prior learning should be included for distributed practice?	Distributed practice increases long-term retention.	3
11.	How will I maximize positive transfer and minimize negative transfer?	Positive transfer assists learning; negative transfer interferes.	4
12.	Have I identified the critical attributes of this concept?	Critical attributes help distinguish one concept from all others.	4
13.	Are the concepts or skills too similar to each other?	Concepts and skills that are too similar should not be taught together.	4
14.	How will I show students how they can use (transfer) this learning in the future?	The prospect of future transfer increases motivation and meaning.	4
15.	Is it appropriate to use a metaphor with this objective?	Metaphors enhance transfer, hemispheric integration, and retention.	4
16.	Have I included activities that are multisensory?	Using many senses increases retention.	5
17.	Would a concept map help here?	Concept maps help hemispheric integration and retention.	5
18.	Am I using strategies that promote imaging and imagining?	Imaging and imagining help establish meaning, promote novelty, and increase retention.	6
19.	Would some music be appropriate? If so, what kind and when?	Some music assists processing and cooperative learning activities.	6

	Question	Rationale	Chapter
20.	How will I move this objective up Bloom's Taxonomy?	The taxonomy's upper levels involve higher-order thinking and are more interesting.	7
21.	What emotions (affective domain) need to be considered or avoided in learning this objective?	Emotions play a key role in student acceptance and retention of learning.	7
22.	How do I integrate technology into the lesson to improve student engagement and learning?	Technology can be an effective motivator and tool for engagement, while giving students access to new information.	All

UNIT PLANNING

Teacher's Work Sample

Federal and state initiatives to ensure that teachers are highly qualified have prompted some teacher training institutions to develop designs that assist beginning teachers in planning instructional units. Called the Teacher Work Sample, the design can also be used for daily lessons, and some of its components parallel the modified Hunter model discussed earlier. One sample, developed by the Renaissance Partnership for Improving Teacher Quality, contains the following elements:

- **Contextual Factors.** The teacher lists information about the community, school, and characteristics of students, including their prior learning and learning styles.
- **Learning Goals.** The teacher sets significant and challenging learning objectives that are clear, appropriate for the specific student population, and consistent with national, state, and local standards.
- **Assessment Plan.** The teacher indicates the technically sound multiple assessments to determine student learning before, during, and after instruction.
- **Design for Instruction.** The teacher designs the unit's lesson plans that use a variety of instructional methods, activities, assignments, and resources, including technology.
- **Instructional Decision Making.** The teacher uses ongoing analysis of student progress to make instructional decisions and ensure that any adjustments to instruction are consistent with the learning objectives.
- **Analysis of Student Learning.** The teacher uses assessment data to profile student learning by using graphs to compare the preassessment and assessment results for individuals and for the class.
- **Reflection and Self-Evaluation.** The teacher reflects on the instruction to determine what went well and why, what needs to be changed and why, and what implications there are for future decisions on teaching practice and assessment.

Teacher work samples are particularly helpful in assisting novice and veteran teachers in assessing their skills, refining their craft, and improving their classroom presentations. They also serve to measure the training outcomes of professional development initiatives and to validate new teaching practices.

MAINTAINING SKILLS FOR THE FUTURE

This book suggests strategies that teachers can try in order to enhance the effectiveness of the teaching-learning process. The strategies have been derived from the current research on how we learn. Teachers who try these strategies for the first time may need support and feedback on the effectiveness of their implementation. The school-based support system is very important to maintaining teacher interest and commitment, especially if the new strategies don't produce the desired results in the classroom right away.

The Building Principal's Role

Building principals and head teachers play a vital role in establishing a school climate and culture that are receptive to new instructional strategies and in maintaining the support systems necessary for continuing teacher development. Providing opportunities for teachers to master an expanded repertoire of research-based instructional techniques is an effective way for principals to foster collaboration, establish their role as an instructional leader, and enhance the teaching staff's pursuit of professional inquiry. Such opportunities can include peer coaching, in-building study groups, action research projects, and workshops that keep the staff abreast of continuing discoveries about the teaching-learning process. For more detailed suggestions about the building principal's role, see Sousa (2003).

Types of Support Systems

Peer Coaching

This structure pairs two teachers who periodically observe each other in class. During the lesson, the observing teacher is looking for the use of a particular strategy or technique that was identified in a preobservation conference. After the lesson, the observing teacher provides feedback on the results of the implementation of the strategy. The nonthreatening and supportive nature of this peer relationship encourages teachers to take risks and to try new techniques that they might otherwise avoid for fear of failure or administrative scrutiny. Peer coaches undergo initial training in how to set the observation goal at the preconference and on different methods for collecting information during the observation. Numerous studies attest to the effectiveness of properly implemented peer coaching (e.g., Kretlow, Cooke, & Wood, 2012; Neumerski, 2013; Stormont, Reinke, Newcomer, Marchese, & Lewis, 2015).

Study Groups

Forming small groups of teachers and administrators to study a particular topic further is an effective means of expanding understanding and methods of applying new strategies. The group members seek out new research on the topic and exchange and discuss information, data, and experiences in the group setting. Each group focuses on one or two topics, such as wait time, attention, memory, transfer, and retention techniques. Groups within a school or district can use cooperative learning procedures as a means of sharing information across groups.

Action Research

As discussed more fully in the Introduction, conducting small research studies in a class or a school can provide teachers with the validation they may need to incorporate new strategies permanently into their repertoire. Action research gives the practitioner a chance to be a researcher and to investigate specific problems that affect teaching and learning.

For example, deliberately changing the length of the wait time after posing questions yields data on how the amount and quality of student responses vary with the wait time. If several teachers carry out this research and exchange data, they will have the evidence to support the continued use of longer wait time as an effective strategy. Action research on the use of humor and music in the classroom can help teachers determine the value of these strategies on student performance. Teachers can then share their results with colleagues at faculty meetings or study group sessions. This format also advances the notion that teachers should be involved in research projects as part of their professional growth.

Workshops on New Research

Periodic workshops that focus on new research findings in the teaching and learning process are valuable for updating teachers' knowledge base. Areas such as the transfer and transformation of learnings, reflection, memory, and concept development are the targets of extensive research at this time and should be monitored to determine if new findings are appropriate for district and school workshops.

When educators encourage ongoing staff development activities, such as study groups and action research, they are recognizing that our understanding of the teaching-learning process is in continual change as the research yields more data on how the amazing brain learns. True professionals are committed to updating their knowledge base constantly, and they recognize individual professional development as a personal and lifelong responsibility that will enhance their effectiveness. This is the essence of a professional learning community.

CONCLUSION

The potential contributions of neuroscience to educational practice continue to accumulate. The very fact that neuroscientists and educators are meeting and talking to each other regularly is evidence that we have crossed a new frontier in our profession. There are, of course, no magic answers that make the complex processes of teaching and learning successful all the time. Educators recognize that numerous variables affect this dynamic interaction, many of which are beyond the teacher's influence or control. What teachers *can* control is their own behavior. Although a few students can learn on their own, most of them rely heavily on the instructional talents of their teachers to learn information and skills. For them, the quality of their learning rarely exceeds the quality of teaching. My hope is that this book provides teachers with some new information, strategies, and insights that will increase their chances of success with more students.

> *The quality of learning rarely exceeds the quality of teaching.*

HAPPY TEACHING AND LEARNING!

PRACTITIONER'S CORNER

Reflections on Lesson Design

Here's a sample lesson design using the information processing model in Chapter 2.

Objective: The learner will be able to describe verbally the major parts of the brain processing model in the text *How the Brain Learns*.

Anticipatory Set: "Take a moment to think about whether it is important for teachers to know how we believe the brain selects and processes information. Then discuss your thoughts with your partner."

Purpose: "The purpose of this lesson is to give you some of the latest research we have on how we think the brain processes information so that you can be more successful in choosing those teacher actions that are more likely to result in learning."

Input: The teacher describes major steps in the process, including uptake by senses, interplay of the perceptual register and short-term memory, working memory, long-term storage, the cognitive belief system, and self-concept. Emphasizes the importance of sense and meaning, as well as of past experiences, throughout the entire process.

Modeling: Teacher explains the four metaphors (venetian blinds, clipboard, work table, and filing cabinets). Uses examples of working memory capacity, uses hands as model, and shows the model brain.

Check for Understanding: Teacher has students fill in the function sheet after several parts of the model are covered, and has them use the synergy strategy to discuss with their partners.

Guided Practice: Teacher gives examples of sense and meaning differences, and of positive and negative self-concept differences, to determine the extent of application of the model.

Closure: "Take a few minutes to quietly summarize in your mind the major parts of the brain processing model and be prepared to explain them."

CHAPTER 8: PUTTING IT ALL TOGETHER

Key Points to Ponder

Jot down on this page key points, ideas, strategies, and resources you want to consider later. This sheet is your personal journal summary and will help to jog your memory.

_____

_____

_____

_____

_____

_____

_____

_____

_____

_____

_____

Resources

BOOKS

Damasio, A. (2010). *Self comes to mind: Constructing the conscious brain.* New York, NY: Pantheon.

Dehaene, S. (2010). *Reading in the brain: The new science of how we read.* New York, NY: Penguin.

Eagleman, D. (2015). *The brain: The story of you.* New York, NY: Pantheon.

Patel, A. D. (2010). *Music, language, and the brain.* New York, NY: Oxford University Press.

Ramachandran, V. S. (2011). *The tell-tale brain: A neuroscientist's quest for what makes us human.* New York, NY: W. W. Norton.

Ratey, J. J. (2008). *Spark: The revolutionary new science of exercise and the brain.* New York, NY: Little, Brown.

Sousa, D. A. (Ed.). (2010). *Mind, brain, and education: Neuroscience implications for the classroom.* Bloomington, IN: Solution Tree Press.

Sousa, D. A. (2016). *Engaging the rewired brain.* West Palm Beach, FL: Learning Sciences International.

Sweeney, M. S. (2009). *Brain: The complete mind.* Washington, DC: National Geographic.

Sylwester, R. (2007). *The adolescent brain: Reaching for autonomy.* Thousand Oaks, CA: Corwin.

Sylwester, R. (2010). *A child's brain: The need for nurture.* Thousand Oaks, CA: Corwin.

INTERNET SITES

Note: All sites were active at time of publication.

American Educational Research Association (AERA): Brain, Neurosciences and Education Special Interest Group

http://aera.net

This special interest group promotes neuroscience research in the educational community that has implications for educational practice and provides a forum for issues and controversies connecting these fields.

Brain Institutes

Allen Institute for Brain Science: http://www.alleninstitute.org/what-we-do/brain-science/

Brain and Cognitive Sciences, MIT: http://bcs.mit.edu

Brain and Creativity Institute, University of Southern California: http://www.usc.edu/schools/college/bci

Brain Institute, University of Utah: http://brain.utah.edu/portal/site/brain

McDonnell Network for Cognitive Neuroscience, University of Oxford: http://www.cogneuro.ox.ac.uk

The Zanvyl Krieger Mind/Brain Institute, Johns Hopkins University: http://krieger.jhu.edu/mbi

Southwest Center for Mind, Brain and Education, University of Texas at Arlington: https://www.uta.edu/coed/curricandinstruct/research-community/mind-brain/

Vanderbilt Brain Institute: http://braininstitute.vanderbilt.edu

The Center for Applied Linguistics

http://www.cal.org

This is a private, nonprofit organization that uses the findings of linguistics and related sciences in identifying and addressing language-related problems. CAL carries out a wide range of activities including research, teacher education, analysis and dissemination of information, design and development of instructional materials, technical assistance, and program evaluation.

The Center for Arts Education

https://centerforartsed.org

This center is committed to restoring, stimulating, and sustaining quality arts education as an essential part of every child's education. It identifies, funds, and supports exemplary partnerships and programs that demonstrate how the arts contribute to learning and student achievement. Although the center mainly supports New York City's schools, its website has useful information about arts programs and resources.

Dana Alliance for Brain Initiatives

http://www.dana.org/About/DABI

This site is sponsored by the Dana Foundation and is dedicated to promoting public awareness and education about the progress and promise of brain research.

Discovery Education

http://www.discoveryeducation.com/teachers

This site offers numerous free classroom resources that encourage students to take charge of their learning through engaging contests, puzzles, interactive games, videos, and lesson plans.

Education Resources Information Center (ERIC)

http://www.eric.ed.gov

This is the U.S. Department of Education's research site that contains research reports on all topics related to education.

Flipped Classroom

http://www.flippedclassroom.org

This site shares videos, forums, events, and best practices for educators using the flipped learning classroom approach.

Inspiration Software, Inc.

http://inspiration.com

This company produces software that helps students construct all types of visual organizers for improving comprehension and building thinking skills. *Kidspiration* is designed for Grades K through 5, and *Inspiration* is for Grade 6 and higher. Demonstration versions can be downloaded to computers and other digital devices from the site.

International Mind, Brain, and Education Society

http://www.imbes.org

This organization facilitates worldwide collaboration among researchers in biology, education, and the cognitive and developmental sciences to examine research findings and to explore ways such findings might apply to educational practice.

Learning and the Brain Conferences/Seminars

http://www.learningandthebrain.com

This organization sponsors conferences and seminars around the United States that feature prominent scientists, researchers, and educators discussing topics in the field of educational neuroscience.

National Institutes of Health

http://www.nih.gov

This site provides reports and research studies on issues regarding mental and physical health as well as information on learning disorders.

National Network for
Early Language Learning (NNELL)

http://www.nnell.org

This is an organization for educators involved in teaching foreign languages to children. The organization facilitates cooperation among organizations directly concerned with early language learning; facilitates communication among teachers, teacher educators, parents, program administrators, and policymakers; and disseminates information and guidelines to assist in developing programs of excellence.

Neuroscience for Kids

http://faculty.washington.edu/chudler/neurok.html

This resource-rich and entertaining site for students and teachers provides a wide range of information about the structures and functions of the nervous and sensory systems. Portions of the site are available in about a dozen languages.

Parents as Teachers

http://www.parentsasteachers.org

This site provides parents with current research, training, curriculum, and advocacy for early childhood education.

The Society for Neuroscience

http://www.sfn.org

Educators will find useful information about brain research in the publications of this organization.

STEM to STEAM

http://www.stemtosteam.org

This site is sponsored by the Rhode Island School of Design and provides information, case studies, events, and resources relating to the STEM to STEAM initiative.

Thematic Units Sites

Lesson Plans for K–12 teachers by the hundreds in nearly all subject areas:

http://csus.libguides.com/content.php?pid=669780

A to Z Teacher Stuff/Themes: http://atozteacherstuff.com/Themes/

Teachers First: http://teachersfirst.com

Whole Brain Atlas

http://www.med.harvard.edu/AANLIB/home.html

Hundreds of different types of scans to illustrate typical and atypical brains are available on this site.

Glossary

Action research. A systematic process for evaluating the effectiveness of classroom practices using the techniques of research.

Alphabetic principle. The understanding that spoken words can be broken down into phonemes and that written letters represent the phonemes of spoken language.

Amygdala. The almond-shaped structure in the brain's limbic system that encodes emotional messages to long-term storage.

Angular gyrus. A brain structure that decodes visual information about words so they can be matched to their meanings.

Aphasia. The loss of the ability to understand or express speech.

Apoptosis. The genetically programmed process that destroys unneeded or unhealthy brain cells.

Associative learning. A learning situation whereby a response gets linked to a specific stimulus.

Astrocyte. A type of glial cell in the brain that regulates the rate of neuron signaling and forms part of the blood-brain barrier.

Axon. The neuron's long and unbranched fiber that carries impulses from the cell to the next neuron.

Brain stem. A major part of the brain that receives sensory input and monitors vital functions such as heartbeat, body temperature, and digestion.

Cerebellum. A major part of the brain that coordinates muscle movement.

Cerebrum. The largest major part of the brain that controls sensory interpretation, thinking, and memory.

Chunking. The ability of the brain to perceive a coherent group of items as a single item or chunk.

Circadian rhythm. The daily pattern of body functions, such as breathing, the sleep-wake cycle, and body temperature.

Closure. The teaching strategy that allows learners quiet time in class to mentally reprocess what they have learned during a lesson.

Cochlea. A spiral-shaped structure of the internal ear containing hairlike cells that convert sound vibrations to nerve impulses.

Cognitive belief system. The unique construct one uses to interpret how the world works, on the basis of experience.

Computerized axial tomography. An instrument that uses X-rays and computer processing to produce a detailed cross section of brain structure. Also known as CT or CAT scan.

Confabulation. The brain's replacement of a gap in long-term memory by a falsification that the individual believes to be correct.

Constructivist. An approach to learning stating that active learners use past experiences and chunking to construct sense and meaning from new learning, thereby building larger conceptual schemes.

Corpus callosum. The bridge of nerve fibers that connects the left and right cerebral hemispheres and allows communication between them.

Cortex. The thin but tough layer of cells covering the cerebrum that contains all the neurons used for cognitive and motor processing.

Critical attribute. A characteristic that makes one concept different from all others.

Declarative memory. Knowledge of events and facts to which we have conscious access.

Delayed sleep-phase syndrome (DSPS). A chronic condition caused mainly by a shift in an adolescent's sleep cycle that results in difficulty falling asleep at night and waking up in the morning.

Dendrite. The branched extension from the cell body of a neuron that receives impulses from nearby neurons through synaptic contacts.

Distributed practice. The repetition of a skill over increasingly longer periods of time to improve performance.

Educational neuroscience. A new field of inquiry that examines how neuroscientific findings can affect the curricular, instructional, and assessment decisions of educational practitioners.

Electroencephalography (EEG). An instrument that charts fluctuations in the brain's electrical activity via electrodes attached to the scalp.

Emotional memory. The retention of the emotional components of an experience.

Endorphins. Opiate-like chemicals in the body that lessen pain and produce pleasant and euphoric feelings.

Engram. The permanent memory trace that results when brain tissue is anatomically altered by an experience.

Episodic memory. Knowledge of events in our personal history to which we have conscious access.

Fissure. A deep groove or fold in the brain.

Flashbulb memory. A vivid memory of the circumstances surrounding a shocking or an emotionally charged experience.

Flipped classroom. An instructional model whereby students learn new material at home via video lectures and use classroom time to engage in discussions, projects, and creative activities.

Frontal lobe. The front part of the brain that monitors higher-order thinking, directs problem solving, and regulates the excesses of the emotional (limbic) system.

Functional magnetic resonance imaging (fMRI). An instrument that measures blood flow to the brain to record areas of high and low neuronal activity.

Glial cells. Special "glue" cells in the brain that surround each neuron providing support, protection, and nourishment.

Gray matter. The thin but tough covering of the brain's cerebrum also known as the cerebral cortex.

Guided practice. The repetition of a skill in the presence of the teacher, who can give immediate and specific feedback.

Gyrus. An elevated fold in the brain.

Hippocampus. A brain structure that compares new learning to past learning and encodes information from working memory to long-term storage.

Hypothalamus. A small brain structure at the base of the limbic area that regulates body functions in response to internal and external stimuli.

Imagery. The mental visualization of objects, events, and arrays.

Immediate memory. A temporary memory where information is processed briefly (in seconds) and subconsciously, then either blocked or passed on to working memory.

Independent practice. The repetition of a skill on one's own outside the presence of the teacher.

Information avoidance. A condition that results when one becomes frustrated or paralyzed by an overwhelming amount of information.

Laterality. The notion that the two cerebral hemispheres are specialized and process information differently.

Limbic area. The structures at the base of the cerebrum that control emotions.

Long-term potentiation. The increase in synaptic strength and sensitivity that endures as a result of repeated, frequent firings across a synapse between two associated neurons. As of now, it is the accepted mechanism for explaining long-term storage.

Long-term storage. The areas of the cerebrum where memories are stored permanently.

Magnetic resonance imaging (MRI). An instrument that uses radio waves to disturb the alignment of the body's atoms in a magnetic field to produce computer-processed, high-contrast images of internal structures.

Massed practice. The repetition of a skill over short time intervals to gain initial competence.

Mnemonic. A word or phrase used as a device for remembering unrelated information, patterns, or rules.

Modality preferences. The notion that many individuals tend to prefer using one sense over the others when learning.

Motivation. The influence of needs and desires on behavior.

Motor cortex. The narrow band across the top of the brain from ear to ear that controls movement.

Myelin. A fatty substance that surrounds and insulates a neuron's axon.

Neural efficiency. The ability of the brain to use fewer neurons to accomplish a repetitive task.

Neurogenesis. The birth of new neurons, occurring mostly during prenatal development, but sometimes continuing into adulthood, especially in the hippocampus.

Neuron. The basic cell making up the brain and nervous system, consisting of a cell body, a long fiber (axon) that transmits impulses, and many shorter fibers (dendrites) that receive them.

Neuroplasticity. The brain's lifelong ability to reorganize neural networks as a result of new experiences.

Neurotransmitter. One of several dozen chemicals stored in axon sacs that transmit impulses from neuron to neuron across the synaptic gap.

Nonassociative learning. A learning whereby the individual responds unconsciously to a stimulus.

Nondeclarative memory. Knowledge of motor and cognitive skills to which we have no conscious access, such as riding a bicycle.

Number sense. In its limited form, the ability to recognize that an object has been added or removed from a collection, without counting.

Perceptual representation system. A form of nondeclarative memory in which the structure and form of objects and words can be prompted by prior experience.

Phonemes. The minimal units of sound in a language that combine to make syllables.

Phonemic awareness. The ability to hear, identify, and manipulate phonemes in spoken syllables and words.

Phonological awareness. The ability (in addition to phonemic awareness) to recognize that sentences are composed of words, words are composed of syllables, and syllables are composed of onsets and rimes that can be broken down into phonemes.

Plasticity. *See* neuroplasticity.

Positron-emission tomography. Technology that traces the metabolism of radioactively tagged sugar in brain tissue producing a color image of cell activity. Also known as a PET scan.

Practice. The repetition of a skill to gain speed and accuracy.

Primacy-recency effect. The phenomenon whereby one tends to remember best that which comes first in a learning episode and second best that which comes last.

Prime-time. The time in a learning episode when information or a skill is more likely to be remembered.

Procedural memory. A form of nondeclarative memory that allows the learning of motor (riding a bicycle) and cognitive (learning to read) skills.

Prosody. The rhythm, cadence, accent patterns, and pitch of a language.

Psychological-cognitive cycle. One of the body's circadian rhythms that determines the degree of focus one has during cognitive processing.

Rate of learning. The amount of time it takes one to learn cognitive information with sufficient confidence that it will be consolidated into long-term memory.

Rate of retrieval. The amount of time it takes one to recall information from long-term memory to working memory.

Rehearsal. The reprocessing of information in working memory.

Retention. The preservation of learning in long-term storage in such a way that it can be identified and recalled quickly and accurately.

Reticular activating system (RAS). The dense formation of neurons in the brain stem that controls major body functions and maintains the brain's alertness.

Self-concept. Our perception of who we are and how we fit into the world.

Semantic memory. Knowledge of facts and data that may not be related to any event.

Sensory memory. The short-lived (usually in milliseconds) retention of information, such as recalling what someone just said to us, although we were not paying attention to the speaker.

Spacing effect. The experience whereby one is better able to recall items studied a few times over longer periods, rather than repeatedly in a short period.

Specialization. The notion that certain brain regions, such as Broca's area, are mainly dedicated to accomplishing specific tasks.

STEM to STEAM. The STEAM curriculum initiative enhances creativity and critical thinking skills by incorporating the "A" for arts into sciences, technology, engineering, and mathematics (STEM) instruction.

Stereotype threat. A concern that one will be evaluated based on a negative stereotype.

Strategic abandonment. The removal from the curriculum of topics of little importance to allow more time for in-depth study of important topics.

Sulcus (plural, sulci). A shallow groove or fold in the brain.

Suprachiasmatic nuclei. A tiny cluster of neurons (located just above where the optic nerves cross on their way to the visual cortex) that monitors the intensity of signals along the optic nerve to determine the intensity of external light and start the sleep cycle.

Synapse. The microscopic gap between the axon of one neuron and the dendrite of another.

Synaptic pruning. *See* apoptosis.

Task switching. The brain's ability to quickly shift its attention from one task to another, a behavior often misinterpreted as multitasking.

Thalamus. A part of the limbic system that receives all incoming sensory information, except smell, and shunts it to other areas of the cortex for additional processing.

Transfer. The influence that past learning has on new learning, and the degree to which the new learning will be useful in the learner's future. Positive transfer aids, and negative transfer inhibits, the acquisition of new learning.

Wait time. The period of teacher silence that follows the posing of a question before the first student is called to respond.

White matter. The support tissue that lies beneath the cerebrum's gray matter (cortex).

Window of opportunity. An important period during which the young brain responds to certain types of input to create or consolidate a neural network.

Working memory. The temporary memory wherein information is processed consciously.

References

Abeles, H. F. (2009). *Year VIII assessment report: New Jersey Symphony Orchestra's Early Strings Program.* New York, NY: Center for Arts Education Research, Columbia University.

Aben, B., Stapert, S., & Blokland, A. (2012, August). About the distinction between working memory and short-term memory. *Frontiers in Psychology, 3,* 301. Retrieved from http://doi.org/10.3389/fpsyg.2012.00301

ACT. (2014). *The condition of college and career readiness 2014.* Iowa City, IA: Author. Retrieved from http://www.act.org/research

Aheadi, A., Dixon, P., & Glover, S. (2009). A limiting feature of the Mozart effect: Listening enhances mental rotation abilities in non-musicians but not musicians. *Psychology of Music, 38,* 107–117.

Akyol, M. E., & Gündüz, H. B. (2014, October). The motivation level of the teachers according to the school managers' senses of humour. *Procedia–Social and Behavioral Sciences, 152,* 205–213.

Al-Hashimi, O., Zanto, T. P., & Gazzaley, A. (2015, October). Neural sources of performance decline during continuous multitasking. *Cortex, 71,* 49–57.

Alloway, T. P., Williams, S., Jones, B., & Cochrane, F. (2014, September). Exploring the impact of television watching on vocabulary skills in toddlers. *Early Childhood Education Journal, 42*(5), 343–349.

Altmann, E. M., Trafton, J. G., & Hambrick, D. Z. (2014, February). Momentary interruptions can derail the train of thought. *Journal of Experimental Psychology: General, 143*(1), 215–226.

Anderman, E. M., & Gray, D. (2015). Motivation, learning, and instruction. In J. Wright (Ed.), *International encyclopedia of the social & behavioral sciences* (2nd ed., pp. 928–935). Waltham, MA: Elsevier.

Anderson, J. R., Lee, H. S., & Fincham, J. M. (2014, August). Discovering the structure of mathematical problem solving. *NeuroImage, 97,* 163–177.

Anderson, L. W. (Ed.), Krathwohl, D. R. (Ed.), Airasian, P. W., Cruikshank, K. A., Mayer, R. E., Pintrich, P. R., . . . Wittrock, M. C. (2001). *A taxonomy for learning, teaching, and assessing: A revision of Bloom's Taxonomy of Educational Objectives* (Complete edition). New York, NY: Longman.

Angulo-Perkins, A., Aubé, W., Peretz, I., Barrios, F. A., Armony, J. L., & Concha, L. (2014, October). Music listening engages specific cortical regions within the temporal lobes: Differences between musicians and non-musicians. *Cortex, 59,* 126–137.

Anvari, S. H., Trainor, L. J., Woodside, J., & Levy, B. A. (2002). Relations among musical skills, phonological processing, and early reading ability in preschool children. *Journal of Experimental Child Psychology, 83,* 111–130.

Archila-Suerte, P., Zevin, J., & Hernandez, A. E. (2015, February). The effect of age of acquisition, socioeducational status, and proficiency on the neural processing of second language speech sounds. *Brain and Language, 141*, 35–49.

Ashkenazi, S., Black, J. M., Abrams, D. A., Hoeft, F., & Menon, V. (2013, November/December). Neurobiological underpinnings of math and reading learning disabilities. *Journal of Learning Disabilities, 46*(6), 549–569.

Averell, L., & Heathcote, A. (2011, February). The form of the forgetting curve and the fate of memories. *Journal of Mathematical Psychology 55*(1), 25–35.

Bailey, D. H., Littlefield, A., & Geary, D. C. (2012, September). The codevelopment of skill at and preference for use of retrieval-based processes for solving addition problems: Individual and sex differences from first to sixth grades. *Journal of Experimental Child Psychology, 113*(1), 78–92.

Balderas, I., Rodriguez-Ortiz, C. J., & Bermudez-Rattoni, F. (2015, May).Consolidation and reconsolidation of object recognition memory. *Behavioural Brain Research, 285*, 213–222.

Balu, D. T., & Lucki, I. (2009, March). Adult hippocampal neurogenesis: Regulation, functional implications, and contribution to disease pathology. *Neuroscience & Biobehavioral Reviews, 33*, 232–252.

Baron-Cohen, S. (2003). *The essential difference: The truth about the male and female brain.* New York, NY: Basic Books.

Baroody, A. J., Eiland, M., & Thompson, B. (2009). Fostering at-risk preschoolers' number sense. *Early Education and Development, 20*(1), 80–128.

Barros, R. M., Silver, E. J., & Stein, R. E. K. (2009). School recess and group classroom behavior. *Pediatrics, 123*, 431–436.

Bassok, D., Latham, S., & Rorem, A. (2016, January–March). Is kindergarten the new first grade? *AERA Open, 1*(4), 1–31.

Bauer, P. J. (2015, December). Development of episodic and autobiographical memory: The importance of remembering forgetting. *Developmental Review, 38*, 146–166.

Bauerlein, M. (2011). Too dumb for complex texts? *Educational Leadership, 68*, 28–32.

Bayliss, D. M., Bogdanovs, J., & Jarrold, C. (2015, May). Consolidating working memory: Distinguishing the effects of consolidation, rehearsal and attentional refreshing in a working memory span task. *Journal of Memory and Language, 81*, 34–50.

Beal, S. (2013, August 11). Turn STEM to STEAM: *Why science needs the arts.* Retrieved from http://www.huffingtonpost.com/stephen-beal/turn-stem-to-steam_b_3424356.html

Beilock, S. L., & Maloney, E. A. (2015, October). Math anxiety: A factor in math achievement not to be ignored. *Policy Insights From the Behavioral and Brain Sciences, 2*(1), 4–12.

Bein, O., Reggev, N., & Maril, A. (2014, November). Prior knowledge influences on hippocampus and medial prefrontal cortex interactions in subsequent memory. *Neuropsychologia, 64*, 320–330.

Bergelson, E., & Swingley, D. (2012, February). At 6–9 months, human infants know the meanings of many common nouns. *Proceedings of the National Academy of Sciences, 109*(9), 3253–3258.

Bergmann, L. S., & Zepernick, J. (2007). Disciplinarity and transfer: Students' perceptions of learning to write. *WPA: Writing Program Administration, 31*(102), 124–149.

Bishop, D. V. M. (2015, May). The interface between genetics and psychology: Lessons from developmental dyslexia. *Proceedings of the Royal Society B: Biological Sciences, 282*(1806), 1–8.

Bloch, C., Kaiser, A., Kuenzli, E., Zappatore, D., Haller, S., Franceschini, R., . . . Nitsch, C. (2009). The age of second language acquisition determines the variability in activation elicited by narration in three languages in Broca's and Wernicke's area. *Neuropsychologia, 47,* 625–633.

Bloom, B. S. (1976). *Human characteristics and school learning.* New York, NY: McGraw-Hill.

Bloom, B. S. (Ed.), Engelhart, M. D., Furst, E. J., Hill, W. H., & Krathwohl, D. R. (1956). *Taxonomy of educational objectives: The classification of educational goals. Handbook I: Cognitive domain.* New York, NY: David McKay.

Bloom, B. S., Mesia, B. B., & Krathwohl, D. R. (1964). *Taxonomy of educational objectives: The affective domain and the cognitive domain.* New York, NY: David McKay.

Bonin, R. P., & De Koninck, Y. (2015, June). Reconsolidation and the regulation of plasticity: Moving beyond memory. *Trends in Neurosciences, 38*(6), 336–344.

Bor, D., Duncan, J., Wiseman, R. J., & Owen, A. M. (2003). Encoding strategies dissociate prefrontal activity from working memory demand. *Neuron, 37,* 361–367.

Bos, M. G. N., van Goethem, T. H. J., Beckers, T., & Kindt, M. (2014, December). Cortisol response mediates the effect of post-reactivation stress exposure on contextualization of emotional memories. *Psychoneuroendocrinology, 50,* 72–84.

Botto, M., Basso, D., Ferrari, M., & Palladino, P. (2014, May). When working memory updating requires updating: Analysis of serial position in a running memory task. *Acta Psychologica, 148,* 123–129.

Bowen, D. H., Greene, J. P., & Kisida, B. (2014, January/February). Learning to think critically: A visual art experiment. *Educational Researcher, 43*(1), 37–44.

Bower, J. M., & Parsons, L. M. (2003). Rethinking the lesser brain. *Scientific American, 289,* 51–57.

Brady, T. F., Konkle, T., & Alvarez, G. A. (2009). Compression in visual working memory: Using statistical regularities to form more efficient memory representations. *Journal of Experimental Psychology, 138,* 487–502.

Brannon, E. M. (2005). The independence of language and mathematical reasoning. *Proceedings of the National Academy of Sciences, 102,* 3177–3178.

Brooks, J. G., & Brooks, M. G. (1999). *In search of understanding: The case for constructivist classrooms.* Alexandria, VA: ASCD.

Brown, C. P., & Weber, N. B. (2016, May/June). Struggling to overcome the state's prescription for practice: A study of a sample of early educators' professional development and action research projects in a high-stakes teaching context. *Journal of Teacher Education, 67*(3), 183–202.

Brown, E. D., Benedett, B., & Armistead, M. E. (2010). Arts enrichment and school readiness for children at risk. *Early Childhood Research Quarterly, 25*(1), 112–124.

Brucker, B., Scheiter, K., & Gerjets, P. (2014, July). Learning with dynamic and static visualizations: Realistic details only benefit learners with high visuospatial abilities. *Computers in Human Behavior, 36,* 330–339.

Burman, D. D., Bitan, T., & Booth, J. R. (2008). Sex differences in neural processing of language among children. *Neuropsychologia, 46*(5), 1349–1362.

Burns, M. K., Kanive, R., & DeGrande, M. (2012, May/June). Effect of a computer-delivered math fact intervention as a supplemental intervention for math in third and fourth grades. *Remedial and Special Education, 33*(3), 184–191.

Burnside, R. D., Pasion, R., Mikhail, F. M., Carroll, A.J., Robin, N. H., Youngs, E. L., . . . Butler, M. G. (2011). Microdeletion/microduplication of proximal 15q11.2 between BP1 and BP2: A susceptibility region for neurological dysfunction including developmental and language delay. *Human Genetics, 130,* 517–528.

Buzan, T. (1989). *Use both sides of your brain* (3rd ed.). New York, NY: Penguin.

Cahill, L. (2005). His brain, her brain. *Scientific American, 292,* 40–47.

Calvert, M., & Sheen, Y. (2015, March). Task-based language learning and teaching: An action-research study. *Language Teaching Research, 19*(2), 226–244.

Campbell, S. (2006). Language in the nondominant hemisphere. In K. Brown (Ed.), *Encyclopedia of language and linguistics* (2nd ed., pp. 529–536). Oxford, UK: Elsevier.

Campitelli, G., Gobet, F., Head, K., Buckley, M., & Parker, A. (2007). Brain localization of memory chunks in chess players. *International Journal of Neuroscience, 117,* 1641–1659.

Cantarero, G., Tang, B., O'Malley, R., Salas, R., & Celnik, P. (2013, March). Motor learning interference is proportional to occlusion of LTP-like plasticity. *Journal of Neuroscience, 33*(11), 4634–4641.

Cappelletti, M., & Price, C. J. (2014). Residual number processing in dyscalculia. *NeuroImage: Clinical, 4,* 18–28.

Carpenter, S. K., Pashler, H., & Cepeda, N. J. (2009). Using tests to enhance 8th grade students' retention of U.S. history facts. *Applied Cognitive Psychology, 23,* 760–771.

Carretti, B., Borella, E., Cornoldi, C., & De Bene, R., (2009, June). Role of working memory in explaining the performance of individuals with specific reading comprehension difficulties: A meta-analysis. *Learning and Individual Differences, 19*(2), 246–251.

Carskadon, M. A., Acebo, C., Wolfson, A. R., Tzischinsky, O., & Darley, C. (1997). REM sleep on MSLTS in high school students is related to circadian phase. *Sleep Research, 26,* 705.

Catmur, C. (2015, November). Understanding intentions from actions: Direct perception, inference, and the roles of mirror and mentalizing systems. *Consciousness and Cognition, 36,* 426–433.

Catterall, J. S., Dumais, S. A., & Hampden-Thompson, G. (2012). *The arts and achievement in at-risk youth: Findings from four longitudinal studies* (Research Report No. 55). Washington, DC: National Endowment for the Arts.

Ceulemans, A., Titeca, D., Loeys, T., Hoppenbrouwers, K., Rousseau, S., & Desoete, A. (2015, April). The sense of small number discrimination: The predictive value in infancy and toddlerhood for numerical competencies in kindergarten. *Learning and Individual Differences, 39,* 150–157.

Chapin, H., Jantzen, K., Kelso, A. S., Steinberg, F., & Large, E. (2010). Dynamic emotional and neural responses to music depend on performance expression and listener experience. *PLoS One, 5*(12), e13812. doi: 10.1371/journal.pone.0013812

Chapman, C. (1993). *If the shoe fits: Developing the multiple intelligences classroom.* Thousand Oaks, CA: Corwin.

Chapman, C., & King, R. (2000). *Test success in the brain compatible classroom.* Tucson, AZ: Zephyr.

Check, E. (2005). Genetics: The X factor. *Nature, 434,* 266–267.

Chen, X., Sachdev, P. S., Wen, W., & Anstey, K. J. (2007). Sex differences in regional gray matter in healthy individuals aged 44–48 years: A voxel-based morphometric study. *NeuroImage, 36,* 691–699.

Cheour, M., Ceponiene, R., Lehtokoski, A., Luuk, A., Allik, J., Alho, K., & Näätänen, R. (1998). Development of language-specific phoneme representations in the infant brain. *Nature Neuroscience, 1,* 351–353.

Chicago Arts Partnerships in Education (CAPE). (2016). *Increasing achievement for low performing students.* Retrieved from http://www.pairresults.org/downloads/researchsummary.pdf

Christakis, D. A. (2011, October). The effects of fast-paced cartoons. *Pediatrics, 124*(4), 772–774.

Christodoulou, J., & Burke, D. M. (2016, February). Mood congruity and episodic memory in young children. *Journal of Experimental Child Psychology, 142,* 221–229.

Chung, S.-C., Tack, G.-R., Choi, M.-H., Lee, S.-.J, Choi, J-S., Yi, J.-H. . . . Park, S.-J. (2009). Changes in reaction time when using oxygen inhalation during simple visual matching tasks. *Neuroscience Letters, 453*(3), 175–177.

Clarke, B., Doabler, C. T., Nelson, N. J., & Shanley, C. (2015, May). Effective instructional strategies for kindergarten and first-grade students at risk in mathematics. *Intervention in School and Clinic, 50*(5), 257–265.

Clawson, H. J., & Coolbaugh, K. (2001, May). The YouthARTS Development Project. *Juvenile Justice Bulletin.* Washington, DC: U.S. Department of Justice.

Clemow, D. B., & Walker, D. J. (2014, September). The potential for misuse and abuse of medications in ADHD: A review. *Postgraduate Medicine, 126*(5), 64–81.

Cohen, L., Lehéricy, S., Henry, C., Bourgeois, M., Larroque, C., Saint-Rose, C., . . . Hertz-Panier, L. (2004, December). Learning to read without a left occipital lobe: Right-hemispheric shift of visual word form area. *Annals of Neurology, 56*(6), 890–894.

Cole, M. W., Bagic, A., Kass, R., & Schneider, W. (2010). Prefrontal dynamics underlying rapid instructed task learning reverse with practice. *The Journal of Neuroscience, 30*(42), 14245–14254.

Common Sense Media. (2015, November). *Media use by tweens and teens.* San Francisco, CA: Author. Retrieved from http://www.commonsensemedia.org

Costa, A. L., & Kallick, B. (2009). *Learning and leading with habits of mind: 16 essential characteristics.* Alexandria, VA: Association for Supervision and Curriculum Development.

Costanzo, E. Y., Villarreal, M., Drucaroff, L. J., Ortiz-Villafañe, M., Castro, M. N., Goldschmidt, M.,. . . Guinjoan, S. M. (2015, July). Hemispheric specialization in affective responses, cerebral dominance for language, and handedness: Lateralization of emotion, language, and dexterity. *Behavioural Brain Research, 288,* 11–19.

Courage, M. L., & Howe, M. L. (2010, June). To watch or not to watch: Infants and toddlers in a brave new electronic world. *Developmental Review, 30*(2), 101–115.

Cowan, N. (2009). Sensory and immediate memory. In W. Banks (Ed.), *Encyclopedia of consciousness* (pp. 327–339). New York, NY: Academic Press.

Cowan, N. (2010). The magical mystery four: How is working memory capacity limited, and why? *Current Directions in Psychological Science, 19,* 51–57.

Cowan, N., Hismjatullina, A., AuBuchon, A. M., Saults, J. S., Horton, N., Leadbitter, K., & Towse, J. (2010). With development, list recall includes more chunks, not just larger ones. *Developmental Psychology, 46,* 1119–1131.

Cowan, N., Saults, J. S., & Clark, K. M. (2015, July). Exploring age differences in visual working memory capacity: Is there a contribution of memory for configuration? *Journal of Experimental Child Psychology, 135,* 72–85.

Cubelli, R., & Della Sala, S. (2013, January). Flashbulb memories: Sorry, no Flash! *Cortex, 49*(1), 356–357.

Cuevas, J. (2015, November). Is learning styles-based instruction effective? A comprehensive analysis of recent research on learning styles. *Theory and Research in Education, 13,* 308–333.

Curci, A., & Conway, M. A. (2013, January). Playing the flashbulb memory game: A comment on Cubelli and Della Sala. *Cortex, 49*(1), 352–355.

Cusack, J. P., Williams, J. H. G., & Neri, P. (2015, February). Action perception is intact in autism spectrum disorder. *Journal of Neuroscience, 35*(5), 1849–1857.

Dahlin, E., Neely, A. S., Larsson, A., Bäckman, L., & Nyberg, L. (2008). Transfer of learning after updating training mediated by the striatum. *Science, 320,* 1510.

Daly, I., Williams, D., Hallowell, J., Hwang, F., Kirke, A., Malik, A., . . . Nasuto, S. J. (2015, December). Music-induced emotions can be predicted from a combination of brain activity and acoustic features. *Brain and Cognition, 101,* 1–11.

Darki, F., Peyrard-Janvid, M., Matsson, H., Kere, J., & Klingberg, T. (2014, October). DCDC2 polymorphism is associated with left temporoparietal gray and white matter structures during development. *Journal of Neuroscience, 34*(43), 14455–14462.

Darrow, A.-A. (2014, October). Promoting social and emotional growth of students with disabilities. *General Music Today, 28*(1), 29–32.

Deemer, E. D., Thoman, D. B., Chase, J. P., & Smith, J. L. (2014, April). Feeling the threat: Stereotype threat as a contextual barrier to women's science career choice intentions. *Journal of Career Development, 41*(2), 141–158.

Dehaene, S. (2009). *Reading in the brain.* New York, NY: Viking.

Dehaene, S. (2010). The calculating brain. In D. A. Sousa (Ed.), *Mind, brain, & education: Neuroscience implications for the classroom* (pp. 179–198). Bloomington, IN: Solution Tree Press.

Delaney, P. F., Goldman, J. A, King, J. S., & Nelson-Gray, R. O. (2015, September). Mental toughness, reinforcement sensitivity theory, and the five-factor model: Personality and directed forgetting. *Personality and Individual Differences, 83,* 180–184.

Deng, W., Aimone, J. B., & Gage, F. H. (2010). New neurons and new memories: How does adult hippocampal neurogenesis affect learning and memory? *Nature Reviews Neuroscience, 11*(5), 339–350.

DePasque, S., & Tricomi, E. (2015, October). Effects of intrinsic motivation on feedback processing during learning. *NeuroImage, 119,* 175–186.

Derntl, B., Windischberger, C., Robinson, S., Kryspin-Exner, I., Gur, R. C., Moser, E., & Habel, U. (2009). Amygdala activity to fear and anger in healthy young males is associated with testosterone. *Psychoneuroendocrinology, 34,* 687–693.

DeSoto Independent School District. (2016). *What is iSTEAM3D?* Retrieved from http://www.desotoisd.org/

Desrivières, S., Lourdusamy, A., Tao, C., Toro, R., Jia. T., Loth. E., . . . Schumann, G. (2015, February). Single nucleotide polymorphism in the neuroplastin locus associates with cortical thickness and intellectual ability in adolescents. *Molecular Psychiatry, 20*(2), 263–274.

Devine, A., Fawcett, K., Szucs, D., & Dowker, A. (2012, July). Gender differences in mathematics anxiety and the relation to mathematics performance while controlling for test anxiety. *Behavioral and Brain Functions, 8,* 3–42.

Dindar, M., & Akbulut, Y. (2016, February). Effects of multitasking on retention and topic interest. *Learning and Instruction, 41,* 94–105.

DiPiro, J. T. (2009, December). Why do we still lecture? *American Journal of Pharmacy Education, 73*(8), 137.

Dixon, L. Q., Zhao, J., Shin, J.-Y., Wu, S., Su, J.-H., Burgess-Brigham, R., . . . Snow, C. (2012, March). What we know about second language acquisition: A synthesis from four perspectives. *Review of Educational Research, 82*(1), 5–60.

Doabler, C. T., & Fien, H. (2013, May). Explicit mathematics instruction: What teachers can do for teaching students with mathematics difficulties. *Intervention in School and Clinic, 48*(5), 276–285.

Dole, M., Meunier, F., & Hoen, M. (2014, July). Functional correlates of the speech-in-noise perception impairment in dyslexia: An MRI study. *Neuropsychologia, 60,* 103–114.

Dong, S., Reder, L. M., Yao, Y., Liu, Y., & Chen, F. (2015, August). Individual differences in working memory capacity are reflected in different ERP and EEG patterns to task difficulty. *Brain Research, 1616,* 146–156.

Dosenbach, N. U., Nardos, B., Cohen, A. L., Fair, D. A., Power, J. D., Church, J. A., . . . Schlaggar, B. L. (2010). Prediction of individual brain maturity using fMRI. *Science, 329,* 1358–1361.

Doyon, J., Albouy, G., Vahdat, D., & King, B. R. (2015). Neural correlates of motor skill acquisition and consolidation. *Brain Mapping, 3,* 493–500.

Duch, H., Fisher, E. M., Ensari, L., Font, M., Harrington, A., Taromino, C., & Rodriguez, C. (2013, September). Association of screen time use and language development in Hispanic toddlers: A cross-sectional and longitudinal study. *Clinical Pediatrics, 52*(9), 857–865.

Duffau, H., Leroy, M., & Gatignol, P. (2008). Cortico-subcortial organization of language networks in the right hemisphere: An electrostimulation study in left-handers. *Neuropsychologia, 46,* 3197–3209.

Dumay, N. (2016, January). Sleep not just protects memories against forgetting, it also makes them more accessible. *Cortex, 74,* 289–296.

Dunn, R., & Dunn, K. (1993). *Teaching secondary students through their individual learning styles: Practical approaches for grades 7–12.* Boston, MA: Allyn & Bacon.

Durisko, C., & Fiez, J. A. (2010). Functional activation in the cerebellum during working memory and simple speech tasks. *Cortex, 46*(7), 896–906.

Durkin, K., & Conti-Ramsden, G. (2014, June). Turn off or tune in? What advice can SLTs, educational psychologists and teachers provide about uses of new media and children with language impairments? *Child Language Teaching and Therapy, 30*(2), 187–205.

Dweck, C. (2006). *Mindset: The new psychology of success.* New York, NY: Random House.

Dweck, C. (2012/2013). Mindsets: How to motivate students (and yourself). *Educational Horizons, 91*(2), 16–21.

Dwyer, D. B., Harrison, B. J., Yücel, M., Whittle, S., Zalesky, A., Pantelis, C., . . . Fornito, A. (2014, October). Large-scale brain network dynamics supporting adolescent cognitive control. *Journal of Neuroscience, 34*(42), 14096–14107.

Dyson, N. I., Jordan, N. C., & Glutting, J. (2013, March/April). A number sense intervention for low-income kindergartners at risk for mathematics difficulties. *Journal of Learning Disabilities, 46*(2), 166–181.

Eisner, E. (2002a). *The arts and the creation of mind.* New Haven, CT: Yale University Press.

Eisner, E. (2002b). What the arts do for the young. *School Arts, 102,* 16–17.

El Haj, M., Antoine, P., & Kapogiannis, D. (2015, January). Similarity between remembering the past and imagining the future in Alzheimer's disease: Implication of episodic memory. *Neuropsychologia, 66,* 119–125.

Elliott, G., Isaac, C. L., & Muhlert, N. (2014, May). Measuring forgetting: A critical review of accelerated long-term forgetting studies. *Cortex, 54,* 16–32.

Ellis, A. W., Ansorge, L., & Lavidor, M. (2007). Words, hemispheres, and dissociable subsystems: The effects of exposure duration, case alternation, and continuity of form on word recognition in the left and right visual fields. *Brain and Language, 103,* 292–303.

Eren, B. (2015, July). The use of music interventions to improve social skills in adolescents with autism spectrum disorders in integrated group music therapy sessions. *Procedia–Social and Behavioral Sciences, 197,* 207–213.

Everett, C., & Madora, K. (2012, January/Feburary). Quantity recognition among speakers of an anumeric language. *Cognitive Science, 36*(1), 130–141.

Everhart, D. E., Shucard, J. L., Quatrin, T., & Shucard, D. W. (2001). Sex-related differences in event-related potentials, face recognition, and facial affect processing in prepubertal children. *Neuropsychology, 15,* 329–341.

Farrugia, N., Jakubowski, K., Cusack, R., & Stewart, L. (2015, September). Tunes stuck in your brain: The frequency and affective evaluation of involuntary musical imagery correlate with cortical structure. *Consciousness and Cognition, 35*, 66–77.

Fegen, D., Buchsbaum, B. R., & D'Esposito, M. (2015, January). The effect of rehearsal rate and memory load on verbal working memory. *NeuroImage, 105*, 120–131.

Fine, J. G., Semrud-Clikeman, M., & Zhu, D. C. (2009). Gender differences in BOLD activation to face photographs and video vignettes. *Behavioural Brain Research, 201*, 137–146.

Finlayson, M. (2014). Addressing math anxiety in the classroom, *Improving Schools, 17*(1), 99–115.

Finn, A. S., Kalra, P. B., Goetz, C., Leonard, J. A., Sheridan, M. A., & Gabrieli, J. D. E. (2016, February). Developmental dissociation between the maturation of procedural memory and declarative memory. *Journal of Experimental Child Psychology, 142*, 212–220.

Fisher, D., & Frey, N. (2008). *Better learning through structured teaching: A framework for the gradual release of responsibility.* Alexandria, VA: ASCD.

Flom, R., & Pick, A. D. (2012, December). Dynamics of infant habituation: Infants' discrimination of musical excerpts. *Infant Behavior and Development, 35*(4), 697–704.

Flore, P. C., & Wicherts, J. M. (2015, February). Does stereotype threat influence performance of girls in stereotyped domains? A meta-analysis. *Journal of School Psychology, 53*(1), 25–44.

Frank, C. K., Baron-Cohen, S., & Ganzel, B. L. (2015, January). Sex differences in the neural basis of false-belief and pragmatic language comprehension. *NeuroImage, 105*, 300–311.

Freeman, S., Eddy, S. L., McDonough, M., Smith, M. K., Okoroafora, N., Jordt, H, & Wenderoth, M. P. (2014). Active learning increases student performance in science, engineering, and mathematics. *Proceedings of the National Academy of Sciences, 111*(23), 8410–8415.

Fulton, K. (2012). Upside down and inside out: Flip your classroom to improve student learning. *Learning & Leading with Technology, 39*(8), 12–17.

Gallup. (2015). *2015 Gallup student poll—overall report.* Retrieved from http://www.gallupstudentpoll.com

Gardner, H. (1993). *Frames of mind: The theory of multiple intelligences* (Rev. ed.). New York, NY: Basic Books.

Gazzaniga, M. S. (1998a). *The mind's past.* Berkeley: University of California Press.

Gazzaniga, M. S. (1998b). The split brain revisited. *Scientific American, 279*, 48–55.

Gazzaniga, M. S., Ivry, R. B., & Mangun, G. R. (2002). *Cognitive neuroscience: The biology of the mind* (2nd ed.). New York, NY: W. W. Norton.

Geday, J., & Gjedde, A. (2009). Attention, emotion, and deactivation of default activity in inferior medial prefrontal cortex. *Brain and Cognition, 69*, 344–352.

Gee, C. J. (2010). How does sport psychology actually improve athletic performance? A framework to facilitate athletes' and coaches' understanding. *Behavior Modification, 34*(5), 386–402.

Geil, C. R., Hayes, D. M., McClain, J. A., Liput, D. J., Marshall, S. A., Chen, K. Y., & Nixon, K. (2014, October). Alcohol and adult hippocampal neurogenesis: Promiscuous drug, wanton effects. *Progress in Neuro-Psychopharmacology and Biological Psychiatry, 54*, 103–113.

Geist, E. (2010, March). The anti-anxiety curriculum: Combating math anxiety in the classroom. *Journal of Instructional Psychology, 37*, 24–31.

George, E. M., & Coch, D. (2011). Music training and working memory: An ERP study. *Neuropsychologia, 49*, 1083–1094.

Gerbier, E., & Toppino, T. C. (2015, September). The effect of distributed practice: Neuroscience, cognition, and education. *Trends in Neuroscience and Education, 4*(3), 49–59.

Gerraty, R. T., Davidow, J. Y., Wimmer, G. E., Kahn, I., & Shohamy, D. (2014, August). Transfer of learning relates to intrinsic connectivity between hippocampus, ventromedial prefrontal cortex, and large-scale networks. *Journal of Neuroscience, 34*(34), 11297–11303.

Gersten, R., & Chard, D. (1999). Number sense: Rethinking arithmetic instruction for students with mathematical disabilities. *Journal of Special Education, 33,* 18–28.

Gibson, P. A., Stringer, K., Cotten, S. R., Simoni, Z., O'Neal, L. J., & Howell-Moroney, M. (2014, February). Changing teachers, changing students? The impact of a teacher-focused intervention on students' computer usage, attitudes, and anxiety. *Computers & Education, 71,* 165–174.

Gilchrist, A. L., Cowan, N., & Naveh-Benjamin, M. (2009). Investigating the childhood development of working memory using sentences: New evidence for the growth of chunk capacity. *Journal of Experimental Child Psychology, 104,* 252–265.

Gilmore, A. W., Nelson, S. M., & McDermott, K. B. (2015, September). A parietal memory network revealed by multiple MRI methods. *Trends in Cognitive Sciences, 19*(9), 534–543.

Gittler, G., & Fischer, G. (2011). IRT-based measurement of short-term changes of ability, with an application to assessing the "Mozart effect." *Journal of Educational and Behavioral Statistics, 36,* 33–75.

Gooding, L. F. (2010). Using music therapy protocols in the treatment of premature infants: An introduction to current practices. *The Arts in Psychotherapy, 37,* 211–214.

Gotts, S. J., Jo, H. J., Wallace, G. L., Saad, Z. S., Cox, R. W., & Martin, A. (2013, September). Two distinct forms of functional lateralization in the human brain. *Proceedings of the National Academy of Sciences, 110*(36), E3435–E3444.

Gradisar, M., Smits, M. G., & Bjorvatn, B. (2014, June). Assessment and treatment of delayed sleep phase disorder in adolescents: Recent innovations and cautions. *Sleep Medicine Clinics, 9*(2), 199–210.

Graziano, A. B., Peterson, M., & Shaw, G. L. (1999). Enhanced learning of proportional math through music training and spatial-temporal training. *Neurological Research, 21,* 139–152.

Greene, R. L. (2008). Repetition and spacing effects. In J. Byrne (Ed.), *Learning and memory: A comprehensive reference, 2008* (pp. 65–78). Oxford, UK: Elsevier.

Griffin, S. (2002). The development of math competence in the preschool and early school years: Cognitive foundations and instructional strategies. In J. M. Roher (Ed.), *Mathematical cognition: Current perspectives on cognition, learning, and instruction* (pp. 1–32). Greenwich, CT.: Information Age.

Groeschel, S., Vollmer, B., King, M. D., & Connelly, A. (2010). Developmental changes in cerebral grey and whiter matter volume from infancy to adulthood. *International Journal of Developmental Neuroscience, 28,* 481–489.

Grotheer, M., Ambrus, G. G., & Kovács, G. (2016, May). Causal evidence of the involvement of the number form area in the visual detection of numbers and letters. *NeuroImage, 132,* 314–319.

Guerrero, S. M., & Palomaa, K. (2012). First-grade methods of single-digit addition with two or more addends. *Journal of Research in Childhood Education, 26*(1), 1–17.

Gur, R., Turetsky, B., Matsui, M., Yan, M., Bilker, W., Hughett, P., & Gur, R. E. (1999). Sex differences in brain gray and white matter in healthy young adults: Correlations with cognitive performance. *The Journal of Neuroscience, 19,* 4065–4072.

Gur, R. C., Alsop, D., Glahn, D., Petty, R., Swanson, C. L., Maldjian, J. A., . . . Gur, R. E. (2000). An fMRI study of sex differences in regional activation to a verbal and a spatial task. *Brain and Language, 74*, 157–170.

Haier, R. J., Jung, R. E., Yeo, R. A., Head, K., & Alkire, M. T. (2004). Structural brain variation and general intelligence. *NeuroImage, 23*, 425–433.

Hamari, J., Shernoff, D. J., Rowe, E., Coller, B., Asbell-Clarke, J., & Edwards, T. (2016, January). Challenging games help students learn: An empirical study on engagement, flow and immersion in game-based learning. *Computers in Human Behavior, 54*, 170–179.

Hambrick, D. Z., Macnamara, B. N., Campitelli, G., Ullén, F., & Mosing, M. A. (2016). Beyond born versus made: A new look at expertise. *Psychology of Learning and Motivation, 64*, 1–55.

Hamrick, P. (2015, December). Declarative and procedural memory abilities as individual differences in incidental language learning. *Learning and Individual Differences, 44*, 9–15.

Hannon, E. E., & Johnson, S. P. (2005). Infants use meter to categorize rhythms and melodies: Implications for musical structure learning. *Cognitive Psychology, 50*, 354–377.

Hansen, M., Wallentin, M., & Vuust, P. (2013, November). Working memory and musical competence of musicians and non-musicians. *Psychology of Music, 41*(6), 779–793.

Harbard, E., Allen, N. B., Trinder, J., & Bei, B. (2016). What's keeping teenagers up? Prebedtime behaviors and actigraphy-assessed sleep over school and vacation. *Journal of Adolescent Health, 58*(4), 426–432.

Hart, S. A., Petrill, S. A., Willcutt, E., Thompson, L. A., Schatschneider, C., Deater-Deckard, K., & Cutting, L. E. (2010, November). Exploring how symptoms of attention-deficit/hyperactivity disorder are related to reading and mathematics performance: General genes, general environments. *Psychological Science, 21*, 1708–1715.

Hattie, J. (2012). *Visible learning for teachers: Maximizing impact on learning.* New York, NY: Routledge.

Hautzel, H., Mottaghy, F. M., Specht, K., Müller, H.-W., & Krause, B. J. (2009). Evidence of a modality-dependent role of the cerebellum in working memory? An fMRI study comparing verbal and abstract n-back tasks. *NeuroImage, 47*(4), 2073–2082.

Hawkins, J., & Blakeslee, S. (2004). *On intelligence.* New York, NY: Times Books.

He, C., & Trainor, L. J. (2009). Finding the pitch of the missing fundamental in infants. *The Journal of Neuroscience, 29*(24), 7718–8822.

Hecht, D. (2010). Depression and the hyperactive right-hemisphere. *Neuroscience Research, 68*, 77–87.

Helene, A. F., & Xavier, G. F. (2006). Working memory and acquisition of implicit knowledge by imagery training, without actual task performance. *Neuroscience, 139*(1), 401–413.

Helmrich, B. H. (2010). Window of opportunity? Adolescence, music, and algebra. *Journal of Adolescent Research, 25*(4), 557–577.

Henderson, L., Weighall, A., & Gaskell, G. (2013, November). Learning new vocabulary during childhood: Effects of semantic training on lexical consolidation and integration. *Journal of Experimental Child Psychology, 116*(3), 572–592.

Henkel, L. A., & Mather, M. (2007). Memory attributions for choices: How beliefs shape our memories. *Journal of Memory and Language, 57*, 163–176.

Henry, G. T., Campbell, S. L., Thompson, C. L., Patriarca, L. A., Luterbach, K. J., Lys, D. B., & Covington, V. M. (2013, November/December). The predictive validity of measures of teacher candidate programs and performance: Toward an evidence-based approach to teacher preparation. *Journal of Teacher Education, 64*(5), 439–453.

Hermans, E. J., Battaglia, F. P., Atsak, P., de Voogd, L. D., Fernández, G., & Roozendaal, B. (2014, July). How the amygdala affects emotional memory by altering brain network properties. *Neurobiology of Learning and Memory, 112*, 2–16.

Herreid, C. F., & Schiller, N. A. (2013). Case studies and the flipped classroom. *Journal of College Science Teaching, 42*(5), 62–66.

Hertrich, I., Mathiak, K., & Ackermann, H. (2016). The role of the cerebellum in speech perception and language comprehension. In P. Mariën & M. Manto (Eds.), *The linguistic cerebellum* (pp. 33–50). Cambridge, MA: Academic Press.

Hetland, L. (2000). Learning to make music enhances spatial reasoning. *Journal of Aesthetic Education, 34*, 179–238.

Hewitt, D. (2012, October). Young students learning formal algebraic notation and solving linear equations: Are commonly experienced difficulties avoidable? *Educational Studies in Mathematics, 81*, 139–159.

Hirano, M., Kubota, S., Tanabe, S., Koizume, Y., & Funase, K. (2015, November/December), Interactions among learning stage, retention, and primary motor cortex excitability in motor skill learning. *Brain Stimulation, 8*(6), 1195–1204.

Ho, C., Mason, O., & Spence, C. (2007). An investigation into the temporal dimension of the Mozart effect: Evidence from the attentional blink task. *Acta Psychologica, 125*, 117–128.

Ho, Y.-C., Cheung, M.-C., & Chan, A. S. (2003). Music training improves verbal but not visual memory: Cross-sectional and longitudinal explorations in children. *Neuropsychology, 17*, 439–450.

Hockley, W. E., & Bancroft, T. D. (2015). Context dependent memory. In J. Wright (Ed.), *International encyclopedia of the social & behavioral sciences* (2nd ed., pp. 778–785). Waltham, MA: Elsevier.

Hollier, L. P., Maybery, M. T., Keelan, J. A., Hickey, M., & Whitehouse, A. J. O. (2014, December). Perinatal testosterone exposure and cerebral lateralisation in adult males: Evidence for the callosal hypothesis. *Biological Psychology, 103*, 48–53.

Holloway, J. D., Price, G. R., & Ansari, D. (2010, January). Common and segregated neural pathways for the processing of symbolic and nonsymbolic numerical magnitude. An fMRI study. *NeuroImage, 49*, 1006–1017.

Hornsby, A. K. E., Redhead, Y. T., Rees, D. J., Ratcliff, M. S. G., Reichenbach, A., Wells, T., . . . Davies, J. S. (2016, January). Short-term calorie restriction enhances adult hippocampal neurogenesis and remote fear memory in a Ghsr-dependent manner. *Psychoneuroendocrinology, 63*, 198–207.

Huang, M., Baskin, D. S., & Fung, S. (2016, May). Glioblastoma presenting with pure alexia and palinopsia involving the left inferior occipitotemporal gyrus and visual word form area evaluated with fMRI and DTI tractography. *World Neurosurgery, 89*, 725.e5–725.e10.

Huijgen, J., & Samson, S. (2015, March). The hippocampus: A central node in a large-scale brain network for memory. *Revue Neurologique, 171*(3), 204–216.

Hunter, M. (2004). *Mastery teaching.* Thousand Oaks, CA: Corwin.

Hyde, S. J., & Linn, C. M. (2009). Diversity: Gender similarities in mathematics and science. *Science, 314*, 599–600.

Hyerle, D. (1996). *Visual tools for constructing knowledge.* Alexandria, VA: Association for Supervision and Curriculum Development.

Hyerle, D. (2004). *Student successes with thinking maps: School-based research, results, and models for achievement using visual tools.* Thousand Oaks, CA: Corwin.

Iacoboni, M. (2015). The use of brain imaging to investigate the human mirror neuron system. *Brain Mapping, 3*, 119–124.

Ilieva, I. P., Hook, C. J., & Farah, M. J. (2015, June). Prescription stimulants' effects on healthy inhibitory control, working memory, and episodic memory: A meta-analysis. *Journal of Cognitive Neuroscience,27*(6), 1069–1089.

Ingalhalikar, M., Smith, A., Parker, D., Satterthwaite, T. D., Elliott, M. A., Ruparel, K. . . . Verma, R. (2014, January). Sex differences in the structural connectome of the human brain. *Proceedings of the National Academy of Sciences, 111*(2), 823–828.

Institute of Medicine. (2013). *Educating the student body: Taking physical activity and physical education to school.* Washington, DC: Author. Retrieved from http://www.iom.nationalacademies.org

Ison, M. J., Quiroga, R. Q., & Fried, I. (2015, July). Rapid encoding of new memories by individual neurons in the human brain. *Neuron, 87,* 220–230.

Israel, D. (2009). *Staying in school: Arts education and New York City high school graduation rates.* New York, NY: Center for Arts Education.

Jauk, E., Benedek, M., & Neubauer, A. C. (2012, May). Tackling creativity at its roots: Evidence for different patterns of EEG alpha activity related to convergent and divergent modes of task processing. *International Journal of Psychophysiology, 84*(2), 219–225.

Jaušovec, N., Jaušovec, K., & Gerlič, I. (2006). The influence of Mozart's music on brain activity in the process of learning. *Clinical Neurophysiology, 117*(12), 2703–2714.

Jeder, D. (2015, May). Implications of using humor in the classroom. *Procedia–Social and Behavioral Sciences, 180,* 828–833.

Johnson, D. W., Johnson, R. T., & Holubec, E. J. (2007). *The nuts & bolts of cooperative learning* (2nd ed.). Minneapolis, MN: Interaction Book Company.

Jordan, N. C., Kaplan, D., Ramineni, C., & Locuniak, M. N. (2009). Early math matters: Kindergarten number competence and later mathematics outcomes. *Developmental Psychology, 45,* 850–867.

Jovanovic, D., & Matejevic, M. (2014, September). Relationship between rewards and intrinsic motivation for learning: Researches review. *Procedia–Social and Behavioral Sciences, 149,* 456–460.

Kaldenberg, E. R., Watt, S. J., & Therrien, W. J. (2015, August). Reading instruction in science for students with learning disabilities: A meta-analysis. *Learning Disability Quarterly, 38*(3), 160–173.

Kang, S. H. K. (2016, March). Spaced repetition promotes efficient and effective learning: Policy implications for instruction. *Policy Insights from the Behavioral and Brain Sciences, 3*(1), 12–19.

Kaufman, S. B., Quilty, L. C., Grazioplene, R. G., Hirsh, J. B., Gray, J. R., Peterson, J. B., & DeYoung, C. G. (2016, April). Openness to experience and intellect differentially predict creative achievement in the arts and sciences. *Journal of Personality, 84*(2), 248–258.

Keller, K., & Menon, V. (2009). Gender differences in the functional and structural neuroanatomy of mathematical cognition. *NeuroImage, 47,* 342–352.

Kelley, J., & Demorest, S. M. (2016, April). Music programs in charter and traditional schools: A comparative study of Chicago elementary schools. *Journal of Research in Music Education, 64*(1), 88–107.

Kenna, M. A. (2015, December). Acquired hearing loss in children. *Otolaryngologic Clinics of North America, 48*(6), 933–953.

Kent, B. A., Oomen, C. A., Bekinschtein, P., Bussey, T. J., & Saksida, L. M. (2015, August). Cognitive enhancing effects of voluntary exercise, caloric restriction and environmental enrichment: A role for adult hippocampal neurogenesis and pattern separation? *Current Opinion in Behavioral Sciences, 4,* 179–185.

Kibbe, M. M., & Feigenson. L. (2016, January). Infants use temporal regularities to chunk objects in memory. *Cognition, 146,* 251–263.

Killgore, W. D. S. (2010). Effects of sleep deprivation on cognition. *Progress in Brain Research, 185,* 105–129.

Kim, H. (2016, January). Default network activation during episodic and semantic memory retrieval: A selective meta-analytic comparison. *Neuropsychologia, 80,* 35–46.

Kim, K. H., (2011). The creativity crisis: The decrease in creative thinking scores on the Torrance Tests of Creative Thinking. *Creativity Research Journal, 23*(4), 285–295.

Kitamura, T., Mishina, M., & Sugiyama, H. (2006). Dietary restriction increases hippocampal neurogenesis by molecular mechanisms independent of NMDA receptors. *Neuroscience Letters, 393*(2–3), 94–96.

Klassen, J. A., Liang, Y., Tjosvold, L., Klassen, T. P., & Hartling, L. (2008). Music for pain and anxiety in children undergoing medical procedures: A systematic review of randomized controlled trials. *Ambulatory Pediatrics, 8,* 117–128.

Konrad, M., Joseph, L. M., & Itoi, M. (2011, January). Using guided notes to enhance instruction for all students. *Intervention in School and Clinic, 46*(3), 131–140.

Kopasz, M., Loessl, B., Hornyak, M., Riemann, D., Nissen, C., Piosczyk, H., & Voderholzer, U. (2010). Sleep and memory in healthy children and adolescents: A critical review. *Sleep Medicine Reviews, 14,* 167–177.

Korol, D. L., & Gold, P. E. (1998). Glucose, memory, and aging. *American Journal of Clinical Nutrition, 67,* 764S–771S.

Kreeger, K. Y. (2002). Deciphering how the sexes think: It's not necessarily about who is better at what, but why the sexes process some stimuli in dissimilar ways. *The Scientist, 16,* 28–29.

Kretlow, A. G., Cooke, N. L., & Wood, C. L. (2012, November/December). Using in-service and coaching to increase teachers' accurate use of research-based strategies. *Remedial and Special Education, 33*(6), 348–361.

Kreutzmann, J. C., Havekes, R., Abel, T., & Meerlo, P. (2015, November). Sleep deprivation and hippocampal vulnerability: Changes in neuronal plasticity, neurogenesis and cognitive function. *Neuroscience, 309,* 173–190.

Krishnan, S. S., & Sitaraman, R. K. (2012). *Video stream quality impacts viewer behavior: Inferring causality using quasi-experimental designs.* Retrieved from http://people.cs.umass.edu/~ramesh/Site/HOME_files/imc208-krishnan.pdf

Kucian, K. (2016). Developmental dyscalculia and the brain. In D. B. Berch, D. C. Geary, & K. Mann Koepke (Eds.), *Development of mathematical cognition* (pp. 165–193). Cambridge, MA: Academic Press.

Kumar, N., Wheaton, L. A., Snow, T. K., & Millard-Stafford, M. (2016, January). Carbohydrate ingestion but not mouth rinse maintains sustained attention when fasted. *Physiology & Behavior, 153,* 33–39.

Kwon, S. H., Scheinost, D., Lacadie, C., Sze, G., Schneider, K. C., Dai, F., . . . Ment, L. R. (2015, March). Adaptive mechanisms of developing brain: Cerebral lateralization in the prematurely-born. *NeuroImage, 108,* 144–150.

Lachmair, M., Dudschig, C., de la Vega, I., & Kaup, B. (2014, May). Relating numeric cognition and language processing: Do numbers and words share a common representational platform? *Acta Psychologica, 148,* 107–114.

Lai, M.-C., Lombardo, M. V., Chakrabarti, B., Ecker, C., Sadek, S. A., Wheelwright, S. J. . . . Baron-Cohen, S. (2012, July). Individual differences in brain structure underpin empathizing–systemizing cognitive styles in male adults. *NeuroImage, 61*(4), 1347–1354.

Landerl, K., Göbel, S. M., & Moll, K. (2013, June). Core deficit and individual manifestations of developmental dyscalculia (DD): The role of comorbidity. *Trends in Neuroscience and Education, 2*(2), 38–42.

Langer, N., Peysakhovich, B., Zuk, J., Drottar, M., Sliva, D. D., Smith, S., . . . Gaab, N. (2015, December). White matter alterations in infants at risk for developmental dyslexia. *Cerebral Cortex*, doi:10.1093/cercor/bhv281

Lee, B. K., Patall, E. A., Cawthon, S. W., & Steingut, R. R. (2015, March). The effect of drama-based pedagogy on preK–16 outcomes: A meta-analysis of research from 1985 to 2012. *Review of Educational Research, 85*(1), 3–49.

Leight, H., Saunders, C., Calkins, R., & Withers, M. (2012, December). Collaborative testing improves performance but not content retention in a large-enrollment introductory biology class. *CBE-Life Sciences Education, 11*(4), 392–401.

Lengel, T., & Kuczala, M. (2010). *The kinesthetic classroom: Teaching and learning through movement.* Thousand Oaks, CA: Corwin.

Leppänen, P. H. T., Hämäläinen, J. A., Salminem, H. K., Eklund, K. M., Guttorm, T. K., Lohvansuu, K. . . . Lyytinen, H. (2010, November/December). Newborn brain event-related potentials revealing atypical processing of sound frequency and the subsequent association with later literacy skills in children with familial dyslexia. *Cortex, 46*(10), 1362–1376.

Leventon, J. S., Stevens, J. S., & Bauer, P. J. (2014, October). Development in the neurophysiology of emotion processing and memory in school-age children. *Developmental Cognitive Neuroscience, 10*, 21–33.

Lewis, P. A., Critchley, H. D., Smith, A. P., & Dolan, R. J. (2005). Brain mechanisms for mood congruent memory facilitation. *NeuroImage, 25*, 1214–1223.

Lewy, A. J., Emens, J. S., Songer, J. B., & Rough, J. N. (2009). The neurohormone melatonin as a marker, medicament and mediator. In D. W. Pfaff, A. P. Arnold, A. M. Etgen, S. E. Fahrbach, & R. T. Rubin (Eds.), *Hormones, Brain and Behavior,* San Diego, CA: Academic Press, pp. 2505–2526.

Libertus, M. E., Odic, D., & Halberda, J. (2012, November). Intuitive sense of number correlates with math scores on college-entrance examination. *Acta Psychologica, 141*(3), 373–379.

Liikkanen, L. A. (2012, March). Musical activities predispose to involuntary musical imagery. *Psychology of Music, 40*(2), 236–256.

Limb, C. J., & Braun, A. R. (2008). Neural substrates of spontaneous musical performance: An fMRI study of jazz improvisation. *PLoS ONE 3*(2), e1679. doi: 10.1371/journal.pone.0001679

Lin, L.-Y., Cherng, R.-J., Chen, Y.-J., Chen, Y.-J., & Yang, H.-M. (2015, February). Effects of television exposure on developmental skills among young children. *Infant Behavior and Development, 38*, 20–26.

Lindberg, S. M., Hyde, J. S., Petersen, J. L., & Linn, M. C. (2010). New trends in gender and mathematics performance: A meta-analysis. *Psychological Bulletin, 136*, 1123–1135.

Lindell, A. K., & Lum, J. A. G. (2008). Priming vs. rhyming: Orthographic and phonological representations in the left and right hemispheres. *Brain and Cognition, 68*, 193–203.

Livingston, G. (2014, December). *Fewer than half of U.S. kids today live in a "traditional" family.* Washington, DC: Pew Research Center. Retrieved from http://www.pew research.org

Lu, C., Qi, Z., Harris, A., Weil, L. W., Han, M., Halverson, K., . . . Gabrieli, J. D. E. (2016, March). Shared neuroanatomical substrates of impaired phonological working memory across reading disability and autism. *Biological Psychiatry: Cognitive Neuroscience and Neuroimaging, 1*(2), 169–177.

Ludden, A. B., & Wolfson, A. R. (2010). Understanding adolescent caffeine use: Connecting use patterns with expectancies, reasons, and sleep. *Health Education & Behavior, 37*, 330–342.

Lust, J. M., Geuze, R. H., Groothuis, A. G., & Bouma, A. (2011, March). Functional cerebral lateralization and dual-task efficiency-testing the function of human brain lateralization using fTCD. *Behavioural Brain Research, 217*(2), 293–301.

Lutchmaya, S., Baron-Cohen, S., & Raggatt, P. (2002). Fetal testosterone and vocabulary size in 18- and 24-month-old infants. *Infant Behavior and Development, 24,* 418–424.

MacLean, P. D. (1990). *The triune brain in evolution: Role in paleocerebral functions.* New York, NY: Plenum Press.

Magnussen, S. (2015). Psychology of visual memory. In J. Wright (Ed.), *International encyclopedia of the social & behavioral sciences* (2nd ed., pp. 175–180). Waltham, MA: Elsevier.

Malin, J. L., Cabrera, N. J., & Rowe, M. L. (2014). Low-income minority mothers' and fathers' reading and children's interest: Longitudinal contributions to children's receptive vocabulary skills. *Early Childhood Research Quarterly, 29*(4), 425–432.

Mansi, G., & Levy, Y. (2013, June). Do instant messaging interruptions help or hinder knowledge workers' task performance? *International Journal of Information Management, 33*(3), 591–596.

Marsolek, C. J. (2015), Implicit memory. In J. Wright (Ed.), *International encyclopedia of the social & behavioral sciences* (2nd ed., pp. 709–713). Waltham, MA: Elsevier.

Martinez, S., & Guzman, S. (2013, August). Gender and racial/ethnic differences in self-reported levels of engagement in high school math and science courses. *Hispanic Journal of Behavioral Sciences, 35,* 407–427.

Marvel, C. L., & Desmond, J. E. (2016). The cerebellum and verbal working memory. In P. Mariën & M. Manto (Eds.), *The linguistic cerebellum* (pp. 51–62). Cambridge, MA: Academic Press.

Mason, C. Y., Steedly, K. M., & Thormann, M. S. (2008). Impact of arts integration on voice, choice, and access. *Teacher Education and Special Education, 31,* 36–46.

Mayseless, N., Aharon-Peretz, J., & Shamay-Tsoory, S. (2014, November). Unleashing creativity: The role of left temporoparietal regions in evaluating and inhibiting the generation of creative ideas. *Neuropsychologia, 64,* 157–168.

Mazzocco, M. M. M., & Hanich, L. B. (2010, April). Math achievement, numerical processing, and executive functions in girls with Turner syndrome. Do girls with Turner syndrome have math learning disability? *Learning and Individual Differences, 20,* 70–81.

McCullough, A. M., Ritchey, M., Ranganath, C., & Yonelinas, A. (2015, September). Differential effects of stress-induced cortisol responses on recollection and familiarity-based recognition memory. *Neurobiology of Learning and Memory, 123,* 1–10.

McNamara, G. I., & Isles, A. R. (2014). Influencing the social group: The role of imprinted genes. *Advances in Genetics, 86,* 107–134.

McPherson, G. E., & Hendricks, K. S. (2010). Students' motivation to study music: United States of America. *Research Studies in Music Education, 32,* 201–213.

Medina, J. (2008). *Brain rules.* Seattle, WA: Pear Press.

Melby-Lervåg, M., & Hulme, C. (2013, February). Is working memory training effective? A meta-analytic review. *Developmental Psychology, 49*(2), 270–291.

Meldrum, R. C., & Restivo, E. (2014, June). The behavioral and health consequences of sleep deprivation among U.S. high school students: Relative deprivation matters. *Preventive Medicine, 63,* 24–28.

Mellalieu, S. D., Hanton, S., & Thomas, O. (2009). The effects of a motivational general-arousal imagery intervention upon performance symptoms in male rugby union players. *Psychology of Sport and Exercise, 10*(4), 175–185.

Menon, V., & Levitin, D. J. (2005). The rewards of music listening: Response and physiological connectivity of the mesolimbic system. *NeuroImage, 28,* 175–184.

Mestre, J. (2002). *Transfer of learning: Issues and research agenda.* Arlington, VA: National Science Foundation.

Metcalfe, J., Kornell, N., & Son, L. K. (2007). A cognitive-science based programme to enhance study efficacy in a high and low-risk setting. *European Journal of Cognitive Psychology, 19,* 743–768.

Midgley, K. J., Holcomb, P. J., & Grainger, J. (2009). Language effects in second language learners and proficient bilinguals investigated with event-related potentials. *Journal of Neurolinguistics, 22,* 281–300.

Mihov, K. M., Denzler, M., & Förster, J. (2010). Hemispheric specialization and creative thinking: A meta-analytic review of lateralization of creativity. *Brain and Cognition, 72*(3), 442–448.

Miller, D. I., & Halpern, D. F. (2014, January). The new science of cognitive sex differences. *Trends in Cognitive Sciences, 18*(1), 37–45.

Miller, G. A. (1956). The magical number seven, plus-or-minus two: Some limits on our capacity for processing information. *Psychological Review, 101,* 343–352.

Moll, K., Hasko, S., Groth, K., Bartling, J., & Schulte-Körne, G. (2016, April). Letter-sound processing deficits in children with developmental dyslexia: An ERP study. *Clinical Neurophysiology, 127*(4), 1989–2000.

Monk, C. A., Trafton, J. G., & Boehm-Davis, D. A. (2008). The effect of interruption duration and demand on resuming suspended goals. *Journal of Experimental Psychology: Applied, 14*(4), 299–313.

Monroy, L. L. (2015, February). Teaching creativity. *Procedia—Social and Behavioral Sciences, 174,* 2795–2797.

Moons, W. G., & Mackie, D. M. (2007). Thinking straight while seeing red: The influence of anger on information processing. *Personality and Social Psychology Bulletin, 33,* 706–720.

Mueller, P. A., & Oppenheimer, D. M. (2014, June). The pen is mightier than the keyboard: Advantages of longhand over laptop note taking. *Psychological Science, 25,* 1159–1168.

Mulder, M. J., Baeyens, D., Davidson, M. C., Casey, B. J., Van Den Ban, E., Van Engeland, H., & Durston, S. (2008). Familial vulnerability to ADHD affects activity in the cerebellum in addition to the prefrontal systems. *Journal of the American Academy of Child & Adolescent Psychiatry, 47,* 68–75.

Myers, N. E., Stokes, M. G., Walther, L., & Nobre, A. C. (2014, June). Oscillatory brain state predicts variability in working memory. *Journal of Neuroscience, 34*(23), 7735–7743.

Nagel, B. J., Herting, M. M., Maxwell, E. C., Bruno, R., & Fair, D. (2013, June). Hemispheric lateralization of verbal and spatial working memory during adolescence. *Brain and Cognition, 82*(1), 58–68.

Nahum, N., Bouzerda-Wahlen, A., Guggisberg, A., Ptak, R., & Schnider, A. (2012, August). Forms of confabulation: Dissociations and associations. *Neuropsychologia, 50*(10), 2524–2534.

National Center for Education Statistics. (2012). *The nation's report card: Science 2011.* Washington, DC: U.S. Department of Education.

National Center for Education Statistics. (2013). *The nation's report card: 1990 to 2013 assessment results in mathematics.* Washington, DC: U.S. Department of Education.

National Center for Education Statistics. (2014). *Average national assessment of educational progress in mathematics scale scores.* Washington, DC: U.S. Department of Education.

National Center for Education Statistics. (2015). *The nation's report card: 2015 mathematics and reading assessments.* Washington, DC: U.S. Department of Education.

National Governors Association Center for Best Practices & Council of Chief State School Officers. (2010). *Common core state standards for mathematics.* Washington, DC: Author. Retrieved from http://www.corestandards.org/Math

National Institute on Deafness and Other Communication Disorders. (2010). *Speech and language developmental milestones.* Retrieved May 23, 2011, from http://www.nidcd.nih.gov/health/voice/speechandlanguage.html

National Survey of Student Engagement. (2015). *Engagement insights: Survey findings on the quality of undergraduate education.* Bloomington: Indiana University Center for Postsecondary Research.

Navawongse, R., & Eichenbaum, H. (2013, January). Distinct pathways for rule-based retrieval and spatial mapping of memory representations in hippocampal neurons. *Journal of Neuroscience, 33*(3), 1002–1013.

Nee, D. E., & Jonides, J. (2014, June). Frontal–medial temporal interactions mediate transitions among representational states in short-term memory. *Journal of Neuroscience, 34*(23), 7964–7975.

Neubauer, A. C., Grabner, R. H., Fink, A., & Neuper, C. (2005). Intelligence and neural efficiency: Further evidence of the influence of task content and sex on the brain-IQ relationship. *Cognitive Brain Research, 25,* 217–225.

Neumerski, C. M. (2013, April). Rethinking instructional leadership, a review: What do we know about principal, teacher, and coach instructional leadership, and where should we go from here? *Educational Administration Quarterly, 49*(2), 310–347.

Neves, G., Cooke, S. F., & Bliss, T. V. (2008). Synaptic plasticity, memory and the hippocampus: A neural network approach to causality. *Nature Reviews Neuroscience 9*(1), 65–75.

Newbury, D. F., & Monaco, A. P. (2010). Genetic advances in the study of speech and language disorders. *Neuron, 68,* 309–320.

Newman, S. D., & Green, S. R. (2015). Complex problem solving. *Brain Mapping, 3,* 543–549.

Nguyen, D. K., & Disteche, C. M. (2006). High expression of the mammalian X chromosome in brain. *Brain Research, 1126,* 46–49.

Njemanze, P. C. (2005). Cerebral lateralization and general intelligence: Gender differences in a transcranial Doppler study. *Brain and Language, 92,* 234–239.

Norman-Haignere, S., Kanwisher, N. G., & McDermott, J. H. (2015, December). Distinct cortical pathways for music and speech revealed by hypothesis-free voxel decomposition. *Neuron, 88*(6), 1281–1296.

Norton, A., Winner, E., Cronin, K., Overy, K., Lee, D. J., & Schlaug, G. (2005). Are there pre-existing neural, cognitive, or motoric markers for musical ability? *Brain and Cognition, 59,* 124–134.

Norton, A., Zipse, L., Marchina, S., & Schlaug, G. (2009). Melodic intonation therapy: Shared insights on how it is done and why it might help. *Annals of the New York Academy of Sciences, 1169,* 431–436.

Nussbaumer, D., Grabner, R. H., & Stern, E. (2015, May/June). Neural efficiency in working memory tasks: The impact of task demand. *Intelligence, 50,* 196–208.

Oberauer, K., & Bialkova, S. (2009, February). Accessing information in working memory: Can the focus of attention grasp two elements at the same time? *Journal of Experimental Psychology, 138,* 64–87.

Oberauer, K., & Hein, L. (2012, June). Attention to information in working memory. *Current Directions in Psychological Science, 21*(3), 164–169.

Oberauer, K., & Kliegl, R. (2004). Simultaneous cognitive operations in working memory after dual-task practice. *Journal of Experimental Psychology: Human Perception and Performance, 30,* 689–707.

Ogden, C. L., Carroll, M. D., Kit, B. K., & Flegal, K. M. (2014, February). Prevalence of childhood and adult obesity in the United States, 2011–2012. *Journal of the American Medical Association, 311*(8), 806–814.

Olson, I. R., & Berryhill, M. (2009). Some surprising findings on the involvement of the parietal lobe in human memory. *Neurobiology of Learning and Memory, 91,* 155–165.

Omar, N., Mohamad, M. M., & Paimin, A. N. (2015, August). Dimension of learning styles and students' academic achievement. *Procedia—Social and Behavioral Sciences, 204,* 172–182.

Ornstein, R., & Thompson, R. (1984). *The amazing brain.* Boston: Houghton Mifflin.

Ossowski, A., & Behrmann, M. (2015, November). Left hemisphere specialization for word reading potentially causes, rather than results from, a left lateralized bias for high spatial frequency visual information. *Cortex, 72,* 27–39.

Palmiero, M., Nori, R., & Piccardi, L. (2016, February). Visualizer cognitive style enhances visual creativity. *Neuroscience Letters, 615,* 98–101.

Pancsofar, N., & Vernon-Feagans, L. (2006). Mother and father language input to young children: Contributions to later language development. *Journal of Applied Developmental Psychology, 27,* 571–587.

Panzer, S., & Shea, C. H. (2008). The learning of two similar complex movement sequences: Does practice insulate a sequence from interference? *Human Movement Science, 27,* 873–887.

Park, J., DeWind, N. K., Woldorff, M. G., & Brannon, E. M. (2016, February). Rapid and direct encoding of numerosity in the visual stream. *Cerebral Cortex, 26*(2), 748–763.

Park, S., Lee, J.-M., Baik, Y., Kim, K., Yun, H. J., Kwon, H., . . . Kim, B.-N. (2015, November). A preliminary study of the effects of an arts education program on executive function, behavior, and brain structure in a sample of nonclinical school-aged children. *Journal of Child Neurology, 30*(13), 1757–1766.

Parrott, C. A. (1986). Visual imagery training: Stimulating utilization of imaginal processes. *Journal of Mental Imagery, 10,* 47–64.

Patihis, L., Lilienfeld, S. O., Ho, L. Y., & Loftus, E. F. (2014, October). Unconscious repressed memory is scientifically questionable. *Psychological Science, 25*(10), 1967–1968.

Pavlicevic, M., O'Neil, N., Powell, H., Jones, O., & Sampathianaki, E. (2014, March). Making music, making friends: Long-term music therapy with young adults with severe learning disabilities. *Journal of Intellectual Disabilities, 18*(1), 5–19.

Pearson, P. D., & Gallagher, M. C. (1983). The instruction of reading comprehension. *Contemporary Educational Psychology, 8,* 317–344.

Pereira, A. C., Huddleston, D. E., Brickman, A. M., Sosunov, A. A., Hen, R., McKhann, G. M., . . . Small, S. A. (2007). An in vivo correlate of exercise-induced neurogenesis in the adult dentate gyrus. *Proceedings of the National Academy of Sciences USA, 104,* 5638–5643.

Pereltsvaig, A. (2011). *Linguistic diversity and language endangerment in Papua New Guinea.* Retrieved from http://www.languagesoftheworld.info/australia-and-papua-new-guinea

Perkins, D., & Salomon, G. (1988). Teaching for transfer. *Educational Leadership, 46,* 22–32.

Petrosini, L., Graziano, A., Mandolesi, L., Neri, P., Molinari, M., & Leggio, M. G. (2003). Watch how to do it! New advances in learning by observation. *Brain Research Reviews, 42,* 252–264.

Petersson, K. M., & Hagoort, P. (2012, July). The neurobiology of syntax: Beyond string sets. *Philosophical Transactions of the Royal Society B: Biological Sciences, 367*(1598), 1971–1983.

Phillips, L. (2013, January 23). *Top 10 skills children learn from the arts.* Retrieved from https://www.washingtonpost.com/news/answer-sheet/wp/2013/01/22/top-10-skills-children-learn-from-the-arts/

Pietschnig, J., Voracek, M., & Formann, A. K. (2010). Mozart effect–Shmozart effect: A meta-analysis. *Intelligence, 38*(3), 314–323.

Pinker, S. (1994). *The language instinct: How the mind creates language.* New York, NY: Harper Perennial.

Piro, J. M., & Ortiz, C. (2009). The effect of piano lessons on the vocabulary and verbal sequencing skills of primary grade students. *Psychology of Music, 37*(3), 325–347.

Polikoff, M. S. (2012, December). The redundancy of mathematics instruction in U.S. elementary and middle schools. *Elementary School Journal, 113*, 230–251.

Poppenk, J., Köhler, S., & Moscovitch, M. (2010). Revisiting the novelty effect: When familiarity, not novelty, enhances memory. *Journal of Experimental Psychology: Learning, Memory, and Cognition, 36*, 1321–1330.

Portowitz, P., Lichtenstein, O., Egorova, L., & Brand, E. (2009). Underlying mechanisms linking music education and cognitive modifiability. *Research Studies in Music Education, 31*, 107–129.

Portrat, S., Barrouillet, P., & Camos, V. (2008). Time-related decay or interference-based forgetting in working memory? *Journal of Experimental Psychology: Learning, Memory, and Cognition, 34*, 1561–1564.

Posner, M., Rothbart, M. K., Sheese, B. E., & Kieras, J. (2008). How arts training influences cognition. In C. Asbury & B. Rich (Eds.), *Learning, arts, and the brain* (pp. 1–10). New York, NY: Dana Press.

Postle, B. R. (2016). The hippocampus, memory, and consciousness. *The neurology of consciousness* (2nd ed., pp. 349–363). Cambridge, MA: Academic Press.

Powell, S. R. (2015, November). Connecting evidence-based practice with implementation opportunities in special education mathematics preparation. *Intervention in School and Clinic, 51*(2), 90–96.

Preston, J. L., Molfese, P. J., Frost, S. J., Mencl, W. E., Fulbright, R. K., Hoeft, F., . . . Pugh, K. R. (2016, January). Print-speech convergence predicts future reading outcomes in early readers. *Psychological Science, 27*(1), 75–84.

Pulvermüller, F. (2010). Brain embodiment of syntax and grammar: Discrete combinatorial mechanisms spelt out in neuronal circuits. *Brain and Language, 112*, 167–179.

Purpura, D. J., & Lonigan, C. J. (2013, February). Informal numeracy skills: The structure and relations among numbering, relations, and arithmetic operations in preschool. *American Educational Research Journal, 50*, 178–209.

Purpura, D. J., & Reid, E. E. (2016). Mathematics and language: Individual and group differences in mathematical language skills in young children. *Early Childhood Research Quarterly, 36*, 259–268.

Quaglia Institute for Student Aspirations. (2014). *My voice national student report 2014 (Grades 6–12).* Portland, ME: Author.

Quinn, J. M., & Wagner, R. K. (2015, July/August). Gender differences in reading impairment and in the identification of impaired readers: Results from a large-scale study of at-risk readers. *Journal of Learning Disabilities,48*(4), 433–445.

Rabkin, N., & Redmond, R. (2004). *Putting the arts in the picture: Reforming education in the 21st century.* Chicago, IL: Columbia College.

Ramón y Cajal, S. (1989). *Recollections of my life.* Cambridge, MA: MIT Press.

Ranganathan, R., Wieser, J., Mosier, K. M., Mussa-Ivaldi, F. A., & Scheidt, R. A. (2014, June). Learning redundant motor tasks with and without overlapping dimensions: Facilitation and interference effects. *Journal of Neuroscience, 34*(24), 8289–8299.

Ratey, J. J. (2008). *Spark: The revolutionary new science of exercise and the brain.* New York, NY: Little, Brown.

Rauscher, F. H., Shaw, G. L., & Ky, K. N. (1995, February). Listening to Mozart enhances spatial-temporal reasoning: Towards a neurophysiological basis. *Neuroscience Letters, 185,* 44–47.

Rauscher, F. H., Shaw, G. L., Levine, L. J., Wright, E. L., Dennis, W. R., & Newcomb, R. L. (1997). Music training causes long-term enhancement of preschool children's spatial-temporal reasoning. *Neurological Research, 19,* 2–8.

Rauscher, F. H., & Zupan, M. A. (2000). Classroom keyboard instruction improves kindergarten children's spatial-temporal performance: A field experiment. *Early Childhood Research Quarterly, 15,* 215–228.

Reber, P. J. (2013, August). The neural basis of implicit learning and memory: A review of neuropsychological and neuroimaging research. *Neuropsychologia, 51*(10), 2026–2042.

Redick, T. S., Shipstead, Z., Harrison, T. L., Hicks, K. L., Fried, D. E., Hambrick, D. Z., . . . Engle, R. W. (2013). No evidence of intelligence improvement after working memory training: A randomized, placebo-controlled study. *Journal of Experimental Psychology: General, 142*(2), 359–379.

Rémy, F., Wenderoth, N., Lipkens, K., & Swinnen, S. P. (2010). Dual-task interference during initial learning of a new motor task results from competition for the same brain areas. *Neuropsychologia, 48,* 2517–2527.

Respress, T., & Lutfi, G. (2006). Whole brain learning: The fine arts with students at risk. *Reclaiming Children and Youth, 15,* 24–31.

Restak, R. M. (2003). *The new brain: How the modern age is rewiring your mind.* New York, NY: Rodale.

Rickford, J. R., Duncan, G. J., Gennetian, L. A., Gou, R. Y., Greene, R., Katz, L. F., . . . Ludwig, J. (2015, September). Neighborhood effects on use of African-American Vernacular English. *Proceedings of the National Academy of Sciences, 112*(38), 11817–11822.

Ridderinkhof, K. R., & Brass, M. (2015, February/June). How kinesthetic motor imagery works: A predictive-processing theory of visualization in sports and motor exper- tise. *Journal of Physiology-Paris, 109*(1–3), 53–63.

Ringo, J. L., Doty, R. W., Demeter, S., & Simard, P. Y. (1994). Time is of the essence: A conjecture that hemispheric specialization arises from interhemispheric conduc- tion delays. *Journal of the Cerebral Cortex, 4,* 331–343.

Rinne, L., Gregory, E., Yarmolinskaya, J., & Hardiman, M. (2011, June). Why arts integra- tion improves long-term retention of content. *Mind, Brain, and Education, 5*(2), 89–96.

Rizzolatti, G., Fadiga, L., Gallese, V., & Fogassi, L. (1996, March). Premotor cortex and the recognition of motor actions. *Cognitive Brain Research, 3*(2), 131–141.

Roelofs, A., Piai, V., Rodriguez, G. G., & Chwilla, D. J. (2016, March). Electrophysiology of cross-language interference and facilitation in picture naming. *Cortex, 76,* 1–16.

Root-Bernstein, R. S. (1997, July 11). Art for science's sake. *Chronicle of Higher Education,* B6.

Rossa, K. R., Smith, S. S., Allan, A. C., & Sullivan, K. A. (2014, August). The effects of sleep restriction on executive inhibitory control and affect in young adults. *Journal of Adolescent Health, 55*(2), 287–292.

Rowe, M. B. (1974). Wait-time and rewards as instructional variables, their influ- ence on language, logic, and fate control: Part one—wait-time. *Journal of Research in Science Teaching,* 81–94.

Ruch, S., Markes, O., Duss, S. B., Oppliger, D., Reber, T. P., Koenig, . . . Henke, K. (2012, August). Sleep stage II contributes to the consolidation of declarative memories. *Neuropsychologica, 50*(10), 2389–2396.

Ruigrok, A. N. V., Salimi-Khorshidi, G., Lai, M.-C., Baron-Cohen, S., Lombardo, M. V., Tait, R. J., & Suckling, J. (2014, February). A meta-analysis of sex differences in human brain structure. *Neuroscience & Biobehavioral Reviews 39*, 34–50.

Russell, P. (1979). *The brain book.* New York, NY: E. P. Dutton.

Rydell, R. J., Van Loo, K. J., & Boucher, K. L. (2014, March). Stereotype threat and executive functions: Which functions mediate different threat-related outcomes? *Personality and Social Psychology Bulletin, 40*(3), 377–390.

Saggar, M., Quintin, E.-M., Kienitz, E., Bott, N. T., Sun, Z., Hong, W.-C., . . . Reiss, A. L. (2015, May). Pictionary-based fMRI paradigm to study the neural correlates of spontaneous improvisation and figural creativity. *Scientific Reports, 5.* doi:10.1038/srep10894

Sahari, S. H., & Johari, A. (2012). Improvising reading classes and classroom environment for children with reading difficulties and dyslexia symptoms. *Procedia—Social and Behavioral Sciences, 38*, 100–107.

Sara, S. J. (2015, December). Locus coeruleus in time with the making of memories. *Current Opinion in Neurobiology, 35*, 87–94.

Saraa-Zawyah, T., Badli, T., & Dzulkifli, M A. (2013, November). The effect of humour and mood on memory recall. *Procedia—Social and Behavioral Sciences, 97*, 252–257.

Sargent, J., Dopkins, S., Philbeck, J., & Cichka, D. (2010). Chunking in spatial memory. *Journal of Experimental Psychology: Learning, Memory, and Cognition, 36*, 576–589.

Sato, H., Yahata, N., Funane, T., Takizawa, R., Katura, T., Atsumori, H. . . . Kasai, K. (2013, December). A NIRS–fMRI investigation of prefrontal cortex activity during a working memory task. *NeuroImage, 83*, 158–173.

Satterthwaite, T. D., Wolf, D. H., Erus, G., Ruparel, K., Elliott, M. A., Gennatus, E., . . . Gur, R. E. (2013, October). Functional maturation of the executive system during adolescence. *Journal of Neuroscience, 33*(41), 16249–16261.

Schacter, J., & Jo, B. (2016, February). Improving low-income preschoolers mathematics achievement with Math Shelf, a preschool tablet computer curriculum. *Computers in Human Behavior, 55*, Part A, 223–229.

Schiff, R., & Vakil, E. (2015, April). Age differences in cognitive skill learning, retention and transfer: The case of the Tower of Hanoi Puzzle. *Learning and Individual Differences, 39*, 164–171.

Schlaug, G. (2015). Chapter 3—Musicians and music making as a model for the study of brain plasticity. *Progress in Brain Research, 217*, 37–55.

Schmithhorst, V. J., & Holland, S. K. (2004). The effect of musical training on the neural correlates of math processing: A functional magnetic resonance imaging study in humans. *Neuroscience Letters, 354*, 193–196.

Scholey, A., Macpherson, H., Sünram-Lea, S., Elliott, J., Stough, C., & Kennedy, D. (2013, January). Glucose enhancement of recognition memory: Differential effects on effortful processing but not aspects of "remember-know" responses. *Neuropharmacology, 64*, 544–549.

Schroder, H. S., Moran, T. P., Donnellan, M. B., & Moser, J. S. (2014, December). Mindset induction effects on cognitive control: A neurobehavioral investigation. *Biological Psychology, 103*, 27–37.

Schroeder, J. H., Desrocher, M., Bebko, J. M., & Cappadocia, C. (2010). The neurobiology of autism: Theoretical applications. *Research in Autism Spectrum Disorders, 4*(4), 555–564.

Schulte-Körne, G., & Bruder, J. (2010, November). Clinical neurophysiology of visual and auditory processing in dyslexia: A review. *Clinical Neurophysiology, 121*(110), 1794–1809.

Schutte, G. M., Duhon, G. J., Solomon, B. G., Poncy, B. C., Moore, K., & Story, B. (2015, April). A comparative analysis of massed vs. distributed practice on basic math fact fluency growth rates. *Journal of School Psychology, 53*(2), 149–159.

Scott-Simmons, D., Barker, J., & Cherry, N. (2003). Integrating research and story writing. *The Reading Teacher, 56*, 742–745.

Seabrook, R., Brown, G. D. A., & Solity, J. E. (2005). Distributed and massed practice: From laboratory to classroom. *Applied Cognitive Psychology, 19*, 107–122.

Semenza, C., Delazer, M., Bertella, L., Granà, A., Mori, I., Conti, F. M., . . . Mauro, A. (2006). Is math lateralized on the same side as language? Right hemisphere aphasia and mathematical abilities. *Neuroscience Letters, 406*, 285–288.

Shargorodsky, J., Curhan, S. G., Curhan, G. C., & Eavey, R. (2010). Changes in prevalence of hearing loss in U.S. adolescents. *Journal of the American Medical Association, 304*(7), 772–778.

Sharma, H. P., Bansil, S., & Uygungil, B. (2015, December). Signs and symptoms of food allergy and food-induced anaphylaxis. *Pediatric Clinics of North America, 62*(6), 1377–1392.

Shaywitz, S. E. (2003). *Overcoming dyslexia: A new and complete science-based program for reading problems at any level.* New York, NY: Knopf.

Shen, J., Zhang, G., Yao, L., & Zhao, X. (2015, March). Real-time fMRI training-induced changes in regional connectivity mediating verbal working memory behavioral performance. *Neuroscience, 289*, 144–152.

Sheriff, K. A., & Boon, R. T. (2014, August). Effects of computer-based graphic organizers to solve one-step word problems for middle school students with mild intellectual disability: A preliminary study. *Research in Developmental Disabilities, 35*(8), 1828–1837.

Shillingsburg, M. A., Bowen, C. N., Peterman, R. K., & Gayman, M. D. (2015, March). Effectiveness of the direct instruction language for learning curriculum among children diagnosed with autism spectrum disorder. *Focus on Autism and Other Developmental Disabilities, 30*(1), 44–56.

Sidaway, B., Bates, J., Occhiogrosso, B., Schlagenhaufer, & Wilkes, D. (2012, July). Interaction of feedback frequency and task difficulty in children's motor skill learning. *Physical Therapy, 92*(7), 948–957.

Simmons-Stern, N. R., Budson, A. E., & Ally, B. A. (2010). Music as a memory enhancer in patients with Alzheimer's disease. *Neuropsychologia, 48*(10), 3164–3167.

Singh, A. M., Neva, J. L., & Staines, W. R. (2016, March). Aerobic exercise enhances neural correlates of motor skill learning. *Behavioural Brain Research, 301*, 19–26.

Singh, L. (2008). Influences of high and low variability on infant word recognition. *Cognition, 106*, 833–870.

Siu, K.-C., Suh, I. H., Mukherjee, M., Oleynikov, D., & Stergiou, N. (2010). The effect of music on robot-assisted laparoscopic surgical performance. *Surgical Innovation, 17*, 306–311.

Skoe, E., & Kraus, N. (2012). A little goes a long way: How the adult brain is shaped by musical training in childhood. *The Journal of Neuroscience, 32*(34), 11507–11510.

Slavin, R. E. (2015). Cooperative learning in schools. In J. Wright (Ed.), *International encyclopedia of the social & behavioral sciences* (2nd ed., pp. 881–886). Waltham, MA: Elsevier.

Sluming, V., Brooks, J., Howard, M., Downes, J. J., & Roberts, N. (2007). Broca's area supports enhanced visuospatial cognition in orchestral musicians. *The Journal of Neuroscience, 27*(14), 3799–3806.

Smetackova, I. (2015, May). Gender stereotypes, performance and identification with math. *Procedia—Social and Behavioral Sciences, 190,* 211–219.

Smith, M. A., Riby, L. M., van Eekelen, J., & Foster, J. K. (2011). Glucose enhancement of human memory: A comprehensive research review of the glucose memory facilitation effect. *Neuroscience & Biobehavioral Reviews, 35,* 770–783.

Smith, S. M., & Moynan, S. C. (2008). Forgetting and recovering the unforgettable. *Psychological Science, 19,* 462–468.

Soderstrom, N. C., & Bjork, R. A. (2015, March). Learning versus performance: An integrative review. *Perspectives on Psychological Science, 10*(2), 176–199.

Solopchuk, O., Alamia, A., Olivier, E., & Zénon, A. (2016, March). Chunking improves symbolic sequence processing and relies on working memory gating mechanisms. *Learning & Memory, 23*(3), 108–112.

Sousa, D. A. (2003). *The leadership brain: How to lead today's schools more effectively.* Thousand Oaks, CA: Corwin.

Sousa, D. A. (2011). *How the ELL brain learns.* Thousand Oaks, CA: Corwin.

Sousa, D. A. (2014). *How the brain learns to read* (2nd ed.). Thousand Oaks, CA: Corwin.

Sousa, D. A. (2015a). *How the brain learns mathematics* (2nd ed.). Thousand Oaks, CA: Corwin.

Sousa, D. A. (2015b). *Brain-friendly assessments: What they are and how to use them.* West Palm Beach, FL: Learning Sciences International.

Sousa, D. A. (2016). *Engaging the rewired brain.* West Palm Beach, FL: Learning Sciences International.

Sparks, A. & Reese, E. (2013 February). From reminiscing to reading: Home contributions to children's developing language and literacy in low-income families. *First Language, 33*(1), 89–109.

Spearman, C. (1904). General intelligence, objectively determined and measured. *The American Journal of Psychology 15*(2), 201–292.

Spencer, R. C., Devilbiss, D. M., & Berridge, C. W. (2015, June). The cognition-enhancing effects of psychostimulants involve direct action in the prefrontal cortex. *Biological Psychiatry, 77*(11), 940–950.

Sperry, R. (1966). Brain bisection and consciousness. In J. Eccles (Ed.), *How the self controls its brain.* New York: Springer-Verlag.

Stahl, R. J. (1985). *Cognitive information processes and processing within a uniprocess superstructure/microstructure framework: A practical information-based model.* Unpublished manuscript, University of Arizona, Tucson.

Standley, J. M. (2008). Does music instruction help children learn to read? Evidence of a meta-analysis. *Update: Applications of Research in Music Education, 27,* 17–32.

Starr, A., Libertus, M. E., & Brannon, E. M. (2013, November). Number sense in infancy predicts mathematical abilities in childhood. *Proceedings of the National Academy of Sciences, 110*(45), 18116–18120.

Steinbrink, C., Vogt, K., Kastrup, A., Müller, H.-P., Juengling, F. D., Kassubek, J., & Riecker, A. (2008, November). The contribution of white and gray matter differences to developmental dyslexia: Insights from DTI and VBM at 3.0 T. *Neuropsychologia, 46*(13), 3170–3178.

Stemmer, B. (2015). Lateralization of language as demonstrated by brain imaging procedures. In J. Wright (Ed.), *International encyclopedia of the social & behavioral sciences* (2nd ed., pp. 398–409). Waltham, MA: Elsevier.

Stephane, M., Ince, N. F., Kuskowski, M., Leuthold, A., Tewfik, A. H., Nelson, K., . . . Tadipatri, V. A. (2010). Neural oscillations associated with the primacy and recency effects of verbal working memory. *Neuroscience Letters, 473,* 172–177.

Stern, E. (2015). Intelligence, prior knowledge, and learning. In J. Wright (Ed.), *International encyclopedia of the social & behavioral sciences* (2nd ed., pp. 323–328). Waltham, MA: Elsevier.

Sternberg, R. (1985). *Beyond IQ: A triarchic theory of human intelligence.* New York, NY: Cambridge University Press.

Sternberg, R. J., Ferrari, M., Clinkenbeard, P. R., & Grigorenko, E. L. (1996). Identification, instruction, and assessment of gifted children: A construct validation of a triarchic model. *Gifted Child Quarterly, 40,* 129–137.

Sternberg, R. J., Grigorenko, E. L., Jarvin, L., Clinkenbeard, P., Ferrari, M., & Torfi, B. (2000, Spring). The effectiveness of triarchic teaching and assessment. *National Research Center on the Gifted and Talented Newsletter,* 3–8.

Stevens, D., Anderson, D. I., O'Dwyer, N. J., & Williams, A. M. (2012, September). Does self-efficacy mediate transfer effects in the learning of easy and difficult motor skills? *Consciousness and Cognition, 21*(3), 1122–1128.

Stichter, J. P., Randolph, Kay, D., & Gage, N. (2009). The use of structural analysis to develop antecedent-based interventions for students with autism. *Journal of Autism and Developmental Discord,* 883–896.

Stoodley, C. J. (2016). The role of the cerebellum in developmental dyslexia. In P. Mariën & M. Manto (Eds.), *The linguistic cerebellum* (pp. 199–221). Cambridge, MA: Academic Press.

Stormont, M., Reinke, W. M., Newcomer, L., Marchese, D., & Lewis, C. (2015, April). Coaching teachers' use of social behavior interventions to improve children's outcomes: A review of the literature. *Journal of Positive Behavior Interventions, 17*(2), 69–82.

Sun, J., & van Es, E. A. (2015). An exploratory study of the influence that analyzing teaching has on preservice teachers' classroom practice. *Journal of Teacher Education, 66*(3), 201–214.

Sünram-Lea, S. I., Dewhurst, S. A., & Foster, J. K. (2008). The effect of glucose administration on the recollection and familiarity components of recognition memory. *Biological Psychology, 77,* 69–75.

Swanson, E., Wanzek, J., Vaughn, S., Roberts, G., & Fall, A.-M. (2015, July). Improving reading comprehension and social studies knowledge among middle school students with disabilities. *Exceptional Children, 81*(4), 426–442.

Sweeney, M. S. (2009). *Brain: The complete mind.* Washington, DC: National Geographic.

Tang, T., Jiao, Y., Wang, X., & Lu, Z. (2013, November). Gender versus brain size effects on subcortical gray matter volumes in the human brain. *Neuroscience Letters, 556,* 79–83.

Taras, H. (2005). Physical activity and student performance at school. *Journal of School Health, 75,* 214–218.

Terry, W. S. (2005). Serial position effects in recall of television commercials. *Journal of General Psychology, 132,* 151–163.

Thomas, K., Singh, P., & Klopfenstein, K. (2015, November). Arts education and the high school dropout problem. *Journal of Cultural Economics, 39*(4), 327–339.

Thomas, L. (1979). *The Medusa and the snail.* New York: Viking Press.

Thompson, W. L., Slotnick, S. D., Burrage, M. S., & Kosslyn, S. M. (2009). Two forms of spatial imagery: Neuroimaging evidence. *Psychological Science, 20,* 1245–1253.

Tierney, A., & Kraus, N. (2013). Music training for the development of reading skills. *Progress in Brain Research, 207,* 209–241.

Tierney, A., Krizman, J., & Kraus, N. (2015, August). Music training alters the course of adolescent auditory development. *Proceedings of the National Academy of Sciences, 112*(32), 10062–10067.

Timmann, D., Drepper, J., Frings, M., Maschke, M., Richter, S., Gerwig, M., & Kolb, F. P. (2010, July–August). The human cerebellum contributes to motor, emotional and cognitive associative learning. *Cortex, 46*(7), 845–857.

Tomlinson, C. A. (1999). *The differentiated classroom: Responding to the needs of all learners.* Alexandria, VA: Association for Supervision and Curriculum Development.

Tomlinson, M. M. (2015, December). Transmodal redesign in music and literacy: Diverse multimodal classrooms. *Journal of Early Childhood Literacy, 15*(4), 533–567.

Tosto, M. G., Malykh, S., Voronin, I., Plomin, R., & Kovas, Y. (2013, October). The etiology of individual differences in maths beyond IQ: Insights from 12-year-old twins. *Procedia—Social and Behavioral Sciences, 86*, 429–434.

Trappe, H. J. (2010). The effects of music on the cardiovascular system and cardiovascular health. *Heart, 96*(23), 1868–1871.

Treur, J., & van Wissen, A. (2013, October). Conceptual and computational analysis of the role of emotions and social influence in learning. *Procedia—Social and Behavioral Sciences, 93*, 449–467.

Trezise, K., & Reeve, R. A. (2014, May). Working memory, worry, and algebraic ability. *Journal of Experimental Child Psychology, 121*, 120–136.

Truong, H. M. (2016, February). Integrating learning styles and adaptive e-learning system: Current developments, problems and opportunities. *Computers in Human Behavior, 55*(B), 1185–1193.

Tsuei, M. (2012, May). Using synchronous peer tutoring system to promote elementary students' learning in mathematics. *Computers in Education, 58*, 1171–1182.

Tuma, R. S. (2005, July–August). An eye on shut-eye. *Brain Work, 15*, 6.

Ullman, H., Almeida, R., & Klingberg, T. (2014, January). Structural maturation and brain activity predict future working memory capacity during childhood development. *Journal of Neuroscience, 34*(5), 1592–1598.

Upson, S. (2014, November/December). Human cyborgs reveal how we learn. *Scientific American Mind, 25*(6), 32–35.

Uzer, T. (2016, February). Retrieving autobiographical memories: How different retrieval strategies associated with different cues explain reaction time differences. *Acta Psychologica, 164*, 144–150.

Valentin, C. M., & Mihaela, C. (2015). The relationship between blood glucose levels and performance at cognitive processing and motor coordination tasks. *Procedia—Social and Behavioral Sciences, 187*, 777–782.

Van de Cavey, J., & Hartsuiker, R. J. (2016, January). Is there a domain-general cognitive structuring system? Evidence from structural priming across music, math, action descriptions, and language. *Cognition, 146*, 172–184.

van den Heuvel, M. P., & Sporns, O. (2013, September). An anatomical substrate for integration among functional networks in human cortex. *Journal of Neuroscience, 33*(36), 14489–14500.

Van der Mark, S., Klaver, P., Bucher, K., Maurer, U., Schulz, E., Brem, S., . . . Brandeis, D. (2011, February). The left occipitotemporal system in reading: Disruption of focal fMRI connectivity to left inferior frontal and inferior parietal language areas in children with dyslexia. *NeuroImage, 54*(3), 2426–2436.

van Ermingen-Marbach, M., Grande, M., Pape-Neumann, J., Sass, K., & Heim, S. (2013). Distinct neural signatures of cognitive subtypes of dyslexia with and without phonological deficits. *NeuroImage: Clinical, 2*, 477–490.

Van Overwalle, F., & Mariën, P. (2016, January). Functional connectivity between the cerebrum and cerebellum in social cognition: A multi-study analysis. *NeuroImage, 124*, Part A, 248–255.

van Praag, H., Fleshner, M., Schwartz, M. W., & Mattson, M. P. (2014, November). Exercise, energy intake, glucose homeostasis, and the brain. *Journal of Neuroscience, 34*(46), 15139–15149.

Vargas, M. E. R. (2015, February). Music as a resource to develop cognition. *Procedia— Social and Behavioral Sciences, 174*, 2989–2994.

Vaughn, K. (2000, Fall). Music and mathematics: Modest support for the oft-claimed relationship. *Journal of Aesthetic Education, 34*, 149–166.

Verrusio, W., Ettorre, E., Vicenzini, E., Vanacore, N., Cacciafesta, M., & Mecarelli, O. (2015, September). The Mozart Effect: A quantitative EEG study. *Consciousness and Cognition, 35*, 150–155.

Vukovic, R. K., Kieffer, M. J., Bailey, S. P., & Harari, R. R. (2013, January). Mathematics anxiety in young children: Concurrent and longitudinal associations with mathematical performance. *Contemporary Educational Psychology, 38*, 1–10.

Vukovic, R. K., & Lesaux, N. K. (2013, June). The language of mathematics: Investigating the ways language counts for children's mathematical development. *Journal of Experimental Child Psychology, 115*(2), 227–244.

Wandell, B., Dougherty, R. F., Ben-Shachar, M., Deutsch, G. K., & Tsang, J. (2008). Training in the arts, reading, and brain imaging. In C. Asbury & B. Rich (Eds.), *Learning, arts, and the brain* (pp. 51–59). New York, NY: Dana Press.

Wang, D., Buckner, R. L., & Liu, H. (2014, September). Functional specialization in the human brain estimated by intrinsic hemispheric interaction. *Journal of Neuroscience, 34*(37), 12341–12352.

Wang, M., & Holcombe, R. (2010). Adolescents' perceptions of school environment, engagement, and academic achievement in middle school. *American Educational Research Journal, 47*, 633–662.

Wang, S. S.-H., Kloth, A. D., & Badura, A. (2014, August). The cerebellum, sensitive periods, and autism. *Neuron, 83*(3), 518–532.

Watts, T. W., Duncan, G. J., Siegler, R. S., & Davis-Kean, P. E. (2014, October). What's past is prologue: Relations between early mathematics knowledge and high school achievement. *Educational Researcher, 43*(7), 352–360.

Webb, N. (1997). *Criteria for alignment of expectations and assessments on mathematics and science education.* Research Monograph 6. Washington, DC: Council of Chief State School Officers.

Weinberger, N. M. (2004, November). Music and the brain. *Scientific American, 291*, 89–95.

Wessing, I., Rehbein, M. A., Romer, G., Achtergarde, S., Dobel, C., Zwitserlood, P., . . . Junghöfer, M. (2015, June). Cognitive emotion regulation in children: Reappraisal of emotional faces modulates neural source activity in a frontoparietal network. *Developmental Cognitive Neuroscience, 13*, 1–10.

West, C. K., Farmer, J. A., & Wolff, P. M. (1991). *Instructional design: Implications from cognitive science.* Englewood Cliffs, NJ: Prentice Hall.

Wiggins, G. (2012, January). *Transfer as the point of education.* Retrieved from https:// grantwiggins.wordpress.com/2012/01/11

Wiggins, G. (2015, April). *Why do so many high school history teachers lecture so much?* Retrieved from https://grantwiggins.wordpress.com/2015/04/24

Wiggins, G., & McTighe, J. (2005). *Understanding by design.* Alexandria, VA: Association for Supervision and Curriculum Development.

Wilcox, L. J., He, K., & Derkay, C. S. (2015, December). Identifying musical difficulties as they relate to congenital amusia in the pediatric population. *International Journal of Pediatric Otorhinolaryngology, 79*(12), 2411–2415.

Wilhelm, I., Diekelmann, S., Molzow, I., Ayoub, A., Mölle, M., & Born, J. (2011). Sleep selectively enhances memory expected to be of future relevance. *The Journal of Neuroscience, 31,* 1563–1569.

Wilkinson, L., Steel, A., Mooshagian, E., Zimmermann, T., Keisler, A., Lewis, J. D., & Wassermann, E. M. (2015, October). Online feedback enhances early consolidation of motor sequence learning and reverses recall deficit from transcranial stimulation of motor cortex. *Cortex, 71,* 134–147.

Willcutt, E. G., Petrill, S. A., Wu, S., Boada, R., DeFries, J. C., Olson, R. K., & Pennington, B. F. (2013, November/December). Comorbidity between reading disability and math disability: Concurrent psychopathology, functional impairment, and neuropsychological functioning. *Journal of Learning Disabilities, 46,* 500–516.

Winner, E., Hetland, L., Veenema, S., Sheridan, K., & Palmer, P. (2006). Studio thinking: How visual arts teaching can promote disciplined habits of mind. In P. Locher, C. Martindale, L. Dorfman, & D. Leontiev (Eds.), *New directions in aesthetics, creativity, and the arts* (pp. 189–205). New York, NY: Baywood.

Witney, A. G. (2004). Internal models for bi-manual tasks. *Human Movement Science, 23,* 747–770.

Witt, K., Margraf, N., Bieber, C., Born, J., & Deuschl, G. (2010). Sleep consolidates the effector-independent representation of a motor skill. *Neuroscience, 171,* 227–234.

Wixted, J. T. (2004). The psychology and neuroscience of forgetting. *Annual Review of Psychology, 55,* 235–269.

Wright, B. A., Bowen, R. W., & Zecker, S. G. (2000). Nonlinguistic perceptual deficits associated with reading and language disorders. *Current Opinion in Neurobiology, 10,* 482–486.

Wright, R., John, L., Ellenbogen, S., Offord, D. R., Duku, E. K., & Rowe, W. (2006). Effect of a structured arts program on the psychosocial functioning of youth from low-income communities: Findings from a Canadian longitudinal study. *The Journal of Early Adolescence, 26,* 186–205.

Wymbs, N. F., Bastian, A, J., & Celnik, P. A. (2016, February). Motor skills are strengthened through reconsolidation. *Current Biology, 26*(3), 338–343.

Yamaguti, Y. & Tsuda, I. (2015, February). Mathematical modeling for evolution of heterogeneous modules in the brain. *Neural Networks, 62,* 3–10.

Yan, V. X., Thai, K-P., & Bjork, R. A. (2014, September). Habits and beliefs that guide self-regulated learning: Do they vary with mindset? *Journal of Applied Research in Memory and Cognition, 3*(3), 140–152.

Yang, C. F., & Shah, N. M. (2014, April). Representing sex in the brain, one module at a time. *Neuron, 82*(2), 261–278.

Yarbro, J., Arfstrom, K. M., McKnight, K., & McKnight, P. (2014). *Extension of a review of flipped learning.* South Bend, IN: Flipped Learning Network.

Yee, M. (2007). *Learning phoneme discrimination at the end of words in typical developing infants.* Pittsburg, PA: Carnegie Mellon University.

Yeung, H. H., & Werker, J. F. (2009, November). Learning words' sounds before learning how words sound: 9-month-olds use distinct objects as cues to categorize speech information. *Cognition, 113,* 234–243.

Zamarian, L., Ischebeck, A., & Delazer, M. (2009, June). Neuroscience of learning arithmetic: Evidence from brain imaging studies. *Neuroscience & Biobehavioral Reviews, 33,* 909–925.

Zenasni, F., & Lubart, T. (2011). Pleasantness of creative tasks and creative performance. *Thinking Skills and Creativity, 6,* 49–56.

Zhang, D., Zhao, H., Bai, W., & Tian, X. (2016, January). Functional connectivity among multi-channel EEGs when working memory load reaches the capacity. *Brain Research, 1631,* 101–112.

Zhao, J., de Schotten, M. T., Altarelli, I., Dubois, J., & Ramus, F. (2016, March). Altered hemispheric lateralization of white matter pathways in developmental dyslexia: Evidence from spherical deconvolution tractography. *Cortex, 76,* 51–62.

Zheng, X., Flynn, L. J., & Swanson, H. L. (2013, May). Experimental intervention studies on word problem solving and math disabilities: A selective analysis of the literature. *Learning Disability Quarterly, 36*(2), 97–111.

Zheng, Y., & Cleveland, H. H. (2015, December). Differential genetic and environmental influences on developmental trajectories of antisocial behavior from adolescence to young adulthood. *Journal of Adolescence, 45,* 204–213.

Zhu, W., Zhao, L., Zhang, J., Ding, X., Liu, H., Ni, E., . . . Zhou, C. (2008). The influence of Mozart's sonata K.448 on visual attention: An ERP study. *Neuroscience Letters, 434*(1), 35–40.

Index

Abandonment, strategic, 298–299
Accountability, **76**
  synergy and, **83**
Acetylcholine, 22
Acquired amusia, 258
Acquired dyscalculia, 226
Action research, 9–10, **14,** 323
  on block lessons, 104
Active participation, **144**
ACT test, 34
Administrators and humor, **74**
Adrenaline, 96
Advantages and disadvantages
  chunking, **149**
Age, variations in processing with,
  61–62
Allergies, food, 32
Alphabetic principle, 208, **238**
Alzheimer's disease, 19, 23, 88
  declarative memory and, 93
  directed forgetting and, 131
  episodic memory and, 91
Amazing Brain, The, 43
Amusia, 258
Amygdala, 19–20, **39**
  emotional memory and, 93
  fight-or-flight reaction and, 294
  gender differences, 193–194, 195
  sense of smell and, 48
Analogies, 166, **179, 180**
  maps, **234**
Androgen, 196
Angular gyrus, 206
Anticipatory set, 316
Anxiety, math, 61, 164
Aphasia, 16
Apoptosis, 25, 26
Arrays chunking, **149**
Artificial meaning, **78**
Arts, 243–244
  ability to shift goals in process of, 247
  acceptance of operating within constraints
    and, 247
  aesthetic perspective and, 247

attention to nuance and nonverbal
  communication, 246
as basic to the human experience,
  244–245
cognitive growth through,
  246–248
collaborative skills and, 247
confidence and, 247
constructive feedback and, 247
creativity and, 248–250
development of perseverance
  through, 247
different learning preferences
  and, 254
with disaffected and disadvantaged
  students, 253–255
impact on student learning and behavior,
  251–255
included in all lessons, **273**
key points to ponder, **281**
perception of relationships and, 246
and permission to make decisions in the
  absence of a rule, 247
personal and interpersonal connections
  and, 254–255
problem solving and, 246
sciences needing the, 250
sustained focus and, 246
visual, 266–268, **273**
why teach the, 245–250
and the young brain, 245–246
See also Music
Aspartame, 32
Assessment
  formative, 114
  math anxiety and, 226
Associative learning, 93, 163–164
Astrocytes, 21–22
Attention, technology effects on, 33
Attention Deficit/Hyperactivity Disorder,
  88, 89
  cerebellum and, 269
  dyscalculia and, 227
  reading problems and, 214

Auditory processing, 106, 107
listening to music, 257–258
speed differences, 212–213
Autism, 269
Avoidance, information, 285
Axons, 22
memory formation and, 87–88
Ayoub, A., 116

Baron-Cohen, S., 197
Bauerlein, 34–35
Biological rhythms, 5, 115–119, **145–146**
Block scheduling, 104, **141–142**
Bloom's Taxonomy of the Cognitive Domain, **12**, 288–289, **301–302**
cognitive and emotional thinking in, 293–294
connecting complexity and difficulty to ability, 296–298
constructivism and, 298
critical difference between complexity and difficulty and, 295–298, **304, 306–308**
curriculum changes to accommodate, 298–299
dimensions of thinking and, 295
higher-order thinking and, 299
important characteristics of revised model for, 293
increasing complexity and levels of, **305**
levels, 289–290, 295
loosening of hierarchy, 293
other ways to view levels in, 293
structure and revision, 289–292
take a concept/situation, **303**
testing understanding of, 294–295
tips on using revised, **304**
Bogen, J., 188
Born, J., 116
Boyer, E. L., 243
Brace maps, **235**
Brain, the
activity during motor skill acquisition, 108–109
amygdala, 19–20, **39**, 48, 93, 193–194
area functions, **39**
cells, 21–24
cerebellum, 21, **39**
cerebrum, 20–21, **37, 39**
effects of technology on, 32
gender and, 193–198
grey matter, 121
hippocampus, 19, 36, **39**, 156, 194
importance of physical exercise for, 36
key points to ponder, **42**
lateralization of, 188–199
left and right hemisphere processing, 189–190
lesions in, 213

limbic system, 18–20, **37**
lobes, 16–18, **39**
midbrain, 16, 156
motor cortex and somatosensory cortex, 18
movement and, 269–270
neural systems involved in reading, 206–207
as novelty seeker, 30–36
preparation for test taking, **41**
size, **37**
stem, 18, 25, **37, 39**
structural differences in, 213
students understanding, 312–313
teaching to the whole, **229–232**
windows of opportunity in development of, 26–30
Brain-compatible teaching, **13**
Brain damage, 16, 17, 19
Brain-derived neurotrophic factor (BDNF), 36
Brain fuel, 25, **73**
Brain imaging
arts training and, 248, 249
episodic and semantic memories, 91
gender and, 193
intelligence and, 120–121
lesions, 213
music training and, 263
neural systems involved in reading and, 206
number sense, 227
problems in learning to read and, 209–210
rehearsal process, 98
second language learning and, 204
structural differences in the brain, 213
transfer of learning, 156
types of, 2–4
Brain organization
causes of differences in, 191
gender differences in, 193–198
key points to ponder, **242**
language-oriented schools and, 198
laterality, 188–190
learning mathematics and, 215–228
learning to read and, 205–215
left and right hemisphere processing, 189–190
mathematics and science programs and, 199
schools and, 198–199
second language learning and, 204–205
specialization, 188, 191–193
spoken language organization, 199–205
Brainstorming, **179, 180**
Brain-training programs, 133–134
Breakfast, importance of, 25
Bridging, **179–180**
Broca, P., 200
Broca's area, 200, 205, 248, 261

Brooks, 298
Building principals, 322
Bulletin boards, **231**
Buzan, T., 105, **278**

Caffeine, 32
    sleep deprivation and, 117
Carroll, L., 55
Categorical chunking, **148–149**
Cells, brain, 21–24
Cerebellum, 21, 25, **39**
    motor skill acquisition and, 108
    movement and, 269
    reading problems and, 214
Cerebrum, 20–21, **37, 39**
    motor skill acquisition and, 108
Chain maps, **233, 234**
Checking for understanding, 317
Chicago Arts Partnerships in Education
    (CAPE), 253
Children
    changing environment of, 31–36
    emotional control window, 28–29
    importance of breakfast for, 25
    instrumental music window, 30
    language acquisition window, 29
    mathematics and logic window, 29–30
    motor development window, 27–28
    neuron development in, 25–30
    vocabulary window, 29
    windows of opportunity in, 26–30
Chomsky, N., 202
Chunking, 126–129, **148–149**
    categorical, **148–149**
    cramming as, 129
    effect of past experiences on, 127–129
    pattern, **148**
Circadian rhythms, 5, 115–116, 117,
    145–146
Classical conditioning, 91, 92–93
Classroom, flipped, xii, 313–314
Classroom climate
    arts and, 255
    circadian rhythms and, **146**
    conducive to learning, **71**
    guidelines for teaching the emotional brain
        and, **135**
    mathematics instruction and, 225–226
    thinking skills in, 287–288
    using humor to enhance, **73–74**
Closure, **79**, 98, 317
    in collaborative learning, 114
Coaching, peer, 322
Cochlea, 257
Cognitive belief system, 58–59, 87
Cognitive capacity, 53
    music and, 259
Cognitive growth through the arts, 246–248
Cognitive skills and procedural memory, 92
Collaborative learning, 114, 247

Collage, **172**
Common Core State Standards for Mathematics,
    222, 223, 225, 228
Communication competence, **237**
Community artists, **273**
Complexity and difficulty, critical difference
        between, 295–298, **304, 306–308**
Comprehension, text, 208, **238, 240**
Computerized axial tomography (CAT), 2
Concept attainment, 315
Concept mapping, **233–235**
Conclusion forming, 286
Conditioning, classical, 91, 92–93
Confabulation, 132–133
Confidence, 247
Conflicting messages, **230**
Congenital amusia, 258
Conscious memory. *See* Declarative memory
Consolidation in motor skill acquisition,
    108–109
Constructivism, 9
    Bloom's taxonomy and, 298
    transfer and, 167
Context
    and degree of original learning effect on
        transfer, 160
    -dependent memory, 124
    imagery, **276**
    of metaphors, **183**
    of retrieval, 124
Contingency learning, **181, 182**
Convergent thinking, 285–286
Cooperative learning groups, 9, 315
Corpus callosum, 20, 188, 191, 192, 195
Cortex, 20, 25
Costa, A., 299
Cramming, 129
Creative thinking, 286, 295
Creativity, 5, 286
    arts and, 248–250
    brain hemispheres and, 192
    intelligence versus, 119
    perception of relationships and, 246
Critical attributes effect on transfer,
    162–163, **175–178**
Critical periods, 26
Critical thinking, 286, 295
Cues, retrieval, 123
Cumulative repetition, **137**
Curriculum
    changes to accommodate Bloom's
        Taxonomy, 298–299
    connected to emotions, 94–95
    repetition of subject matter in
        mathematics, 225

Daily planning, 314–321
Dance and theater, **273**
Declarative memory, 90, 91
    system of storage, 124

Degree of learning, **76**
Dehaene, S., 215
Delay, language, 203–204
Delayed sleep phase syndrome (DSPS), 118–119, **146**
Demonstration, 315
Dendrites, 22–23
    memory formation and, 88
Depth of Knowledge (DoK), 300
Developmental dyslexia, 210, 213
Diekelmann, S., 116
Differentiated instruction, 9
Dimensions of thinking, 285–288, 295
Directed forgetting, 131
Direct instruction in reading, **240**
Direct teaching, 315
Discourse competence, **237, 239**
Discovery lessons, 316
Distributed practice, 113
Divergent thinking, 285–286
Domain-specific knowledge, 286, 295
Dopamine, 22
    deficiency problems, 88
Drill and practice, 315
Drugs, smart, 88–89
Dunn, K., 62
Dunn, R., 62
Dweck, C., 60, **67**
Dyscalculia, 226, 227
Dyslexia, developmental, 210, 213

Earworms, 258
Ebbinghaus, H., 53, 100, 130
Educational neuroscience, xii, 6
Elaborative rehearsal, 98–99, 106
    strategies, **137–138**
Electroencephalography (EEG), 2, 3
    arts training and, 248, 249
    music and, 256
    neural efficiency and, 121
Emotional memory, 93–96
    flashbulb memories, 95–96
    gender differences in, 194
    learning and, 93–95
Emotions
    associated with learning, 164
    brain development and, 28–29
    connecting content to, 94–95
    effects on retrieval, 124
    endorphins and, 22, **73,** 94
    gender differences in recalling, 194
    and guidelines for teaching the emotional brain, **135**
    memory and, 5, 28–29
    thinking and, 284
    and threats affecting memory processing, 50–51
Empathizing female, 197
Endorphins, 22, **73,** 94

English language learners (ELLs)
    mathematics for, 227–228
    transfer and, 167–168
Engram, 88
Environmental factors
    difficulties in learning mathematics and, 223–226
    gender differences in brain development and, 197
    novelty and, 31–36
Epinephrine, 22
Episodic memory, 91
Event-related potential (ERP), 2
Every Student Succeeds Act, 30, 288
Exclusivity, specialization differentiated from, 191–193
Exercise
    brain development and, 5, 36
    brain performance and, 269–270
    motor skill acquisition and, 109
    test-taking preparation and, **41**
Explicit memory. *See* Declarative memory
Expository lessons, 316
Expository visuals, **277**
Extrinsic motivation, **75**

Facial recognition and expressions, 194, 195
Farmer, J. A., **183, 233, 276**
Federal Trade Commission, U.S., 134
Feedback, **76**
    arts and constructive, 247
    interactive lecture and direct teaching, 106
    practice and, 112
Fight-or-flight reaction, 294
Fissures, 20
Flashbulb memories, 95–96
Flipped classroom, xii, 313–314
Fluency, 208
Fluid intelligence, 122
Focus, sustained, 246
Focused instruction, 114
Food allergies, 32
Forebrain, 16
Forgetting, 129–133
    directed, 131
Formative assessments, 114
Frontal lobes, 16–17, **39,** 121
Fruit, 25, **41**
Functional magnetic resonance imaging (fMRI), 3, 4, 24
    brain lesions, 213
    gender and, 193
    inhibition and, 249
    music training and, 263
    neural systems involved in reading and, 206
    number sense and, 227
    problems in learning to read and, 209–210
    rehearsal process, 98

second language learning and, 204
transfer of learning, 156
Functional magnetic resonance spectroscopy
(fMRS), 3, 4

Gardner, H., 119–120, 122
Gazzaniga, M., 187, 188
Gender
brain organization and, 193–198
brain structural and developmental
differences, 193–194, 195
empathizing female/systematizing male
and, 197
impact on mathematics and science
programs, 199
performance differences, 194
possible causes of differences in brain
organization by, 196–198
reading problems and, 213
Generalizing, 286
Genetics
intelligence and, 120
mathematics problems and, 227
reading problems and, 213
Geniuses, 125
G factor, 119
Gifted students, 125, 255
Glial cells, 21
Glucose as brain fuel, 25, **41, 73**
Glutamate, 22
Goal setting, **231**
Gradual Release of Responsibility (GRR)
model, xii, 114–115
Grammar, 202–203, **237**
Graphic organizers, **172, 277**
concept mapping, **233–235**
Gray matter, 191, 193, 195
Grey matter, 121
Guided instruction, 114
Guided practice, 112, 317
Gyri, 20

Habits of mind, 299–300
Habituation, 93
Hands-on learning, **232**
Hart, L. A., 15
Hawkins, J., 120–121
Hemispheres, brain. *See* Lateralization, brain
Heredity. *See* Genetics
Hierarchy maps, **233, 234**
Higher-order thinking, 299
activities to stimulate, **310**
questions to stimulate, **309**
High School Survey of Student
Engagement, 35
Hindbrain, 16
Hippocampus, 19, **39**
exercise and, 36
gender differences, 194, 195
transfer of learning and, 156

Homeostasis, 19
Hormones, 196
Hugging, **181–182**
Humor, **40,** 164
enhancing climate through, **73–74**
physiological benefits of, **73**
psychological, sociological, and
educational benefits of, **73**
sarcasm versus, **74**
Hunter, M., 6, **76,** 112, **143,** 153, 165, **175,**
315–316, 321
Hyerle, D., **278**
Hypothalamus, 19, **39**

Imagery, **183,** 266–267, 268, **276**
Immediate memory, 48, 49–51, **65,** 90
Implicit memory. *See* Nondeclarative memory
Incoming information, **65**
chunking of, 126–129
forgetting, 130
Independent practice, 112, 317
Independent tasks, 115
Individualized instruction, 315
Information, incoming, **65**
Information avoidance, 285
Information Processing Model, **65**
cognitive belief system, 58–59
inadequacy of computer model, 46–47
key points to remember, **85**
learning profiles and, 62–64
limitations, 45–46
origins, 44
rate of learning, 124–125
redesigning the, **66**
self-concept, 59–61
senses in, 47
sensory register, 47–48
short-term memory, 48–57
usefulness, 44–45
variations in processing with age, 61–62
Inhibition, 249
Initial rehearsal, 97–98
Input, learning, 317
Instrumental music window of
opportunity, 30
Integrated thematic units, 9
Intelligence, 5, 119
different views of, 119–122
fluid, 122
heredity and, 120
mastery through practice and, 111
Mozart effect on, 259
neural efficiency and, 121–122
retrieval and, 119–122
Interaction, imagery, **276**
Interactive lecture and direct teaching, 106
Interdisciplinary approach to curriculum, 9
Interest, generating, **75**
Interference, learning, 110
Interviews, **172**

Intrinsic motivation, **75**
Iowa test of Basic Skills, 253

Jordan, M., 109
Journal writing for transfer, 167, **185**

Kallick, B., 299
Keyboard training, 263
Key points to ponder, **42, 85, 152, 242, 281, 311, 326**
Knowledge/knowing, 91
    domain-specific, 286
K-W-L maps, **234**

Language
    acquisition, 5, 29
    acquisition of secondary, 204–205, **236–237**
    areas in the brain, 193–195
    delay, 203–204
    mathematics learning and, 216–217
    oriented schools, 198
    specialization, spoken, 199–205
Lateralization, brain, 188–189
Learning
    accepting or rejecting, 60–61
    associative, 93, 163–164
    climate, 94
    collaborative, 114, 247
    complexity of link between, 166
    connecting to past, **172**
    contingency, **181, 182**
    creating meaning in new, **78**
    daily biological rhythms and, 5, 115–119
    degree of, **76**
    developing classroom climate conducive to, **71**
    developing students' growth mindset for, **67**
    by doing/practice, 107
    emotional memory and, 93–95
    emotions associated with, 164
    forgetting and, 129–133
    generating interest in, **75**
    grammar, 202–203
    hands-on, **232**
    interference, 110
    key points to remember, **152**
    maintaining skills for the future and, 322–323
    mathematics, 215–228
    modality preferences, 62
    motor skills, 108–115
    nonassociative, 91, 93
    objective, 316
    past experiences and, 57
    phonemes, 201–203
    preferences and the arts, 254
    primacy-recency effect and, 100–101, **139–140**
    prime-time, 100–102
    profiles, 62–64
    rate of, 124–125
    re-, **144**
    to read, 205–215
    retention and, 96–108
    rote, 160, 169
    second language, 204–205, **236–237**
    sensory preferences, 62, 63–64, **68, 68–70**
    spoken language, 201–204
    transfer during, 128, 154–155
    transfer of, 156–157
    un-, 112
    using synergy to enhance, **82–83**
    visual arts and, 267–268
Learning disabilities, direct instruction for, 106
Lecture/direct instruction, 106–108
Left hemisphere of brain, 189–190
Lesions, brain, 213
Lessons, 8
    circadian rhythm and planning of, **145**
    components for different teaching methods, 318–319
    components to consider in designing, 318
    daily design, 314–319
    design, reflections on, **325**
    discovery, 316
    expository, 316
    humor in, **74**
    including the arts in all, **273**
    length of, 102–105
    novelty and, **40**
    primacy-recency effect on, 100–101, **139–140**
    questions to ask during planning of, 319–321
    teaching for transfer, 157–158
    teaching to the whole brain, **229–232**
Level of concern, **76**
Lewin, R., 282
Lighting, classroom, **146**
Limbic system, 18–20, **37**
    emotional memory and, 93, 194
Literary devices, **273**
Literature, **239**
Lobes, brain, 16–18
    intelligence and, 121
Logic, 192, **232**
    brain development and, 29–30
    used in discussing concepts, **230**
Lombardi, V., 112
Long-term memory, **12**, 90
    emotional component of, 19–20
    hippocampus and, 19
    long-term storage versus, 58
    rehearsal and, 99
    task switching and, 33–34
    transfer of information from, **12**

Long-term potentiation (LTP), 88
Long-term storage, 19, **65**
    cognitive belief system, 58–59
    criteria for, 54–55
    long-term memory versus, 58
    process of, 57–58
    testing whether information is in, **80–81**
    See also Retrieval

MacLean, P., 16
Magnetic resonance imaging (MRI), 2
    structural differences in the brain, 213
Magnetoencephalography (MEG), 2, 3
Mapping
    concept, **233–235**
    mind, **278**
Massed practice, 112–113, **143**
Mastery Teaching, 153
Math anxiety, 61, 164, 224–226
Mathematics
    brain development and, 29–30
    declarative approach to, 220–221
    difficulties in learning, 223–227
    for English language learners, 227–228
    environmental factors in difficulties with
        learning, 223–226
    in high school grades, 222
    instructional strategies, 225, **241**
    in intermediate grades, 220–221
    learning to calculate and, 216–217
    music and, 262–265
    neurological factors in difficulties with
        learning, 226–227
    number sense, 215–218
    in primary grades, 219
    reasoning skills, 221
    teaching brain-friendly, 218–222
McTighe, J., 300
Meaning
    artificial, **78**
    closure and, **79**
    context and, 155
    creating, **78**
    intermediate grades mathematics
        and, 220
    sense and, 55–57, **79**
Medusa and the Snail, The, 1
Memorization, rote, 160, 169
Memory, 86–87
    in brain's lobes, 16–18
    classical conditioning, 91, 92–93
    confabulation, 132–133
    context-dependent, 124
    declarative, 90, 91, 124
    emotional, 93–96
    emotions effects on, 5, 28–29
    engram, 88
    flashbulb, 95–96
    forgetting and, 130–132
    formation, 87–88

glucose and, 25
    key points to remember, **152**
    long-term potentiation (LTP), 88
    multitasking and, 33–34
    music creation as beneficial for, 261–262
    nondeclarative, 90, 91–93
    Perceptual Representation System (PRS),
        91, 92
    primacy-recency effect, 100–101
    procedural, 91–92
    reconsolidation, 123
    repressed, 133
    smart drugs to enhance, 88–89
    stages of, 90
    temporary stimulus and, 87–88
    See also Immediate memory; Long-term
        memory; Retention; Retrieval;
        Working memory
Mental practice, **181, 182**
Mestre, J., 165
Metacognition, **179, 180**, 286
Metaphors, 166
    for enhancing transfer, **183–184**
    teaching to the whole brain using, **231**
Midbrain, 16
    transfer of learning and, 156
Miller, G., 51
Mimicry, **304**
Mind mapping, **278**
Mindset and self-concept, 60, **67**
Mirror neurons, 24
Mixed metaphors, **183**
Mnemonic devices, **78, 150–151**
Modality preferences, 62
Modeling, **78, 82**, 317
    imagery, **276**
    thinking skills, 287–288
Models, **172**
Mölle, M., 116
Molzow, I., 116
Motivation
    extrinsic, **75**
    increasing processing time through,
        75–77
    intrinsic, **75**
    for practice, 111
Motor coordination and reading
        problems, 214
Motor cortex, 18
Motor development window, 27–28
Motor skills
    avoiding teaching two very similar, **136**
    brain and learning, 108–115
Movement, **40**, 269–272, **273**
    brain performance and, 269–270
    cerebellum and, 269
    creating synergy, **82**
    recess and, 271–272
    strategies for using, **279–280**
Mozart effect, 259

Multisensory activities, 63, **231**
Multitasking, 33–34
Mural, **172**
Music, **273**
  benefits of listening to, 258–260
  connecting to past learnings, **172**
  creating, 260–265
  effects of listening to versus creating, 256–257
  how the brain listens to, 257–258
  as inborn, 255–256
  instrumental, 30
  in lesson design, **40**
  mathematics and, 262–265
  motor skill acquisition and, 109
  neuron development and, 23
  perseverance with, 247
  practice time and mastery of, 111
  reading and, 265
  student attitudes toward, 265–266
  temporal lobes and, 17
  use in the classroom, **274–275**
  See also Arts
Myelin layer, 25
Myelin sheath, 22

National Assessment of Educational Progress (NAEP), 228, 252
National Endowment for the Arts, 253
Natural selection, 196–197
Negative transfer, 110, 156
Neural efficiency, 121–122
NeuroBingo, **84**
Neurogenesis, 19
Neurons, 21–23, **38**, 86
  development in children, 25–30
  memory formation and, 87–88, 89
  mirror, 24
  neural efficiency and, 121–122
Neuroplasticity, 5, 26, 33
  aerobic exercise and, 109
  intelligence and, 120
Neuroscience, educational, xii, 6
Neurotransmitters, 22
  memory formation and, 88
Neutotransmitters, 3
No Child Left Behind law, 30
Noise, detection of target sounds in, 214
Nonassociative learning, 91, 93
Nondeclarative memory, 90, 91–93
  emotional memory as, 93
Nootropics, 88
Notebook design, **278**
Note taking, **137**
  visualized, **277–278**
Novelty, 30, **75**
  environmental factors that enhance, 31–36
  used in lessons, **40**
Number sense, 215–218

Obesity, 32
Objective, learning, 316
Observing, 286
Occipital lobes, 17
Old mammalian brain, 18
Onomatopoeia, 101
Ornstein, R., 43
Oxygen as brain fuel, 25, **73**

Pairing and synergy, **83**
Paraphrasing, **137**
Parentese, 201
Parietal lobes, 18
Parkinson's disease, 88
Parrott, C. A., **276**
Past experiences
  chunking and, 127–129
  creating meaning in new learning, **78**
  new learning and, 57
  self-concept and, 59–60
Patterns
  chunking, **148**
  finding, 286
Pavlov's dog, 92–93
Peer coaching, 322
Perceptual filtering, 48
Perceptual Representation System (PRS), 91, 92
Perkins, D., 154, 165, **179, 181**
Perseverance, 247
Pew Research Survey, 31
Phonemes, 201–202
  words from, 202
Phonemic awareness, 207–208, **238**
Phonics, 208, **238**
Phonological awareness, 207–208, **239**
Phonological deficits and reading, 212
Physical exercise. *See* Exercise
Planning
  daily, 314–321
  questions to ask during lesson, 319–321
  unit, 321–322
Plasticity, 26
Plot diagrams, **235**
Positive transfer, 155
Positron-emission tomography (PET), 2, 4, 19
  amygdala, 193–194
  gender and, 193
  music and, 256
  neural efficiency and, 121–122
Postsynaptic terminal, 22
Practice
  avoiding teaching two very similar motor skills and, **136**
  Bloom's Taxonomy and, **304**
  conditions for successful, 111, **143**
  distributed, 113
  drill and, 315

Gradual Release of Responsibility (GRR)
model, 114–115
guided, 112, 317
independent, 112, 317
learning by, 107
for maintaining mastery, 110–111
massed, 112–113, **143**
mental, **181, 182**
and rehearsal over time increasing
retention, 112–113
See also Rehearsal
Predicting, **138**
Prefrontal cortex, 16–17
Preoccupation, 54
Primacy-recency effect, 100–101,
139–140
Prime-time, 100–104
Principals, building, 322
Procedural memory, 91–92
motor skill acquisition and, 108
Prompting, imagery, **276**
Prosody, 201
Psychological-cognitive cycle, 115
Punctuality, **231**
Purpose, learning, 316

Questioning, **138**
Quiz games, **40**

Ramón y Cajal, S., 20
Rapid-eye movement (REM) stage of sleep,
116
delayed sleep phase syndrome and,
118–119
Rate of retrieval, **12**, 124–125
Rauscher, F., 259
Reading, 5
balanced approach in teaching, **238–239**
considerations for teaching, **238–239**
direct instruction in, **240**
guidelines for all teachers, **240**
inadequate instruction in, 210–211
music and, 265
as natural ability, 205–206
neural systems involved in, 206–207
phases of learning, 209
physical causes of problems with,
212–214
problems in learning, 209–214
skills involved in, 207–209
social and cultural causes of problems
with, 211–212
Reasoning, mathematical, 221
Recall, 123
Recess, 271–272
Reciprocal teaching, 228
Recognition, 123
Reconsolidation, 123
Reduction mnemonics, **151**
Reflection, **82**

Rehearsal, 52
elaborative, 98–99, 106, **137–138**
enhancing retention, 97–99, **137**
Gradual Release of Responsibility (GRR)
model, 114–115
metaphors and, **183**
rote, 98, **137**
time for initial and secondary, 97–98
See also Practice
Reinforcement, imagery, **276**
Remembering, 91
Repetition, simple and cumulative, **137**
Representational system, thinking as, 284
Repressed memory, 133
Retention, **12**, 57
chunking and, 126–129, **148–149**
closure and, **79**, 98
defined, 97
higher-order thinking increasing, 299
journal writing for, **185**
key points to remember, **152**
learning and, 96–108
during learning episode, 99–101
mnemonics for, **78, 150–151**
practice and rehearsal over time
increasing, 112–113
rehearsal and, 97–99, **137**
testing whether information is in long-
term storage and, **80–81**
using humor to promote, **73–74**
varying with teaching method, 105–108
See also Memory
Reticular activating system (RAS), 18, 48
Retrieval, 122–123
confabulation and, 132–133
context of, 124
cues, 123
factors affecting, 123–124
intelligence and, 119–122
mood and belief effects on, 124
rate, **12**, 124–125
relearning through, **144**
students with fast, 125
students with slow, 125
underachievers and, 125
wait time and, **144, 147**
See also Long-term storage
Rhyming mnemonics, **150**
Right hemisphere of brain, 190
Ringo, J., 191
Rizzolatti, G., 24
Role-playing, **280**
Rote learning, 160, 169
Rote rehearsal, 98, **137**
Rowe, M. B., **147**
Russell, P., 54

Salomon, G., 154, 165, **179, 181**
Sarcasm, **74**, 164
Scheduling, block, 104, **141–142**

Schopenhauer, A., 86
Sciences needing the arts, 250
Secondary rehearsal, 97–98
Second language learning, 204–205,
    236–237
Selecting and note taking, **137**
Self-concept, 59
    accepting or rejecting new learning and,
        60–61
    feedback and, **76**
    mindset and, 60, **67**
    past experiences and, 59–60
    slower retrieval and, 124
    variations in processing with age and,
        61–62
Self evaluation, 9
Semantic level in reading, **239**
Semantic memory, 91
Sense and meaning, 55–57, **79**
Senses, the, 47
Sensitization, 93
Sensory filtering, 48
Sensory memory, 48, 90
    See also Immediate memory
Sensory preferences, 62, 63–64, **68, 68–70**
Sensory register, 47–48, **65**
    accepting or rejecting new learning,
        60–61
Sequential sounds, perception of, 214
Serial position effect, 100
Sex chromosomes, 196
Shakespeare, W., 158
Shaw, G., 259
Shaywitz, S. E., 205
Short stories, **172**
Short-term memory, 48
    immediate memory and, 48, 49–51
    See also Working memory
Similarity
    avoiding teaching concepts with,
        173–174
    differences chunking and, **149**
    effect on transfer, 160–162
    metaphor and, **183**
Simile, 166
Simple repetition, **137**
Simulation games, **181, 182**, 315
Sleep, 5, 32
    classroom lighting and, **146**
    delayed sleep phase syndrome,
        118–119, **146**
    importance in learning and memory,
        116–117
    later school start times and, **145**
    REM stage, 116, 118–119
Smart drugs, 88–89
Social and cultural causes of reading
        problems, 211–212
Sociolinguistic competence, **237**
Socratic method, 315

Somatosensory cortex, 18
Sound-frequency discrimination, 214
Sousa, D. A., 205, 215, 322
Spacing effect, 113
Spearman, C., 119
Specialization, 188
    causes of, 191
    examples of, 192
    versus exclusivity, 191–193
    implications for teachers, 192–193
    spoken language, 199–205
Sperry, R., 188–189
Spider maps, **233, 234**
Split Brain Revisited, The, 187
Spoken language specialization, 199–205
Sports
    motor skill acquisition and, 109
    practice and mastery of, 111
Stahl, R., 44
STEAM (science, technology, engineering,
        arts, and mathematics), xii, 252–253
STEM (science, technology, engineering, and
        mathematics), xii, 251–253
Stem, brain, 18, 25, **37, 39**
Stereotype threat, 199
Sternberg, R., 119, 120, 122
Stickperson symbol, **277**
Story maps, **234**
Strategic abandonment, 298–299
Strategic competence, **237**
Strings training, 263–264
Structure and function chunking, **149**
Student-to-student interaction, 107, **232**
Study groups, 323
Sulcus, 20
Summarizing, **138**
Supplemental textbooks, **240**
Support systems, 322–323
Suprachiasmatic nuclei, 115
Sustained focus, 246
Synapses, 22
    memory formation and, 88
Synaptic pruning, 25
Synaptic vesicles, 22
Synergy, **82–83**
Syntax level in reading, **239**
Systemizing male, 197

Tabula rasa, 29
Talking as reading tool, **240**
Target sounds, detection of, 214
Task switching, 33
    complex texts and, 34–35
Taxonomies chunking, **149**
Teacher work sample, 321–322
Teaching others as practice, 107
Technology
    affecting how students think, 285
    effects on attention, 33
    effects on student brain, 32–35

intermediate grades mathematics and, 221
multitasking and, 33–34
schools changing with increased, 35
transfer and, 168–169
Television, 203
Temporal lobes, 17
Temporary stimulus and memory formation, 87–88
Testing
   cramming for, 129
   gender differences in, 194, 195
   misuse of, **80–81**
   preparation for, **41**
   time of day for, **146**
   transfer and high-stakes, 169
   whether information is in long-term storage, **80–81**
Testosterone, 196
Textbooks, supplemental, **240**
Text comprehension, 208, **238, 240**
Thalamus, 18, **39,** 48
Thinking
   characteristics of human, 282–285
   cognitive and emotional, 293–294
   creative, 286, 295
   critical, 286, 295
   critical difference between complexity and difficulty in, 295–298
   Depth of Knowledge (DoK) and, 300
   designing models of, 285–286
   dimensions of, 285–288, 295
   emotion and, 284
   habits of mind and, 299–300
   higher-order, 299, **309–310**
   key points to ponder, **311**
   metacognition, **179, 180,** 286, 295
   as representational system, 284
   skills modeled in the classroom, 287–288
   teaching skills in, 286–287
   technology affecting, 285
   types of, 283
   Understanding by Design (UbD) and, 300
Thomas, L., 1
Thompson, R., 43
Threats and emotions effect on memory processing, 50–51
Time limits of working memory, 53–54
Toffler, A., 312
Tomlinson, C. A., 62
Torrance Tests of Creative Thinking, 285
Transfer, 128, 153
   association and, 163–164
   avoiding teaching concepts that are similar and, **173–174**
   bridging and, **179–180**
   complexity of link between learnings and, 166
   constructivism and, 167
   context and degree of original learning and, 160

critical attributes effect on, 162–163, **175–178**
English language learners and, 167–168
factors affecting, 159–164
general guidelines on teaching for, **171**
hugging and, **181–182**
journal writing for, 167, **185**
during learning, 154–155
of learning, 156–157
metaphors for enhancing, **183–184**
negative, 156
from past to present, 165, **172**
positive, 155
power of, **186**
from present to future, 165–166
rote memorization and, 169
similarity effect on, 160–162
teaching for, 157–158, **232**
technology and, 168–169
as two-part process, 154
types of, 155–156

Underachievers, 125
Understanding by Design (UbD), 300
Unit planning, 321–322
Unlearning and relearning skills, 112

Venn diagrams, **235**
Verbal processing, 106–107
Verbal to physical tug-of-war, **280**
Visual arts, 266–268, **273**
Visualized note taking, **277–278**
Visual material, **240**
   retention and, 106
   teaching to the whole brain, **229, 232**
Visual processing, 63
   mathematics learning and, 216
   retention and, 106–107
   speed differences, 212–213
Visuals, expository, **277**
Visual working memory, 53
Vocabulary
   brain development and, 29
   building using movement, **280**
   learning to read and, 208, **240**
Vogel, P., 188

Wait time, **144, 147**
Water, 25, **41**
Webb, N., 300
Wernicke, C., 200
Wernicke's area, 200–201, 206, 248, 261
West, C. K., **183, 233, 276**
White matter, 191, 193, 195
Wiggins, G., 165, 300
Wilhelm, I., 116
Windows of opportunity, 26–30
   emotional control, 28–29
   instrumental music, 30
   language acquisition, 29

mathematics and logic, 29–30
motor development, 27–28
vocabulary, 29
Wolff, P. M., **183, 233, 276**
Word from phonemes, 202
Working memory, **65,** 90
    capacity, **12,** 51–53
    chunking and, 126–129
    closure and, **79**
    cramming and, 129
    criteria for long-term storage,
        54–55
    immediate memory and,
        48, 49–51
    implications for teaching, 53

    increasing processing time through
        motivation, **75–77**
    music and, 262
    not overloaded with imagery, **276**
    preoccupation, 54
    rehearsal, 52
    relearning through recall, **144**
    short-term memory and, 48
    task switching and, 33–34
    time limits of, 53–54
    visual, 53
Work sample, teacher, 321–322
Workshops, teacher, 323

YouthARTS Development Project, 253

A SAGE Publishing Company

CORWIN HAS ONE MISSION: to enhance education through intentional professional learning.

We build long-term relationships with our authors, educators, clients, and associations who partner with us to develop and continuously improve the best evidence-based practices that establish and support lifelong learning.

How the Brain Learns

Fifth Edition

Other Books From Corwin and David A. Sousa

The Leadership Brain: How to Lead Today's Schools More Effectively, 2003

How the Brain Influences Behavior: Management Strategies for Every Classroom, 2009

How the Gifted Brain Learns, Second Edition, 2009

How the ELL Brain Learns, 2011

How the Brain Learns to Read, Second Edition, 2014

How the Brain Learns Mathematics, Second Edition, 2015

How the Special Needs Brain Learns, Third Edition, 2016

Brain-Compatible Activities for Mathematics, Grades K–1, 2010

Brain-Compatible Activities for Mathematics, Grades 2–3, 2010

Brain-Compatible Activities for Mathematics, Grades 4–5, 2010

Brain Compatible Activities, Grades K–2, 2008

Brain-Compatible Activities, Grades 3–5, 2008

Brain-Compatible Activities, Grades 6–8, 2008